1975

Youth, Crime, and Society

is book may be kept

Youth, Crime, and Society

edited by

James A. Gazell
and
G. Thomas Gitchoff

*California State University
San Diego*

Holbrook Press, Inc.
Boston

Acknowledgments

Robert M. Carter and G. Thomas Gitchoff, "An Alternative to Youthful Mass Disorder," *The Police Chief*, 37 (July, 1970), pp. 52-56. Reprinted by permission.

J. L. Simmons and Barry Winograd, "The Hang-Loose Ethic," in *It's Happening* (Santa Barbara, California: Marc-Laird, 1966), pp. 6-30. Reprinted by permission.

Joseph Paul Kimble, "Night Thoughts of a Police Chief," *The Nation*, 210 (April 27, 1970), pp. 490-492. Reprinted by permission.

Marvin E. Wolfgang, "The Culture of Youth," in Ronald Steel (ed.), *New Light on Juvenile Delinquency* (New York: The H. W. Wilson Company, 1967), pp. 101-107. Reprinted by permission.

Theodore Roszak, "Technocracy's Children," from *The Making of a Counter Culture*, by Theodore Roszak, copyright © 1968, 1969 by Theodore Roszak, pp. 1-41, Anchor edition. Reprinted by permission of Doubleday and Company, Inc.

David Matza, "Position and Behavior Patterns of Youth," in Robert E. L. Faris (ed.), *Handbook of Modern Sociology*, © 1964 by Rand McNally & Company, Chicago, pp. 191-193, 198-216. Reprinted by permission.

Orrin E. Klapp, "Style Rebellion and Identity Crisis," from Tamotsu Shibutani, Editor, *Human Nature and Collective Behavior: Papers in Honor of Herbert Blumer*, © 1970. Reprinted by permission of Prentice-Hall, Inc., Englewood Cliffs, New Jersey.

Paul Goodman, "The Missing Community," from *Growing Up Absurd*, by Paul Goodman. Copyright © 1960 by Paul Goodman. Reprinted by permission of Random House, Inc.

James A. Michener, pp. 19-31 from *America vs. America* by James A. Michener, copyright © 1968, 1969, by Marjay Productions, Inc. By arrangement with The New American Library, Inc.

Edgar Z. Friedenberg, "The Revolt Against Democracy," *Change in Higher Education*, 1 (May-June, 1969), pp. 1-10. Reprinted by permission.

Acknowledgments

Daniel Seligman, "A Special Kind of Rebellion," *Fortune*, 79, pp. 67-68, 172-175. Reprinted from the January, 1969, issue of *Fortune Magazine* by special permission; © 1968 Time, Inc.

Kenneth Keniston, "Personal Roots: Turmoil, Success, and the End of the Line," from *Young Radicals*, copyright © 1968, by Kenneth Keniston. Reprinted by permission of Harcourt Brace Jovanovich, Inc.

Ralph W. England, Jr., "A Theory of Middle Class Juvenile Delinquency," reprinted by special permission from the *Journal of Criminal Law, Criminology and Police Science* (Northwestern University School of Law), copyright © 1960, Volume 50, Number 6, pp. 535-540.

Jackson Toby, "Affluence and Adolescent Crime," in *The President's Commission on Law Enforcement and the Administration of Justice. Task Force Report: Juvenile Delinquency* (Washington, D. C.: Government Printing Office), pp. 132-144.

Robert M. Carter, "Delinquency in the Upper and Middle Classes," *General Practice*, 37 (March, 1968), pp. 122-129. Reprinted by permission.

Edmund W. Vaz, "Delinquency and the Youth Culture: Upper- and Middle-Class Boys," reprinted by special permission from the *Journal of Criminal Law, Criminology and Police Science* (Northwestern University School of Law), copyright © 1969, Volume 60, Number 1, pp. 33-46.

Fred J. Shanley, "Middle-Class Delinquency as a Social Problem," *Sociology and Social Research*, 51 (January, 1967), pp. 185-198. Reprinted by permission.

G. Thomas Gitchoff, "Kids vs. Cops: Delinquency Prevention and the Police Function," in *Kids, Cops, and Kilos*, San Diego, California: Malter-Westerfield Publishing Company, 1969), pp. 109-125. Reprinted by permission.

Roy W. Menninger, Jr., "The Dilemma of the Generations," address given August 18, 1967. An adapted version entitled "What Troubles Our Troubled Youth?" appeared in *Mental Hygiene*, 52 (July, 1968), pp. 323-329. Reprinted by permission.

Contents

Preface

This collection of articles seeks to realize three principal aims. First, it attempts to assemble and to interrelate the latest and most reputably professional thought about a problem that is proving increasingly troublesome to American society: the disaffection of numerous youths that often is expressed in rebellion and crime. Second, it tries to examine the societal influences that generate such disturbing behavior. Third, it seeks to explore what, if any, may be done by individuals and groups outside as well as inside governmental units to alleviate this social crisis.

This reader aims for audiences found largely within the social sciences. More specifically, it seeks to inform and to interest such people as criminologists, police scientists, social psychologists, sociologists, psychologists, correctional experts, and public administrators. Moreover, the essays are sufficiently nontechnical to interest the general reader. Both audiences may find this reader significant because it represents the most recent effort to fulfill the aims cited above.

The authors wish to acknowledge their indebtedness to the late Joseph D. Lohman, Dean of the School of Criminology at the University of California at Berkeley, and Dr. Robert M. Carter, Associate Professor of Public Administration at the University of Southern California, for their inspiration and encouragement. We would like to express our gratitude to the following talented research assistants: Mr. Fred Glatstein, Mrs. Elsie Ellenbogen, Mr. Richard Shope, Mr. Chester Baldiga, Mrs. June Kaiser, Mrs. Romney Cohen, and Maj. James Rattigan (U.S.M.C., Ret.).

James A. Gazell

G. Thomas Gitchoff

Introduction

Like many concepts, the behavior of youth eludes a simple explanation. Its scope is large enough to include the following: radicalism, bohemianism, delinquency, and deviance. We define these terms as does sociologist David Matza in his article in Section III. *Radicalism* encompasses an anti-capitalist, anti-imperialist orientation. *Bohemianism* embraces a pervasive indifference to a contemporary economic order, especially if the Protestant Ethic is an underpinning of it. *Delinquency* incorporates the violations of capitalistic property arrangements. *Deviance* may denote, in its most generic sense, any conduct to which some authority or norm objects.

We selected articles and book excerpts for this reader on the basis of five main criteria. First, we tended to favor material most recently published. Second, the editors sought empirical materials, but accepted impressionistic articles and excerpts of particular insightfulness. Third, we sought articles by the most eminent scholars in this field. Fourth, we selected materials of widely varying difficulty. Finally, fairly short articles (under twenty-five pages) were chosen so that they could include as wide a variety of viewpoints as possible.

Rebellious Youth: Subcultural Dimensions

A discussion of the subcultural dimensions of rebellious youth requires that we first consider, albeit briefly, the nature of culture. Most definitions of culture stress the comprehensiveness of this term, for it is usually equated with the totality of man's conscious existence in contrast to his animal existence. One of the oldest definitions of this concept belongs to sociologist E. B. Taylor, who, in 1871, aserted that "culture, or civilization,...is that complex whole which includes knowledge, belief, art, law, morals, customs, and any other capabilities and habits acquired by man as a member of society."[1] A more recent definition comes from sociologist Leslie A. White, who viewed culture as an organization of phenomena with five main components: symbols, acts (such as behavior patterns), objects (such as tools and items made with tools), ideas (such as beliefs and knowledge), and sentiments (such as attitudes and values).[2] In short, culture centers on man's ideational existence, which necessarily includes his aspirations, attitudes, beliefs, and values.

A subculture is a segment of a cultural totality. It is the culture of a fairly well-defined entity within the total society. Moreover, a subculture differs in some significant respects from the conventional mores, laws, and folkways prevailing in the larger society. A subculture may explicitly or implicitly reject the larger whole. One contemporary illustration is the "hippie" subculture, which differs from the culture of the rest of society in

3

at least seven respects: physical appearance, dress, demeanor, sexual morality, racial attitudes, drugs, and an indifference toward money. In subcultures, as in cultures, there is a consensus on a set of norms governing behavior.

This section contains four articles which examine some dimensions of the subcultures of rebellious youth. The first selection by criminologists Robert M. Carter and G. Thomas Gitchoff suggests that subcultures of rebellious youths are *not* pervasively and irreconcilably different from the dominant culture. These scholars contend that such subcultures are temporary aberrations — the responses of ordinary young people to a fusillade of unusual social, economic, political, and military circumstances. However, although these academicians provide considerable informal documentation to buttress such a thesis, one still must ask why millions of ordinary youths retain orthodox life styles despite such circumstances. Nevertheless, this central theme may partially explain the deviant behavior of numerous youths. Furthermore, these writers supply three notable corollaries to this thesis. First, adults — like youths — frequently and publicly protest governmental actions or inactions by drastic methods, although they usually do not proceed so far as to adopt bizarre life styles. Second, since society generates these subcultures, it can also reintegrate them into its mainstream if it really seeks that end. Finally, these authors describe a proposal (the establishment of youth commissions in American communities), which, if adopted widely, will take a modest step toward achieving such reunification.

The second selection by sociologists J. L. Simmons and Barry Winograd, like the Roszak essay in Section III, focuses on the implied question: What kind of life style will be embraced by the subcultures of people rebelling against conventional ways? The authors suggest that some aspects of the subculture have already become apparent: an irreverence for conventionality, an espousal of humanism, the pursuit of experience (rather than reading about experience) as a means of learning and growing, spontaneity, a tolerance of other persons' attitudes and practices as long as they do not interfere with one's own, a repudiation of property, and a willingness to fulfill commitments only if one wants to. Together these dimensions constitute what the authors call "The Hang-Loose Ethic." For these writers youth subcultures are considerably more structured than Roszak would have us believe.

The third selection, by police chief Joseph Paul Kimble, unlike the first two selections, focuses not on subcultures generally, but on countercultural attitudes toward the preeminent institution of domestic authority: the police. In trying to interpret their views from his position of power, the author implies that the counterculture attributes at least eight shortcomings to this institution. First, it has failed to increase the stability of society which, in Kimble's view, most youths are seeking. Second, it has not rejected extremist ideas and practices. Third, it constitutes a threat to the young. Fourth, although it may not be corrupt, it is biased against ethnic minorities. Fifth, it is not competent to cure inveterate social problems, which other governmental agencies have long neglected. Sixth, it needs to be far more effective than it has been. Seventh, it has to eschew the tendency to stereotype people and to cease treating them monolithically. Finally, it has to acknowledge the serious social problems confronting this country before it can help to alleviate them.

The fourth selection, by sociologist Marvin E. Wolfgang, like the Roszak article, suggests that the subcultural dimensions of rebellious youth are, on the whole, highly amorphous. Wolfgang implies that millions of adolescents are in anomie—an indefinite and permeating limbo. He intimates that these youths face two main choices: to refit themselves into the society which disenchants them or to form subcultural norms which will prove tolerable to them. He suggests that as long as widespread and quick technological and social changes continue to weaken the traditional adult role of youth counselor without supplanting it with another role, and as long as there are no new roles to supplant the traditional youth role of novices learning how to fit into society, the latter choice will have to be made.

NOTES

1. E. B. Taylor, *Primitive Culture* (London: John Murray, 1871), p. 1.
2. Leslie A. White, "Cultural vs. Psychological Interpretations of Human Behavior," *American Sociological Review*, 12 (December 1947), pp. 686-98.

An Alternative to Youthful Mass Disorder

Robert M. Carter
G. Thomas Gitchoff

It has become increasingly common to discuss the "decline in respect for law and order," particularly among American youth. Attention to this apparent change toward our total legal and social system is of ever-increasing concern to those among us who are concerned with youth. In every quarter, and with increasing intensity, we hear that the citizenry, for reasons as yet unclear, is not only failing to honor specific laws, but also displays a mounting disregard for the "rule of law" itself as an essential aspect of the democratic way of life. But even as we echo this common concern, it is not clear that we are all agreed as to what is meant by "decline in respect for law and order," or precisely to whom or to what we are referring.

Lack of respect for law is very often assumed to be evidence of a willful disregard for legitimate authority and probably evidence of some personal defect or shortcoming. We have much to learn however about the mysteries by which a society generates an abnormal response within its own circles. But this has become increasingly apparent: *it is society which itself contributes significantly to such behavior.* Indeed, it is the self-same social structure expressing its force and influence in an ambivalent manner which produces on one hand the conforming individual— the person respectful of the social and legal codes—and on the other, the deviant and lawbreaker who are disrespectful of the law. It may be that a large amount of what we observe and label "disrespect for law" is, in fact, *a normal reaction of normal persons to an abnormal condition or situation!*[1]

The mass media has portrayed for us—live and in color— segments of our youthful society in revolt. From the burning ghettoes of Los Angeles, Detroit, and Newark to campuses as far flung as Columbia and Wisconsin to Berkeley and San Francisco, we have and continue to witness mass civil disorder unparalleled in recent times. We have observed our young people in revolt against such seemingly varied objects as the war in Vietnam, the grape industry, selective service, marihuana laws, presidential candidates, and Dow Chemical. We have seen these youths defy authority ranging from the President of the United States to local law enforcement. We have observed rebellion against the establishment in forms encompassing freedom riders in the South to looters in the North. American youth in increasing numbers have withstood tear gas and mace, billy clubs and bullets, insults and assaults, jail and prison in order to lie-down in front of troop trains, sit-in at a university administration building, love-in in public parks, wade-in at non-integrated beaches, and lie-in within our legislative buildings. These youths have challenged the establishment on such issues as the legal-oriented entities of the draft, the right of Negroes to use the same restrooms and drinking fountains as whites, the death penalty, and free speech. They have also challenged socially-oriented norms with "mod" dress and hair styles, language, rock music, and psychedelic colors, forms, and patterns. We have watched the development of the hippy and yippy, the youthful drug culture, black, yellow, brown and red power advocates and organizations such as the Third World Liberation Front, the Peace and Freedom Party, and Black Studies Departments on the campus. We have been exposed to violence, vandalism, assault, destruction, looting, disruption, and chaos on our streets.

An outsider viewing the current American scene might well believe that we have all gone mad. A commentary by that outsider would be dominated by terms which describe a growing distance between man and his former objects of affection. It is clear that the terms in use today—alienation, estrangement, anomie, withdrawal, disengagement, separation, non-involvement, apathy, indifference—point to a sense of loss and a widening gap between man and his social world. This estrangement is not restricted to the poor, or the black, or the unemployed; it is beginning to encompass the average, the adjusted, and even the affluent American. The fortunate, the talented, and the privileged have all come under the spell of a society which is seemingly disaffected with itself. We do not know whether the computers, the Apollo missions, the hot lines and the red phones, the pill or the other products of our great technology, or even the generation gap, have brought on this great unrest.

But this unrest is not restricted to youth alone. Increasingly, adults are becoming rebels against the establishment. One need look no further than the recent slow-downs, work stoppages, and strikes of such tradition-oriented groups as police and fire officials, sanitation personnel, social workers, and teachers. Adults from varied social and economic backgrounds have joined protest movements—and counter protest movements—in a similar, but generally more moderate fashion than youth. Some adult protest against the establishment has been through membership in liberal political organizations of a left-wing orientation; others have joined the conservative right-wing organizations of the Birch Society or Minutemen. Millions of adult Americans protested against the political establishment by either voting for a third or fourth party candidate or not voting at all in the 1968 elections.

We can agree that protest and confrontation have become part of the American way of life—for adults as well as youth. This is true even if we disregard those protests and confrontations which are generated by subversive individuals and groups, the mentally deranged, anarchists, and those among us who thrive on conflict for the sake of conflict alone. Even apart from those persons, and apart from those immature youth who may have been used by those persons, we are faced with confrontation in almost every direction and against almost every conceivable issue.

Youth have been particularly susceptible to involvement in various causes and movements. No one can state definitively or with certainty why this is so, but we offer three observations which may have some relevance to the phenomenon. Initially, American youth have a capacity to see, with a particularly clear vision, the numerous inconsistencies which exist in our society— even though they, themselves, may not be personally affected. While they may not be able to verbalize these discrepancies, they feel them and are sensitive to them. Secondly, there is a gut-level emotion which urges that they should be involved in a meaningful fashion in generating changes which will improve the lot of their fellow man. There is an immediacy about this emotion. Finally, youth have seldom been given an opportunity to participate in decision-making; they do not generally ask to make the decisions, but rather to be involved in the process of making decisions.[2]

What are some of these inconsistencies that have "turned on" youth to protest? An incomplete list would include:

—The waging of a land war in a remote corner of Asia that has now taken more than 30,000 American and an unknown number of enemy lives over an issue variously described as "preserving democracy everywhere," and "stopping the spread of Communism,"but has not, after years of conflict, "even been dignified" by a declaration of war by the Congress.

—The assassination by shooting of a president, a senator, and a civil rights leader on one hand, and the near impossibility of congressional approval of meaningful gun legislation on the other.

—The inequities of demands for law and order when in fact the demand should be for law and justice: a need brought to the attention of adults by youth who recognized clear abuses in the application of law to those among us who are socially or economically disadvantaged.

—The contradiction between law and society which severely penalizes one type of drug user—the marihuana smoker for example—and tolerates and encourages the use of other substances reputedly more dangerous, such as alcohol and tobacco.

—The inconsistency of poverty and hunger among large segments of the most affluent society which has ever existed on the face of this earth. Concurrent with this is the expenditure of some 70 to 80 billions of dollars on the military establishment and an expenditure perhaps only 1/100th of that amount for such programs as Vista and the Peace Corps.

—The peculiarities of a society which on one hand formally and theoretically endorses the importance of marriage and continuity of the family and certain standards of sexual behavior, but on the other, finds in practice an ever increasing divorce rate coupled with infidelity, adultery, and discord. Coupled with the officially sanctioned sexual morality are inconsistencies of behavior revealed by the use of sex for fun and profit—in the cinema, on television, and in marketing and advertising.

—The absurdity of such governmental "helping" programs as urban renewal, which in fact means replacing Negroes with trees in our central cities, or welfare systems which not only assuredly perpetuate themselves with mediocity, but trap their clientele into second and third generation welfare recipients.

—The incongruence of a selective service system which sets the minimum age for military service at eighteen and a social and political system which denies the eighteen-year-old the right to vote /no longer true/. Youth ask whether a societal license to kill and be killed in combat for one's country should not also enable the licensee to cast his ballot in the democratic tradition.

—Educational programs from grammar school through the university which are tied to a paternalistic past and pattern and guarantee that only certain portions of our society will ever reap their benefits.

—The inconsistency in application of the principle that all men are created equal, for even the most casual observer will note that equal opportunity for housing, education, employment, and the like are not uniformly distributed among our people but rather are reserved—by both formal and informal processes—for those of us of a particular ethnic, racial, social or cultural background.

This has not been a complete list of the concerns of our young people. There are other issues and we will become aware of them—not through dialogue—but rather by new confrontations described and reported upon by the mass media. This is predictable with almost absolute certainty, for we have not made any provisions for expressions of concern by our young people through legitimate channels. As long as such channels are non-existent, youth will be heard through the process of protest and confrontation.

There is no question but that each one of us is concerned with and condemns the violence which has spread across the country. While adults may not agree with the significance of the issues being raised or believe that our youth have taken the correct position on a particular issue, we can certainly find consensus that the proper resolution of the issues must be an approach considerably more rational than mass disorder. Again, the deranged, anarchists, and subversives aside, there is no question that our youth intends to be heard. Might not it be worthwhile to explore the possibility of opening such channels of communication?

This is not to be construed as suggesting that youth be given total decision-making power, but rather that they be given an opportunity to be involved in decisions on those issues and concerns where they have a particular interest or talent. If we assume first that youth are aware of some of the more important issues of our times and second, that they feel a mandate to be involved in the resolution of these issues, only two courses of action are open. There can be a denial of opportunity for youth to participate legitimately in problem-solving, which will insure a continuation of conflict, or there can be the creation of opportunities for participation which will channel the enormous energy of a large and growing segment of our population into the resolution of problems. And in deciding which might be the most appropriate of the alternatives—continued conflict or integrated involvement with adults—we would do well to note that the only thing worse than the dynamic interest of youth in American social, economic, and political problems and the problems of their fellow men everywhere would be indifference to such problems.

The involvement of youth through legitimate methods is not to be seen as permissiveness run wild, nor is it to be viewed as a sell-out. We have an absolute right to demand a cessation of violence on our campuses and streets and to support whatever steps are necessary to restore some semblance of sanity to our communities. Concurrently, we have an obligation to explore the possibilities of directing the energies of our youth into more meaningful patterns for resolution of problems. Indeed, as a practical matter, such an approach would probably insure that the "legitimate" protestors—the non-psychopaths and anarchists— would join with adults in the pursuit of resolution of issues through reasonable channels, leaving the professional agitators standing by themselves, isolated, in relatively small numbers. But, the "sincere" protestors cannot be separated as long as they are without legitimate alternatives.

While it is not particularly difficult to envision the creation of systems for legitimate youthful involvement, it will be considerably more difficult to adjudicate the communication or generation gap. Many adults are disappointed, disaffected, or "downright" disgusted with the behavior of youth. In large measure this may be attributed to the current wave of mass disorders, but there may be one or more reasons, considerably more subtle and perhaps more important, for these feelings. Adults may be "down" on youth because that generation has focused attention on issues which upset long-standing tradition.

There is a certain embarrassment brought on by exposure of flaws in the American system. Our system, no more and no less than any other, is imperfect, but our imperfections were hidden from view until protest about poverty, civil rights, and other issues dramatically pointed them out. The upset and challenge of cherished traditions are, of course, painful. It is equally distressing to observe youth actively and sincerely involved in issues toward which adults have been either indifferent or only casually concerned. It is awkward to note that youth have the time, or have taken the time, to be meaningfully involved, particularly when many adults are without meaningful involvement of any sort.

We can be certain that no single activity or methodology can bridge the communication or generation gap, but we can be equally certain that some effort must be directed toward resolution of the conflict. If the mass disorders on the streets of this and other countries are precursors of a third world revolution—a youth revolution—paralleling in significance the impact of the agricultural and industrial revolutions, we are in for continued and intensified conflict. There are many who believe the third revolution has begun and evidence is cited to show that the activities of older youth in the community and on the campus are now being imitated by younger teenagers of high school and junior high school age. If such is the case, the opening of channels of communication—the building of bridges—between adults and youth may be too late. But if we are witness to something less than a worldwide revolt of youth against the standards and moralities of adults, these channels and bridges are essential.

The following is a description of a specific community-based approach which may be designed and implemented to open legitimate channels for youth involvement. This approach centers about creation of local youth commissions.[3] Although such commissions cannot possibly negotiate the termination of the war in Vietnam or provide resolution of poverty and civil rights issues, they can provide an opportunity—a legitimate one—for youth to participate in the affairs of their own community. And perhaps it is appropriate that their interests and concerns about issues and problem-solving begin in the local community. Several communities have initiated youth commissions; clear guidelines for establishment and operation of such commissions are available. If there is a single concept which may be seen as the hallmark of a youth commission, it is one of dialogue between adults and youth. It is neither a matter of being patronizing nor condescending, but rather the joining together of two major forces in the life of a community to share insights and understandings about the community and to develop techniques for coping with the problems within the community which have been unearthed by such dialogue. It assumes that the exposure of problems and inconsistencies in the life of the community will be tolerated by young and old alike. Youth commissions require equal participation of youth and adults, mutual respect, and tolerance; there is no requirement for excessive investments of time and money or other personal resources. The traditionalized adult and exuberant youth may not always blend together smoothly; thus there is also a requirement for empathy, rationality, and concern.

A number of cities, most notably in California, have created youth commissions or youth councils.[4] These have frequently been directed toward a particular aspect of community life or created for a specific purpose, such as serving recreation needs or reducing delinquency. The reports of these various commissions suggest certain principles which are related to achievement or non-achievement of stated objectives. Assuming that youth commissions are being contemplated for a community, the following guidelines have usually been applied with some success:

1. The most important single characteristic of a successful youth commission centers about the joint and co-equal participation of youth and adults in determining activities and functions. Simply stated, when adults control commissions, or when youth have more than an appropriate amount of responsibility, an imbalance is created, frequently with adverse effects.
2. Successful youth commissions have avoided utilizing youth as "advisors," but rather have formally involved them in commission activities. For example, a fifteen-member youth commission might most appropriately be organized with an approximately equal number of adults and youth, each member having an equal voice and vote. This would be a superior arrangement than a structure centered upon fifteen-well-meaning, but often naive, adults who on occasion "consult" with or seek advice from youth.

3. The legitimatization of a youth commission through local government action is important. It is desirable to have a youth commission created by city ordinance or charter in a manner similar to appointment of other local commissions, e.g., fire commissions, park and recreation commissions, and the like. The capacity for accomplishment of objectives by a commission is considerably enhanced by formal recognition and status in a community.

4. The objectives and activities of a youth commission should be broadly, rather than narrowly, conceived. An attack on delinquency, for example, must deal with recreation, housing, education, employment, and like activities. It cannot be isolated as though it is a single cell cancer in the community. In short, approaching total problems is more appropriate than small individual segments of community life.

5. Membership on a youth commission should, as far as possible, represent and be a cross-section of the community. A commission consisting only of "square kids," "little old ladies," and successful businessmen may be more comfortable to work with, but it will have overlooked the important consideration that a community consists of other significant and diverse groups.

6. Fortunately, operational youth commisssions are but a recent development in dealing with community problems. We have no heritage to be tied to, no tradition to overcome, no pattern which must be followed. We, therefore, have a license to be as imaginative, innovative, and creative as possible in organizational matters, approaches, and activities. The limits are yet to be developed.

7. Finally, there must be a caution expressed—for the establishment of youth commissions is by no means an answer to the multiple problems which confront our communities and nation. Youth commissions may make a significant contribution, but they are not to be conceived of as a cure-all or panacea.

Previously, the idea was expressed that much of what appears to be a revolution among young Americans may be a normal response of normal people to an abnormal situation. If we return to this observation for just a moment, is it not possible that we are witnessing a normal response to a society which abnormally denies a large segment of its population any participation in decision-making, particularly when the decision-making is focused upon a long history and tradition of inconsistencies? Some of these inconsistencies—at least those expressed by youth—have been identified. Almost without exception, we have asked—indeed, demanded—that our youth accept adult judgments on important national concerns. As long as we deny youth a chance to participate in our political system of shared decisions, they will find alternative ways to be heard. And, as many youth indicate, adults frequently do not hear except by loud voices and destructive behavior.

In short, we are suggesting that the concerns of youth be heard through legitimate social and political systems—by these concerns about campus, community, or other phases of social life. It should be clear that our young men and women—whether we agree with their beliefs or not—are going to be heard. The choice of adults at this point is simply limited to audio techniques; we can hear what our youth have to say through confrontations at Berkeley and Watts, or we can devise some alternatives. Youth commissions, for example, are in a small way, alternatives. But time is running short.

NOTES

1. William E. Amos, and Charles F. Wellford, (ed.). *Delinquency Prevention: Theory & Practice* (Englewood Cliffs, N.J.: Prentice Hall, 1967), p. xv.
2. See G. T. Gitchoff, *Kids, Cops and Kilos: A Study of Contemporary Suburban Youth.* (San Diego: Malter-Westerfield, 1969), for an indepth discussion on youth involvement in the decision-making process.
3. *Ibid.,* pp. 29.
4. Joseph D. Johnson, and Robert Carter, *et al.* "Middle-Class Delinquency: An Experiment in Community Control," *Research Monograph.* (Berkeley: Univ. of Calif. School of Criminology, 1969).

READING 2

The Hang-Loose Ethic

J.L. Simmons
Barry Winograd

. . .*[*There is*]* an emerging new ethos in American society which seems most aptly called "the hang-loose ethic." It is cool and irreverent and it reflects a good deal of disaffection toward many of our more traditional roots. For this reason, it is perhaps more worrisome to parents, educators, and officials than the mere wildness or deviant flirtations of youth.

A barefooted man with a beard and a surplus Navy jacket that has "Love IS" written on the back of it was walking down the main street of a small midwestern city, digging the sunlight and thinking that the heat was really pleasant when you got out into it. A group of high school kids rode by him in a car and began shouting to him. "Hey beatnik." "Hey, you're high man." "What color's your dingy?" And, from one of the less imaginative boys, "Why don't you go fly a kite?"

The man looked up musingly, jaywalked across the street to a dime store, bought a kite and some luminous paint and two thousand feet of string. He took them to his battered car and drove around the adjacent suburbs for awhile, rounding up kids to fly the kite with him. Some parents looked him over and scurried their kids away, shaking their heads about the invasion of perverts; others looked into his face and saw nothing evil there, so consented. They drove to the top of a hill overlooking the town, painted the kite with bright psychedelic colors, sent it up and flew it all afternoon. Toward sunset, they cut loose the string and watched their *objet d'art* disappear into the aerial world above them.

The thing about this story is that the young man didn't turn upon his assailants and by opposing them become their like. Nor did he go into a foetal crouch over a beer, pitying himself as a sensitive and misunderstood soul (which he is) and condemning

17

the society which trains even its children to put down the unusual. He transcended the harassment, rather than succumbing to it by being roused to self-pity or anger.

The emerging ethic is hang-loose in a number of senses, but, its deep running feature is that things once taken for granted as God-given or American Constitution-given—those basic premises about the world and the way it works—are no longer taken for granted or given automatic allegiance. In other words, many Americans are hanging a bit loose from traditional Americana.

This new ethos is still in the process of forming and emerging; the adherents themselves are mostly unaware of the credo they are participating in making and are already living by. For instance, if you went up to many of the likely young people about town and said, "Say, are you an adherent of the hang-loose ethic?", many of them would look at you oddly and wonder what the hell you were talking about.

Well, if this thing is still so amorphous and you can only speculate about it, and the supposed followers are hardly even aware of it, why bother?

Because we want to see what lies beneath the legion of different concrete happenings. A society can be portrayed in a number of different ways and each gives a different picture of what the society is. It can be done by sketching the material objects, the streets, the buildings, the childhood and adult toys. It can be done by describing the typical behavior, the activities, the rituals, the average life-course of an ordinary member. It can also be done by trying to ferret out the underlying ideology or ethos, which comes forth in a thousand and one different ways and which is the wellspring from which flows the other things, the toys, the scenes, the lives, the typical attitudes and responses. Our attempt to ferret out the ideology behind the happenings is an attempt, then, to dive beneath the trappings and veneers down to the basic world view of the people who are making them happen.

At first glance, it might seem as if the hang-loose ethic is the absence of any morality, that it rejects every ideology, that the followers have no rudder and no star except the swift gratification of all impulses. At a second glance it appears only as a bewildering melange of scenes in various locales. But upon closer examination, one can see that it does embody some values and some guiding principles which, although still ill-formed and vaguely expressed, shape the attitudes and actions of the followers. However, to convey a fuller picture of this ethos, we must sketch the previous American ethics from which it emerged.

Europeans and Americans of the past few centuries have been characterized by most writers as human beings who subscribed to and lived by what is called the Protestant Ethic. This Protestant Ethic was a way of life and a view of life which stressed the more somber virtues, like the quiet good feeling of a hard day's work well done, the idea that the good man always more than earned his pay, and a kind of fierce pragmatism in which the hard and fast, here and now, seeable, touchable, aspects of reality were the only things given the name of reality.

Another thing about the Protestant Ethic was a kind of positive moderatism. Moderation wasn't just a safe course between extremes; moderation was an optimum, positive, good in-and-of-itself thing. Moderation was raised almost to a first principle of ethics. It was a mandate on how to conduct your life.

Anything which veered very far from this somber dignity in oneself and one's accumulations was thought of as bad and suspect. We will see, for example, when we discuss "tripping" that whereas most of the world has regarded exceptional behavior that strays beyond the mundane with an awe combining wonder and terror, in the Western world the wonder has until very recently dropped away and it was suppressed as altogether dangerous. Western man neglected what other times and places made a good deal of, the positive aspects which exceptional experiences might have.

This moderatism carried over into virtually every aspect of the lives of the people. Even in religion and young love, anything smacking too much of mysticism was suspect. The West has relied mostly upon dogma rather than experience in its religious institutions and, despite our hungry romanticism, most of our marriages and other sexual liasons have been made largely by arrangement.

This Protestant Ethic seems to have characterized the majority of our forefathers although there was always a "lunatic" fringe and a subterranean stratum composed of those at the bottom of the social ladder and of outsiders. And, like all people everywhere, the adherents didn't entirely live up to their own ideals. But, the Protestants ran the schools and the courts, and the country and the fringe was contained and circumscribed, largely kept at the fringe.

Then, as the decades passed and we moved into the present century, America began to undergo a secularization which involved not only a dwindling of the force of religion, but also a dwindling of the force of the work ethic and the rather stiff personal code which surrounded it. Particularly in the mushrooming urban areas after the Second World War, something grew up which William F. Whyte termed "the Social Ethic."

The Social Ethic (or perhaps more aptly, the Sociable Ethic) was a kind of jocular, benign, superficial, "we're all in the same boat," goodwill. But it shared many things with the Portestant Ethic from which it evolved under the impact of modern times. It was still taken for granted that getting ahead in the Establishment was the thing to do, and that the accumulation of material wealth was a good thing in and of itself. Whyte used the "organization man" living in the new suburbs as his prototypic example and he made a good argument that this was tending to become the overweening American ethos. Work and play, family and politics, each of these were supposed to be a good thing, a fun thing, a comfortable thing. The Sociable Ethic was a secularization of the Protestant ideology combined with a feeling of comfort and goodwill which is easy to generate in a luxuriant society such as ours.

Risk is minimized in the Sociable Ethic. All parties join in a collusion which reduces the change of great failure and great success once you've been hooked into the system. Of course, there were some dark counterthemes in this portrait: those thirty percent of the people who were not in any real sense beneficiaries of the luxuriant system. And it certainly was not a comfortable place for them—it was as Baldwin has suggested, another country. This didn't just mean the Negro of the South; it also included most Northern Negroes, the uneducated, the abysmally poor, those who lacked the skills to sell themselves, to make themselves an attractive enough package to get recruited into the system.

But the majority of Americans were in it and were doing

fairly well. And the continuities with the earlier ethic remained. There still existed a kind of blandness, a real distrust for the exceptional and the bizarre, and there still remained a real distrust for doing something, let's say, "just for kicks." We had in the fifties almost the Utopian culmination of the principle of moderation. Moderate in politics, moderate in work—not too much because it doesn't really pay, not too little because you might get dropped. Moderate in family which involved a kind of thing where you were moderately attached to your spouse and children and moderately concerned with their welfare and you were moderately unfaithful and moderately blasphemous. But you also gave a moderate allegiance to your family and your company and your country.

This was not a picture window nightmare. Most of those involved were probably moderately comfortable and moderately happy.

Does this mean that these people were apathetic and uninvolved, just going through some motions?

No. They were moderately involved in many things. they cried a little and they cared a little and they strove a little and were proud a little and ashamed a little. You see, these people were veterans of hard times; a world depression which was tough, a world war which was tough, an uncertain time afterwards which was tough. And so at last they arrived in their ranch houses and they could afford cocktails on the way home without much worrying about the price. It was, in a sense, the indulgence of a dream, the dream of building an affluent society. Because in the fifties that's exactly what we had—fantastically affluent compared with anything that had ever existed before.

Certainly, there were a few hot social movements and protests about the thirty percent who weren't "in." But, we must realize that in most times and countries it's been 90 percent or 98 percent. So only thirty percent left out is pretty damn good and something brand new in history. And the first scattered appearance of the beats and the freedom cats must not obscure the fact that the vast majority were (moderately) good Americans in the small sense of not rocking any boats.

Yet even as the sociable ideology was crystallizing and taking hold and Eisenhower was virtually proclaiming moderation the

21

cornerstone of our national policy, a new kind of feeling was beginning to stir across the land—a feeling which had many ties with the past but which was also new.

Although there were precursors in the late fifties when Ginsberg was telling people he'd seen the best minds of his generation driven mad, and hip talk (and an inevitable bit of the philosophy behind it) was being picked up by teenagers, the hang-loose ethos really belongs to the sixties because this is the decade in which it is emerging and spreading throughout our society.

When we search for the "philosophy" which is the common denominator running through the variety of happenings—the implicit code of values pushing those involved toward some things and away from other things—some of the characteristics of this yet crystallizing view can be discerned.

One of the fundamental characteristics of the hang-loose ethic is that it is *irreverent*. It repudiates, or at least questions, such cornerstones of conventional society as Christianity, "my country right or wrong," the sanctity of marriage and premarital chastity, civil obedience, the accumulation of wealth, the right and even competence of parents, the schools, and the government to head and make decisions for everyone—in sum, the Establishment. This irreverence is probably what most arouses the ire and condemnation of the populace. Not only are the mainstream institutions and values violated, but their very legitimacy is challenged and this has heaped insult upon moral injury in the eyes of the rank and file.

Sin, as the violation of sacred beliefs and practices, is nothing new and most of us have had at least a few shamefully delightful adventures somewhere along the way. But what is qualitatively new is that the very truth and moral validity of so many notions and practices, long cherished in our country, are being challenged. When caught by parents or authorities, youths are no longer hanging their heads in shame. Instead, they are asserting the rightness, at least for themselves, of what they're doing. And they are asking what right do their elders have to put them down.

And not infrequently the irreverence takes a form which goes beyond this openly aggressive challenging. An increasing number of happeners have reached a level of disrespect so thoroughgoing that they don't even bother to "push their cause." Not only have they dropped their defensive posture, but their own assertiveness has become quiet, even urbane, in its detachment and indifference toward the "other morality." This withdrawal has aroused some of the greatest resentment and opposition since it is perhaps the gravest affront to an established ethic not to be taken seriously. To be defied is one thing; to be simply ignored and dismissed out of hand is something else. The spread of this more fullblown irreverence testifies to the fact that a good many happeners are managing to set up a life that is relatively independent of conventional society.

Another basic aspect of the hang-loose ethic is a diffuse and pervasive *humanism* which puts great store upon the value of human beings and human life. Adherents don't necessarily proclaim the rationality of men or their inherent "goodness," but they do claim that people are precious and that their full development is perhaps the most worthwhile of all things.

Killing is a heinous violation of this ethos and so is any action which puts others down, except under extreme circumstances. The most approved method of defense and retaliation is to turn one's oppressors onto the good life they're condemning and to help them resolve hangups which prevent this from happening. If this fails, one may attempt to "blow their minds," to shock their preconceptions and prejudices in some way and hence force them to open their eyes, to re-evaluate, and hopefully to grow. The happeners refuse under most circumstances to employ the weapons of their adversaries because they feel that by so doing they would merely become like them. Instead, they try to transform their adversaries into fellows. The only really endorsed aggression is to try and force your enemies to become your friends. Only in extreme cases is putting down—the main strategy of the Establishment—even partly acceptable.

Ideally, the happeners do not fill the role of modern missionaries, though their practice in conversation and contact reminds one of historical attempts at persuasion and conversion. When approaching others, they welcome acceptance as well as adoption, but this does not imply that happeners resemble the adventurous, pioneering missionaries of established religions or ideologies. The few actual organizations existing in the happening world are there, first, to serve their "constituents" and, second, to espouse and inform.

This humanism, combined as it is with irreverence, produces a passive resistance toward the Establishment and the persuasive efforts of straights, rather than an active rebellion. The happeners are more transcendent than antagonistic; more indifferent and benevolently contemptuous than negative and bitter. Bitterness does occur over concrete immediate cases of harassment or "for your own good" busts, commitments, and putdowns. But it fades rather quickly again into the more general mood of simple wariness. The mood is not grim, although there is a diffuse paranoia toward the established social order which waxes and wanes as the scene gets hot and cools down again.

Another basic aspect of the hang-loose ethic is the pursuit of *experience* both as a thing in itself and as a means of learning and growing. The idea is that a great variety and depth of experience is beneficial and not at all harmful as long as you can handle it. This entails a heightened attention to the present ongoing moment and far less concern with the past or future. It also involves a mistrust of dogmas and principles which tend to obscure the richness of life. For this reason, they also often reject the categorizing and generalizing which is so rampant in our educational system. Within the drug scenes, for instance, there is full awareness that LSD-25 can trigger "bad trips," for some people. But, again the fact of experience alone, whether guided officially by researchers or informally by "guides," overrides the application of a generalized rule about the possible detrimental effects of such drugs.

This courting of raw experience is what gives many people the impression that those participating in the happenings are without any morals whatsoever; that they are selfishly pursuing swift gratification of their impulses. And it is true that the unabashed seeking of experiences will frequently lead the seeker to violate what other people consider proper. But such judgments are one-sided. Although they see that swingers are breaking standards, they entirely miss the point that swingers are following another, different set of standards; so that arguments between the camps are in reality debates between conflicting ideologies.

As part and parcel of the importance placed on directly experiencing oneself and the world, we find that *spontaneity*, the ability to groove with whatever is currently happening, is a highly valued personal trait. Spontaneity enables the person to give himself up to the existential here and now without dragging along poses and hangups and without playing investment games in hopes of possible future returns. The purest example of spontaneity is the jazz musician as he stands up and blows a cascade of swinging sounds.

Another facet of the hang-loose ethic is an untutored and unpretentious *tolerance*. Do whatever you want to as long as you don't step on other people while doing it. A girl is free to wet her pants or play with herself openly while she's up on an acid trip and no one will think less of her for it. A man can stand and stare at roadside grass blowing in the wind and no one will accuse him of being the village idiot. If you like something that I don't like, that's fine, that's your bag; just don't bring me down.

The swingers, when you come down to it, are anarchists in the fullest sense. They chafe at virtually all restrictions because they see most every restriction that modern man has devised as a limitation on directions people can travel and grow. They feel that the irony of contemporary society is that the very restrictions necessary to curb an immature populace prevent that same populace from becoming mature enough to live without restrictions, just as a girdle weakens the muscles it supports.

Even clothes are regarded by some as mostly a nuisance and swingers have led the whole Western world toward simplicity and ease in styles and makeup. And over weekends and vacations, small groups will often go up together to back country retreats where whoever wants to can run around naked.

Without the fuss or the self-righteousness so common among Establishment liberals, the happeners have come closer to integrating the races, religions, and the sexes than any other group one can think of. A fierce equality is practiced among them, which is appreciative of differences in backgrounds and temperaments. Equality and tolerance aren't abject attempts to make people feel comfortable or wanted; they are dispositions that permit things and relationships to just happen without deliberate forethought and planning. In most happening circles, a Negro is not the recipient of conscious liberal acceptance, but an individual in and of himself who may or may not be a "good" person. Acceptance and participation is based more on how the individual presents himself within the context of the scene, not by preconceived and nurtured stereotypes about the way he is expected to be.

One's past is not held against one and one's reputation is not spoiled by the fact that one might have served time in a prison or mental institution, had an abortion, or perhaps a homosexual affair.

This doesn't mean that the swingers will indiscriminately associate with anyone. Like everybody else, they choose their friends, their lovers, their acquaintances and the people they avoid by how well they get along with one another and enjoy doing things together. But they are less down on the people they don't choose to associate with than others generally are.

But the tolerance stops if somebody is stepping on other people. For instance, if a guy shows up in a particular scene and starts tooling around with other people's minds or bum tripping them just for his own kicks, several people are likely to get together and elect themselves to deal with him by busting *his* mind. And such a guy can quickly be shut out of virtually the entire happenings in that specific scene.

The ideal person in the hang-loose view embodies traits that are difficult to combine. Being as spontaneous as a child yet being sophisticated and worldwise; being fully self-expressive yet being always in control of oneself. This is the ambiguity of being cool. Being able to dig the ongoing present as it unfolds yet being able to get things done and maintain a competent life of fulfilled commitments and involvements. Being hang-loose from any constraining orthodoxy, yet being courageous enough to follow your own path wherever it may lead and whatever the travails it plunges you into.

The heroes are those who have managed to swing in some eminent way, especially if they did so in spite of tough conditions. The distinguished outsiders of history, avant-garde artists, the leaders of unpopular social movements. The list of admirable people would include figures such as Aldous Huxley, Allen Ginsberg, Gandhi, John F. Kennedy, Fidel Castro, Alpert and Leary, and Bob Dylan. But such people are not so much heroes in the ordinary sense because, although they are much admired, they are not so much worshipped, and because they are critically discussed as well as fondly quoted.

The fact that swingers operate at least partly outside the Establishment and often even outside the law produces a certain admiration and sympathy among them for other categories of alienated and disaffiliated people, such as the Negroes, the poor, the mentally disturbed, the delinquent, the sexual deviant, and the peoples of underdeveloped countries. They do not necessarily approve of what these people do, but they do see them as victims of Establishments.

These sympathies, coupled with their tolerance and op-position to restrictiveness, lead the happeners to take a "liberal" stand on almost every question and issue, from welfare measures to disarmament, to the legalization of pot and abortions, to racial integration and civil liberties generally, to recognition of Red China and negotiations with the Viet Cong, to sexual per-missiveness and progressive education, to socialized medicine and the exploration of space.

But most of them are not self-conscious "liberals." They take these stands for granted as the only reasonable and sensible ones, but they usually don't work within organized political parties to bring them about and they are not very happy with the com-promising Establishment liberals who do. They support such men as Governor Brown, Clark Kerr and Bobby Kennedy only as the best of the poor choices available, all of whom are really more alike than different, and none of whom are really worth a good God damn.

But they are not pro-Communist either, although sym-pathetic toward revolutionaries in underdeveloped countries. They see communism as at least as odious and repressive as the societies of the West and probably a good deal more so.

The hang-loose people are not joiners; indeed this is one of their defining attributes. They tend to shy away from any kind of conventional ideologies or fanaticisms, seeing them as unfree compulsions and obsessions rather than noble dedications. They regard those who are too intensely and doggedly involved, in even such highly approved causes as integration and peace, a little askance and happeners will sometimes describe their own past involvements in these movements as something of a psychological hangup.

The villains in the hang-loose view are people and social forces which put other people down and hang them up, which teach people to be stolid and dignified rather than swinging, self-righteous and moralistic rather than responsible, dutiful rather than devoted. Those who, for the sake of some ideology, will set fire to other people's kids; who, for the sake of some ideology, will slap their own children into becoming something less than they might have been. The villains are those who pass their own hangups onto those around them and thus propagate a sickness, "for your own good."

This seems to be the still amorphous and emerging ethos which is the basis of the happenings we're concerned with. Admirable in some ways, perhaps a bit idealistic and innocent and even silly in others, still in the process of forming and changing, and creating many problems for everyone. And perhaps as inevitable, given current conditions, as the spring winds which stir its adherents.

And it is a set of ideals which, like all people, the adherents are not able to live up to. Sometimes when things get uptight, they betray themselves and each other. Sometimes, they can't resist selling out for a better package deal. Sometimes, despite their utterances they can become as provincial and arrogant as any tribesman who thinks he has the monopoly on truth. And sometimes they are driven by other motives to cheat and exploit one another. But such shortcomings are panhuman and can be leveled at any group including the United States Senate or the medical profession. And this should not obscure the fact that ideals are a potent social force which have a major hand in making people what they are. Ideals, aside from having a part in making individual attitudes, attachments and adjustments, also serve to categorize people as runners along certain tracks of life. What is today called deviant is tomorrow only eccentric. What harps upon and tortures the older ethics and ideologies, can eventually become an accepted, if not generally followed, belief system.

Like all ideologies, this ethos is sometimes used as a rationalization and justification. Irresponsibility can be excused as freedom. Apathy can be called being cool. Lack of dependability can be called spontaneity and so can boorishness and sloth. And virtually any behavior can be justified on the grounds that it is experience and will lead in some way to personal growth.

But then pointing out these blindspots may be a pot calling a kettle black, for all ideologies are so misused and the misuse doesn't destroy the fact that they are also faithfully followed.

Those following under the banner of the hang-loose ethic are not of one stripe. Sometimes it is the spontaneous pose of a youth who is drunk on his own vaulting life-energy. Sometimes it is the final vision which has resulted from long training in some Eastern philosophy. Sometimes it is the whimsical realization that your hard work has produced a degree of comfort and success but that you're growing older and that things are perhaps just too uncertain to lay too much store upon the alleged joys of the future or the hereafter. Sometimes it is a temporary fling in what will prove to be an otherwise pedestrian life. Sometimes it is a later stage in a journey which has led a youth through romantic idealism, folksong clubs and science fiction, protest movements, a period of disenchantment, wandering, and psychedelic drugs while still in his teens. And sometimes it is the stony and even vicious hipsterism of the slum ghetto.

The hang-loose attitude is simply not a uniform thing. One can hang-loose happily or bitterly, stoicly or desperately, wisely or floundering, as a posing actor or as a blithe spirit. Sometimes it is mixed with defiance; sometimes loving tolerance; and sometimes it embodies an indifference which smacks of callous unconcern for the fate of others. And sometimes it is tinged with the pathos of the feeling that in another, better world things would be different.

This ethos will have a somewhat different flavor in different groups and in different regions of the country. On the Eastern seaboard, it is likely to be more cosmopolitan and Eureopean in temperament. In the Midwest it is more likely to be a reaction to the stolid Dirksonesque environment. In the South, it tends to combine the effete with the rustic. And in the West it is likely to be more gaudy and mystical. Among students it tends to be more self-reflective and among dropouts it tends to be more starkly hedonistic. Among the lower classes it tends to be a proletarian disaffiliation, among the middle and upper classes it tends to combine the *Playboy* hipsterism with psychoanalytic self-realization. Among teenagers it is likely to be the following of fads, among youth it is more likely to be a search for meanings and recipes, among adults it is likely to be more cautious and more straight, and among older people it is likely to be hobbies and vitriolic conversations in the sun.

Among Negroes, Mexicans and Puerto Ricans it will tend to be more angry and physical and immediate, among whites it will probably be more sedentary and compromising and tolerant because it is more their society. Among Catholics it will involve "soul trouble"; among Protestants, a Nietzchean debate over whether God is dead; among Jews, an agnostic urbanity; and among the uncommitted, a search for alternative faiths.

In the urban slums it is explosive and a source of constant potential violence. Among middle class youth it is a source of scandals, a recruiting ground for protests of all kinds, and a susceptibility toward the milder, unharmful forms of deviance, and personal problems. And among suburban adults it is a careful but sometimes determined minority voice within the Establishment, and an "aw, come on!" ambivalence toward the Great Society bit.

American suburbs aren't the places of other-directed conformity as Whyte and Reisman depicted them in the fifties. Perhaps they never altogether were. But the stereotype of the jovial empty-spirited organization man which may have had a good deal of truth a decade ago, now fits only a plurality at most — and a plurality that is no longer in the center of things, but off to the side as a disinherited conservatism.

In today's suburbs one finds a widespread diffidence toward job, background, and other external tags and badges. People are unwilling to think of themselves or others as merely the sum of their statuses and nothing more. A few years ago you might ask "what do you do?"; be answered, "I'm an accountant"; and say, "Oh, that's nice." But now you'd say, "Well, yes, but what do *you* do, who are *you*?"

Fromm's classic thesis that contemporary people are only using their freedom from the chains of tradition to package and sell their external selves until the package becomes the person and there's nothing left but a gaudy shell, is no longer so true either. In almost any neighborhood gathering, one can find plenty of evidence for a growing disaffection with external symbols (which were the main unit of currency in the heyday of the Sociable Ethic). Expressions of a certain distance from one's job and other positions and a conspiratorial show of fellow humanness have in fact become the newest gambit in advertising, salesmanship and interpersonal relations generally.

There is of course a good deal of the older ideologies still around and certain facets of them still ring faintly even among the most far out followers of the hang-loose view. Among those followers who are working within the Establishment there is still moderate disapproval of doing things just for kicks. Swinging should be "constructive," either by refreshing you so that you can return zestfully to the playful fray of your workaday world, or by helping you resolve psychoanalytic hangups so that you can move on to the next stage of growth.

And with a bit of pendulum swinging from the gregarious outwardness of the Sociable Ethic to the fierce individualism of our puritan predecessors, the current swingers in schools and suburbs are less concerned with courting the offhand opinions and tepid acceptance of the crowds they encounter. They are not immune to the smiles and frowns of others, especially people they like, but they are not enslaved by them either, and much of the time they groove along with an inner-directedness that would delight Reisman.

There is also an appreciation of affluence as with the Sociable Ethic, and in fairly sharp distinction to the self-conscious poverty of most of the Beats during the fifties. But this is more of a taken-for-granted that the world is full of material baubles which can be very useful, than a deliberate striving to accumulate them. The current swingers take national affluence for granted and only strive to have it distributed more widely and with less necessity of selling oneself to get a part of it.

The modern happeners like many of the things which our shopping-center society produces in so great a quantity, such as cars and clothes and stereos and prints and books, and they do not share the anti-television stance of the intellectuals during the last decade. But they don't want to struggle too hard to get them and they will freely loan and borrow them. So this shared appreciation of affluence shouldn't lead us to neglect what is now so different— namely that swingers have broken away from the high valuation of property which has been the cornerstone of every Western society since the Reformation and the rise of the middle classes. Property is not something designed to dominate an individual's life; it is something to be lived with and used, not as a focus of existence, but as incidental to the fact that humans are alive and dynamic. A young man, who like many others is only involved in some of the happening scenes, once commented, "do you realize that legally we can kill for the sake of property? What gives us the right to say that if a burglar is stealing a damned TV set we can go ahead and blow his brains out. Property, not human life, has become the most sacred thing in our society."

Along with the repudiation of property as something to work and live for, the hang-loose people feel less honor bound to fulfill commitments unless they are coupled with personal involvements and attachments. This makes them less dependable workers and spouses, and their lack of steadfastness creates part of their bad reputation in a society which still harkens to the Calvinist idea of duty. But swingers will not discharge their duties as students, workers, lovers, or citizens just because someone else says they *should.* "Should" isn't good enough unless it is coupled with "want to," stemming either from personal desire or personal convictions. Concretely, this means that they will break a law they disagree with, will desert a spouse or friend they no longer love, will cheat on a test they feel is unjust, will walk off a job they find odious, and will speak against a war they feel is dishonorable. The swingers will, because of expediency, often cool it by fulfilling obligations they do not feel personally bound to, but if they don't have to, they frequently won't.

Hence, an obvious strategy for those in the opposition wishing the demise of happening scenes and their tangential attributes, would involve making these people "want to" do something or discharge some particular responsibility. Sadly it is too infrequently recognized that unless those with the hang-loose philosophy are, at a minimum, tolerated, little progress in the above direction can be made. You can't call somebody a lunatic, beatnik, dope addict, or radical and expect them to jump to your beck and call. Regardless of how much reason and substance are part of the opposition doctrines, they will get nowhere until debate goes beyond mutual debasement and vilification.

In the hang-loose view, the main problems besides hassles with the Establishment and its blue-frocked representatives, are the personal hang-ups which prevent people from living as fully and spontaneously as they otherwise might. This is a more general and extreme form of the ideals of individualism, self-determination and self-realization which have been kicking around Western Civilization for several centuries and which have been such a prominent part of psychoanalysis. These ideals when carried to their logical extreme by the swingers, however, put them in opposition to a good many of the rules and practices of the Establishment, which, like societies everywhere, grants personal freedom only within limits and which labels those who go beyond these limits, deviant.

And this is the dilemma of the swinger. In the very process of attempting to resolve his hang-ups, he will usually move further outside the pale of conventional society and will become more deviant, immoral and dangerous in the eyes of the general populace.

Happeners are aware of this dilemma and spend long hours talking with each other about how it might be resolved. An individual solution is to become exceedingly cool—to develop the skills and habits to swing yet evade the eye of the Establishment by being discreet and by being able to play straight when necessary.

But this is only a makeshift solution, temporary and high in personal cost. The long-term solution almost all swingers agree is to turn the world on. Their dream is to live in a world of beautiful people in which everyone grooves on their own things and doesn't interfere with anyone else in doing it. Where people will say "no" only because they want to and not because of fear or tie-ups. Where people don't make it their business to screw each other up over some decrepit dogma. Where children aren't stunted by "education" and "training" into growing up absurd, sad caricatures of their possible selves. Where people are free enough and fearless enough to grow their own trees.

If you think this dream is a little naive and foolish and fantastic, you are right: If you think it neglects and glosses over many of the realities of present world conditions and that it is a bit pretentious and unlikely, given the facts of history, you are right again. And if you find nothing good or true or beautiful about it, you can go to hell.

There is a storm of violent opposition to the hang-loose ethos and the behavior that stems from it. This storm of opposition seems to be of two kinds, and the first kind is moral.

A good many people feel that those participating in the happenings are morally depraved. Bratty overgrown kids crying for the freedom to play with each other underneath the streetlights. Arrogant but innocent youngsters who think they know more than they do and who are easy prey for dope peddlers, sexual perverts, and Communist agitators. A few more rapped knuckles, stiffer curfews and supervision, a few more jail sentences to set examples, and a stint in the army might make men (and women) out of them. But right now they're spoiled, oversexed, smart aleck brats who aren't worth their pay on a job of work and who are unfit to inherit our great country.

In the rush of controversy and opposition to what's happening, the swingers become *objects* for explanation, condescending sympathy, or condemnation. But because the happeners don't themselves own or have much access to communication channels for reaching the general public, the fact that they are active *subjects* who are in turn evaluating their evaluators is lost sight of. So their turnabout indictments seldom reach the ears of the general public, although they are widely circulated and discussed among the swingers themselves. When they are quoted by officials or the mass media, it is usually only to illustrate their alienation, willfulness, or delinquency. The quotes are treated only as graphic evidence of their sickness and depravity. Attempts for example, to legalize the use of marijuana receive the sarcastic and superior attention of smiling commentators on the 11 o'clock news. But, for those even partially involved in the drug world such activity is serious business that is a frequent subject of conversation, if not direct action. Although they might discuss it with a measure of frivolity, fearful of taking themselves *too* seriously, marijuana legalization has become a meaningful aspect of personal commitment and not some deviant's practical joke.

Parents and other concerned adults are discussing and fretting over what is becoming of today's youth and turning to each other, to experts (usually self-proclaimed) and to their officials for advice.

And youth are discussing and fretting over their elders and they turn to each other and to those rare experts and officials who are in any sense "where it's at" for advice. Restless and uncertain they are; unsure of themselves, of their beliefs, and of their futures. But they are more self-assured in their feelings that parents and mentors, neighbors and newscasters, officials and presidents of the United States cannot be taken at face-value. They suspect—dimly or consciously—that their elders are not altogether honest, wise or competent to run the world and give advice, though many sincerely wish they were.

To the widespread charges that they are being immoral, irresponsible, and irreverent, they turn about and reply: "Look at you, blowing up whole countries for the sake of some crazy ideologies that you don't live up to anyway. Look at you, mind-fucking a whole generation of kids into getting a revolving charge account and buying your junk. (Who's a junkie?) Look at you, needing a couple of stiff drinks before you have the balls to talk with another human being. Look at you, making it with your neighbor's wife on the sly just to try and prove that you're really alive. Look at you, hooked on *your* cafeteria of pills, and making up dirty names for anybody who isn't in your bag, and screwing up the land and the water and the air for profit, and calling this nowhere scene the Great Society! *And you're gonna tell us how to live?* C'mon, man, you've got to be kidding!"

(This collage was made from a multitude of remarks dropped in a wide variety of different scenes. The remarks were usually reactions to specific events such as McNamara's proposal to draft the world or Reagan's promises of suppression, Dirkson's Biblical pronouncements or the sentencing of a youth for smoking a casual weekend joint. Ill-will is more of a temporary reaction than an intrinsic attitude among happeners.)

And the oldsters in their turn reply: "Well what are you doing that's so meaningful? Aren't you maybe on a hundred roads to nowhere too?" And the host of individual debates that go to make up the Great Debate continue all over our country.

The other kind of opposition is a practical concern. Who's going to be left to run the world if everybody turns on? This question bothers many people who are otherwise not so concerned about the morality or immorality of what's happening. They fear that nobody will be left to mind the store, to do those thousand-and-one routine but necessary things that keep society's wheels turning, her goods flowing and her children growing. Who will hold the world together?

Maybe nobody will hold the *present* world together. Who wants to? How much of it do we really need? How many of our proud items are only consolation prizes? Maybe a newer social order could evolve in which we would have the real things that we talk about on rainy nights but never quite seem to achieve?

The worry that the present social order cannot continue unless the happenings are checked is counter-balanced by the worry among happeners that the present social order may well persist in spite of their wishes and efforts to change things, and that the current social order at the worst may destroy the world in a thermonuclear light that would dim any prospect of an enlightened future. Here we find a true opposition and conflict between those who want to preserve the present moral order and those who wish to transform it.

Many among the older cohort worry whether today's youth are training and preparing themselves for the adult roles they are soon to occupy. This worry contains some validity, for many swingers are pretty unimpressive even judged in terms of their own values and ideals. A three year collection of *Wonder Woman* comics is perhaps trippy, but it doesn't make the world a cleaner, greener land.

But the worry is also ethnocentric and historically arrogant because the young needn't accept or strive to fill adult roles as the oldsters choose to define them—and it might even be best if they didn't. On this issue youth *is* rebellious as it tries to revamp the more traditional conceptions of a "man," a "woman," a "career," a "citizen," a "human being." In their uncertain experimentations some swingers are probably stumbling toward what will prove to be more realistic and effective roles which may better fit the upcoming times.

Perhaps the most curious irony about the hang-loose ethic is that it is distilled from many of the highest ideals of Western man and our national heritage, carried out to their logical conclusion. America, is now, in a sense, confronted by a legion of youths who are trying in their own fumbling way to practice what generations of fatuous graduation speakers have been preaching. This emerging ethos which seems so heretical at first glance is partly a restatement of some of the highest ideals and values which the great middle classes struggled for during the Industrial Revolution and which have since served all too often as a covering rationalization for self-seeking exploitation; the ideals we learn to bend and compromise in the process of "growing up" and "learning the ropes" and becoming "mature." The irony is not that Americans have failed to teach the upcoming generation but that they have been perhaps too successful in their training and must now confront their fervent pupils.

READING 3

Night Thoughts of a Police Chief
Joseph Paul Kimble

If one were asked to characterize this past decade, it might be fair to say that it has been a period of thrashing about. A search for stability, a longing for the "normalcy" of the pre-nuclear years, has rendered a substantial part of our population uncomfortable, unsure and extremely anxious. As a result, the arc of our social spectrum grows wider and wider. And, like a tired metronome, opinion becomes increasingly disposed to stick at one or the other extreme.

In many ways it is a relief to identify the sources of one's discontent by a simplistic "Them vs. Us" identification. As we gulp our social and political tranquilizers, as we readjust our conscience, the world momentarily resumes the sound and shape and shadows of the distant past.

We come to depend upon these periods of euphoria as an escape from the hurting present. We come to rely upon the prescriptions of the vocal extremes. After a while we cease to question the efficacy of what we ingest. It becomes easier to let others think for us; it becomes more comfortable to let others act for us. The only volition we cling to is the right to reject—to reject, or even hate, anyone or anything that might threaten our great and sovereign state of Rationalization. It is understandable, then, that certain segments of the population, when they find that the reasonableness of *their* great crusade is doubted, threatened, or even attacked, react with indignation. The greatest blow of all, of course, is to find a comfortable perch on the radical Right, or the radical Left, jeopardized by those subversive young people of the radical middle! The foregoing characterization is not intended to be facetious—the fact is that the anguished protestation of modern youth is largely directed against the ideology of extremism in *either sector*. It is also directed against the silent, ambivalent middle, that by default perpetuates the extremes.

At the risk of generalizing, I would say that the majority of American youth are protesting the addiction to uncompromising viewpoints. They are protesting an unhealthy obsession with the past, with self-indulgence and self-hypnosis. They are protesting inertia, indifference, and the compromise of integrity for the sake of expediency. It is unfortunate that their protests generate overreaction in some quarters, even when they are *not* accompanied by violence or unreasonable conduct. Many young people are protesting those forces and conditions that *generate* radical reaction. Unhappily, it has become so unfashionable in today's society to question the *status quo*, that the motives of those who protest become automatically suspect.

What is it that perceptive young Americans are so intent on bringing to our attention? What are some of the urgent messages being semaphored from the urban and academic wilderness? My experience with young people indicates that their concerns touch many areas, but I shall focus for the present on my own field of law enforcement.

Young people tend to view traditional law enforcement in a nontraditional way. Ignoring the precepts of past generations, they too often view police as a threat, rather than as a constructive force. Their position is that police, as a group, are too conservative, too resistant to change. Impressed more by what they see than by what they're told, the young are frank to state that some police agencies are ineffective and inconsistent. They keep hearing loud pronouncements regarding modern investagatory methods, crime laboratories, computers, space-age gimmickry, training and correctional and rehabilitation programs. In spite of such boasts, they observe that crime is increasing, clearance rates for major crimes are still below 30 percent, some cops still "hassle" people on the street, and very few serious offenders are rehabilitated to any meaningful degree. They hear the police side of drugs and other issues, but they have access to bodies of knowledge that provide different and sometimes better answers.

Others question the honesty of a few police agencies across the country—not necessarily that they are corrupt but that their response to certain community problems is biased. For example, do officers in some areas show particular deference to certain segments of the community? Have they one code for the majority and another for ethnic minorities? Do their hiring policies and requirements tend to exclude minority groups? Are observed acts inconsistent with official policies? Do too many agencies stress training, rather than education, for their officers? Are too many agencies operated on the military general staff concept, as opposed to a department that is open—responsive to and held accountable by the community? These are just a few of the misgivings expressed by young people about justice and the police.

In spite of the sometimes brash and self-righteous tone of their inquiry, young people, more than any other group, understand the need for a redefinition of the police role, and the need for a new kind of policeman.

It is painfully obvious that we are no longer a tranquil, rural society. It follows that 18th-century police practices (or 18th-century governmental practices) are irrelevant. For example, we are experiencing the mass movement of people on an unprecedented scale. One million blacks moved out of the South in ten years. Some 400,000 young people converged on the Catskills in one week to attend a "rock festival." Nearly 40 million citizens—more than 12 million households—move every year in the United States! These are staggering figures when one remembers that before 1900 most people never left the area in which they were born. Now, only one person in five still lives within 50 miles of where he was born.

The movement is mostly to the cities, and this has resulted in an influx of people who are ill-equipped to cope with the frustrating, abrasive urban life. Their children, in turn, are even less willing to tolerate the stress, regulation and loss of dignity that is inherent in being hopelessly bogged in metropolitan poverty. It is understandable, then, that traditional police approaches and reactions to the new problems of the central city and its suburbs fall short of the mark. It is reasonable to say—and it is often said—that the police *shouldn't* be expected to deal with these broader community problems; but in fact they are forced to do so because the community as a whole chooses to pretend that the problems don't even exist.

It is no secret to policemen that ghettos, whether they trap white or black, are the urban cancer. The police recognize that this disease is perilously close to the terminal stage in many of our cities. Yet the police have been asked to practice medicine without a license—a license the community has failed to issue in terms of support and involvement. Too many people, young and old, look to the police to cure problems created by years of rejection and indifference. Concerned police officers *are* attempting to reach solutions, but is has become evident that there is a need not only for more policemen but for more effective policemen.

Young people acknowledge this need in their statements of what they expect from the police. These expectations include the enforcement of law in a legal, ethical and humane fashion, by officers with a broadened social outlook and an awareness of the changing world around them. They envision qualified and positive leadership, directing an organization composed of individuals who care about other people, individuals who are emotionally, intellectually and morally competent to deal effectively with the complex problems of this society. Young people want law enforcement that is contemporary and constitutional. They are asking for what the President's Crime Commission recommended in 1967—a rational restructuring of law enforcement.

Although the police are the subject of a great deal of attention by young people, the rest of the community is not exempted from their scrutiny. One of their loudest blasts is directed against the categorization of people and institutions. Too many Americans have succumbed to the dangerous practice of stereotyping. In rebuttal, young people reply that:

¶ Not all people of "hippie appearance" are degenerates, thieves, addicts, or even hippies! (particularly in California).

¶ Not all policemen are racist, Fascist, honky, pig cops; not all policemen are biologically, physiologically and intellectually inferior; not all policemen want to marry your daughters.

¶ Not all governmental institutions are insensitive, inappropriate or nonresponsive; not all critics of government are effete snobs.

¶ Not all wars are good simply because we happen to be involved in them.

¶ Not all young people who are trying to change the Establishment are intent on destroying it.

¶ Law and order, without reason and justice, denies the best of our system.

¶ There is no generation gap; there is a communication and an image reality gap.

¶ People over 30 can be trusted; it's sad, however, that people over 30 attach so little importance to that trust.

Even the church is examined in a critical light. The young observe that too many of them are stained-glass filling stations, where people occasionally stop to fill their spiritual tanks and inflate their egos. The clergy seems oblivious of the problems of civil rights and social justice in the world outside their holy precincts.

My concluding observation concerns the expectations young people hold for the American public. Their greatest hope, I'm told, is that America will at last acknowledge its basic problems, as a first step to finding solutions for its dilemmas. Many young people would like the country as a whole to say: "As a result of a number of circumstances and events, we are, at this point in time, a racist society, a violent society, a criminal society." (It is a terribly difficult statement to make.)

The young contend, first of all, that this country is basically racist, and document their charge with a series of reports and observations, most of which are embodied in the Kerner Report. The Kerner Report, young people are quick to point out, came as a shock to the white, middle-class public. It came as a shock to black people, they say, only because so much money was spent to reach a conclusion that was self-evident.

Young people point out that we are, in too many ways, a violent country. We have never viewed violence as a monopoly of the state, but see it in general as the logical solution when all other solutions fail. During the last decade we have experienced an almost uninterrupted level of domestic violence, and have now apparently reached the point where we are willing to tolerate it, if not excuse it, as an unavoidable side effect of a stress society. Eons ago man crept from his cave as he overcame his fear of his environment. Now, it appears, the violence of our world is forcing him back inside. If you think this a metaphor, I suggest you visit the nearest "total security" apartment complex, "total security" retirement community, or "total security" vacation spa.

It would be fair to characterize ours as a criminal society. We condemn it, we lament it, but as with the weather, we do little more than talk about it. Our legislators use it as emotional fuel for their election drives. They're either waving their hands or sitting on them; nothing substantial happens. It is also safe to suggest that politicians don't really appreciate the relationship of education, housing, jobs, health and poverty to crime. The Safe Streets and Crime Bill offered the greatest hope of the 20th century in unifying efforts against crime. Its partisan emasculation, however, left it measurably less effective than it was destined to be. It is to the discredit of the Congress, past and present, that its members insist on "legislation without appropriation." If one wants evidence of congressional apathy, one can look at the situation in the District of Columbia, which is the only city where the federal government has direct responsibility for combating crime. While rates for serious crime in the nation have increased 11 percent, in the District of Columbia they have jumped 29 percent. On the day the present Congress adjourned, Washington, D.C., had eighty robberies in twenty-four hours.

In this respect, as in most respects, Congress mirrors the American public. Last year it spent $12 billion on alcohol, $8 billion on tobacco, and less than $4 billion on the total administration of justice! Perhaps Pogo was right when he said, "We have met the enemy—and he is us!"

Reasonable people will probably agree that we have explored our world, and we have exploited our world, but we have yet to make it safe. In an urgent search for security we may overlook the important messages given us by concerned young adults. I would earnestly suggest that we don't tune out the truths to which they have addressed themselves. In our lifetime there have been rivers of blood and years of darkness. There has been a tendency to let democracy slowly slip away. It always comes as a bitter surprise that once any part of our liberty is lost, the task of regaining it is agonizingly difficult. We can get it all back—we can make democracy work as it was intended to work if we end the fragmentation and polarization that is destroying us. As Dr. King once said, "We must learn to live together as brothers, or we die together as fools."

We can do it, but will we? I am curious—blue.

The Culture of Youth

Marvin E. Wolfgang

Gertrude Stein is alleged to have said that the United States is the oldest country in the world because it has had the most experience with modern industrial society and its complex consequences. With similar perception, Dwight Macdonald has said that the United States was the first to develop the concept of the teenager, a concept which is still not well accepted in Europe, and that we have had the longest experience with the subculture of youth. The way we handle a nearly "overdeveloped" society with transportation, bureaucratization, impersonal, automated living, and the way we learn to understand the new problems of youth and the existence of poverty to remind us of our social imperfection, will be lessons of value to underdeveloped or newly developed countries. Despite our longer experience with modernity and the teenage subculture, we still have lessons to learn about the problems created by both, and the particular interrelation of modern youth and modern poverty is especially important and striking in many ways.

Our youth in general are richer today than they have ever been and have more alternatives of action and more privileges. The list of privileges usurped by youth has not only increased but has shifted downward in age. The high school student of today has the accouterments of the college student of yesteryear—cars, long pants, money, and more access to girls. This downward shift in privileges, precocious to younger ages, is a phenomenon well known to every parent whose own youth subculture was devoid of them.

Not only are our youth more privileged and richer, but they have for some time constituted an increasingly significant portion of American purchasing power. The statistics of consumption of lipsticks and brassieres, even by twelve- and thirteen-year-olds, are well known, as are those of records, used cars, popular

43

magazines, and transistor radios. The magnified purchasing power of young teenagers is one of the factors that tends to make them want to grow up faster or not at all, which is suggestive of Reuel Denney's credit-card viewpoint of "grow up now and pay later."

The ambivalence of the analyzers regarding whether our youth become adultlike too early or behave as adolescent children too long is a scholastic debate that has not yet been resolved by empirical data. Moreover, a valid appraisal of the "youth problem" is also made difficult by the existence of conflicting cultural prescriptions for youth. We appear to want teenagers to act like young adults in our society, yet we are increasingly stretching the whole socialization process from childhood to adulthood. And the number of people involved in the subculture stretch is increasingly large. There are nearly seventy million persons in the United States under eighteen years of age, or nearly one-third of the nations population.

The number reaching age eighteen each year has, however, doubled within a decade. There were two million in 1956 and four million in 1965, the result of the "baby boom" of the late forties. Of the more than 1.5 million who graduate from high school, about half will register for college, and the 25 percent of the sixteen-twenty-four age group now in college will increase. One could say with Denney that the age of extended socialization is already in full swing.

It is of correlative interest that the public has become disturbed by the announced figure of 7.5 million school dropouts during the 1960s, despite some queries about whether we really want to or can prevent all school dropouts. The middle-class and middle-aged producers of prescriptions for youth want to keep them in, or return them to school for reasons that extend from a genuine belief that all youth should benefit from more formal education to fears that dropout youths inundate the labor market and thereby contribute to delinquency and crime. Our society would apparently like more children to go to college, often without commensurate concern for how the extended period of dependency, socialization, and an indiscriminate density of college population may contribute to producing mediocrity of educational standards. Yet, without continued education, the dropouts are commonly dependent in other ways. As Lucius Cervantes has very recently pointed out, although the dropout group cuts across social class, ethnic, and geographic lines, most come from the blue- and lower-white-collar economic classes. In summarizing, he says:

> The dropout rate nationally is between 30 and 40 percent. The rate is higher in the South than in the North; higher among boys than girls (53 percent versus 47 percent); higher in the slums than in the suburbs. Most dropouts withdraw from school during or before their sixteenth year. There is ten times the incidence of delinquency among the dropouts as there is among the stayins. In view of society's educational expectations for modern youth and dropout youth's inability to get a job while "just waiting around for something to happen," the very state of being a dropout has all but become by definition a condition of semidelinquency.

On the one hand, then, the privileges and age roles are being extended by being lowered, and young teenagers are as sophisticated or cynical, as fantasy-filled and joyriding as our older teenagers used to be. On the other hand, and at the other end of the range of the youth age, the period of their not moving into adult roles is also being extended.

This extended socialization is accompanied by the problem of poor adult models. Throughout the social classes, it appears that the search for the adult to be emulated is often a desperate and futile quest. Part of the reason for this futility is due to the very rapid social and technological changes occuring in our society which make it more difficult for the adult to perform his traditional role of model and mentor to youth. Social change is so rapid, says Kenneth Keniston, that growing up no longer means learning how to fit into society because the society into which young people will someday fit has not yet been developed or even, perhaps, cannot properly be imagined. Many youths feel forced into detachment and premature cynicism because society seems to offer youth today so little that is stable, relevant, and meaningful. They often look in vain for values, goals, means, and institutions to which they can be committed because their trust for commitment is strong. Youth can be a period of fruitful idealism, but there are few of what Erik Erikson would call "objects of fidelity" for our youth; so that "playing it cool" is more than an ephemeral expression—it becomes a way of avoiding damaging commitments to goals and life styles of the parent generation which may be outmoded tomorrow. Times and viewpoints shift rapidly, and many of our children resemble world-weary and jaded adults at age fourteen. The social isolation, social distance, alienation, and retreat from the adult world are increased by many social and technological mechanisms operating to encourage a youth sub-culture. As the numbers and intensity of value sharing in the youth subculture increase, the process of intergenerational alienation also escalates. Parents have almost always been ac-cused of not understanding their children. What may be new is that more parents either do not care that they do not understand, or that it is increasingly impossible for them to understand. Perhaps, then, it is not that the parents are poor models for the kinds of lives that the youths will lead in their own mature years; parents may simply be increasingly irrelevant models for their children. So rapid is current social change that the youth of today have difficulty projecting a concept of themselves as adults . . . .

THE MASCULINE PROTEST AND ITS TRANSFORMATION

Social scientists have long stressed the importance of the theme of masculinity in American culture and the effect that this image of the strong masculine role has had on child rearing and the general socialization process. The inability of the middle-class male child to match himself to this masculine model and the neuroticism that is the consequence of this increasingly futile struggle was vividly brought to our attention years ago by Arnold Green. . . . There is reason to believe, however, that this once dominating culture theme is dissipating, especially in the central or middle-class culture, and that this dissipation is diffusing downwards through the lower classes via the youth subculture. It may be argued that in the United States, while the status of the sexes in many social spheres of activity has been approaching equality, there has been an increasing feminization of the general culture. Instead of females becoming more like males, males have increasingly taken on some of the roles and attributes formerly assigned to females. It is not so much that maleness is reduced as a goal motivating young boys; rather, physical aggressiveness, once the manifest feature of maleness, is being reduced and the meaning of masculinity is thereby being changed to more symbolic forms. The continued diminution of the earlier frontier mores which placed a premium on male aggressiveness has been replaced by other attributes of masculinity. The gun and fist have been substantially replaced by financial ability, by the capacity to manipulate others in complex organizations, and by intellectual talents. The thoughtful wit, the easy verbalizer, even the striving musician and artist are, in the dominant culture, equivalents of male assertiveness where broad shoulders and fighting fists were once the major symbols. The young culture heroes may range from Van Cliburn to the Beatles, but Billy the Kid is a fantasy figure from an earlier history.

It may well be true that in many lower-class communities violence is associated with masculinity and may not only be acceptable but admired behavior. That the rates of violent crimes are high among lower-class males suggests that this group still strongly continues to equate maleness with overt physical aggression. In the Italian slum of the Boston West End, Herbert Gans describes families dominated by the men and where mothers encourage male dominance. On the other hand, lower-class boys who lack father or other strong male figures, as is the case with many boys in Negro families, have a problem of finding models to imitate. Rejecting female dominance at home and at school, and the morality which they associate with women, may be the means such boys use to assert their masculinity, and such assertion must be performed with a strong antithesis of femininity, namely. by being physically aggressive. Being a bad boy . . . /it has been/ said, can become a positive goal if goodness is too closely identified with femininity.

Whatever the reasons for this stronger masculine role among lower-class youth, its retention will continue to result in violence, because the young male is better equipped physically to manifest this form of masculinity than the very young, the middle-aged, or the very old. Because he needs no special education to employ the agents of physical aggression (fists, agility), and because he seeks, as we all do, reinforcement from others for his ego and commitment, in this case to the values of violence, a youth often plays violent games of conflict within his own age-graded violent subcultural system. So do others play games, of course; the artist when he competes for a prize, the young scholar for tenure, the financier for a new subsidiary, and a nation for propaganda advantage. But the prescribed rules for street fighting produce more deadly quarrels with weapons of guns and knives than do competitions among males who use a brush, a dissertation, or a contract. . . .

Should the lower classes become more like the middle class in value orientation, family structure, and stability, there is reason to believe the emphasis on masculine identification through physical prowess and aggression will decline. . . . As the disparity in life style, values, and norms between the lower and middle classes is reduced, so too will be reduced the subculture of violence that readily resorts to violence as an expected form of masculine response to certain situations.

If this social prognosis proves correct, there may not always be functional and virtuous expertise in the masculine symbolism. We could witness, for example, a shift from direct physical violence to detached and impersonalized violence or to corruption. The dominant, middle-class culture has a considerable tolerance for distant and detached violence expressed in ways that range from dropping heavy bombs on barely visible targets, to the stylized, bloodless violence of film and television heroes, and to the annual slaughter of 50,000 persons on our highways. This same culture, for reasons too complex to detail here, not only tolerates but sometimes creates structural features in its social system that seem to encourage corruption, from tax evasion to corporate crime. To transform the theme of male aggressiveness may mean assimilation with the larger culture, but this may merely increase the distance between the user and consumer of violence, and increase the volume of contributors to corruption. It may be hoped, of course, that changes in the current direction of the dominant culture may later produce a more sanguine description of this whole process.

YOUTH AND VIOLENT CRIME

There is little more than faulty and inadequate official delinquency statistics to answer basic questions about the current extent and character of youth crime. Recording techniques have changed, more juvenile police officers are engaged in handling young offenders, more methods are used for registering such minor juvenile status offenses as running away from home, being incorrigible, or truant. For over a decade most city police departments have used a dichotomy of "official-nonofficial arrest" or "remedial-arrest" or "warned-arrest" for apprehending juveniles, but not for adults. Yet both forms of juvenile disposition are recorded and rates of delinquency are computed in the total. . . .

The public image of a vicious, violent juvenile population producing a seemingly steady increase in violent crime is not substantiated by the evidence available. There may be more juvenile delinquency recorded today, but even that is predominantly property offenses. Rather consistently we are informed by the Uniform Crime Reports, published by the Federal Bureau of Investigation, that two-thirds of automobile thefts and about one-half of all burglaries and robberies are committed by persons under eighteen years of age. Among crimes of personal violence, arrested offenders under age eighteen are generally low: for criminal homicide they are about 8 percent; for forcible rape and aggravated assault, about 18 percent.

What this actually means is not that these proportions of these crimes are committed by juveniles, but that among persons who are taken into custody for these offenses, these proportions hold. Most police officers agree that it is easier to effect an arrest in cases involving juveniles than in cases involving adults. Most crimes known to the police, that is, complaints made to them or offenses discovered by them, are not "cleared by arrest," meaning cleared from their records by taking one or more persons into custody and making them available for prosecution. The general clearance rate is roughly 30 percent. Thus, the adult-juvenile distribution among 70 percent of so-called major crimes (criminal homicide, forcible rape, robbery, aggravated assault, burglary, larceny over $50, auto theft) is not known and cannot safely be projected from the offenses cleared or the age distribution of offenders arrested.

In addition, very often the crude legal labels attached to many acts committed by juveniles give a false impression of the seriousness of their acts. For example, a "highway robbery" may be a $100 theft at the point of a gun and may result in the victim's being hospitalized from severe wounds. But commonly, juvenile acts that carry this label and are used for statistical compilation are more minor. Typical in the files of a recent study were cases involving two nine-year-old boys, one of whom twisted the arm of the other on the school yard to obtain twenty-five cents of the latter's lunch money. This act was recorded and counted as "highway robbery.". . .

The data needed to describe the volume of youth crime are inadequate at present, but an alarmist attitude does not appear justified. Age-specific and weighted rates are required before trends can be validly presented and analyzed, but because of the known rise in the present adolescent population due to high fertility rates of the late 1940s, there is reason to suspect that any overall increase in juvenile delinquency can be largely attributed to the population increase in the ages from fourteen to eighteen. The absolute amount of delinquency can be expected to increase for some time, for this same reason, but there is no basis for assuming that rates of juvenile violence will increase.

Moreover, as the suburban population increases, the amount of juvenile delinquency can be expected to rise in these areas even without a rate increase. In addition, as the social class composition of suburbs changes, as it has been, from being predominantly upper class to containing more middle- and lower-middle-class families, the rates of delinquency of the last migrating class will travel with them. . . . What is often viewed as middle-class delinquency is not middle class in the sense of the traditional middle-class value system or life style but only in terms of a middle-income group. . . .

Finally, with respect to delinquency, it might be said that a certain amount of this form of deviancy has always existed, will continue to exist, and perhaps should exist. . . . Not only does the existence of delinquency provide the collective conscience an opportunity to reinforce its norms by applying sanctions, but the presence of deviancy reflects the existence of something less than a total system of control over individuals. Moreover, there appear to be personality traits among many delinquents that could be viewed as virtues if behavior were rechanneled. For instance, Sheldon and Eleanor Glueck noted, in *Unraveling Juvenile Delinquency*, that among five hundred delinquents compared to five hundred nondelinquents, the delinquent boys were characterized as hedonistic, distrustful, aggressive, hostile and, as boys who felt they could manage their own lives, were socially assertive, and defied authority. The nondelinquents were more banal, conformistic, neurotic, felt unloved, insecure, and anxiety-ridden. The attributes associated with the delinquents sound similar to descriptions of the Renaissance man who defied the authority and static orthodoxy of the Middle Ages, who was also aggressive, richly assertive, this-world rather than other-world centered, and was less banal, more innovative, than his medieval predecessors. The Glueck delinquents also sound much like our nineteenth century captains of industry, our twentieth century political leaders and corporation executives. The freedom to be assertive, to defy authority and orthodoxy may sometimes have such consequences as crime and delinquency. But it is well to remember that many aspects of American ethos, our freedom, our benevolent attitude toward rapid social change, our heritage of revolution, our encouragement of massive migrations, our desire to be in or near large urban centers, and many other values that we cherish, may produce the delinquency we deplore as well as the many things we desire.

Rebellious Youth:
Context of Rebellion

The "context of youthful rebelliousness" is a phrase which refers to the complex of social variables associated with this kind of behavior. Generally, the context encompasses the social and personal milieu which accompany varying degrees of non-conformist conduct. This milieu includes at least five sets of factors. One set of factors centers on the effects of social position on the propensity of many youth to be rebellious. For instance, it may be hypothesized that such behavior is a function of lower-class position and ghetto living conditions. A second set includes socialization patterns and their socialization pattern determinants. Under this category fall such considerations as a father's occupational status, his disciplinary practices, and the extent of a youth's involvement in peer-group activity. A third set of factors focus on the impact of situational forces and chance variables on the probability of rebellious behavior. Such conduct may be a function of the availability of automobiles to steal and weapons to use. A fourth set includes the circumstances under which a youth moves from isolated rebellious acts to adopting the role of rebel. Doubtless many youths engage in rebellious acts from time to time without becoming inveterate rebels. Frequently, when a community begins to identify and treat a youth as rebellious, he may respond by thinking of himself in that role. The fifth and last set of factors is the impact of peer groups on the likelihood of rebellious conduct by youths. Such behavior is more common in groups of peers than when one is alone. Although this enumeration of factors is far from comprehensive, it does infuse substantial content into the phrase *context of rebellion*. The following eight selections focus on this context. A few comments about each essay may prove beneficial.

The first selection by Roszak suggests that all contemporary youth subcultures have a common source: a protest or revolt against the larger technocratic society with its numerous experts whose authority, power, and status depend on their appeal to science, its mechanization of men, its conscious and subliminal dehumanization, its pervasive impersonality, the inaccessibility of the masses to its power, its many unaccountable political and economic power centers, and its worship of efficiency, order, and rational control. Furthermore, the author implies that revolt against technocracy derives from numerous tributaries: parental default, the growing youthfulness of society, the spread of leisure, the emergence of teenage economic power, the adolescentization of dissenters, permissive childrearing, and a higher degree of social consciousness. For Roszak these streams overlap, and his separation of them for analysis is unavoidably artificial. Finally, he intimates that the technocratic rebels are more certain about what they oppose than about what they would substitute for the dominant society. He suggests that the norms of the emerging subcultures are also in flux and will probably remain in that condition indefinitely. The dimensions of these subcultures are presently fragmented and are only now beginning to crystallize.

The second selection, by sociologist David Matza, implies that the context of youthful rebellion is a fairly uniform milieu. It is one of reduced dependency, prolonged aspirations, more opportunities for diversion, partial autonomy from parental control, and a continuing pursuit of an identity. Furthermore, he suggests that all youth—the scrupulous youth, the studious youth, the athlete, the rebel, the radical, the bohemian, and the delinquent—operate within this ambience.

The third essay by sociologist Orrin E. Klapp complements Matza's article. Whereas Matza analyzes the contextual characteristics and prototypes of rebellious youth, Klapp centers his attention on one facet of this context: the style rebellion. He uses this term to denote youthful resentments, as expressed in clothing, against middle-class morality, hard work, thrift, material success, conventional religion, militarism, and respect for numerous experts.

The fourth essay, by social critic Paul Goodman, makes explicit what Klapp leaves tacit: the heterogeneity and amorphousness of the context of youthful rebellion. For Goodman this context is basically a compromised revolution which has left American society disheveled, disorganized, and seemingly irrational to youth. Old values have been discarded with no widely acceptable surrogates. Such a revolution is not only political, but also economic and social. This revolution generates rebellious youths as a concomitant of pervasive anomie. Furthermore, Goodman hints that this context cannot be changed in a neat, orderly manner. However, he does furnish a prescription as to how this context may be made more tolerable for youth through pervasive decentralization and by the delegation of authority in huge institutions.

The fifth selection, by novelist James Michener, supplements the first four essays by expounding on the amorphousness permeating the context of youthful rebellion. Like the previous selections, this one suggests that youths know more about what they resent than about what they would substitute. However, Michener does provide a concise list of the values against which many youths are rebelling: puritanism, formal education, material success, a reverence for competence, respect for authority, responsibility, faith in accumulation, and pervasive optimism.

The sixth essay, by sociologist Edgar Z. Friedenberg, subscribes to the views in the previous selections regarding the characteristics of the context of rebellion. However, like Klapp, Friedenberg proceeds meticulously, analyzing one segment of the total context. Whereas Klapp focuses on the style of rebellion, Friedenberg concentrates on the rebellion against what many youths regard as fundamentally illegitimate authority. He implies that such perceived illegitimacy results mainly from a government which purports to be democratic, but which is pervasively undemocratic in fact. In this context there is an increasing use of force by officials to maintain their authority and the hostility of lower-class Americans to democratic values, especially civil liberties.

The seventh selection, by journalist Daniel Seligman, discusses the same segment of the context of youthful rebellion as does Friedenberg. However, Seligman supplies empirical evidence to support the impressions stated in the previous essays.

The eighth article, by psychologist Kenneth Keniston, was included in this reader because it offers a perspective on the context of youth rebellion that the previous articles do not. The perspective of the previous selections was basically sociological, regardless of the authors' professional background. The perspective of the Keniston essay, by contrast, is largely individual-oriented rather than societal. He describes the inner turmoil experienced by rebellious youths and supplies insight into the normative makeup of rebellious personalities.

Technocracy's Children

Theodore Roszak

The struggle of the generations is one of the obvious constants of human affairs. One stands in peril of some presumption, therefore, to suggest that the rivalry between young and adult in Western society during the current decade is uniquely critical. And yet it is necessary to risk such presumption if one is not to lose sight of our most important contemporary source of radical dissent and cultural innovation. For better or worse, most of what is presently happening that is new, provocative, and engaging in politics, education, the arts, social relations (love, courtship, family, community), is the creation either of youth who are profoundly, even fanatically, alienated from the parental generation, or of those who address themselves primarily to the young. It is at the level of youth that significant social criticism now looks for a responsive hearing as, more and more, it grows to be the common expectation that the young should be those who act, who make things happen, who take the risks, who generally provide the ginger. It would be of interest in its own right that the age-old process of generational disaffiliation should now be transformed from a peripheral experience in the life of the individual and the family into a major lever of radical social change. But if one believes, as I do, that the alienated young are giving shape to something that looks like the saving vision our endangered civilization requires, then there is no avoiding the need to understand and to educate them in what they are about.

The reference [of *The Making of a Counter Culture*] is primarily to America, but it is headline news that generational antagonism has achieved international dimensions. Throughout the West (as well as in Japan and parts of Latin America) it is the young who find themselves cast as the only effective radical opposition within their societies. Not all the young, of course: perhaps only a minority of the university campus population. Yet no analysis seems to make sense of the major political upheavals of the decade other than that which pits a militant minority of dissenting youth against the sluggish consensus-and-coalition politics of their middle-class elders. This generational dichotomy is a new fact of political life, one which the European young have been more reluctant to accept than their American counterparts. The heirs of an institutionalized left-wing legacy, the young radicals of Europe still tend to see themselves as the champions of "the people" (meaning the working class) against the oppression of the bourgeoisie (meaning, in most cases, their own parents). Accordingly, they try valiantly to adapt themselves to the familiar patterns of the past. They reach out automatically along time-honored ideological lines to find allies—to the workers, the trade unions, the parties of the left . . . only to discover that these expected alliances strangely fail to materialize and that they stand alone and isolated, a vanguard without a following.

In Germany and Italy the major parties of the left opposition have allowed themselves to be co-opted into the mainstream of respectable politicking—perhaps even to the point of joining governing coalitions. Despite the fact that German students (less than 5 percent of whom come from working-class families) risk the wrath of the police to crusade beneath banners bearing the names of Rosa Luxemburg and Karl Liebknecht, the backlash their street politics produces is as sharp among the workers as the bourgeoisie. When Berlin students demonstrate against the war in Vietnam, the trade unions respond (as in February 1968) with counter-demonstrations supporting Washington's version of "peace and freedom" in Southeast Asia.

In Britain, the Aldermaston generation and its disillusioned successors have long since had to admit that the Labor Party, angling always for the now decisive middle-class vote, is little more than Tweedledum to the Tories' Tweedledee. As for the British working class, the only cause that has inspired a show of fighting spirit on its part during the sixties (other than the standard run of wages and demarcation grievances) is the bloody-minded cry to drive the colored immigrants from the land.

In France, the battle-scarred students of the May 1968 Rebellion have had to watch the much-mellowed CGT and PC conniving to function as President de Gaulle's labor lieutenants in the maintenance of responsible, orderly government against the meance of "anarchy" in the streets. If the students march by rebellious thousands to the barricades, their cautious parents march in behalf of the status quo by the tens of thousands and vote by the millions for the general and the managerial elite he has recruited from the *Ecole polytechnique* for the purpose of masterminding the new French affluence. Even the factory workers who swelled the students' ranks from thousands to millions during the early stages of the May 1968 General Strike seem to have decided that the essence of revolution is a bulkier pay envelope.

Over and again it is the same story throughout Western Europe: the students may rock their societies; but without the support of adult social forces, they cannot overturn the established order. And that support would seem to be nowhere in sight. On the contrary, the adult social forces—including those of the traditional left—are the lead-bottomed ballast of the status quo. The students march to the Internationale, they run up the red flag, they plaster the barricades with pictures of Marxist heroes old and new . . . but the situation they confront stubbornly refuses to yield to a conventional left-right analysis. Is it any wonder that, in despair, some French students begin to chalk up the disgruntled slogan *"Je suis marxiste, tendance Groucho"* ("I'm a Marxist of the Groucho variety")? At last they are forced to admit that the entrenched consensus which repels their dissent is the generational phenomenon which the French and German young have begun to call "daddy's politics."

If the experience of the American young has anything to contribute to our understanding of this dilemma, it stems precisely from the fact that the left-wing of our political spectrum has always been so pathetically foreshortened. Our young are therefore far less adept at wielding the vintage rhetoric of radicalism than their European counterparts. But where the old categories of social analysis have so little to tell us (or so I will argue here), it becomes a positive advantage to confront the novelty of daddy's politics free of outmoded ideological preconceptions. The result may then be a more flexible, more experimental, though perhaps also a more seemingly bizarre approach to our situation. Ironically, it is the American young, with their underdeveloped radical background, who seem to have grasped most clearly the fact that, while such immediate emergencies as the Vietnam war, racial injustice, and hard-core poverty demand a deal of old-style politicking, the paramount struggle of our day is against a far more formidable, because far less obvious, opponent, to which I will give the name "the technocracy"—a social form more highly developed in America than in any other society. The American young have been somewhat quicker to sense that in the struggle against *this* enemy, the conventional tactics of political resistance have only a marginal place, largely limited to meeting immediate life-and-death crises. Beyond such front-line issues, however, there lies the greater task of altering the total cultural context within which our daily politics takes place.[1]

• • •

By the technocracy, I mean that social form in which an industrial society reaches the peak of its organizational integration. It is the ideal men usually have in mind when they speak of modernizing, up-dating, rationalizing, planning. Drawing upon such unquestionable imperatives as the demand for efficiency, for social security, for large-scale co-ordination of men and resources, for ever higher levels of affluence and ever more impressive manifestations of collective human power, the technocracy works to knit together the anachronistic gaps and fissures of the industrial society. The meticulous systematization Adam Smith once celebrated in his well-known pin factory now extends to all areas of life, giving us human organization that matches the precision of our mechanistic organization. So we arrive at the era of social engineering in which entrepreneurial talent broadens its province to orchestrate the total human context which surrounds the industrial complex. Politics, education, leisure, entertainment, culture as a whole, the unconscious drives, and even as we shall see, protest against the technocracy itself: all these become the subjects of purely technical scrutiny and of purely technical manipulation. The effort is to create a new social organism whose health depends upon its capacity to keep the technological heart beating regularly. In the words of Jacques Ellul:

> Technique requires predictability and, no less, exactness of prediction. It is necessary, then, that technique prevail over the human being. For technique, this is a matter of life and death. Technique must reduce man to a technical animal, the king of the

slaves of technique. Human caprice crumbles before this necessity; there can be no human autonomy in the face of technical autonomy. The individual must be fashioned by techniques, either negatively (by the adaptation of man to the technical framework), in order to wipe out the blots his personal determination introduces into the perfect design of the organization.[2]

In the technocracy, nothing is any longer small or simple or readily apparent to the non-technical man. Instead, the scale and intricacy of all human activities—political, economic, cultural— transcends the competence of the amateurish citizen and inexorably demands the attention of specially trained experts. Further, around this central core of experts who deal with large-scale public necessities, there grows up a circle of subsidiary experts who, battening on the general social prestige of technical skill in the technocracy, assume authoritative influence over even the most seemingly personal aspects of life: sexual behavior, child-rearing, mental health, recreation, etc. In the technocracy everything aspires to become purely technical, the subject of professional attention. The technocracy is therefore the regime of experts—or of those who can employ the experts. Among its key institutions we find the "think-tank," in which is housed a multi-billion-dollar brainstorming industry that seeks to anticipate and integrate into the social planning quite simply everything on the scene. Thus, even before the general public has become fully aware of new developments, the technocracy has doped them out and laid its plans for adopting or rejecting, promoting or disparaging.[3]

Within such a society, the citizen, confronted by bewildering bigness and complexity, finds it necessary to defer on all matters to those who know better. Indeed, it would be a violation of reason to do otherwise, since it is universally agreed that the prime goal of the society is to keep the productive apparatus turning over efficiently. In the absence of expertise, the great mechanism would surely bog down, leaving us in the midst of chaos and poverty.... The roots of the technocracy reach deep into our cultural past and are ultimately entangled in the scientific world-view of the Western tradition. But for our purposes here it will be enough to define the technocracy as that society in which those who govern justify themselves by appeal to technical experts who, in turn, justify themselves by appeal to scientific forms of knowledge. And beyond the authority of science, there is no appeal.

Understood in these terms, as the mature product of technological progress and the scientific ethos, the technocracy easily eludes all traditional political categories. Indeed, it is characteristic of the technocracy to render itself ideologically invisible. Its assumptions about reality and its values become as unobtrusively pervasive as the air we breathe. While daily political argument continues within and between the capitalist and collectivist societies of the world, the technocracy increases and consolidates its power in both as a transpolitical phenomenon following the dictates of industrial efficiency, rationality, and necessity. In all these arguments, the technocracy assumes a position similar to that of the purely neutral umpire in an athletic contest. The umpire is normally the least obtrusive person on the scene. Why? Because we give our attention and passionate allegiance to the teams, who compete within the rules; we tend to ignore the man who stands above the contest and who simply interprets and enforces the rules. Yet, in a sense, the umpire is the most significant figure in the game, since he alone sets the limits and goals of the competition and judges the contenders.

The technocracy grows without resistance, even despite its most appalling failures and criminalities, primarily because its potential critics continue trying to cope with these breakdowns in terms of antiquated categories. This or that disaster is blamed by Republicans on Democrats (or vice versa), by Tories on Laborites (or vice versa), by French Communists on Gaullists (or vice versa), by scientists on capitalists (or vice versa), by Maoists or Revisionists (or vice versa). But left, right, and center, these are quarrels between technocrats or between factions who subscribe to technocratic values from first to last. The angry debates of conservative and liberal, radical and reactionary touch everything except the technocracy, because the technocracy is not generally perceived as a political phenomenon in our advanced industrial societies. It holds the place, rather, of a grand cultural imperative which is beyond question, beyond discussion.

When any system of politics devours the surrounding culture, we have totalitarianism, the attempt to bring the whole of life under authoritarian control. We are bitterly familiar with totalitarian politics in the form of brutal regimes which achieve their integration by bludgeon and bayonet. But in the case of the technocracy, totalitarianism is perfected because its techniques become progressively more subliminal. The distinctive feature of the regime of experts lies in the fact that, while possessing ample power to coerce, it prefers to charm conformity from us by exploiting our deep-seated commitment to the scientific world-view and by manipulating the securities and creature comforts of the industrial affluence which science has given us.

So subtle and so well rationalized have the arts of technocratic domination become in our advanced industrial societies that even those in the state and/or corporate structure who dominate our lives must find it impossible to conceive of themselves as the agents of a totalitarian control. Rather, they easily see themselves as the conscientious managers of a munificent social system which is, by the very fact of its broadcast affluence, incompatible with any form of exploitation. At worst, the system may contain some distributive inefficiencies. But these are bound to be repaired...in time. And no doubt they will be. Those who gamble that either capitalism or collectivism is, by its very nature, incompatible with a totally efficient technocracy, one which will finally eliminate material poverty and gross physical exploitation, are making a risky wager. It is certainly one of the oldest, but one of the weakest radical arguments which insists stubbornly that capitalism is *inherently* incapable of laying golden eggs for everyone.

The great secret of the technocracy lies, then, in its capacity to convince us of three interlocking premises. They are:

1. That the vital needs of man are (contrary to everything the great souls of history have told us) purely technical in character. Meaning: the requirements of our humanity yield wholly to some manner of formal analysis which can be carried out by specialists possessing certain impenetrable skills and which can then be translated by them directly into a congeries of social and economic programs, personnel management procedures, merchandise, and mechanical gadgetry. If a problem does not have such a technical solution, it must not be a *real* problem. It is but an illusion...a figment born of some regressive cultural tendency.
2. That this formal (and highly esoteric) analysis of our needs has now achieved 99 percent completion. Thus, with minor hitches and snags on the part of irrational elements in our midst, the prerequisites of human fulfillment have all but been satisfied. It

is this assumption which leads to the conclusion that wherever social friction appears in the technocracy, it must be due to what is called a "breakdown of communication." For where human happiness has been so precisely calibrated and where the powers that be are so utterly well intentioned, controversy could not possibly derive from a substantive issue, but only from misunderstanding. Thus we need only sit down and reason together and all will be well.

3. That the experts who have fathomed our heart's desires and who alone can continue providing for our needs, the experts who *really* know what they're talking about, all happen to be on the official payroll of the state and/or corporate structure. The experts who count are the certified experts. And the certified experts belong to headquarters.

One need not strain to hear the voice of the technocrat in our society. It speaks strong and clear, and from high places. For example:

> Today these old sweeping issues have largely disappeared. The central domestic problems of our time are more subtle and less simple. they relate not to basic clashes of philosophy or ideology, but to ways and means of reaching common goals—to research for sophisticated solutions to complex and obstinate issues....
>
> What is at stake in our economic decisions today is not some grand warfare of rival ideologies which will sweep the country with passion, but the practical management of a modern economy. What we need are not labels and cliches but more basic discussion of the sophisticated and technical questions involved in keeping a great economic machinery moving ahead....
>
> I am suggesting that the problems of fiscal and monetary policy in the Sixties as opposed to the kinds of problems we faced in the Thirties demand subtle challenges for which technical answers—not political answers—must be provided.[4]

Or, to offer one more example, which neatly identifies elitist managerialism with reason itself:

> Some critics today worry that our democratic, free societies are becoming overmanaged. I would argue that the opposite is true. As paradoxical as it may sound, the real threat to democracy comes, not from overmanagement, but from undermanagement. To undermanage reality is not to keep free. It is simply to let some force other than reason shape reality. That force may be unbridled emotion; it may be greed; it may be aggressiveness; it may be hatred; it may be ignorance; it may be inertia; it may be anything other than reason. But whatever it is, if it is not reason that rules man, then man falls short of his potential.

> Vital decision-making, particularly in policy matters, must remain at the top. This is partly, though not completely, what the top is for. But rational decision-making depends on having a full range of rational options from which to choose, and successful management organizes the enterprise so that process can best take place. It is a mechanism whereby free men can most efficiently exercise their reason, initiative, creativity and personal responsibility. The adventurous and immensely satisfying task of an efficient organization is to formulate and analyze these options.[5]

Such statements uttered by obviously competent obviously enlightened leadership, make abundantly clear the prime strategy of the technocracy. It is to level life down to a standard of so-called living that technical expertise can cope with—and then, on that false and exclusive basis, to claim an intimidating omnicompetence over us by its monopoly of the experts. Such is the politics of our mature industrial societies, our truly *modern* societies, where two centuries of aggressive secular skepticism, after ruthlessly eroding the traditionally transcendent ends of life, has concomitantly given us a proficiency of technical means that now oscillates absurdly between the production of frivolous abundance and the production of genocidal munitions. Under the technocracy we become the most scientific of societies; yet, like Kafka's K., men throughout the "developed world" become more and more the bewildered dependents of inaccessible castles wherein inscrutable technicians conjure with their fate. True, the foolproof system again and again bogs down in riot or apathetic rot or the miscalculations of overextended centralization; true, the chronic obscenity of thermonuclear war hovers over it like a gargantuan bird of prey feeding off the bulk of our affluence and intelligence. But the members of the parental generation, storm-tossed by depression, war, and protracted war-scare, cling fast to the technocracy for the myopic sense of prosperous security it allows. By what right would they complain against those who intend only the best, who purport to be the agents of democratic consensus, and who invoke the high rhetorical sanction of the scientific world view, our most unimpeachable mythology? How does one take issue with the paternal beneficence of such technocratic Grand Inquisitors? Not only do they provide bread aplenty, but the bread is soft as floss: it takes no effort to chew, and yet is vitamin-enriched.

To be sure, there are those who have not yet been cut in on the material advantages, such as the "other Americans" of our own country. Where this is the case, the result is, inevitably and justifiably, a forceful, indignant campaign fixated on the issue of integrating the excluded into the general affluence. Perhaps there is an exhausting struggle, in the course of which all other values are lost sight of. But, at last (why should we doubt it?), all the disadvantaged minorities are accommodated. And so the base of the technocracy is broadened as it assimilates its wearied challengers. It might almost be a trick, the way such politics works. It is rather like the ruse of inveigling someone you wish to capture to lean all his weight on a door you hold closed. . .and then, all of a sudden, throwing it open. He not only winds up inside, where you want him, but he comes crashing in full tilt.

In his analysis of this "new authoritarianism," Herbert Marcuse calls our attention especially to the technocracy's "absorbent power": its capacity to provide "satisfaction in a way which generates submission and weakens the rationality of protest." As it approaches maturity, the technocracy does indeed seem capable of anabolizing every form of discontent into its system.

Let us take the time to consider one significant example of such "repressive desublimation" (as Marcuse calls it). The problem is sexuality, traditionally one of the most potent sources of civilized man's discontent. To liberate sexuality would be to create a society in which technocratic discipline would be impossible. But to thwart sexuality outright would create a widespread, explosive resentment that required constant policing; and besides, this would associate the technocracy with various puritanical traditions that enlightened men cannot but regard as superstitious. The strategy chosen, therefore, is not harsh repression, but rather the *Playboy* version of total permissiveness which now imposes its image upon us in every slick movie and posh magazine that comes along. In the affluent society, we have sex and sex galore—or so we are to believe. But when we look more closely we see that this sybaritic promiscuity wears a special social coloring. It has been assimilated to an income level and social status avilable only to our well-heeled junior executives and the jet set. After all, what does it cost to rent these yachts full of nymphomaniacal young things in which our playboys sail off for orgiastic swimming parties in the Bahamas? *Real sex*, we are led to believe, is something that goes with the best scotch, twenty-seven-dollar sunglasses, and platinum-tipped shoelaces. Anything less is a shabby substitute. Yes, there is permissiveness in the technocratic society; but it is only for the swingers and the big spenders. It is the reward that goes to reliable, politically safe henchmen of the status quo. Before our would-be playboy can be an assembly-line seducer, he must be a loyal employee.

Moreover, *Playboy* sexuality is, ideally, casual, frolicsome, and vastly promiscuous. It is the anonymous sex of the harem. It creates no binding loyalties, no personal attachments, no distractions from one's primary responsibilities — which are to the company, to one's career and social position, and to the system generally. The perfect playboy practices a career enveloped by noncommittal trivialities: there is no home, no family, no romance that divides the heart painfully. Life off the job exhausts itself in a constant run of imbecile affluence and impersonal orgasms.

Finally, as a neat little dividend, the ideal of the swinging life we find in *Playboy* gives us a conception of femininity which is indistinguishable from social idiocy. The woman becomes a mere playmate, a submissive bunny, a mindless decoration. At a stroke, half the population is reduced to being the inconsequential entertainment of the technocracy's pampered elite.

As with sexuality, so with every other aspect of life. The business of inventing and flourishing treacherous parodies of freedom, joy, and fulfillment becomes an indispensable form of social control under the technocracy. In all walks of life, image makers and public relations specialists assume greater and greater prominence. The regime of experts relies on a lieutenancy of counterfeiters who seek to integrate the discontent born of thwarted aspiration by way of clever falsification.

Thus:

We call it "education," the "life of the mind," the "pursuit of the truth." But it is a matter of machine-tooling the young to the needs of our various baroque bureaucracies: corporate, governmental, military, trade union, educational.

We call it "free enterprise." But it is a vastly restrictive system of oligopolistic market manipulation, tied by institutionalized corruption to the greatest munitions boondoggle in history and dedicated to infantilizing the public by turning it into a herd of compulsive consumers.

We call it "creative leisure": finger painting and ceramics in the university extension, tropic holidays, grand athletic excursions to the far mountains and the sunny beaches of the earth. But it is, like our sexual longings, an expensive adjunct of careerist high-achievement: the prize that goes to the dependable hireling.

We call it "pluralism." But it is a matter of the public authorities solemnly affirming everybody's right to his own opinion as an excuse for ignoring anybody's troubling challenge. In such a pluralism, critical viewpoints become mere private prayers offered at the altar of an inconsequential conception of free speech.

We call it "democracy." But it is a matter of public opinion polling in which a "random sample" is asked to nod or wag the head in response to a set of prefabricated alternatives, usually related to the *faits accompli* of decision makers, who can always construe the polls to serve their own ends. Thus, if 80 percent think it is a "mistake" that we ever "went into" Vietnam, but 51 percent think we would "lose prestige" if we "pulled out now," then the "people" have been "consulted" and the war goes on with their "approval."

We call it "debate." But it is a matter of arranging staged encounters between equally noncommittal candidates neatly tailored to fit thirty minutes of prime network time, the object of the exercise being to establish an "image" of competence. If there are interrogators present, they have been hand-picked and their questions rehearsed.

We call it "government by the consent of the governed." But even now, somewhere in the labyrinth of the paramilitary agencies an "area specialist" neither you nor I elected is dispatching "special advisors" to a distant "trouble-spot" which will be the next Vietnam. And somewhere in the depths of the oceans a submarine commander neither you nor I elected is piloting a craft equipped with firepower capable of cataclysmic devastation and perhaps trying to decide if—for reasons neither you nor I know— the time has come to push the button.

It is called being "free," being "happy," being the Great Society.

From the standpoint of the traditional left, the vices of contemporary America we mention here are easily explained—and indeed too easily. The evils stem simply from the unrestricted pursuit of profit. Behind the manipulative deceptions there are capitalist desperados holding up the society for all the loot they can lay hands on.

To be sure, the desperados are there, and they are a plague of the society. For a capitalist technocracy, profiteering will always be a central incentive and major corrupting influence. Yet even in our society, profit taking no longer holds its primacy as an evidence of organizational success, as one might suspect if for no other reason than that our largest industrial enterprises can now safely count on an uninterrupted stream of comfortably high earnings. At this point, considerations of an entirely different order come into play among the managers, as Seymour Melman reminds us when he observes:

> The "fixed" nature of industrial investment represented by machinery and structures means that large parts of the costs of any accounting period must be assigned in an arbitrary way. Hence, the magnitude of profits shown in any accounting period varies entirely according to the regulations made by the management itself for assigning its "fixed" charges. Hence, profit has ceased to be the economists' independent measure of success or failure of the enterprise. We can define the systematic quality in the behavior and management of large industrial enterprises not in terms of profits, but in terms of their acting to maintain or to extend the production decision power they wield. Production decision power can be gauged by the number of people employed, or whose work is directed, by the proportion of given markets that a management dominates, by the size of the capital investment that is controlled, by the number of other managements whose decisions are controlled. Toward these ends profits are an instrumental device — subordinated in given accounting periods to the extension of decision power.[6]

Which is to say that capitalist enterprise now enters the stage at which large-scale social integration and control become paramount interests in and of themselves: the corporations begin to behave like public authorities concerned with rationalizing the total economy. If profit remains an important lubricant of the system, we should recognize that other systems may very well use different lubricants to achieve the same end of perfected, centralized organization. But in so doing they still constitute *technocratic* systems drawing upon their own inducements.

In the example given above of *Playboy* permissiveness, the instruments used to integrate sexuality into industrial rationality have to do with high income and extravagant merchandizing. Under the Nazis, however, youth camps and party courtesans were used for the same integrative purpose—as were the concentration camps, where the kinkier members of the elite were rewarded by being allowed free exercise of their tastes. In this case, sexual freedom was not assimilated to income level or prestige consumption, but to party privilege. If the communist regimes of the world have not yet found ways to institutionalize sexual permissiveness, it is because the party organizations are still under the control of grim old men whose puritanism dates back to the days of primitive accumulation. But can we doubt that once these dismal characters pass from the scene—say, when we have a Soviet version of Kennedy-generation leadership—we shall hear of topless bathing parties at the Black Sea resorts and of orgiastic goings-on in the *dachas?* By then, the good apparatchiks and industrial commissars will also acquire the perquisite of admission to the swinging life.

It is essential to realize that the technocracy is not the exclusive product of that old devil capitalism. Rather, it is the product of a mature and accelerating industrialism. The profiteering could be eliminated; the technocracy would remain in force. The key problem we have to deal with is the paternalism of expertise within a socioeconomic system which is organized so that it is inextricably beholden to expertise. And, moreover, to an expertise which has learned a thousand ways to manipulate our acquiescence with an imperceptible subtlety.

Perhaps the clearest way to illustrate the point, before we finish with this brief characterization of the technocracy, is to take an example of such technician-paternalism from a non-capitalist institution of impeccable idealism: the British National Health Service. Whatever its shortcomings, the NHS is one of the most highly principled achievements of British socialism, a brave effort to make medical science the efficient servant of its society. But of course, as time goes on, the NHS will have to grow and adapt to the needs of a maturing industrial order. In June 1968, the BBC (TV) produced a documentary study of the NHS which gave special emphasis to some of the "forward thinking" that now transpires among the experts who contemplate the future responsibilities of the service. Among them, the feeling was unmistakably marked that the NHS is presently burdened with too much lay interference, and that the service will never achieve its full potential until it is placed in the hands of professionally competent administrators.

What might one expect from these professionals, then? For one thing, better designed and equipped—notably, more automated—hospitals. Sensible enough, one might think. But beyond this point, the brainstorming surveyed by the documentary became really ambitious—and, mind, what follows are perfectly straight, perfectly serious proposals set forth by respected specialists in their fields. No put-ons and no dire warnings these, but hard-nosed attempts to be practical about the future on the part of men who talked in terms of "realities" and "necessities."

The NHS, it was suggested, would have to look forward to the day when its psychiatric facilities would take on the job of certifying "normal" behavior and of adjusting the "abnormal"— meaning those who were "unhappy and ineffectual"—to the exacting demands of modern society. Thus the NHS would become a "Ministry of Well-Bring," and psychiatric manipulation would probably become its largest single duty.

Further: the NHS would have to take greater responsibility for population planning—which would include administration of a program of "voluntary euthanasia" for the unproductive and incompetent elderly. The NHS might have to enforce a program of compulsory contraception upon all adolescents, who would, in later life, have to apply to the Service for permission to produce children. It would then be the job of the NHS to evaluate the genetic qualities of prospective parents before granting clearance to beget. [7]

How are we to describe thinking of this kind? Is it "left-wing" or "right-wing"? Is it liberal or reactionary? Is it a vice of capitalism or socialism? The answer is: it is none of these. The experts who think this way are no longer part of such political dichotomies. Their stance is that of men who have risen above ideology—and so they have, insofar as the traditional ideologies are concerned. They are simply . . . the experts. They talk of facts and probabilities and practical solutions, their politics *is* the technocracy: the relentless quest for efficiency, for order, for ever more extensive rational control. Parties and governments may come and go, but the experts stay on forever. Because without them, the system does not work. The machine stops. And *then* where are we?

How do the traditional left-wing ideologies equip us to protest against such well-intentioned use of up-to-date technical expertise for the purpose of making our lives more comfortable and secure? The answer is: they don't. After all, locked into this leviathan industrial apparatus as we are, where shall we turn for solutions to our dilemmas if not to the experts? Or are we, at this late stage of the game, to relinquish our trust in science? in reason? in the technical intelligence that built the system in the first place?

It is precisely to questions of this order that the dissenting young address themselves in manifestoes like this one pinned to the main entrance of the embattled Sorbonne in May 1968:

> The revolution which is beginning will call in question not only capitalist society but industrial society. The consumer's society must perish of a violent death. The society of alienation must disappear from history. We are inventing a new and original world. Imagination is seizing power. [8]

• • •

Why should it be the young who rise most noticeably in protest against the expansion of the technocracy?

There is no way around the most obvious answer of all: the young stand forth so prominently because they act against a background of nearly pathological passivity on the part of the adult generation. It would only be by reducing our conception of citizenship to absolute zero that we could get our senior generation off the hook for its astonishing default. The adults of the World War II period, trapped as they have been in the frozen posture of befuddled docility—the condition Paul Goodman has called "the nothing can be done disease"—have in effect divested themselves of their adulthood, if that term means anything more than being tall and debt-worried and capable of buying liquor without having to show one's driver's license. Which is to say: they have surrendered their responsibility for making morally demanding decisions, for generating ideals, for controlling public authority, for safeguarding the society against its despoilers.

Why and how this generation lost control of the institutions that hold sway over its life is more than we can go into here. The remembered background of economic collapse in the thirties, the grand distraction and fatigue of the war, the pathetic if understandable search for security and relaxation afterwards, the bedazzlement of the new prosperity, a sheer defensive numbness in the face of thermonuclear terror and the protracted state of international emergency during the late forties and fifties, the red-baiting and witch-hunting and out-and-out barbarism of the McCarthy years . . . no doubt all these played their part. And there is also the rapidity and momentum with which technocratic totalitarianism came rolling out of the war years and the early cold war era, drawing on heavy wartime industrial investments, the emergency centralization of decision making, and the awe-stricken public reverence for science. The situation descended swiftly and ponderously. Perhaps no society could have kept its presence of mind; certainly ours didn't. And the failure was not only American. Nicola Chiaromonte, seeking to explain the restiveness of Italian youth, observes,

> . . . the young — those born after 1940 — find themselves living in a society that neither commands nor deserves respect. . . . For has modern man, in his collective existence, laid claim to any god or ideal but the god of possession and enjoyment and the limitless satisfaction of material needs? Has he put forward any reason for working but the reward of pleasure and prosperity? Has he, in fact, evolved anything but this "consumer society" that is so easily and falsely repudiated? 9

On the American scene, this was the parental generation whose god Allen Ginsberg identified back in the mid-fifties as the sterile and omnivorous "Moloch." It is the generation whose premature senility Dwight Eisenhower so marvelously incarnated and the disease of whose soul shone so lugubriously through the public obscenities that men like John Foster Dulles and Herman Kahn and Edward Teller were prepared to call "policy." There are never many clear landmarks in affairs of the spirit, but Ginsberg's *Howl* may serve as the most public report announcing the war of the generations. It can be coupled with a few other significant phenomena. One of them would be the appearance of *MAD* magazine, which has since become standard reading material for the junior high school population. True, the dissent of *MAD* often sticks at about the Katzenjammer Kids level: but nevertheless the nasty cynicism *MAD* began applying to the American way of life—politics, advertising, mass media, education—has had its effect. *MAD* brought into the malt shops the same angry abuse of middle-class America which comics like Mort Sahl and Lenny Bruce were to begin bringing into the night clubs of the mid-fifties. The kids who were twelve when *MAD* first appeared are in their early twenties now—and they have had a decade's experience in treating the stuff of their parents' lives as contemptible laughing stock.

At a more significant intellectual level, Ginsberg and the beatniks can be associated chronologically with the aggressively activist sociology of C. Wright Mills—let us say with the publication of Mills' *Causes of World War III* (1957), which is about the point at which Mills' writing turned from scholarship to first-class pamphleteering. Mills was by no means the first postwar figure who sought to tell it like it is about the state of American public life and culture; the valiant groups that maintained radical journals like *Liberation* and *Dissent* had been filling the wilderness with their cries for quite as long. And as far back as the end of the war, Paul Goodman and Dwight Macdonald were doing an even shrewder job of analyzing technocratic America than Mills was ever to do—and without relinquishing their humanitarian tone. But it was Mills who caught on. His tone was more blatant; his rhetoric, catchier. He was the successful academic who suddenly began to cry for action in a lethargic profession, in a lethargic society. He was prepared to step forth and brazenly pin his indictment like a target to the enemy's chest. And by the time he finished playing Emile Zola he had marked out just about everybody in sight for accusation.

Most important, Mills was lucky enough to discover ears that would hear: his indignation found an audience. But the New Left he was looking for when he died in 1961 did not appear among his peers. It appeared among the students—and just about nowhere else. If Mills were alive today, his following would still be among the under thirties (though the Vietnam war has brought a marvelous number of his academic colleagues out into open dissent—but will they stay out when the war finally grinds to its ambiguous finish?).

Admittedly, the dissent that began to simmer in the mid-fifties was not confined to the young. The year 1957 saw the creation at the adult level of resistance efforts like SANE and, a bit later, Turn Toward Peace. But precisely what do groups like SANE and TTP tell us about adult America, even where we are dealing with politically conscious elements? Looking back, one is struck by their absurd shallowness and conformism, their total unwillingness to raise fundamental issues about the quality of American life, their fastidious anti-communism, and above all their incapacity to sustain any significant initiative on the political landscape. Even the Committee of Correspondence, a promising effort on the part of senior academics (formed around 1961) quickly settled for publishing a new journal. Currently the diminishing remnants of SANE and TTP seem to have been reduced to the role of carping (often with a deal of justice) at the impetuous extremes and leftist flirtations of far more dynamic youth groups like the Students for a Democratic Society, or the Berkeley Vietnam Day Committee, or the 1967 Spring Mobilization. But avuncular carping is not initiative. And it is a bore, even if a well-intentioned bore, when it becomes a major preoccupation. Similarly, it is the younger Negro groups that have begun to steal the fire from adult organizations—but in this case with results that I feel are apt to be disastrous.

The fact is, it is the young who have in their own amateurish, even grotesque way, gotten dissent off the adult drawing board. They have torn it out of the books and journals an older generation of radicals authored, and they have fashioned it into a style of life. They have turned the hypotheses of disgruntled elders into experiments, though often without the willingness to admit that one may have to concede failure at the end of any true experiment.

When all is said and done, however, one cannot help being ambivalent toward this compensatory dynamism of the young. For it is, at last, symptomatic of a thoroughly diseased state of affairs. It is not ideal, it is probably not even good that the young should bear so great a responsibility for inventing or initiating for their society as a whole. It is too big a job for them to do successfully. It is indeed tragic that in a crisis that demands the tact and wisdom of maturity, everything that looks most hopeful in our culture should be building from scratch—as must be the case when the builders are absolute beginners.

Beyond the parental default, there are a number of social and psychic facts of life that help explain the prominence of the dissenting young in our culture. In a number of ways, this new generation happens to be particularly well placed and primed for action.

Most obviously, the society is getting younger—to the extent that in America, as in a number of European countries, a bit more than 50 percent of the population is under twenty-five years of age. Even if one grants that people in their mid-twenties have no business claiming, or letting themselves be claimed for the status of "youth," there still remains among the authentically young in the thirteen to nineteen bracket a small nation of twenty-five million people. (As we shall see below, however, there is a good reason to group the mid-twenties with their adolescent juniors.)

But numbers alone do not account for the aggressive prominence of contemporary youth. More important, the young seem to *feel* the potential power of their numbers as never before. No doubt to a great extent this is because the market apparatus of our consumer society has devoted a deal of wit to cultivating the age-consciousness of old and young alike. Teenagers alone control a stupendous amount of money and enjoy much leisure; so, inevitably, they have been turned into a self-conscious market. They have been pampered, exploited, idolized, and made almost nauseatingly much of. With the result that whatever the young have fashioned for themselves has rapidly been rendered grist for the commercial mill and cynically merchandised by assorted hucksters—*including* the new ethos of dissent, a fact that creates an agonizing disorientation for the dissenting young (and their critics) and to which we will return presently.

The force of the market has not been the only factor in intensifying age-consciousness, however. The expansion of higher education has done even more in this direction. In the United States we have a college population of nearly six million, an increase of more than double over 1950. And the expansion continues as college falls more and more into the standard educational pattern of the middle-class young.[10] Just as the dark satanic mills of early industrialism concentrated labor and helped create the class-consciousness of the proletariat, so the university campus, where up to thirty thousand students may be gathered, has served to crystalize the group identity of the young—with the important effect of mingling freshmen of seventeen and eighteen with graduate students well away in their twenties. On the major campuses, it is often enough the graduates who assume positions of leadership, contributing to student movements a degree of competence that the younger students could not muster. When one includes in this alliance that significant new entity, the non-student—the campus roustabout who may be in his late twenties—one sees why "youth" has become such a long-term career these days. The grads and the non-students easily come to identify their interests and allegiance with a distinctly younger age group. In previous generations, they would long since have left these youngsters behind. But now they and the freshmen just out of high school find themselves all together in one campus community.

The role of these campus elders is crucial, for they tend to be those who have the most vivid realization of the new economic role of the university. Being closer to the technocratic careers for which higher education is supposed to be grooming them in the Great Society, they have a delicate sensitivity to the social regimentation that imminently confronts them, and a stronger sense of the potential power with which the society's need for trained personnel endows them. In some cases their restiveness springs from a bread-and-butter awareness of the basic facts of educational life these days, for in England, Germany, and France the most troublesome students are those who have swelled the numbers in the humanities and social studies only to discover that what the society really wants out of its schools is technicians, not philosophers. In Britain, this strong trend away from the sciences over the past four years continues to provoke annoyed concern from public figures who are not the least bit embarrassed to reveal their good bourgeois philistinism by loudly observing that the country is not spending its money to produce poets and Egyptologists—and then demanding a sharp cut in university grants and stipends.[11]

Yet at the same time, these non-technicians know that the society cannot do without its universities, that it cannot shut them down or brutalize the students without limit. The universities produce the brains the technocracy needs; therefore, making trouble on the campus is making trouble in one of the economy's vital sectors. And once the graduate students—many of whom may be serving as low-level teaching assistants—have been infected with qualms and aggressive discontents, the junior faculty, with whom they overlap, may soon catch the fevers of dissent and find themselves drawn into the orbit of "youth."

The troubles at Berkeley in late 1966 illustrate the expansiveness of youthful protest. To begin with, a group of undergraduates stages a sit-in against naval recruiters at the Student Union. They are soon joined by a contingent of non-students, whom the administration then martyrs by selective arrest. A non-student of nearly thirty—Mario Savio, already married and a father—is quickly adopted as spokesman for the protest. Finally, the teaching assistants call a strike in support of the menaced demonstration. When at last the agitation comes to its ambiguous conclusion, a rally of thousands gathers outside Sproul Hall, the central administration building, to sing the Beatles' "Yellow Submarine"—which happens to be the current hit on all the local high-school campuses. If "youth" is not the word we are going to use to cover this obstreperous population, then we may have to coin another. But undeniably the social grouping exists with a self-conscious solidarity.

If we ask who is to blame for such troublesome children, there can be only one answer: it is the parents who have equipped them with an anemic superego. The current generation of students is the beneficiary of the particularly permissive child-rearing habits that have been a feature of our postwar society. Dr. Spock's endearing latitudinarianism (go easy on the toilet training, don't panic over masturbation, avoid the heavy discipline) is much more a reflection than a cause of the new (and wise) conception of proper parent-child relations that prevails in our middle class. A high-consumption, leisure-wealthy society simply doesn't need contingents of rigidly trained, "responsible" young workers. It cannot employ more than a fraction of untrained youngsters fresh out of high school. The middle class can therefore afford to prolong the ease and drift of childhood, and so it does. Since nobody expects a child to learn any marketable skills until he gets to college, high school becomes a country club for which the family pays one's dues. Thus the young are "spoiled," meaning they are influenced to believe that being human has something to do with pleasure and freedom. But unlike their parents, who are also avid for the plenty and leisure of the consumer society, the young have not had to sell themselves for their comforts or to accept them on a part-time basis. Economic security is something they can take for granted — and on it they build a new, uncompromised personality, flawed perhaps by irresponsible ease, but also touched with some outspoken spirit. Unlike their parents, who must kowtow to the organizations from which they win their bread, the youngsters can talk back at home with little fear of being thrown out in the cold. One of the pathetic, but, now we see, promising characteristics of postwar America has been the uppityness of adolescents and the concomitant reduction of the paterfamilias to the general ineffectuality of a Dagwood Bumstead. In every family comedy of the last twenty years, dad has been the buffoon.

The permissiveness of postwar child-rearing has probably seldom met A. S. Neill's standards — but it has been sufficient to arouse expectations. As babies, the middle-class young got picked up when they bawled. As children, they got their kindergarten finger paintings thumbtacked on the living room wall by mothers who knew better than to discourage incipient artistry. As adolescents, they perhaps even got a car of their own (or control of the family's), with all of the sexual privileges attending. They passed through school systems which, dismal as they all are in so many respects, have nevertheless prided themselves since World War II on the introduction of "progressive" classes having to do with "creativity" and "self-expression." These are also the years that saw the proliferation of all of the mickey mouse courses which take the self-indulgence of adolescent "life problems" so seriously. Such scholastic pap mixes easily with the commercial world's effort to elaborate a total culture of adolescence based on nothing but fun and games. (What else could a culture of adolescence be based on?) The result has been to make of adolescence, not the beginning of adulthood, but a status in its own right: a limbo that is nothing so much as the prolongation of an already permissive infancy.

To be sure, such an infantization of the middle-class young has a corrupting effect. It ill prepares them for the real world and its unrelenting if ever more subtle disciplines. It allows them to nurse childish fantasies until too late in life; until there comes the inevitable crunch. For as life in the multiversity wears on for these pampered youngsters, the technocratic reality principle begins grimly to demand its concessions. The young get told they are now officially "grown up," but they have been left too long without any taste for the rigidities and hypocrisies that adulthood is supposed to be all about. General Motors all of a sudden wants barbered hair, punctuality, and an appropriate reverence for the conformities of the organizational hierarchy. Washington wants patriotic cannon fodder with no questions asked. Such prospects do not look like fun from the vantage point of between eighteen and twenty years of relatively carefree drifting. [12]

Some of the young (most of them, in fact) summon up the proper sense of responsibility to adjust to the prescribed patterns of adulthood; others, being incorrigibly childish, do not. They continue to assert pleasure and freedom as human rights and begin to ask aggressive questions of those forces that insist, amid obvious affluence, on the continued necessity of discipline, no matter how subliminal. This is why, for example, university administrators are forced to play such a false game with their students, insisting on the one hand that the students are "grown-up, responsible men and women," but on the other hand knowing full well that they dare not entrust such erratic children with any power over their own education. For what can one rely upon them to do that will suit the needs of technocratic regimentation?

The incorrigibles either turn political or drop out. Or perhaps they fluctuate between the two, restless, bewildered, hungry for better ideas about grown-upness than GM or IBM or LBJ seem able to offer. Since they are improvising their own ideal of adulthood—a task akin to lifting oneself by one's bootstraps—it is all to easy to go pathetically wrong. Some become ne'er-do-well dependents, bumming about the bohemias of America and Europe on money from home; others simply bolt. The FBI reports the arrest of over ninety thousand juvenile runaways in 1966; most of those who flee well-off middle-class homes get picked up by the thousands each current year in the big-city bohemias, fending off malnutrition and venereal disease. The immigration departments of Europe record a constant level over the past few years of something like ten thousand disheveled "flower children" (mostly American, British, German, and Scandinavian) migrating to the Near East and India—usually toward Katmandu (where drugs are cheap and legal) and a deal of hard knocks along the way. The influx has been sufficient to force Iran and Afghanistan to substantially boost the "cash in hand" requirements of prospective tourists. And the British consul-general in Istanbul officially requested Parliament in late 1967 to grant him increased accommodations for the "swarm" of penniless young Englishmen who have been cropping up at the consulate on their way east, seeking temporary lodgings or perhaps shelter from Turkish narcotics authorities. [13]

One can flippantly construe this exodus as the contemporary version of running off with the circus; but the more apt parallel might be with the quest of third-century Christians (a similarly scruffy, uncouth, and often half-mad lot) for escape from the corruptions of Hellenistic society: it is much more a flight *from* than *toward*. Certainly for a youngster of seventeen, clearing out of the comfortable bosom of the middle-class family to become a beggar is a formidable gesture of dissent. One makes light of it at the expense of ignoring a significant measure of our social health.

So, by way of a dialectic Marx could never have imagined, technocratic America produces a potentially revolutionary element among its own youth. The bourgeoisie, instead of discovering the class enemy in its factories, finds it across the breakfast table in the person of its own pampered children. To be sure, by themselves the young might drift into hopeless confusion and despair. But now we must add one final ingredient to this ebullient culture of youthful dissent, which gives it some chance of achieving form and direction. This is the adult radical who finds himself in a plight which much resembles that of the bourgeois intellectual in Marxist theory. In despair for the timidity and lethargy of his own class, Marx's middle-class revolutionary was supposed at last to turn renegade and defect to the proletariat. So in postwar America, the adult radical, confronted with a diminishing public among the "cheerful robots" of his own generation, naturally gravitates to the restless middle-class young. Where else is he to find an audience? The working class, which provided the traditional following for radical ideology, now neither leads nor follows, but sits tight and plays safe: the stoutest prop of the established order. If the adult radical is white, the ideal of Black Power progressively seals off his entree to Negro organizations. As for the exploited masses of the Third World, they have as little use for white Western ideologues as our native blacks—and in any case they are far distant. Unless he follows the strenuous example of a Regis Debray, the white American radical can do little more than sympathize from afar with the revolutionary movements of Asia, Africa, and Latin America.

On the other hand, the disaffected middle-class young are at hand, suffering a strange new kind of "immiserization" that comes of being stranded between a permissive childhood and an obnoxiously conformist adulthood, experimenting desperately with new ways of growing up self-respectfully into a world they despise, calling for help. So the radical adults bid to become gurus to the alienated young or perhaps the young draft them into service.

Of course, the young do not win over all the liberal and radical adults in sight. From more than a few their readiness to experiment with a variety of dissenting life styles comes in for severe stricture—which is bound to be exasperating for the young. What are they to think? For generations, left-wing intellectuals have lambasted the bad habits of bourgeois society. "The bourgeoisie" they have insisted, "is obsessed by greed; its sex life is insipid and prudish; its family patterns are debased; its slavish conformities of dress and grooming are degrading; its mercenary routinization of existence is intolerable; its vision of life is drab and joyless; etc., etc." So the restive young, believing what they hear, begin to try this and that, and one by one they discard the vices of their parents, preferring the less structured ways of their own childhood and adolescence—only to discover many an old-line dissenter, embarrassed by the brazen sexuality and unwashed feet, the disheveled dress and playful ways, taking up the chorus, "No, that is not what I meant. That is not what I meant at all."

For example, a good liberal like Hans Toch invokes the Protestant work ethic to give the hippies a fatherly tongue-lashing for their "consuming but noncontributing" ways. They are being "parasitic," Professor Toch observes, for "the hippies, after all accept—even demand—social services, while rejecting the desirability of making a contribution to the economy."[14] But *of course* they do. Because we have an economy of cybernated abundance that does not need their labor, that is rapidly severing the tie between work and wages, that suffers from hard-core poverty due to maldistribution, not scarcity. From this point of view, why is the voluntary dropping-out of the hip young any more "parasitic" than the enforced dropping-out of impoverished ghetto dwellers? The economy can do abundantly without all this labor. How better, then, to spend our affluence than on those minimal goods and services that will support leisure for as many of us as possible? Or are these hippies reprehensible because they seem to enjoy their mendicant idleness, rather than feeling, as the poor apparently should, indignant and fighting mad to get a good respectable forty-hour-week job? There are criticisms to be made of the beat-hip bohemian fringe of our youth culture—but this is surely not one of them.

It would be a better general criticism to make of the young that they have done a miserably bad job of dealing with the distortive publicity with which the mass media have burdened their embryonic experiments. Too often they fall into the trap of reacting narcissistically or defensively to their own image in the fun-house mirror of the media. Whatever, these things called "beatniks" and "hippies" originally were, or still are, may have nothing to do with what *Time, Esquire, Cheeta,* CBSNBCABC, Broadway comedy, and Hollywood have decided to make of them. Dissent, the press has clearly decided, is hot copy. But if anything, the media tend to isolate the weirdest aberrations *and* consequently to attract to the movement many extroverted poseurs. But what does bohemia do when it finds itself massively infiltrated by well-intentioned sociologists (and we now all of a sudden have specialized "sociologists of adolescence"), sensationalizing journalists, curious tourists, and weekend fellow travelers? What doors does one close on them? The problem is a new and tough one: a kind of cynical smothering of dissent by saturation coverage, and it begins to look like a far more formidable weapon in the hands of the establishment than outright suppression.

Again, in his excellent article on the Italian students quoted above, Nicola Chiaromonte tells us that dissenters

> must detach themselves, and must become resolute "heretics." They must detach themselves quietly, without shouting or riots, indeed in silence and secrecy; not alone but in groups, in real "societies" that will create as far as possible, a life that is independent and wise....It would be...a non-rhetorical form of "total rejection."

But how is one to develop such strategies of dignified secrecy when the establishment has discovered exactly the weapon with which to defeat one's purposes: the omniscient mass media? The only way anybody or anything stays underground these days is by trying outlandishly hard — as when Ed Saunders and a group of New York poets titled a private publication *Fuck You* to make sure it stayed off the newstands. But it can be quite as distortive to spend all one's time evading the electronic eyes and ears of the world as to let oneself be inaccurately reported by them.

Yet to grant the fact that the media distort is not the same as saying that the young have evolved no life style of their own, or that they are unserious about it. We would be surrendering to admass an absolutely destructive potential if we were to take the tack that whatever it touches is automatically debased or perhaps has no reality at all. In London today at some of the better shops one can buy a Chinese Army-style jacket, advertised as "Mao Thoughts in Burberry Country: elegant navy flannel, revolutionary with brass buttons and Mao collar." The cost: £28 . . . a mere $68. Do Mao and the cultural revolution suddenly become mere figments by virtue of such admass larks?

Commercial vulgarization is one of the endemic pests of twentieth-century Western life, like the flies that swarm to sweets in the summer. But the flies don't create the sweets (though they may make them less palatable); nor do they make the summer happen. It will be my contention that there is, despite the fraudulence and folly that collects around its edges, a significant new culture a-borning among our youth, and that this culture deserves careful understanding, if for no other reason than the sheer size of the population it potentially involves.

But there *are* other reasons, namely, the intrinsic value of what the young are making happen. If however, we want to achieve that understanding, we must insist on passing over the exotic tidbits and sensational case histories the media offer us. Nor should we resort to the superficial snooping that comes of cruising bohemia for a few exciting days in search of local color and the inside dope, often with the intention of writing it all up for the slick magazines. Rather, we should look for major trends that seem to outlast the current fashion. We should try to find the most articulate public statements of belief and value the young have made or have given ear to; the thoughtful formulations, rather than the off-hand gossip. Above all, we must be willing, in a spirit of critical helpfulness, to sort out what seems valuable and promising in this dissenting culture, as if indeed it mattered to us whether the alienated young succeeded in their project.

Granted this requires a deal of patience. For what we are confronted with is a progressive "adolescentization" of dissenting thought and culture, if not on the part of its creators, then on the part of much of its audience. And we should make no mistake about how far back into the early years of adolescence these tastes now reach. Let me offer one illuminating example. In December of 1967, I watched a group of thirteen-year-olds from a London settlement house perform an improvised Christmas play as part of a therapeutic theater program. The kids had concocted a show in which Santa Claus had been imprisoned by the immigration authorities for entering the country without proper permission. The knock at official society was especially stinging, coming as it did instinctively from some very ordinary youngsters who had scarcely been exposed to any advanced intellectual influences. And whom did the thirteen-year-olds decide to introduce as Santa's liberators? An exotic species of being known to them as "the hippies," who shiva-danced to the jailhouse and magically released Father Christmas, accompanied by strobelights and jangling sitars.

However lacking older radicals may find the hippies in authenticity or revolutionary potential, they have clearly succeeded in embodying radical disaffiliation — what Herbert Marcuse has called the Great Refusal — in a form that captures the need of the young for unrestricted joy. The hippy, real or as imagined, now seems to stand as one of the few images toward which the very young can grow without having to give up the childish sense of enchantment and playfullness, perhaps because the hippy keeps one foot in his childhood. Hippies who may be pushing thirty wear buttons that read "Frodo Lives" and decorate their pads with maps of Middle Earth (which happens to be the name of one of London's current rock clubs). Is it any wonder that the best and brightest youngsters at Berkeley High School (just to choose the school that happens to be in my neighborhood) are already coming to class barefoot, with flowers in their hair, and ringing with cowbells?

Such developments make clear that the generational revolt is not likely to pass over in a few years' time. The ethos of disaffiliation is still in the process of broadening down through the adolescent years, picking up numbers as time goes on. With the present situation we are perhaps at a stage comparable to the Chartist phase of trade unionism in Great Britain, when the ideals and spirit of a labor movement had been formulated but had not reached anything like class-wide dimensions. Similarly, it is still a small, if boisterous minority of the young who now define the generational conflict. But the conflict will not vanish when those who are now twenty reach thirty; it may only reach its peak when those who are now eleven and twelve reach their late twenties. (Say about 1984.) We then may discover that what a mere handful of beatniks pioneered in Allen Ginsberg's youth will have become the life style of millions of college-age young. Is there any other ideal toward which the young can grow that looks half so appealing?

"Nothing," Goethe observed, "is more inadequate than a mature judgment when adopted by an immature mind." When radical intellectuals have to deal with a dissenting public that becomes this young, all kinds of problems accrue. The adolescentization of dissent poses dilemmas as perplexing as the proletarianization of dissent that bedeviled left-wing theorists when it was the working class they had to ally with in their effort to reclaim our culture for the good, the true, and the beautiful. Then it was the horny-handed virtues of the beer hall and the trade union that had to serve as the medium of radical thought. Now it is the youthful exuberance of the rock club, the love-in, the teach-in.

The young, miserably educated as they are, bring with them almost nothing but healthy instincts. The project of building a sophisticated framework of thought atop those instincts is rather like trying to graft an oak tree upon a wildflower. How to sustain the oak tree? More important, how to avoid crushing the wildflower? And yet such is the project that confronts those of us who are connected with radical social change. For the young have become one of the very few social levers dissent has to work with. This is that "significant soil" in which the Great Refusal has begun to take root. If we reject it in frustration for the youthful follies that also sprout there, where then do we turn?

NOTES

1. For a comparison of American and European student radicalism along the lines drawn here, see Gianfranco Corsini, "A Generation Up in Arms," *The Nation,* June 10, 1968.

   Daniel Cohn-Bendit and his spontaneous revolutionaries in France are something of an exception to what I say here about the young European radicals. Cohn-Bendit's anarchist instincts (which greatly riled the old-line leftist student groups during the May 1968 troubles) provide him with a healthy awareness of "the bureaucratic phenomenon" in modern industrial society and of the way in which it has subtly eroded the revolutionary potential of the working class and of its official left-wing leadership. He therefore warns strongly against "hero-worshipping" the workers. But even so, he continues to conceive of "the people" as the workers, and of the workers as the decisive revolutionary element, the students functioning only as their allies and sparkplugs. This leads him to the conclusion that the subversion of the status quo need not await a total cultural transformation, but can be pulled off by "insurrectional cells" and "nuclei of confrontation" whose purpose is to set an example for the working class. See Daniel and Gabriel Cohn-Bendit, *Obsolete Communism: The Left-Wing Alternatives* (New York: McGraw-Hill, 1969), especially the keen analysis of the working partnership between "empiricist-positivist" sociology and technocratic manipulation, pp. 35-40.

2. Jacques Ellul, *The Technological Society*, trans. John Wilkinson (New York: A.A. Knopf, 1964), p. 138. This outrageously pessimistic book is thus far the most global effort to depict the technocracy in full operation.

3. For a report on the activities of a typical technocratic brain trust, Herman Kahn's Hudson Institute, see Bowen Northrup's "They Think For Pay" in *The Wall Street Journal*, September 20, 1967. Currently, the Institute is developing strategies to integrate hippies and to exploit the new possibilities of programmed dreams.

4. John F. Kennedy, "Yale University Commencement Speech," *New York Times*, June 12, 1962, p. 20.

5. From Robert S. McNamara's recent book *The Essence of Security* (New York: Harper & Row, 1968) pp. 109-10. In the present generation, it is second- and third-level figures like McNamara who are apt to be the technocrats par excellence: the men who stand behind the official facade of leadership and who continue their work despite all superficial changes of government. McNamara's career is almost a paradigm of our new elitist managerialism: from head of Ford to head of the Defense Department to head of the World Bank. The final step will surely be the presidency of one of our larger universities or foundations. Clearly it no longer matters *what* a manager manages; it is all a matter of juggling vast magnitudes of things: money, missiles, students...

6. Seymour Melman, "Priorities and the State Machine," *New University Thought*, Winter 1966-67, pp. 17-18.

7. The program referred to is the documentary "Something for Nothing," produced for BBC-1 by James Burke and shown in London on June 27, 1968. In a 1968 symposium on euthanasia, Dr. Eliot Slater, editor of the *British Journal of Psychiatry*, was of the opinion that even if the elderly retain their vigor, they suffer from the defect of an innate conservatism. "Just as in the mechanical world, advances occur most rapidly where new models are being constantly produced, with consequent rapid obsolescence of the old, so too it is in the world of nature." Quoted in "Times Diary," *The Times* (London), July 5, 1968, p. 10.

8. From *The Times* (London), May 17, 1968: Edward Mortinier's report from Paris.

9. The "falsely" in this quotation relates to Chiaromonte's very astute analysis of a doctrinaire blind spot in the outlook of Italian youth — namely their tendency to identify the technocracy with capitalism, which, as I have suggested, is a general failing of European youth movements. This very shrewd article appears in *Encounter*, July 1968, pp. 25-27. Chiaromonte does not mention the factor of fascism in Italy, but certainly in Germany the cleavage between young and old

has been driven deeper than anything we know in America by the older generation's complicity with Nazism.

10. The rapid growth of the college population is an international phenomenon with Germany, Russia, France, Japan and Czechoslovakia (among the developed countries) equaling or surpassing the increase of the United States. UNESCO statistics for the period 1950-64 are as follows:

	1950	1964	*Increase*
U.S.A.	2.3 million	5 million	2.2x
U.K.	133,000	211,000	1.6x
U.S.S.R.	1.2 million	3.6 million	3.0x
Italy	192,000	262,000	1.3x
France	140,000	455,000	3.3x
W. Germany	123,000	343,000	2.8x
W. Berlin	12,000	31,000	2.6x
Czechoslovakia	44,000	142,000	3.2x
Japan	391,000	917,000	2.3x
India	404,000	1.1 million	2.2x

11. In his 1967 Reith Lectures, Dr. Edmund Leach seeks to account for the steady swing from the sciences. See his *Runaway World,* British Broadcasting Company, 1968. For reflections on the same phenomenon in Germany, see Max Beloff's article in *Encounter,* July 1968, pp. 28-33.

12. Even the Young Americans for Freedom, who staunchly champion the disciplined virtues of the corporate structure, have become too restive to put up with the indignity of conscription. With full support from Ayn Rand, they have set the draft down as "selective slavery." How long will it be before a conservatism that perceptive recognizes that the ideal of free enterprise has nothing to do with technocratic capitalism?

13. For the statistics mentioned, see *Time,* September 15, 1967, pp. 47-49; *The Observer* (London), September 24, 1967; and *The Guardian* (London), November 18, 1967.

14. Hans Toch, "The Last Word on the Hippies," *The Nation,* December 4, 1967. See also the jaundiced remarks of Eric Hoffer in the New York *Post Magazine,* September 23, 1967, pp. 32-33; Milton Mayer writing in *The Progressive,* October 1967; and Arnold Wesker's "Delusions of Floral Grandeur" in the English magazine *Envoy,* December 1967.

READING 6

Position and Behavior Patterns of Youth
David Matza

The surprising thing about youth is how little is known about it despite the considerable number of studies and essays on one or another of its aspects. One may learn a great deal about the correlates of different phases of adolescence or youth (Clausen & Williams, 1963), but he may still know very little directly about these self-same aspects. One knows something about the socialization processes by which children assume one or another youthful style, but considerably less about the variety, shape, and texture of the styles themselves. From the less empirical literature on youth, one may learn much about what is wrong with alleged characteristics of modern youth, but is not enlightened regarding the details of these characteristics and the particular youth to whom they presumably pertain. The present chapter will focus on the shape and texture of these youthful patterns and the position of youth on which the diversity of styles is presumably founded.

"Youth" is here used in a meaning broader than the usual connotation of "adolescence." Rightly or wrongly, adolescence has come to be associated with the teenage years. Youth, however, may, under certain conditions, last well into the thirties or middle-age. Youth ends with the attaining of potentially self-sufficient adulthood. Adolescence has been similarly defined, (Muuss, 1962, p.4), but the word is usually less acceptable when used in such a broad scope. There is less reservation about conceiving of a 13-year-old youth. Such usage is not uncommon. Thus, the present conception of "youth" will be similar to that commonly used with reference to "adolescence" — the period between childhood and adulthood.

Youth is a period in the temporal ordering of society (Moore, 1963). It is a period whose beginnings and end are more or less explicitly punctuated. As Ruth Benedict (1938), and other anthropologists after her, reminded readers, some societies make a great effort to celebrate and ritualize passage into youth and subsequently, into adulthood. Other societies however, are notorious for their lack of activity in these respects. Despite the great variability in the patency of the beginning and end of youth, all societies apparently conceive of the category (Eisenstadt, 1962, pp. 28-29) and manage to supply commonly understood *social indications* of onset and conclusion. These indications may themselves lack consistency and coherence, in which case they are *diffuse,* or they may coincide on a particular point in time, in which case they are *specific.*

Contemporary America tends to the lazy end of the spectrum, allowing the definitions of the beginning and end of youth to lie latent in common understandings and failing to supply a specific occasion on which diverse indications coalesce. But this should not be taken to mean that common understandings of the beginning and end of youth are lacking. The social indications of the start of youth in our society, and many others, have included publicly or privately visible aspects of biological pubescence (Ausubel, 1954; Lander, 1942; Muuss, 1962, pp. 19-23; Sarnoff, 1962, pp. 384-385). Moreover, the beginnings of youth are indicated in the partial subsiding of parental dominance and a concurrent license to utilize guardedly one's new sexual equipment in some pale or playful imitation of adult heterosexuality. Finally, in many modern societies the beginning of youth is indicated by a license — not a right — to engage in some imitation of adult work. Thus indicated, youth is a step, albeit a halting one, toward socially defined adulthood.

The conclusion of youth is obviously the assumption of adult status and, within the limits set by other prevalent systems of stratification, the ascription of first-class citizenship. With adulthood, one is at least a first-class subject within one's estate or caste, and, at best, a first-class citizen in one's community. Excellent and persistent social indicators of the time at which the assumption of adulthood is warranted include the formation of new kinship ties by marriage, the begetting of children, the entrance into the labor force by taking or searching for full-time and permanent employment, and the establishment of a new and separate place of residence.

The conclusion of youth, like its beginning, may be obvious or latent, diffuse or specific, early or late. There is no avoiding this ambiguity and variability — both among and within societies (Muuss, 1962, pp. 8-10). If there are common understandings regarding when entry into and exit from youth take place, it is perhaps risky to rely too heavily on the variable propensities of societies explicitly to ritualize passage in accounting for stressful or tranquil youth. Common understandings of the general conditions of entry and exit may easily substitute for ritualized celebration in assuaging the anxiety presumably felt by youth who lack a concise data of graduation into one or another age grade. To suppose otherwise is to assume that rigid and meticulous social organization is somehow less productive of tension than are flexible and imprecise arrangements.

The Position of Modern Youth

Most analyses of youth have proceeded from a picture of their emergent position in modern society. The problems and potentialities of youth, both as seen from within and by ex-youth, derive from their position in society and their relations with adults. The consequences of the position of youth may be mediated through the special families encountered by them, and mollified or aggravated, but not negated. The position of youth is the general circumstance within which adult agencies of variable character perform their work. Thus, any analysis of youth seems incomplete without a consideration of this position.

A common error in most portrayals of youth is an exaggeration of those aspects of making for stress, turmoil, and subsequently, for deviance and a variety of other psychic misfortunes. Literary essayists and positivist sociologists alike have shared in a common mood which stresses the sense in which growing up in the way preferred by adults is harder and more fraught with obstacles today than at some usually unspecified previous time (Coleman, 1961a; Goodman, 1960). Such a mood should immediately arouse suspicion since it partakes of the general, and for the most part unwarranted, intellectual gloom connected with the negative assessment of modernity (Grana, in press). Moreover, a negative and pessimistic assessment of youth based on a purported degeneration of their position should be subjected to special scrutiny because of the common tendency of ex-youth to romanticize their own experiences and disparage those of succeeding cohorts.

Loose Integration and Partial Autonomy

The term alienation has served to obscure the obvious fact that integration in social systems is a matter of degree. Full alienation connotes, among other things, a feeling of sustained opposition to the system, but this feeling is not necessarily a feature of loosened integration.

Relative freedom from conventional controls initially follows from the normal subsiding of parental domination before the responsibility of self-support has appeared. Relative freedom is further facilitated by the social changes implicit in ameliorated dependence, the potentialities of prolonged and undemanding education, and the combination of resentment and euphoria elicited by these changes.

Eisenstadt (1951; 1962) suggested the general conditions under which youth groups are likely to emerge in society. He felt that they appear in societies in which the family is not directly linked to the productive sectors of the economy. Implicit in his theory is the idea that age periods during which the family subsides in importance and occupation has yet to appear are prone to the development of semiautonomous and relatively unregulated youth groupings.

Youth culture, more properly youth subculture, is neither clearly separated from adult conventions nor unified within itself. Youth subculture is not so separated from adult culture because it is manned by persons who in the past have been dominated by conventional families and look forward, or aspire, to subsequent entry into conventional life. Thus, the leisured diversions which make up much of the substance, temporary for each member, of youth subculture are themselves highly colored by activities and precepts which appear in adult life. Youth subculture is at least in part an adaption of adult sentiments and practices to the special conditions of youthful existence (Elkin & Westley, 1955).

The integration of youth subculture and its separation from conventional adult life are both recognized in Coleman's *Adolescent Society* (1961), despite the fact that Coleman's main purpose was to document the fundamental separation. He related the separation to the "setting-apart" of children in the school system, to the tendency of schools to take on more and more in the form of extracurricular activities, and to the increased duration of education and training. Consequently, suggested Coleman, the adolescent is "cut off from the rest of society, forced inward toward his own age group, made to carry out his whole social life with others of his own age" (Coleman, 1961a, p. 3). Most of the important interactions, according to Coleman, take place within the adolescent society. There are only a few threads of connection with outside adult society" (Coleman, 1961). Coleman suggested that the basic cause of this separation may be found in the emergence and character of the school system. Thus, youth subculture, according to Coleman, is an unintended consequence of the organization of the school system. Youth have been placed in a collective context in which segregation from adult life has been imposed, and they have responded accordingly.

Whether separation is nominal or real, however, depends on the content of youth subculture. If a content different from that of the adult culture appears, one may speak of a separate youth subculture. If the substance of youth subculture is similar to that of adults, then despite the predominance of peer interaction one must exercise considerable caution in conceiving of a separate world of youth. Coleman's (1961a) findings — his data more than his interpretation — indicate a state of affairs somewhere between separation and integration. Coleman was, or course, aware of this, despite the main thrust of his argument which is toward the thesis of separation.

Youth subculture is intertwined with adult culture (Berger, 1963) and is highly pluralistic. Despite its connection with adult sentiments and its internally heterogeneous character, one may nevertheless note the existence of youth subculture and describe some of its manifestations. Youth subculture is by now a world-wide phenomenon, first occurring in advanced countries, but increasingly apparent in emerging nations. Many perceptive observers have correctly stressed the central and initiating role played by American youth (Denny, 1962). Teenage culture has been among the most important exports of the United States. To many Europeans, it has been a disturbing matter.

Youth relations, suggested Smith, "are largely informal and are composed of intimacy and sentiment" (E. Smith, 1962, p.2). The subculture of youth is largely an informal system of highly localized and ephemeral units. It is for the most part not anchored in conventional formal organization, though portions of it may base their operation in one or another adult-sponsored house or area. There is some tendency to avoid adult supervision. Smith, relying heavily on Simmel's (1906, pp. 462-463) assertion regarding the universality of secrecy among youth, suggested the prevalence of youthful inclination to evade regular supervision.

> Solidarity and concealment...may be viewed as universal characteristics of youth culture....The universality of secrecy suggests that youth will manifest varying degrees of withdrawal from adult socializing institutions...The activities and in-

teractions of youth will be hidden behind a veil of secrecy erected to escape the supervision and control of adults. (E. Smith, 1962, p. 2).

Part of what youth are hiding must surely confirm the worst suspicions of their excluded elders; behind the veil they sometimes do disapproved of things. But there are at least two other sorts of activities that are concealed from adults.

First, youth, in a variety of ways, play at being adults. These games take many forms, some of which pay tribute to a public figure, some to members of private and intimate circles. One example of such activity consists of the playful conversion of informal and intimate ball-playing to out-and-out fantasies in which youthful players openly pretend before one another to be grown-up major league baseball stars. Only peculiar and specially defined adults are privy to public fantasies of this sort. Another example consists of the pretenses by which boys and girls are considerably more "grown-up" than they and almost everyone else knows they are. Such aping of adults may be exhibited before peers, but to allow the conventional adult to observe would be embarrassing and in some circles an unpardonable admission of the respect accorded adulthood despite the frequent disclaimers. The staging of disdain of adulthood requires the obscuring of imitation and respect. Many adult observers, their vision being obstructed, have been deceived by the front.

Second, secrecy helps maintain the uncommitted character of youthful identity. Young persons toy with a variety of styles which they later discard. Even during engagement with a particular style, there frequently is little commitment to the precept and practices underlying it. Publicity regarding identity, especially publicity which reaches conventional adults, minimizes the chances of playful engagement and maximizes the chances that character will be typed and lead to commitment.

Thus, seclusion upholds an inner secret of youth: fickle playing rather than commitment to identities. Conventional adults are likely to view the behavior implicit in one or another style completely out of context. They see it as harboring commitment, duration, and, thus, danger or a precocious closing of adolescence. Secrecy is therefore, valuable to the youthful players since it minimizes the possibility that a temporary impression will endure as a stereotype.

THE PURSUIT OF IDENTITY

Adult identity is relatively focused and narrow. Presumably, men find identity in work, or, if work is too stultifying, perhaps in some seriously pursued avocation. Women invest their identity in kinship units, in the perceived occupational status of husbands, in their own roles as housewives, and in the character of their progeny. Increasingly, of course, women seek identity in an occupation or career. Youth, on the other hand, is the period of pursuit of *general* identity, a search which is simultaneously less intellectually demanding and more psychically tiring than that encountered during adulthood. Youth is engaged in self-discovery, except that it is not a self that is typically discovered but rather an already available style with which one's self can be comfortably associated. Identity here consists of generalized *preoccupations* instead of specific occupations (Eisenstadt, 1962; Erikson, 1950; Erikson, 1962; Muuss, 1962).

Because of the emerging position of youth, more or less stable identities have appeared within American life. These identities have grown into traditional styles which have been put aside by one cohort of youth after another. No style claims a majority of youthful adherence. Many youth vacillate among different identities, some of which will be discussed on the following pages, and most include in their wanderings shorter or longer stays in conventional amalgams which combine the features of analytically distinctive styles.

Scrupulosity

Scrupulosity is the most conformist of youthful styles. Among such persons, one finds little trace of the hedonism, expressiveness, and rebellion which presumably characterize youth culture. An expert on the incidence and forms of scrupulosity described it in the following way: "The term scrupulosity is well known to those devoted to pastoral work . . . It may be taken to mean an unhealthy and morbid kind of meticulousness which hampers a person's religious adjustment" (Riffel, 1963, p. 39).

95

For the sociologist, however, the defining element of scrupulosity is the meticulous adherence to religious and moral precepts. Scrupulosity may take the form of meticulous avoidance of temptation, a studied devoutness unbecoming to frivolous youth, a seriousness regarding church and parochial study, or a deeply introspective mentality. Whether such a style masks a deep emotional disorder, as is frequently alleged, is of little concern here, for almost all of the styles of youth to be described have been held by one writer or another to be the manifestation or symptom of a deep or transient disturbance. It remains to be shown, however, that abnormality is more representative of scrupulous youth than, say the occasional athlete who turns out to be a pervert.

Scrupulosity, like most youthful styles, has a putative social base among students in the widespread system of Catholic parochial education. There is undoubtedly scrupulosity among youth who are devoted to other religious or secular faiths, but it is difficult to obtain information on these young people. Thus, the present discussion must focus on Catholic scrupulosity.

The proportion of Catholic youth attending parochial school in America is high. Moreover, the proportion of those engaging in scrupulosity for longer or shorter interludes is sufficiently large to make it an important youthful phenomenon. Numerically, scrupulosity seems of roughly the same order of magnitude as that youthful style at the other end of the spectrum which nowadays attracts so much public attention — juvenile delinquency.

Though it is obviously difficult to know with certainty the frequency with which youth take on the style of scrupulosity, there are a few studies which give a rough idea. The data reported in these studies seem unusually plausible since the conditions of true response are more or less built into the attributes of the style and the generally negative assessment it receives. Scrupulous persons, like delinquents, might have a motive to deny their condition, but unlike delinquents, they cannot because of their scrupulosity.

Riffel summarized the few available reports on the frequency of scrupulosity:

> Though accurate figures on the extent of scrupulosity among
> Catholic adolescent students are hard to obtain, the data of several

reports are available. Mullen (1927) reported in a study of 400 Catholic school girls that 26% of them admitted to habitual scrupulosity. A Fordham study (Riffel, 1958) corroborated this earlier report of Mullen. This study was based on 490 students divided between sophomore high school and sophomore college years . . . . Of the high school students, 26% admitted to current scrupulosity, but in college the number had declined to 14% . . . . Boys and girls were included in the sample and percentage of boys admitting to scrupulosity was almost precisely the same as that for girls (Riffel, 1963, p. 42).

Even if one assumes no scrupulosity whatsoever among parochial students in other denominations, which hardly seems reasonable, and no scrupulosity whatsoever among nonparochial school youth, which is considerably more reasonable, he is still left with a national rate of scrupulosity of at least 2 or 3 percent, which is of the same order of magnitude as that of juvenile delinquency.

Scrupulosity, like delinquency and most other styles of youth, varies in frequency by specific age within the time period of youth. Considerably higher proportions of high school than college youth assume this style. Riffel (1963) stressed the transitory quality of scrupulosity, though he was careful to avoid the common view that it is very short-lived. According to his findings, scrupulosity is a stylistic phase that is assumed and acted on for a year or two, then apparently dispensed for yet another. Some smaller proportion of young persons maintain scrupulosity for somewhat longer periods of time. Scrupulosity, like delinquency, seems to be a passing phase for certain kinds of youth and more or less impervious to correctional intervention. A few persons may develop commitment to the style or for other reasons maintain the identity into adulthood and perhaps even for a lifetime.

Studious Youth

Scholars and achievers, along with the scrupulous, are among the conforming youth. Studious youth conform because they are preoccupied by the official purpose of youth, aspiration and preparation, and for the same reason reduce their participation in diversion and leisure.

Preoccupation with officially-approved study accompanied by the reasonable anticipation of moral success during adulthood would seem calculated to achieve prestige. One might, therefore, expect studious youth to occupy the position of highest prestige among their peers. That they do not seems to be the general conclusion of most research. The findings of research are, in this case as in so many others, similar to those reached by less systematic commentators.

The position of studious youth is tenable, nevertheless, because the rewards and acclaim of scholastic achievement are large and established though not perhaps as high and exclusive as we intellectuals might like. It is also tenable because studious youth are not so rare and isolated as to be unable to form cliques which function to insulate and protect members against the hostility or seduction emanating from nonstudious youth.

Implicit in the view that studious youth are vulnerable is the belief that they are so dispersed as to lack a demographic base for clique structure. This belief gives rise to the oft-expressed fear that initially studious youth run the danger of being discouraged by peers and anti-intellectual adults and thus deterred from serious enterprise. But if a delinquent subculture may flourish, why suppose that a studious subculture nurtured as it is by official authority, cannot also survive. Surely, the demographic base is ample. For youth, both academically-oriented scholars and vocationally-oriented careerists (Clark & Trow, 1960), compose a demographic base for insulated and protective studious cliques. This does not mean they study together, though ocassionally they may; rather, it means that they may support one another's studious propensities. Nor does this imply a separate studious sector within youth subculture. There is shifting from this style to others and vice versa though there is perhaps greater stable commitment to this studious style of youth than to other styles, because it is more adult-like in character, because its preoccupation is more securely linked to the realm of occupation, and because persistent performance — the amassing of a good and steady scholastic record — is a main criterion of success in this style.

Studious youth may hold to a tenable style despite the threats and seductions emanating from other styles and despite the ambivalence and uncertainty which studious youth themselves exhibit. Introspective ambivalency may be an essential and frequently misleading feature of the studious style. Thus, studious youth themselves are among the many critics of their style. They are often in the curious position of verbally wishing for the diversions which abound among the youth who surround them. But denunciation may have little effect on the tenacity with which they pursue study. They know that substantial rewards await scholastic performance. It is that realization that probably accounts for the hostility of nonstudious youth in the first place.

An impression of the proportion of youth who are in some measure oriented to studies may be found in Coleman's *Adolescent Society* (1961). He found that in large high schools about 6 percent of the boys are identified by peers as scholars. Another 1 percent are considered to be both scholars and athletes. In small high schools, a little less than 9 percent are identified as scholars, and another 2 percent are thought of as athlete-scholars. Moreover, the scholars are surrounded by many students whose attitudes seem generally sympathetic to studious enterprise (Coleman, 1961a, p. 147).

Coleman (1961a) suggested that occupational aspirations may be taken as indications of values, some of which provide supportive attitudes to the scholars. Thus, a favorable orientation toward an attractive representative of an occupation which requires conscientious study may indicate a supporting attitude toward scholarship.

The high school students in Coleman's (1961a) study were asked: "If you could be any of these things you wanted, which would you most want to be?" The available responses — jet pilot, nationally famous athlete, missionary, and atomic scientist — may be taken respectively as orientations to adventure, sports, morality, and scholarship. About 25 percent chose atomic scientist. Even if one assumes that all who were identified as scholars chose atomic scientists, and surely many did not, he is left with more than 15 percent of high school youth who, while not scholars, seem sympathetic to scholarship.

The secure status of studious youth and the tenability of the enterprise inherent in that status is indicated in many studies of youthful opinion. Though the interpretations convey a tone of complaint and an expressed wish that the status of studious youth were even higher, the findings themselves leave little doubt regarding their establshment position (Tannenbaum, 1962, Ch. 2). Coleman's (1961a) is one of many studies that legitimately stresses the preponderance of frivolous pursuits among youth, but in so doing minimizes the established and substantial minority given to studious concerns. The secure establishment of a studious style within the subculture is obscured by its minority position, its failure to advertise its advantaged place, and the uncertainty and ambivalence is a response to blandishments and taunts emanating from more diverted youth. Partly, however, the ambivalence is intrinsic to the studious style itself, which, being less distracted by external diversion and more given to solitary study, is perhaps more prone to introspection and self-scrutiny. Some of the anti-studious sentiment which abounds in opinion surveys of youth may actually emanate from studious youth themselves. The ambivalence may function to reduce the level of hostility directed toward the studious. Self-doubt is a mark of the intellectual, which also appears among studious youth. It would be a mistake to suppose that the self-scrutiny and self-doubt of intellectuals, or studious youth, are tantamount to style- or self-rejection.

Tannenbaum's (1962) findings regarding the unfavorable attitudes of high school youth toward the studious are best seen in the light of the ambivalence maintained by youth who are themselves oriented in a studious direction. The students in Tannenbaum's sample were asked to respond in stereotypical fashion to eight adolescent types constructed by dichotomizing three attributes. The attributes were brilliance, conscientiousness or studious effort, and sports-mindedness. The highest-regarded type was the billiant, nonstudious, and sports-minded, while the lowest was brilliant, studious, and nonathletic. Between the two extremes, athletic orientation consistently attracted esteem while studious effort consistently repelled it. Thus far, there is nothing surprising in Tannenbaum's findings. Beyond this, however, he found virtually no relationship

> between character ratings and the respondent's own academic abilities. . . /or/ the educational accomplishments of their parents . . .Correlations hovered around zero. . .indicating that for the population studied, the value of information on intelligence and levels of parental education in predicting character ratings was negligible (Tannenbaum, 1962, p. 58).

This absence of any relation between the rating of the constructed character types and the background and performance of the raters was

> one of the most significant outcomes of the study. Even in the case of the brilliant-studious-non-athlete, rated significantly lower than any of the others, there was no evidence of higher regard shown by those who might identify more closely with this character on the basis of ability and dedication to school work (Tannenbaum, 1962, p. 58).

Tannenbaum (1962) felt that this may indicate a conformity on the part of studious youth to the atmosphere of anti-intellectualism current in high school. Whatever this finding may indicate, it surely demonstrates the persistence of a segment, in this case a large one, of studious youth, whatever their expressed attitude. Tannenbaum's study, as it happens, was of a middle-class high school in Brooklyn, in which the student body was 75 percent Jewish. Jews exemplify, perhaps better than any other American group, a culture which provides support for studious youth. The anti-studious rhetoric of Jewish and other youth seems to be an element of the style of this group. It should not be confused with actual vulnerability to frivolous diversion or rejection of the studious effort implicit in the style.

Sports and Athletes

Sports are perhaps the most important of the conventional styles which divert attention from the officially defined purposes of youth. In the Coleman (1961a) study, the proportion of male youth identified by peers as athletes was slightly under 6 percent in large schools. Another 1 percent combined scholarly with athletic virtuosity. In small schools a little over 9 percent were identified as athletes by peers. An additional 2 percent were seen by their peers as coupling scholarly with athletic skill (Coleman, 1961a, p. 147).

The dominance of sports among American youth has drawn the attention of many observers. Typically, though not always, a disapproval of athletic dominance has accompanied the assertion of its central role in youth (Coleman, 1961a; Gorer, 1958; Laski,

1948). The major basis for this has been the claim that its seductive potency is so high that it diverts energy and attention from studies.

One of Coleman's (1961a) purposes in *Adolescent Society* was to document the prevalence of athletic orientation among high school youth and to designate the limited though large section of youth in which sports predominate.

High school boys were asked: "If you could be remembered here at school for one of the three things below, which one would you want to be?" Of the responses, 31.5 percent of the boys choose brilliant student; 45.1 percent, athletic star; and 23.4 percent, most popular (Coleman, 1961a, pp. 28-29). The responses differ substantially from parental responses to the same question regarding their sons. Of the parents, 77 percent would prefer boys to be remembered as brilliant students; 9 percent as athletic stars; and 14 percent, as the most popular student (Coleman, 1961a, pp. 32-33). Girls were asked: "Suppose you had the chance to go out with . . . [any of the following]. Which one would you rather go out with?" Of their answers 35 percent said star athlete; 17 percent, best student; and 48 percent, best looking boy (Coleman, 1961a, pp. 30-31). Thus, if one granted the utility of such indicators, common sense impressions are supported. A strong case can be made for the predominance of sports among boys, the fact that this predominance is not especially reflected in parental sentiments and that athletic prowess has some limited appeal to girls.

Coleman, among others, tended to view this predominance as a problem or failing and suggested a remedy, or palliative, by intellectual contests to provide prestige for studious youth (Coleman, 1960, pp. 337-347; Coleman, 1961b, pp. 33-43). His desire to ameliorate the position of scholars led him to consider the meaning and appeal of sports among youth. He was forced to consider this question because he wished to provide a structural alternative to sports — something which performs the same variety of functions. The discussion of the basis of athletic appeal is interesting, but incomplete. Thus, his suggested alternative, intellectual contests, remains unconvincing even if one shares the antiathletic bias implicit in Coleman's corrective approach, because intellectual contests do not fulfill the variety of functions performed by sports. Coleman was able to maintain the possibility of substituting intellectual for athletic contests because he ignored many other important functions performed by sports — functions which could not be served by intellectual contests.

Coleman's (1960; 1961b) discussion of the functions of sports and the basis of their appeal is essentially an elaboration of one of the points made by Waller (1932) in *Sociology of Teaching*. Waller's analysis of the appeal of sports is still the fullest and most perceptive attempt by a sociologist to answer the difficult question of the meaning of sports. Waller began, like Coleman, by noting the central role of athletic among youth. He said of the activities of youth within the educational system:

> Of all activities athletics is the chief and most satisfying. It is the most flourishing and most revered culture pattern. It has been elaborated in more detail than any other culture pattern. Competitive athletics has many forms. At the head of the list stands football, still regarded as the most diagnostic test of the athletic prowess of any school. Then comes basketball, baseball, track, etc. (Waller, 1932, pp. 112-113).

Waller went on to consider the basis of athletic preeminence:

> [We may also] account for the favorable influence of athletics upon school life in terms of changes affected in group alignments and the individual attitudes that go with them. It is perhaps as a means of unifying the entire school group that athletics seems most useful from the sociologist point of view. There is a tendency for the school population to split up into its hostile segments of teachers and students and to be fragmented by cliques among both groups. . . . This condition [of potential conflict] athletics alleviates. Athletic games furnish a dramatic spectacle of the struggle of picked men against the common enemy, and thus is a powerful factor in building up a group spirit which includes students of all kinds and degrees and unifies the teachers and the taught (Waller, 1932, pp. 115).

This motion of athletics as a device for enhancing the unity or solidarity of schools was stressed by Coleman (1960; 1961a; 1961b). For Coleman, however, it was the sole basis of athletic appeal, whereas for Waller it was only one of a variety of bases.

Coleman concluded by contrasting the predicament of studious youth with the fortunate position of athletes. It is this contrast which stimulates Coleman's recommendation to promote intellectual contests by which studious youth, too, could serve as collective embodiments of scholastic unity.

The outstanding student, by contrast, has few ways—if any—to bring glory to his school. His victories are purely personal ones, often at the expense of his classmates, who are forced to work harder to keep up with him. Small wonder that his accomplishments gain little reward, and are often met by such ridicule as "curve raiser" or "grind," terms of disapprobation having no analogues in athletics (Coleman, 1961a, p. 309).

By limiting his explanation of the appeals of sports to this single contribution, Coleman (1961a) was not driven to ask why athletics has emerged as *the* agency of school cohesion and therefore had little reason for exercising caution in commending intellectual contests as structural substitutes for football games. As soon as one considers other functions of sports and thus other bases of appeal, the case for intellectual contests is weakened and the case for the continued predominance of sports among youth is strengthened. These other functions are no more speculative, and no less, than the thesis which bases the appeal of sports on its service as a collective representation.

Many of the other possible social functions of sports are discussed by Waller (1932). Waller was able to capture some of the sense in which sports, but not intellectual contests, may exemplify masculinity, heroism, goodness, and danger and thus represent a tenable subject for drama and pageantry.

Waller stressed the contribution made by athletics in supporting an *adult-dominated* scholastic order. Athletic contests in many cases have emerged as increasingly routinized and institutionalized ways of channeling violent rivalries between towns, neighborhoods, and schools (Kittermaster, 1958, pp. 84-85; Rudolph, 1962, p. 378). Early athletic contests were frequently symbolic contests between fierce and violent rivals in which the conflict was increasingly limited by rules of the game and chosen representatives of each side. The routinization of violence in sports has never been quite complete in that there is a persistent tendency for uncontrolled violence to break through the limitations set by the rules, in the form of rough or dirty playing, and for the spectators to join the field of battle. Thus, the athletic contest may occasionally erupt into more total conflict, despite its long institutionalization. Normally, however, the official goal of civil order is well served by the routinized violence embodied in many athletic contests. The contest is still a fight in the crucial sense that physical force and prowess constitute essential elements of sports. The fight is controlled by the rules of the game — the instituted sanctions that attend flagrant violation — and, most important, by the limitation on participation to a few chosen representatives. Thus, as has been argued by some of its defenders, sports have played an important civilizing function. The peculiar and distinctive feature of sports is that it has maintained and encouraged physical force and strength while effectively controlling it.

Waller (1932) suggested the sense in which athletics have been a traditonal means of social control. He also sensed the precariousness with which that purpose is served.

> Competition between schools in athletics comes to a focus on games. The game is in fact disguised war. There is a continual tendency for the game to revert to actual war . . . . Everyone treats the game as a fight, and thinks of it as a fight, except perhaps the referee. It is small wonder that the political order consisting of the rules and the referee to back them, is maintained with such difficulty and only by penalties which impose the direct disabilities upon the offenders. There is, it is true, a whole code of sportsmanship which arises from the conflict situation, a code which internalizes the rule and makes for the principle of fair play (Waller, 1932, pp. 113-114).

Thus, the appeal of sports among youth is enhanced by the fact that it is a forceful contest approved and even applauded by adults and the authorities among them. Sports have been traditionally viewed by adults as a means of stylizing and thus controlling violence. Moreover, athletics, and the associated codes of sportsmanship, have frequently been taken as the playground on which subsequently useful moral precepts are learned. This function can be exaggerated and idealized, but there is some correspondence between the moral demands of adult life and the particular code of sportsmanship prevalent in youthful games. A statement of correspondence or approximation need not be a mindless celebration of sports as character-building.

Waller (1932) suggested that athletics may expedite social control in yet another important sense. Athletes are, by the social definition of their endeavor, discouraged from engaging in many excesses which are commonly associated with youthful deviance. During the athletic seasons, athletes are enjoined to be "in training"; they are to refrain from smoking, drinking, staying out late, and other forms of dissipation which violate the expectations of adult authority and are seen by many as precursors to more serious delinquency. Whether such undesired precocious activity is always controlled by the Spartan requirements of training or whether such regimen is in fact necessary is of little consequence. What is important is that the athlete guided by its stern demands symbolizes the expectations of adults regarding clean-living among youth. Simultaneously, the high position awarded athletes serves to dramatize and glamorize the rewards of avoiding dissipation and other forms of early presumption of adulthood. In this way, as in others, the athlete is doing adult's work.

> Athletes may simplify the problem of police work in school. The group of athletes may . . . furnish a very useful extension of faculty-controlled social order . . . . /There is/ a close correspondence between athletic prowess and clean-living (Waller, 1932, pp. 116-117)

One final service of athletics warrants mention. There has never been any discernible *substantive similarity* between scholastic preparation and occupational goals. Substantive similarity is reserved for apprenticeship systems of preparation and for the small part of our scholastic system, usually in the performing arts or in graduate education, that has maintained important elements of apprenticeship. In almost all of a modern educational system there is little visible substantive connection between studying to be something and actually being that thing. There is formal connection, both direct and indirect, but the tasks of study and preparation bear little resemblance to concrete tasks in any particular occupation. Consequently, though adults expect youth to aspire, the very meaning of aspiration, and thus its impact, is obscure to youth. An important function of athletics is to make real the conception of aspiration.

Thus, sports links aspiration to diversion. Moreover, it joins youth to the adult social order in its functions as an agency of official social control. Athletics are the handmaiden of convention despite their harboring within them the spirit of exuberance, violence, prowess, freedom, and other attributes commonly imputed to youth. Thus, they are among the best examples of the social duplicity by which control is instituted through the illusion of autonomy. The substance of athletics contains within itself —

in its rules, procedures, training, and sentiments — a paradigm of adult expectations regarding youth.

Like most actors who do important work for social systems and are paid in tenuous currency which is not always forthcoming, athletes are not as impressed with their lot as outsiders are. Thus, the high standing attributed to athletic youth does not necessarily result in a subjective feeling of satisfaction and contentment. The imagery of Saturday's hero is quite common among athletic youth, and in a variety of ways they display the same minority mentality as intellectuals or any other group which exists within a pluralistic system and feels its efforts insufficiently rewarded. Like others in their position, athletes are frequently more impressed with the liabilities of their enterprise than its more celetrated perquisites. These liabilities may include the humiliations of persistent defeat, grueling and dull periods devoted to practice and drill, the limitations on free and enjoyable leisure inherent in training regulations, the antiathletic biases of an influential and vocal minority of teachers and students — especially female — which often result in the dehumanizing stereotype of the "jock," the special fears concerning one's fortune after the typically very brief period of celebrity, and the very obvious dangers of incapacitating injury. Thus, the mood of those who maintain the athletic style may as much approximate that emanating from the demeaning ordeal of Sisyphus as that of Olympus.

Rebellious Youth

The final style of youth is a familiar one. Youth are generally known for rebelliousness, and, if one is careful to specify the small proportion who are rebellious, it is useful and informative to describe this contingent. Youth do seem more vulnerable to rebellious posture than either children or adults (Matza, 1961; Matza & Sykes, 1961). During the life cycle, maximum rebelliousness is generally reached during youth (Almond, 1954, pp. 218-220; Bernard, 1957, pp. 421, 444; Dunham & Knauer, 1954; Ernst & Loth, 1952; Lane, 1959, pp. 216-217; McCord, McCord & Zola, 1959, p. 21; Parkinson, 1961, pp. 277-278; Parry, 1933, p. 2). This apparently holds for three forms of rebelliousness — delinquency, radicalism, and bohemianism.

Delinquency, radicalism, and bohemianism are forms of rebelliousness which apparently have a special appeal to youth. Each is a tradition that has distinct anticivil implications. Each is in some sense a threat to the stability and order of an on-going social system, though each threatens different aspects of that system. Delinquency does not denounce bourgeois property arrangements, but it clearly violates them. Moreover, the delinquent rejects bourgeois sentiments of methodism and routine, especially as they appear within the school system, which appears to be his major target of hostility. The bohemian's attitude toward property is typically one of condescending indifference, though he is appalled by the commercialization of art that he associates with property arrangements. His ire is reserved for the puritanical and methodical elements of the bourgeois ethos, especially as they pertain to personal and social relations. Moreover, the bohemian is typically antagonistic to recent trends in bourgeois society. He is opposed to the mechanized, organized, centralized, and increasingly collectivized nature of modern society, Capitalist, Socialist, or Communist. Radicalism, by contrast, envisages a less general denunciation. Particularly in the varieties of revolutionary Marxism, which represent the most important examples of modern radicalism, the primary focus of attack has been on the Capitalist system of economic domination, on the imperialist role allegedly played by such systems, and, most recently, on the threats to world peace presumably initiated or aggravated by Capitalist nations. The methodical, the puritanical, and, especially, the industrial aspects of the bourgeois order have been more or less embraced by most radicals.

Delinquency, radicalism, and bohemianism are most pronounced during youth, but they differ with respect to the specific age of vulnerability within youth. Since the duration of youth turns on the completion of schooling and preparation rather than chronology, it is not surprising that stage of education seems a more decisive point of division than chronological age. Youth who leave school earliest seem most vulnerable to delinquency. Delinquency is primarily a high-school-age phenomenon. Radicalism and bohemianism, especially in America, can be found in institutions of higher education. Its adherents are typically drawn from those whose education terminates during college, with the attainment of a bachelor's degree, or with some graduate work of indeterminable duration. Especially susceptible are persons whose studies are concentrated in areas without a clear-cut career route and without a demanding or exact curriculum. Bohemians seem so regularly concentrated in departments of English, art and music that one is tempted to suggest that their real rebellion is not against society-at-large, but against the faculties in the respective departments and the standards of art they profess.

The modes of rebelliousness, furthermore, differ with respect to their ambitions. Delinquents have no designs on society; there is no desire on the part of delinquents to reconstruct society. Thus, they are aberrant (Merton, 1961, pp. 725-727). Radicals, on the other hand, do wish to reshape society in the form of their own ideological predilections. Thus, they are the archetype of the non-conformist (Merton, 1961, pp. 725-727). Bohemians fall somewhere between, typically wishing to develop a private and insulated way of life, but rarely having any aspiration to convert the rest of society.

Finally the modes of youthful rebelliousness differ with respect to assessments regarding their moral worth. In the case of delinquents, the judgments seem more or less to coincide with those belonging to conventional society (Sykes & Matza, 1957). There is no serious belief in either camp in the moral worth of the delinquent enterprise. There has been, however, considerable dispute regarding the moral value of radicalism and bohemianism. Many intellectuals attribute worth to each of these enterprises, and radicals and bohemians themselves, unlike delinquents, are convinced of the moral value of their doctrines and actions.

Beyond these general similarities and differences, each mode of youthful rebellion may be described separately, remembering that it is extremely unlikely that radicals, bohemians, and delinquents taken together and defined generously constitute even 5 percent of the youthful population.

Juvenile Delinquency. There are many perceptive accounts describing the behavior of juvenile delinquents and their underlying sentiments. Perhaps no style of youth has been better covered and described (Bloch & Niederhoffer, 1958; Bordua, 1961; Cloward & Ohlin, 1960; Cohen, 1955; Cohen & Short, 1958; Finestone, 1957; Griffith, 1948; Kobrin, 1951; Miller, 1958; Shaw

& Moore, 1931; Thrasher, 1936; Yablonski, 1962). Although there have been important differences of opinion in the interpretation placed on various components, there has been some consensus on the content of delinquent values and sentiments.

The distinctive feature of the spirit of delinquency is the celebration of prowess. Each of the themes stressed in the delinquent tradition develops an aspect of the meaning of "prowess." First, delinquents are deeply immersed in a search for excitement, thrills, or "kicks." The approved style of life is an adventurous one. Activities pervaded by displays of daring and charged with danger are highly valued. The fact that an activity involves breaking the law and, thus, an eliciting of the game of "cops and robbers" is often the element that provides the air of excitement. "Kicks" or "action" may come to be defined as "any act tabooed by 'squares' that heightens and intensifies the present moment of experience and differentiates it as much as possible from the humdrum routines of daily life" (Finestone, 1957, p. 5). In courting danger and provoking authorities, the delinquent does not simply endure hazards; he creates them in an attempt to manufacture excitement. For many delinquents, "the rhythm of life fluctuates between periods of relatively routine and repetitive activities and sought situations of greater emotional stimulation" (Miller, 1958, pp. 10-11).

Second, to attain prowess is to seek and receive the material rewards of society while avoiding, in the manner of a leisure class, the canons of school and work with their implicit commitments to methodism, routine, and security. Delinquents commonly exhibit a disdain for "getting on" in the realms of school and work. Instead, there is a sort of aimless drifting or perhaps grandiose dreams of quick success.

The delinquent must be financed if he is to attain the luxury of the sporting life. Although some writers have coupled the delinquent's disdain of work with a disdain of money, it seems unlikely that money is renounced in the delinquent code; more likely, it is treated in a special but not unprecedented way. Money is valued, but not for purposes of a careful series of expenditures or long-range objectives. Money for the delinquent is a luxury. It is something to be attained in windfall amounts and subsequently squandered in gestures of largesse and other exhibitions of conspicuous consumption.

An age-old method of attaining such luxury income is gambling. Most of the other techniques involve victimizing others. Simple expropriation — theft and its variants — must be included, of course, but it is only one of a variety of ways of "scoring" and does not always carry great prestige in the eyes of delinquents (Finestone, 1957). Other forms of prowess include chicanery or manipulation, which may take the form of borrowing from gullible and sympathetic "squares" or more elaborate forms of hustling like exhorbitant initiation fees into otherwise defunct clubs; an emphasis on "pull," frequently with reference to obtaining a "soft" job assumed available only to persons with influential contacts; and the exploitation of females for gain.

A third theme running through the accounts of juvenile delinquency centers on aggressive masculinity. The code of the warrior, which in some ways the delinquent code reflects, calls for aggressive manliness, including reluctance to accept slights on one's honor (Margolis, 1960). The delinquent's readiness for aggression is particularly stressed in the analysis of juvenile gangs in slum areas of large cities. It is in such gangs that one finds the struggle for "turf," and thus, it is in these cases that the applicability of the warrior code is most apparent. Cloward and Ohlin (1960) pointed out that one can be led into error by viewing conflict-oriented delinquents as typical of all delinquents. Yet the gang delinquent's use of honor, or "rep," and the proof of courage or "heart," seems to express in extreme form the idea that aggression is a demonstration of toughness and thus, masculinity. It is this idea which pervades delinquent thought.

Student Radicalism. Relative to the many accounts of delinquency, there are few systematic descriptions of student radicalism in the United States (Iversen, 1959; Wechsler, 1953). Enough exists, however, to proceed with a tentative description of this tradition.

Radicalism among students did not begin in the decade of the thirties, although there is little question that it reached its height during that period. The Intercollegiate Socialist Society was organized in 1905, and in 1921 Calvin Coolidge decried student radicalism (Iversen, 1959, p. 13). Despite the internecine struggles within the revolutionary socialist movement since 1905, some aspects of the radical tradition have remained relatively stable.

111

First among the stable components is the vision of the apocalypse. This refers to "the belief that the evil world as we know it, so full of temptation and corruption, will come to an end one day and will be replaced by a purer and better world" (Shils, 1960, p. 59). This tradition has its origins in the apocalyptic outlook of the prophets of the Old Testament and has been passed down through the early Christians and adherents of heretical sects. Its modern recipients are "the modern revolutionary movements and above all the Marxian movements." The tradition is best reflected in "doctrinaire politics, or the politics of the ideal" (Shils, 1960, p. 60).

Whatever its general importance in revolutionary socialism the politics of the ideal seems peculiarly well suited to the predispositions of youthful rebelliousness. This sort of politics seems consistent with Davis' description of youth's mixture of idealism and cynicism (Davis, 1940; Davis, 1944). In the politics of the ideal, perception and assessment become bifurcated with respect to idealism and cynicism. On this side of the apocalypse, one views and interprets events critically and cynically; on the other side, or in some contemporary foreshadowing of the future, one views and interprets events idealistically and generously.

The second component of the spirit of student radicalism is populism. "Populism is the belief in the creativity and in the superior worth of the ordinary people, of the uneducated and the unintellectual" (Shils, 1960, p. 60). Because of the central role of populism in modern radicalism, revolutionary movements have tended to equate the apocalypse with the liberation of the folk. The particular folk has varied: "In the Russian social revolutionary movement, it was the peasant; in traditional Marxism, it was the industrial proletariat; in the anarchism of Bakunin, it tended to be the *Lumpenproletariat.* American student radicalism, largely unaware of these esoteric distinctions, has tended to lump these populist ideals together in a compote consisting of migrant farm workers, unskilled and semi-skilled industrial workers, and Negroes.

Among students, the appeal of populism is not simply an outgrowth of traditional radical propensities. Just as the apocalyptic mentality has a special appeal to youth, so, too, does populism. Students have a special liking for populism because it is a vehicle for an effective attack on the professional authority and a way of defending against unflattering assessment of themselves.

For the radical, and bohemian, too, a belief in populism allows students who perceive themselves as avant-garde to deflect the contrary judgments of academic elders.

A third component of the student radical spirit is evangelism, which is well suited to the exuberance and impetuosity characteristic of rebellious youth. Without it, radicalism would be too serious an enterprise to compete effectively for rebellious youth. Thus, evangelism seems as important in the bolstering of internal enthusiasms as in its alleged purpose of gaining new adherents. By encouraging excursion, it allows student radicals to stray from the dull routine of the radical enterprise (Wechsler, 1953) and challenges their capacities for argumentation, intimidation, persuasion, and seduction.

The substance of student radicalism is unconventional political action. Its round-of-life consists of taking stands on concrete issues, circulation of petitions, distribution of leaflets, sale of literature, raising funds, demonstrations and rallies, frequent meetings, discussions, debates, and the like. The mundane character of most of these activities is more or less obscured by the context within which they are viewed. This context is provided by the general characteristics of unconventional politics.

Radical politics is less attentive than conventional politics to the administrative bylaws which govern collegiate activity. Thus, elements of excitement and risk are introduced. Moreover, radical politics is revolutionary rather than simply reformist. This adds meaning and drama to concrete activities and provides a basis for vicarious excitement by requiring identification with actual revolutions taking place elsewhere. Furthermore, radical politics is ideological rather than "market" (Bell, 1960) politics, and, thus, a sense of moral superiority attaches to the activities of the enterprise. Finally, radical politics is year-round rather than seasonal, and so imparts a sense of urgency rarely apparent in conventional politics. In summary, each of the characteristics of unconventional politics conspires to transform the mundane to the extraordinary.

Bohemianism. Bohemianism is a socio-artistic enterprise which appeared as a wide-spread phenomenon in the first part of the nineteenth century in France (Parry, 1933, p. ix). Since then it has spread to many parts of the world, but particularly to Europe and the United States. Despite indigenous sources in the United States and internal influences, the periods of rise and fall of American bohemianism have coincided fairly well with its cycles in France (Parry, 1933). "Beat," the most recent form of American bohemianism, is best viewed as a response to recurrent internal conditions, most notably postwar prosperity, as well as a reflection of developments on the French scene, especially the emergence of café existentialism.

The failure to understand the traditional character of bohemianism in selected American locales and to see its ebb and flow as a reflection of recurrent social process, internal and external, has been largely responsible for alarmist interpretations of beat. Beat has been viewed, alternatively, as a sign of incipient nihilist rebellion and a symbol of hedonistic withdrawal from public life. It has been interpreted as a symptom of some deeper malady and a dark foreboding of what is to come. Interpretations of this sort occur whenever deviant patterns are not viewed in their historical context (Sisk, 1961).

The first and major component of bohemianism is romanticism. Romanticism "starts with the appreciation of the spontaneous manifestations of the essence of concrete individuality. Hence it values originality . . . that which is produced from the 'genius' of the individual (or the folk), in contrast with the stereotyped and traditional actions of the philistine" (Shils, 1960, p. 57). The commitment to spontaneity and originality has had many manifestations among traditional bohemians, particularly in the graphic arts (Barrett, 1958; Rosenberg, 1959). Among beats, however, greater stress has been placed on development of originality and spontaneity in other art forms. Most notable among these have been the celebration of improvisation in modern jazz, poetry, and the novel. For this reason, among others, jazz and jazz musicians have occupied an exalted role in the beat realm. Kerouac, the most notable literary exponent of improvisation, has occupied a similarly exalted position (Kerouac, 1957; Kerouac, 1958a; Kerouac, 1958b).

The exaltation of spontaneity in artistic endeavor is reflected in the bohemian view of the folk. Bohemianism, like radicalism, has a distinctive form of populism, which is best termed "primitivism." Its authentic folk hero was, of course, the gypsy.

Because of the gypsy's chronic unavailability, however, it was not long before the notion of primitive folk had expanded to include more available peoples. The closest approximation that could be found in urban society was the Lumpenproletariat, and it is this group that has occupied a central place in the bohemian's primitivist mystique (Malaquais, 1958). In the modern form of bohemianism, the idealized folk is the lower-class Negro (Mailer, 1957). The Negro, however, is not the first American ethnic group to be granted this dubious honor. East European Jews, too, have been perceived by previous bohemians as the incarnation of primitive folk (Parry, 1933, p. 35).

Closely connected to the celebration of the primitive is the tradition of dedicated poverty. "A neighborhood where the poor live, the poor who are resigned to their poverty, is the best environment in which to live 'the life.' This is a cardinal principle which the beat share with the bohemians of the past" (Lipton, 1959, p. 59). Although the dedication to poverty is, in part, a natural outgrowth of a commitment to primitivism, it is simultaneously a conscious way of avoiding the corrupting influence of the commercial world.

A final aspect of romanticism, consistent with primitivism, consists of a more or less complete rejection of bureaucratic-industrial society. This may be referred to as medievalism and is best described as an apocalyptic view without the apocalypse. Medievalism accepts the first part of the apocalyptic formula, man's fall from grace, but makes no provision, as in radicalism, for man's redemption.

The second component of the bohemian tradition is insistence on the expression of authentic inner feelings. Thus, bohemianism has been marked by an intense moodiness. Mood is not to be suppressed or obscured; rather, it is to be indulged, pursued, and exhibited. Mood is a crucial part of inner, or authentic, experience and, thus, deserves unhampered expression. Because of this dedication to the full expression of mood, bohemianism has always been somewhat perplexing to the outsider who expects some consistency of temperament to accompany a reasonably coherent viewpoint.

Bohemianism has long had two faces which, although often combined in the career of the same person, have been manifested in two roughly differentiated streams. There is frivolous bohemianism, reminiscent in many respects of aristocratic "dandyism," and there is morose bohemianism, initiated by Poe and popularized by Baudelaire (Parry, 1933, pp. 11-12). After Baudelaire, the two moods persist and are reflected in beat in the modern distinction between "hot" and "cool":

> By 1948 the hipsters, or beatsters, were divided into cool and hot.... The cool today is your bearded laconic sage... before a hardly touched beer in a beatnik dive, whose speech is low and unfriendly, whose girls say nothing and wear black. The "hot" today is the crazy talkative shining-eyed (often, innocent and open-hearted) nut who runs from bar to bar, pad to pad, looking for everybody, shouting, restless, lushy, trying to "make it" with subterranean beatniks who ignore him (Kerouac, 1961, p. 73).

Thus, in the insistence on the authentic display of mood and in the development of frivolous and morose subtraditions, bohemianism has pushed to the limits of human expression. It has had a manic and a depressive character.

Even for the morose, however, the solitary life receives little authorization in the bohemian view. The unfriendly, laconic sage in Kerouac's description had, after all, "made the scene." Bohemians must have "scenes," since bohemianism has always referred to a collecting of like-minded eccentrics (Lipton, 1959; Parry, 1933; Rigney & Smith, 1961).

Monasticism, which is the formation of insulated communities of adherents, is an explicit attempt on the part of bohemians to regain the sense of community which, according to their ideology, no longer exists in the broader society. The clubs, cafes, dives, or pads, which are their monasteries, are places where the bonds of familiarity can be assumed and, except for the danger of the police interloper, one hardly need "check out" a scene before feeling secure in it. Not all persons are welcome in the places of congregation. Bohemians are not evangelists; on the contrary, the newcomer must prove in a variety of ways that he belongs (Rigney & Smith, 1961).

Bohemians have long realized that both the unauthentic (pretenders or "phonies") and the outright conventional (tourists or "squares") are greatly fascinated by the bohemian life (Rigney & Smith, 1961, p. 181). But because of their stress on authenticity, bohemians have been guarded in their relations with phonies and squares. They are also dimly aware of the fate that, sooner or later, befalls all bohemias. The persistence with which the squares and phonies discover their haunts has meant that virtually no bohemian "monastery" can long survive.

The substance of bohemianism has two important and interrelated elements. First, there is the creation of unconventional art, which may be distinguished from the conventional variety in three major ways. It is disaffiliated from the major institutions which provide the machinery for the production and distribution of art. Among these institutions are the modern university, with its direct and indirect subsidization of the arts, and the modern industries of mass communication which deal commercially in art (publishing firms) and in commercialized art (advertising). Second, stylistic innovation is characteristic of bohemian art. In each of the arts, the bohemian has been an experimenter in new styles of expression.

The third feature of unconventional art applies to its subject matter. Bohemian art has frequently dealt with the forbidden, the censorable. In his attempt to plumb the depths of human existence, the bohemian has often been guilty of confusing or equating the two meanings of "depths." This equivocation was an outgrowth of the bohemian's peculiar style of populism in which authentic life coincides with primitive life, with life as it is lived in the lowest orders of society and the underworld. His own descent into the lowest orders, resulting from his dedicated poverty, allows him to extend the province of his subject matter in an important manner. If the bohemian feared the Lumpenproletariat or if he discovered that their behavior was not always censorable, he could always turn to what is, after all, the most frequent subject matter of bohemian art — bohemians.

This brings us to the second and interrelated element of the bohemian enterprise, the pursuit of unconventional personal experience. It is interrelated, because, whatever its motive among bohemians, it has persistently performed a crucial function for young, aspiring painters, poets, sculptors, and novelists. It has provided them with a subject matter to which to apply their variable talents.

In the pursuit of unconventional personal experience, there is no assurance of success. Some sorts of experience involve higher risks of failure than others — the pursuit of sexual conquest, for instance, is less likely to culminate successfully than is the use of alcohol to lessen inhibitions. Thus, a cataloguing of the forms of experience traditionally pursued by bohemians should not be mistaken for an accurate rendition of what bohemians typically do. More time seems spent in pursuit than in actual experience.

Two sorts of unconventional experience are pursued. First, there is the search for hedonistic experiences which overlap considerably with activities that are currently deemed illegal in the United States. These are generally nonvictimizing offenses and include such misdeeds as sexual excess, homosexuality, intemperate use of alcohol, disturbing the peace, use of narcotics, and speeding in automobiles. Since many of these activities held popularity among bohemians during the nineteenth century (Parry, 1933, p. 11), it should not be assumed that beats have attained new levels of hedonistic experience.

Second, there is a quest for transcendence which is closely related to the problem of creativity and represents an experimenting with the limits to which human perception may be pushed. It is as an attempt to transcend the mundane restrictions on human perception that can best be understood in three highly esoteric activities of the beats: religious mysticism as manifested in Buddhist meditation, or the "Zen kick" (Kerouac, 1958a); the flirtation with and acceptance of psychosis, or the "insanity bit" (Krim, 1960); and the hallucinogenic use of drugs (Lipton, 1959, p. 178).

Conclusion

The aim of this chapter has been to summarize and organize some of the accumulated sociological knowledge regarding youth by means of a description of a variety of styles of youth behavior. Many youth, of course, do not, during most of their younger years, maintain these styles in a pure form. Most youth probably engage in conventional composites, which in varying mixes blend the styles of scrupulosity, scholarship, sports, and one or another mode of rebelliousness. These blends are so varied as to defy enumeration. Moreover, there are other styles about which very little is known.

REFERENCES

Abbott, Grace. *The Child and the State.* Chicago: Univer. of Chicago Press, 1938. 2 vols.

Almond, G.A. *The Appeals of Communism.* Princeton, N.J.: Princeton Univer. Press, 1954.

Ausubel, D.P. *Theory and Problems of Adolescent Development.* New York: Grune & Stratton, 1954.

Barrett, W. *Irrational Man.* New York: Doubleday, 1958.

Bealer, R.C., & Willits, Fern K. "Rural Youth: A case study in the rebelliousness of adolescents." *Ann. Amer. Acad. polit. soc. Sci.,* November, 1961, 338, 63-69.

Becker, H.S. *Man in Reciprocity.* New York: Frederick A. Praeger, 1956.

Becker, H.S. *The Outsiders: Studies in the Sociology of Deviance.* New York: The Free Press of Glencoe, 1963.

Bell D. *End of Ideology.* Glencoe, Ill.: Free Press, 1960.

Benedict, Ruth. "Continuities and Discontinuities in Cultural Conditioning." *Psychiatry,* May, 1938, I, 161-167.

Berger, B.M. "On the youthfulness of Youth Cultures." *Soc. Res.,* Autumn, 1963, 30(3), 319-342.

Berger, B.M. "Adolescence and Beyond: An Essay Review of three books on the problem of growing up." *Soc. Probs.* Spring, 1963

Bernard, Jessie. *Social problem at midcentury.* New York: Dryden, 1957.

Bettelheim, B. "The problem of generation." *Daedalus,* Winter, 1962, 68-96.

Bloch, H., & Niederhoffer, A. *The Gang.* New York: Philosophical Library, 1958.

Bordua, D. "Delinquent Subcultures: Sociological interpretations of gang delinquency." *Ann. Amer. Acad. polit. soc. Sci.,* November, 1961. 338 119-136.

Boys' Club of America. *Needs and interest study of 11, 12, and 13 year old boys club members,* 1963.

Bronfenbrenner, U. "The changing American child. In E. Ginzberg (Ed.), *Values and Ideals of American Youth.* New York: Columbia Univer. Press, 1961. Pp. 71-84.

Bronson, W.C., Katten, E.S., & Livson, N. "Patterns of authority and affection in two generations." *J. abnor. soc. Psycho.,* 1959, 58, 143-152.

Brossard, C. *Who walk in darkness.* New York: New Directions, 1952.

Clark, B.R., & Trow, M. "Determinants of college student subculture." Unpublished manuscript, Berkeley, Center for the Study of Higher Education, 1960.

Clausen, J.A., & Williams, Judith R. "Sociological correlates of child behavior." *Child Psych., 62nd Yearb. nat. Societ. Stud. Educ.* 1963, Part I.

Cloward, R.A. & Ohlin, E.E. *Delinquency and Opportunity.* Glencoe, Ill.: Free Press, 1960.

Cohen, A.K. *Delinquent boys.* Glencoe, Ill.: Free Press, 1955.

Cohen, A.K. & Short, J.F. "Research in delinquent subcultures." *J. Soc. Iss.,* 1958, 14(3), 20-37.

Cohen, A.K., & Short, J.F. "Juvenile delinquency." In R.K. Merton & R.A. Nishet (Eds.), *Contemporary and social problems.* New York: Harcourt, 1961. Pp. 77-126.

Coleman, J. "The adolescent subculture and academic achievement." *Amer. J. Sociol.* January, 1960, 65, 337-347.

Coleman, J. *The Adolescent Society.* Glencoe, Ill.: Free Press, 1961. (a)

Coleman, J. "Athletics in High school." *Ann. Amer. Acad. polit. soc. Sci.,* November, 1961, 338, 33-43. (b)

Dansereau, H. K. "Work and the teen-ager." *Ann. Amer. Acad. polit. soc. Sci.,* November, 1961, 338, 44-52.

Davis. A. "Socialization and adolescent personality." In N.B. Henry (Ed.), *Adolescence, 43rd Yearb. nat. Societ. Stud. Edu.,* 1944. Part I.

Davis, K. "Sociology of parent-youth conflict." *Amer. Sociol. Rev.,* August, 1940, 5, 523-535.

Davis. K. "Adolescence and the social structure." *Ann. Amer. Acad. polit. soc. Sci.,* November, 1944, 236, 8-16.

Denny, R. "American youth today." *Daedalus,* Winter, 1962, 124-144.

Dunham, W.H., & Knauer, M.E. "The juvenile court and its relationship to adult criminality. *Soc. Forces,* March, 1954, 32, 290-296.

Eisenstadt, S.N. *From generation to generation.* Glencoe, Ill.: Free Press, 1956.

Eisenstadt, S.N. "Archetypal patterns of youth." *Daedalus,* Winter, 1962, 28-46.

Elkin, F., & Westley, W.A. "The myth of adolescent culture." *Amer. sociol. Rev.,* December, 1955, 20, 680-684.

Erikson, E. *Childhood and society.* New York: Norton, 1950.

Erikson, E. "Fidelity and diversity." *Daedalus,* Winter, 1962, 5-27.

Ernst, M.L., & Loth, D. *Report on the American Communist.* New York: Holt, 1952.

Feldman, G., & Gartenberg, M. *The beat generation and the angry young men.* New York: Dell, 1958.

Finestone, H. "Cats, kicks, and color." *Soc. Probs.,* 1957, 5, 3-13.

Friedenberg, E. *The vanishing adolescent.* Boston: Beacon, 1959.

Friedenberg, E. "The image of the adolescent minority." *Dissent,* Spring, 1963, 10, 149-158. (a)

Friedenberg, E. "The isolation of the adolescent." In W.C. Bier, S.J. (Ed.) *The adolescent: His search for understanding.* New York: Fordham Univer. Press, 1963, Pp. 11-20. (b)

Goodman, P. *Growing up Absurd.* New York: Random, 1960.

Gorer, G. "The all-American child." In B. Meltzer, H. Doby & P. Smith (Eds.), *Education in society.* New York: Crowell, 1958. Pp. 53-58.

Grana, C. *Bourgeois and bohemia.* New York: Basic Books, in press.

Griffith, Beatrice. *American me.* Boston: Houghton, 1948.

Hess, R.D. & Goldblatt, Irene. "The status of adolescents in American society." *Child Develpm.,* 1957, 28, 459-468.

Hollingshead, A.B. *Elmstown's youth.* New York: Wiley, 1949.

Iversen, R.W. *The Communists and the schools.* New York: Harcourt, 1959.

Keniston, K. "Social change and youth in America." *Daedalus,* Winter, 1962, 145-171.

Kerouac, J. *On the road.* New York: Viking, 1957.

Kerouac, J. *Dharma bums.* New York: Viking, 1958. (a)

Kerouac, J. *The subterraneans.* New York: Grove, 1958. (b)

Kerouac, J. "The Origins of the Beat Generation." In T. Parkinson (Ed.), *A Casebook on the Beat.* New York: Crowell, 1961, Pp. 68-76.

Kittermaster, R. "Sport and Education." In A. Natan (Ed.), *Sport and Society.* London: Bowes and Bowes, 1958. Pp. 82-88.

Knowles. J. *A Separate Peace.* New York: Macmillan, 1960.

Kobrin, S. "The Conflict of Values in Delinquent Areas." *Amer. Sociol. Rev.,* 1951, 16, 653-661.

Kohn, M. "Social Class and the Exercise of Parental Authority." *Amer. Sociol. Rev.,* June, 1959, 24, 352-366.

Krim, S. "The Insanity Bit." In Krim, S. (Ed.), *The Beats.* Greenwich: Fawcett, 1960. Pp. 60-77.

Lander, J. "The Pubertal Struggle Against the Instincts." *Amer. J. Orthopsychiatry.* July, 1942, 12, 456-461.

Lane, R.E. *Political Life,* Glencoe, Ill.: Free Press, 1959.

Laqueur, W.Z. *Young Germany: A History of The German Youth Movement.* New York: Basic Books, 1962.

Laski, H. *American Democracy.* New York: Viking, 1948.

Lemert, E.M. *Social Pathology: A Systematic Approach to the Theory of Sociopathic behavior.* New York: McGraw, 1951.

Lipset, S.M. *Political Man.* Garden City: Anchor, 1963.

Lipton, L. *The Holy Barbarians.* New York: Messner, 1959.

McClelland, D., Atkinson, J., Clark, R., & Lowell, E. *The Achievement Motive.* New York: Appleton-Century-Crofts, 1953.

McCord, W., McCord, Joan, & Zola, I. *Origins of Crime.* New York: Columbia University Press, 1959.

McIntosh, P. C. "The British Attitude to Sport." In A. Natan (Ed.), *Sport and Society.* London: Bowes and Bowes, 1958, Pp. 13-24.

Mailer, N. "The White Negro." *Dissent,* Summer, 1957, 4, 276-293.

Malaquais, Jean. "Critique of White Negro" *Dissent,* Winter, 1958, 5, 73-75.

Margolis, J. "Juvenile Delinquents: Latter-day Knights." *Amer. Schol.,* Spring, 1960, 29, 211-218.

Marshall, T. H. *Citizenship and Social Class, and Other Essays.* Cambridge: Cambridge Univer. Press, 1950.

Matza, D. "Subterranean Traditions of Youth." *Ann. Amer. Acad. polit. soc. Sci.,* November, 1961, 338, 102-118.

Matza, D., & Sykes, G. "Juvenile Delinquency and Subterranean Values." *Amer. Sociol. Rev.,* October, 1961, 26, 712-719.

Merton, R. K. "Social Problems and Sociological Theory." In R.K. Merton & R.A. Nisbet (Eds.), *Contemporary Social Problems.* New York: Harcourt, 1961. Pp. 697-737.

Miller, W. "Lower Class Culture as a Generating Milieu of Gang Delinquents." *J. Soc. Iss.,* 1958, 14 (3), 5-19.

Moore, W. *Man, Time and Society.* New York: Wiley, 1963.

Muuss, R.E. *Theories of Adolescence.* New York: Random House Inc., 1962.

Naegele, K. "Youth and Society." *Daedalus,* Winter, 1962, 47-67.

Parkinson, T. "Phenomenon or Generation." In T. Parkinson (Ed.), *A Casebook on the Beat.* New York: Crowell, 1961. Pp. 276-290.

Parry, A. *Garrets and Pretenders: A History of Bohemianism in America.* New York: Covici-Friede, 1933.

Parsons, T. "Age and Sex in the Social Structure of the United States." *Amer. Sociol. Rev.,* October, 1942, 7, 604-616.

Parsons. T. "Youth in the Context of American Society. *Daedalus,* Winter, 1962, 97-123.

Powers, E., & Witmer, Helen. *An Experiment in the Prevention of Delinquency: The Cambridge-Somerville, Youth Study.* New York: Columbia Univer. Press, 1951.

Reiss, I. L. "Sexual Codes in Teen-Age Culture. *Ann. Amer. Acad. polit. soc. Sci.,* November, 1961, 338, 53-62.

Remmers, H.H. & Radler, D.H. *The American Teenager.* Indianapolis: Bobbs, 1957.

Riffel, P.A. "Sex and Scrupulosity." In W.C. Bier, S.J. (Ed.), *The Adolescent: His Search for Understanding.* New York: Fordham Univer. Press. 1963. Pp. 39-51.

Rigney, F., & Smith, L.D.*The Real Bohemia.* New York: Basic Books, 1961.

Rosenberg, H. *The Tradition of the New.* New York: Horizon, 1959.

Rudolph, R. *The American College and University.* New York: Knopf, 1962.

Sarnoff, I. *Personality Dynamics and Development.* New York: Wiley, 1962.

Shaw, C.R., & Moore, M.E. *The Natural History of a Delinquent Career.* Chicago: Univer. of Chicago Press, 1931.

Shils, E.A. "The Traditions of Intellectuals." In G. de Huszar (Ed.), *The Intellectuals.* Glencoe, Ill.: Free Press, 1960, Pp. 55-61.

Simmel, G., "The Sociology of Secrecy and of Secret Societies. *Amer. J. Sociol.,* January, 1906, 11, 441-497.

Sisk, J.P. "Beatniks and Tradition." In T. Parkinson (Ed.), *A Casebook on the Beat.* New York: Crowell, 1961. Pp. 194-200.

Smith, E.A. *American Youth Culture.* Glencoe, Ill.: Free Press, 1962.

Sykes, G.M, & Matza, D. "Techniques of Neutralization." *Amer. Sociol. Rev.,* December, 1957, 22, 664-670.

Tannenbaum, A. J. *Adolescent Attitudes Toward Academic Brilliance.* New York: Teachers' College, 1962.

Thrasher, F.M. *The Gang.* Chicago: Univer. of Chicago Press, 1936.

Trow, M. "The Second Transformation of American Secondary Education." *Int. J. Comp. Sociol.,* September, 1961, 2, 144-166.

Waller, W. *The Sociology of Teaching.* New York: Wiley, 1932.

Wechsler, J.A. *The Age of Suspicion.* New York: Random House, Inc., 1953.

Werthman, C., & Piliavin, I. "Preadolescent Delinquency as a Relationship to Authority." Unpublished manuscript, Berkeley, Center for the Study of Law and Society, 1963.

Yablonski, L. *The Violent Gang.* New York: Macmillan, 1962.

READING 7

Style Rebellion and Identity Crisis

Orrin E. Klapp

Visiting Russia recently, I was interested to see a band of hippies — about ten long-haired, beard wearing, unkempt young men and women — marching down the Moscow subway, strumming guitars, and singing "Flower Power Will Overcome." It was a jolly good tune and smart tempo. They seemed American and

English. The Russians were amused and did not bother them. I asked a Russian if the USSR had any hippies of its own. He said, "We had one, but they made him cut his hair."

I would not, however, take absence of hippies as a sign that there weren't any — just proof of severely limited self-expression. A hippie there probably has to content himself with something like putting a green border on a red propaganda poster. In freer countries — England, France, Sweden, West Germany, India, Japan, even Yugoslavia — rebels can come out in their true colors.

I don't have to tell you that something odd is going on in the world today — a rebellion which doesn't fit into the usual categories of political protest. There is a wide range of upheaval in styles of clothing, art, music, tastes, morals, and ways of living. Strange slogans like "flower power" and "turn on, tune in, drop out" don't really explain what people are doing; they are as puzzling as the behavior itself. We should not, however, think only of hippies. There is a panorama of rebellion in style in all classes and most of the arts.

We see example in the "mod" fashions of Carnaby Street; the weird garb of the Beatles; or perhaps Lord Snowden in a tight-waisted, knee-length, brown Bonnie and Clyde coat with gangster-style white vertical stripes, and a green and orange striped shirt. "Wham, it hit people straight between the eyes," commented the London *Daily Sketch*. We see mini-skirts, mini-mini-skirts, and nuns wearing mini-habits; bikinies, nokinis, topless and "peekaboo" dresses; Castro-style beards on university students; Moslem fezzes and tribal African garb on American Negroes; and on boys riding motorcycles, black leather jackets, chains, knives, swastikas, and death's head insignia.

In entertainment, too, something odd is happening: "beat" music, loud, strident, catawalling, shocking in themes and lyrics, shattering the ears and producing deafness in some. Folksingers like Joan Baez and Bob Dylan are not celebrating the days of "Tom Dooley" nostalgically, but bitterly protesting what's happening now. A Broadway play, "Hair," features nude people cavorting and facing the audience head on.

Art is producing incomprehensible products, neither meaningful nor pretty; "op" and "pop" styles; "put ons" like Robert Rauschenberg's famous goat — stuffed, with an automobile tire about its middle; "underground" movies on such interesting subjects as an hour viewing a patch of human skin; multi-media "happenings" such as men breaking up an automobile with axes.

Everybody seems to be trying to be more sensational or incomprehensible, to shock and out-shock, in escalation. A girl cellist plays a "topless" concert stripped to the waist, wearing a gas mask. Why the mask? Could it be an expression of distaste for the audience? What next? we ask.

In the midst of this seeming pandemonium, Bob Dylan plunks on his guitar and sings, "Something is happening, and you don't know what it is, do you, Mr. Jones?" — Who is Mr. Jones? (To Greeks he is Papadopoulos.) He is the average one, the ordinary one like you and me; the conventional person who works regular hours, dresses conservatively; doesn't spend his nights attending "love-ins," "be-ins," and "happenings"; and thinks a cigarette is something that gives you only lung cancer, not a "trip" to self-realization. Dylan implies there is a secret of some kind Jones doesn't understand because he's "square," and "straight," that is, accepts things as they are.

Perhaps Dylan is right. We should examine this odd behavior carefully to see if it is saying anything to us.

It used to be that when a person disarranged his costume, let himself go, became dirty and unkempt, and made strange noises, he was locked up. Now he is a "style leader" or "creative artist." The difference is that what would formerly have been rewarded as sheer insanity is being imitated widely and has authority for some. Why is this so? It seems to me that it is because more people now feel an urgent need for self-expression, so it is recognized as legitimate to "let go." A romantic right is growing to express oneself as one pleases.

With this new romanticism, we seem to be entering a new era — not just of science, technology, and material progress, but — of enlarged awareness; delighted acceptance and search for new experiences, seeing things and oneself in new ways, by: travel, scientific discovery, moonshots and undersea exploration, art, religion, sensitivity-training, psychotherapy, and mind-expansion, even by drugs like LSD.

The most startling aspect of this search is style rebellion in the way people dress and live, which is more than merely expressing one's taste in new and creative ways. It is protest which opposes a style by a different style which attacks, rebukes, shocks — "puts down" — prevailing standards. It is aggressive; it makes people angry, it has a flaunting, flouting, defiant quality. It is not simply aesthetic; indeed, it may be shockingly ugly and in bad taste. Its shock value contrasts with smooth fashion whose good taste reflects conformity. Rudi Gernreich, the fashion designer, gives the secret away: "Clothes are not status symbols any longer...Style today is a kind of flaunting of one's personality."

Style rebellion is essentially an attack not on style itself, but on the underlying values of the status quo: middle-class morality, the hard work ethic, the "success" image, conventional religion. We can see this attack in the hippies style. Their uncouthness offends middle-class cleanliness and respectability; their scrounging, carefree, idle existence as free riders and parasites offends the belief that it is good to work hard for one's own living (an idea which kept their forefathers going); "flower power" is a flippant rebuke to militarism and the authority of state; free love is a threat to the monogamous ideal and parent's responsibility; the use of drugs seems unpardonable, selfish, and sensual indulgence, threatening morality and perhaps the entire work structure of productive society; finally, their hair, unkempt, dirty, long in males makes them indistinguishable from females'. As much trouble today seems to be caused by hair as by politics and ideology. For some reason, people got excited about too much, too little, in the wrong places, curled or straight, dyed, or natural. Psychologists and anthropologists say hair is a sexual symbol; maybe that is why people get excited. On boys, especially, it is a problem. Beards, except on priests, are highly suspect these days, since Castro and Che Guevara (they have rather spoilt the Lincoln image). Long hair is regarded as an attack on masculinity. The Syrians made 50 boys cut their hair to preserve them from becoming "soft and effeminate." The Turks turn hippies back to Greece at the border.

However, besides its attack on prevailing values, another feature of style rebellion should be noted. I call it *ego-screaming* — behavior which says, "look at me," "please pay attention to me." This shows the need for recognition, that such people feel ego-deprivation, which is a significant symptom of modern times.

From this we can see that more is going in fashion these days than the usual demand of people for something a little newer and better. Style rebellion is a protest of serious dimensions, not just a normal expression of freedom. It is a sign, I think, of social malaise, that something is wrong which people don't like and want changed. What, then is wrong? What is the protest about?

When we ask, what is wrong with the world, naturally we start looking for injustices, and have no trouble finding them all over the world — displaced Arabs, starved Biafrans, suppressed Czechoslovakians, cheated sharecroppers, and ghetto dwellers everywhere. But the odd thing is that this is not where all, even most, style rebellion and protest are found. Style rebellion is characteristic of rather prosperous people, who enjoy freedom and have money for many indulgences. The middle class provides a large output of rebels: New Left activists, "mods," "beat" musicians, folk singers, hippies, and so on, who are well educated and have been raised with the good things of life. Only a fraction of style rebels today are poor and disprivileged. Nor is there among style rebels (as distinguished from the New Left) an ideology or radical program for remedy of economic and civil industice.

Style rebels appear on the same scene with New Left activists, and there is some collusion between them; but they are not identical and should be distinguished. The distinction is as follows: The New Left are action-oriented, concerned with public affairs; style rebels are expression-oriented, concerned with their own lives. The New Left attacks the Establishment and often attempts to seize power; while style rebels evade responsibility, drop out of the Establishment, and its politics. They are not basically interested in politics. True, style rebellion sometimes verges on political protest when its activities clash with the police and regulations, such as the "filthy speech" rebellion at Berkeley, or when a man smokes marijuana cigarettes on the steps of a court building to express disgust at laws which limit liberty. But, looking at activists of the extreme right and left, as one can see them in news photos or on television, one notes that most are conventionally dressed and do not fit the hippie or extreme "mod" or "beat" categories. What brings them together so often and confuses them in the public mind is their common antagonism to what they call the "Establishment."

But we must ask what is this "Establishment" that they are protesting against? Is it capitalism? A certain government or party? Here we see that it is not so much a political or economic system considered to be working unfairly as it is protest against such things as technology and bureaucracy in general, standardization, and impersonal treatment of humans. The "Establishment" is not so much a class, in Marxian terms, as a way of life which restricts and denies full life for man, as Herbert Marcuse has pointed out. The "Establishment" is a set of middle-class values which college students see in their own teachers and parents — in their own class, not an enemy class.

There is, then, a definite attack on the middle class these days, but the odd thing is that much of it is coming from the middle class itself. It is no proletarian uprising. Two kinds of protest should be distinguished: Lower-class protest is feeling cut off from middle-class values (as we see it when mobs drag television sets from stores). Middle-class protest is alienation from such values already experienced or seen firsthand. The lower middle-class stands appalled at middle-class protest. What's the matter with them? How can one possibly not want to be a business executive or a highly paid white-collar worker, have two cars, three television sets, and live in a nice suburban neighborhood with a patio, barbecue, and swimming pool? Yet, there it is: the prevailing success image has been rejected by many educated young middle-class intellectuals, especially university students; the artistic and literary crowd (outside Madison Avenue); and entertainers. The songs of the Beatles are full of dismal pictures of middle-class life, like "When I'm 64," and "She's Leaving Home." The familiar charges against this way of life we have heard again and again; materialistic, hypocritical, immoral, "square," dull, lacking challenge; and the constant complaint, neglectful of the individual — "Don't fold, spindle, or mutilate."

What I am suggesting is that style rebels are protesting not against the injustice of the world, but the meaninglessness (to them) of a set of values and a style of life (identity) offered by "successful" people in current society. They want to strike out and forge a new identity for themselves. They experiment wildly, sometimes desperately, pathetically, to find something new. In this reaction there is a swing away from the styles of the hard worker, the businessman, the white and blue collar worker, the bureaucrat, toward a more expressive life — in Marcuse's terms, not "one dimensional" but many dimensional man. It is a reaction of boredom against the prevailing image of success and comfortable life of suburbia.

This, then, is what I would call a *meaning problem,* which expressed in terms of the individual is an identity problem. We have to ask, why do modern technological societies so often fail to give meaning and satisfactory identity to their members even when distributing goods adequately? In prosperous societies, troubles seem to shift to the meaning (or, if you prefer, spiritual) sphere.

We are asking, then, why is it that identity problems break out in societies which are materially prosperous, highly modernized and technologized, many of which have philosophies which emphasize the importance of the individual? Unrest is understandable among Rhodesian blacks or overpopulated starving Indians; but it is a paradox that the "have" nations, such as England, France, the United States, Switzerland, the Scandinavian countries, West Germany, Japan, with well-developed economic and welfare systems, many with constitutions emphasizing civil rights, should have abundant identity problems in the middle classes. The paradox seems to be that an individual can get what he wants in terms of material abundance and civil rights, and still have a feeling that he doesn't count.

I can illustrate this by an anecdote about university graduation. The senior class of a California university was rehearsing for the open-air theater for the graduation ceremony that afternoon. The sun was already high, and the prospect was that it would be warm that afternoon. A proposal was made to the class president that, to speed up the ceremony, the calling of names should be dropped, thus saving about 40 minutes. After discussion, the class voted to eliminate name-calling. At this point, a student in one of the upper rows, rose and threw his folding chair down into the arena, narrowly missing the kettle drum of the orchestra. He said, "I have waited four years for this, and I am damned if I will graduate without having my name called!" Then he walked out. There was a moment of stunned silence. Then came a new motion from a member of the class that names be called, which was passed unanimously.

Here we see how easy it is to forget, to lose the individual in the midst of a system designed to educate him for opportunities and give him the good things of life. What had they forgotten?

They had forgotten that there is more to education than facts, skills, and a job; that being appreciated as a person by others is an essential experience every human needs: periodic recognition, standing out from the mass as somebody who counts; having people care emotionally, making one's friends and relatives proud. College graduation is a ceremony to give meaning to a person. It has a sentimental purpose, not a practical one. Abolish it and the individual loses meaning. There is no efficiency in education which ignores identity.

The meaning of an individual — his identity — can be analyzed into two parts: his purpose, the significance of his work and goals; and his self-conception, his sense of his own importance, that he is somebody who counts and that people care about him. Lack of these things creates an identity problem.

The odd thing is that counting people does not make them count; votes and statistics have little value for identity. What gives or takes identity is certain kinds of experience which *others* must give. An individual cannot invent or generate his own importance (unless, of course, he is crazy).

We can here briefly indicate some kinds of things which give the sense of identity and ways in which modern society often fails. I would like to point out briefly six sociological factors disturbing identity all over the world, more in some places than in others — hardly at all, for example, in a village in Crete or a kibbutz in Israel, but very much in modern society characterized by advanced technology, urbanism and mobility. All over the world, disturbances of identity are beginning, but in advanced societies they are often farthest under way because of cumulative effects and the most rapid changes. These identity disturbances feed unrest; they add bitterness to demands of the "have nots" and make middle-class life seem unsatisfactory to many.

The most obviously technological disturbance to identity, perhaps, is *destruction of environment;* places which constitute "home." All over the world, we hear the sound of bulldozers, and jack hammers wiping away familiar landmarks and homes of people. Symbolically, a home is a place where you were raised, rich with childhood and ancestral memories. New housing (architectural design, industrial development, town planning) usually does not replace "home" psychologically, because it has no memories. Sometimes the rich move in where the poor lived and create an entirely new environment. "New towns," suburban tracts, and old people's communities (with names like "Sun Villa") rarely create "home" psychologically. Likewise, social succession, i.e., turnover of people, in urban neighborhoods brings in waves of new dwellers even when buildings remain the same. In five or ten years, an entire population can change, as one sees in Knottinghill Gate, London. The English are appalled to see a village as they knew it destroyed by migrants from the West Indies and Pakistan. The result is that it is coming to be a universal phenomenon that people are finding that they cannot come back to where they were raised to renew themselves by familiar sights and folks back home." One may return to his old neighborhood to find a high-rise building and a parking lot. Even landmarks may be gone, hills flattened, skylines altered, and rivers filled. Strange faces look out from the windows of the old home. The neighbor's children — one's former friends — are gone. Such a man having lost his "home," has lost one of the strands of his identity. He cannot meaningful refer to himself the way a Greek does who says, "I'm a Cretan," and thinks of his village. So, symbolically, masses of modern people, however well housed in material terms, are becoming a homeless generation psychologically. As the adage says, "a house is not a home."

A factor equally disturbing to identity is *loss of contact with the past and tradition.* People are forgetting what kind of people they were, are becoming "people without a past." Ethnic and tribal identities are being abandoned, old customs and ceremonies are being forgotten (though people like Dora Stratou are trying to preserve them), and ancestors and geneologies are losing importance. One may illustrate this with Cleveland Amory's well-known story about the Bostonian who applied to a Chicago firm for a job. He brought with him a letter of recommendation stressing the quality of his ancestry in Boston. But the Chicago office replied that, though they were very impressed with Mr. X's pedigree, they were not interested in using him for breeding purposes. This reply expresses the modern feeling of the practical irrelevance of the past. Old ways are viewed as obsolete, "corny." Modernism is rampant, whose motto is, "away with the old and in with the new." History is becoming abstract knowledge about the past rather than the story of "our people" and our heroes. There is loss of the heroic view of history and the "chosen people" concept.

So the record of the past becomes dead history rather than living tradition. Folklore, folk dance, and song, when revived are not living tradition, but quaint historical study, danced and sung by people who *didn't* learn it from their grandmothers. Hence "folk" today is modern fad, not really living tradition. So, as the sense of continuity with the past is weakened, man loses another thread of identity. He cannot locate himself as a link in a chain of ancestors; he often doesn't even know who his "people" were. He is an ambiguous man who must be what he makes of himself, and is dealt with not as a representative of his people, but statistically in the mass.

But it isn't just what a man does or makes up himself, but how society recognizes him that creates identity. A third factor is *loss of identifying ceremony*. As already illustrated by the college seniors, there is less emphasis today on ceremonies which recognizes the individual — his steps in status, achievements, importance as a person. A whole range of ceremonies can do this: baptisms, birthdays, name-days, religious confirmations, anniversaries, initiations, graduations, honors, retirements, funerals. Some communities still do most of these things. But, somehow — for reasons of "efficiency" or because there are too many people or we don't know people — we find less time for this sort of thing nowadays. Ceremonies of identity are becoming privatized — you do it on your own, the community rarely participates unless it is a man of distinction; each Joseph, George, and Panayotis is on his own. Or the ceremonies are so impersonal that the individual is lost. Even a funeral — that last of all recognition! — may be a quick and efficient disposal procedure with little satisfaction to the community (if they bother to come). Personal eulogies to the deceased are more and more rare. Today, it is a fact that the average person doesn't have nearly enough ceremonies of recognition, and some don't have any at all. So it is not surprising to see a yearning for celebrities (who get what the average man doesn't), ego-screaming in costume and faddism, and some people even commit crimes to get their names in the papers.

A fourth identity-disturbing factor, perhaps most important of all, is the relationship of mobility and numbers of people to *loss of social concern* in day-to-day relationships. We all know people are moving more and more these days, leaving home, crowding into cities, riding around in cars, airplanes, buses, vans, and scooters; homes are being built on wheels. The amount, speed, and radius of movement are increasing rapidly. Contacts with other people are increasing geometrically, accentuated by mass communication. We can easily see this means less time and attention for any *one* person, group, or locality. At the same time, institutions are being redesigned for greater efficiency in handling masses of people. But they don't serve anybody in particular. They are like the scale which gives out a card with your weight and fortune on it. It is not surprising, then, that in the midst of social services, people develop a sense of aloneness — the "lonely crowd" phenomenon, the feeling that "nobody pays any attention to me." It is very hard to get anyone to take an interest in you. Old people, especially, whose children have moved away feel neglected. Machinery and efficient services try to take the place of social concern, but fail. They arouse resentment by their "red tape," and "cold professional" manner. The production line, payroll number, and bureaucratic rubber stamps are all seen as enemies — devices for denying identity. Nor does increase of the number of "friends" with more contacts really remedy the problem. We know acquaintances can't really take the place of friends, let alone kinfolk. Dale Carnegieism is a good political tactic, but no substitute for concern. What I am saying is that as mobility and number of contacts increase, life becomes more like a cocktail party and less like a birthday party; relationships shift toward the casual. What this means is that the chances become good that a large number of people will suffer lack of social concern most of the time; or, as sociologists might say, insufficient rate of meaningful interaction, man-to-man, day-to-day. The sheer amount of interaction isn't the question; you can see a thousand people and not relate to anybody; one phone call or letter can make your day complete. Most people, however, need more than a letter; they need a matrix of frequent affection, support, and emotional sharing — genuine concern — from a sufficient number of people outside their family, especially: teachers, bosses, priests, indicating the approval of superiors and peers as confidants and buddies. The paradox, however, is that a buzzing extroverted society can suffer a lack of concern and not know it, mask it by what sociologists call "false personalization" or "role-playing," for example the pretense of concern by an insurance salesman. Associations and memberships may not mean anything beyond a membership card or being a member of an audience-crowd at meetings. How can one tell if there is genuine concern? Statistics of participation (for example, church attendance) are usually worthless. Some indices, however, can show it, such as the number of personal calls on a person who is sick; few calls invite the conclusion, "I wasn't *that* important." Another sign of lack of concern is that people feel they "can't get through" to others, they talk, but nobody listens. There is a growth of psychotherapeutic programs devoted to breaking through emotional "walls" in modern society. This means inadequate feedback in terms of emotional support, sincere affection, self-expression (to which others listen as distinguished from ego-screaming), and real information needed for personal guidance.

I have tried to explain how modern society could have a high level of involvement along with a low level of concern. Sociologists, since Tonnies and Durkheim, have pointed out that mass society suffers a chronically low level of social concern, that the break up of small groups which are the natural focus of concern (extended family, clan, tribe, village, parish) has not been replaced by associations of modern times like labor union, party, church, or social set. A vacuum persists. So rebels scream and say "look at me!" "Pay attention to me!"

It is not surprising that lack of concern goes with a fifth element in the context of modern identity problems: *shallowness of feeling*, inability to feel sentiments strongly, or to feel that one is living fully. Many writers have noted various signs of emotional shallowness, such as violence and sensation in movies increasing without corresponding shock and depth of tragic feeling, and the passing away of romantic, strictly sentimental, "old fashioned" love. Emotion is privatized. Everyone is trying to be "cool"; it is becoming embarrassing to openly express feelings, "wave the flag," be homesick, "wear one's heart on one's sleeve." Perhaps a reason is lack of emotional support: one sees evidence that others don't really feel what they say; and some say nothing at all, "play it cool." In the background is the fact that our modern society continually overstresses reason, facts, and machinery, at the expense of feeling, impulse, and intuition — the entire inner life. Objectivity is a fetish of science. One is apologetic for poetry, religious faith, artistic sensibility, premonitions, dreams, scruples, and prejudices of all kinds. I don't know all the reasons, but think that the whole feedback network of emotion has become unplugged. So the "batteries" of sentiment don't get changed often enough. If this is so, then it is not surprising to see style rebellion and activism offsetting emotional shallowness by flamboyance, irrational extremes, search for intense experience — even drugs — a wish to feel deeply, genuinely, even painfully, oneself.

Finally, we must consider the effect of entertainers, stars, recordings, films, television, and all that, on the success-image. What does the current worship of celebrities do for identity? It seems plain that mass communication has a strong but confusing impact. It is confusing aspiration among the young by putting up dubious and unworthy ideals in place of the standard success-image which has deteriorated. We can easily see that young people have been offered a variety of models in mass communication today which their parents never heard of and are very doubtful about approving. Some are downright alarming — "rock" musicians and their "birds," playboys and playgirls, etc. Many are "glamorous successes," like the four unwashed boys who with one recording made a million dollars in a week.

Alongside such exciting possibilities is the fact that the standard success-image has become tarnished. I refer to the ideal of the hard-working Horatio Alger hero. Two reasons for the drabness of the standard success-image can be mentioned. One is that literature has dismally depicted the mediocrity of the "organization man" and the bureaucrat, in writings like William F. Whyte's *The Organization Man;* C. Wright Mills' *Whitecollar;* Sloan Wilson's, *Man in the Grey Flannel Suit;* and James Thurber's *Secret Life of Walter Mitty,* or films like "The Graduate." The white-collar worker's career is thus seen as unheroic, boring, restricted, a dreary shuttling between the "ratrace" of business and tame existence of suburbia. Material possessions don't compensate for such restriction; advertisements say "happy life," but that's not what the kids see. The other reason for drabness of the standard success-image is that pile-up of irrelevant information in a technological-scientific society has become an overload in education: boring and irrelevant school studies which discourage students and kill interest. One can almost hear a student say, "look what you have to go through for a job in bureaucracy and a 50-foot lot in suburbia!" The college student feels acutely that he has to memorize the enormous pile of facts, which he feels have no relation to his own life, and "regurgitate" them at examination time (the phrase speaks for his own attitude). "What is the professor 'yakking' about now?" He opens one eye, then goes back to his own dreams. But if he leaves the lecture and goes to the rest of life — television, community affairs, and all that — he finds the same irrelevance, unless he restricts attention to a narrow band of stimuli; such as rock-and-roll music, skin-diving, or some other sport or hobby which for him means intense and meaningful life — "where the action is," "What's happening *now*, baby."

So, putting all this together, we see young people caught in a dilemma between a rather drab career outlook and unrealistic, inappropriate, sometimes demoralizing, career goals offered by celebrities as models in mass communication. This I call the Mitty Syndrome, dreaming of being glamorous TV stars, etc.; but unable to attain this in fact; wanting to be what one can't be, and not wanting to be what one is and has a realistic expectation of being. Such explosion of wishes by mass communication not met by realistic career opportunities means frustration. It is a formula for unhappiness, of dissatisfaction with oneself.

All these six factors — destruction of the "home" environment, loss of contact with tradition, lack of ceremonies recognizing the individual lack of social concern, weakening sentiments, and confusion of aspiration — add up to identity frustrations of the middle class in mass society. They are symbolic disturbances, in the meaning of symbols of the environment and "success" and in communication among people. No amount of pile-up of wealth and welfare services is going to solve these problems unless focused on improving meaningful relationships of people to each other and to their "home" environments, thus reducing psychological and spiritual frustrations.

Once the problem is seen in these terms, the natural question is, what can be done to provide more identifying experience in a mass society? I shall be teaching at a university of 23,000 students, 200 of which I'll face every week. It will be a challenge to me to think of how to focus more on the student's identity as a person — not on new facts in the curriculum, but on how to make facts more relevant to his life. Not by non-academic substitutes, such as football games and riots, but by something going on in the curriculum which the student will regard as too important to be disturbed by football games and riots. If he lets his hair grow long, I hope it will be because he is so interested in studies that he hasn't time for a haircut, not because he wishes to defy society.

How does one produce such an academic miracle? It is the duty of educators to find out what techniques will do this. There is a clear difference between devices which increase "efficiency" of education (as number of students reached times amount of information transmitted), and devices which will *identify* students as persons and help them find what they need to grow as persons. Many highly efficient methods do practically nothing for identity: computerized learning, TV courses, films, machine-scored examinations which call for no more achievement than a check in the right place, and large lecture halls. On the other hand, many methods accentuate identity, such as: debate, creative writing and art, producing and acting dramas, solo performances and competitions, first-name relationships, frank and open discussions, the "cluster principle" of living together in small groups, "self-directed" groups not dominated by the authority of instructors, and cathartic group-sessions and other kinds of group therapy.

I trust that many will be studying the same problem in the factory, bureaucracy, community, church, hospital, welfare agency, and psychotherapy. "Sensitivity training" today is seeking a kind of interaction that will help people get through to others, solve emotional problems, and find themselves. New things are being discovered every day. There is reason to hope that we are on the verge of discoveries of how to make the individual important again, even in a mass society. Already new forms of welfare are appearing, whose motto is, significantly, not a material benefit, but "pride." And we must get over the idea that the focus of social welfare is entirely in the lower classes. Universities are just as much in need of identity programs as slums.

We need, especially, development of youth programs which will put back into growing up, family life, and school experience, all of the identity-giving features which have been lost by the mass society, namely: a "home" environment, contact with tradition and pride in the past and ancestors, ceremonies of recognition, genuine social concern, strong sentiments, and clear and satisfying models of aspiration.

If we can do this, in my opinion, style-rebellion and hippieism will disappear.

READING LIST

Identify Problems of Modern Times

Bennett, John F. *In Search of Identity* (University of Minnesota Press, 1958).

Erikson, Erik. *Childhood and Society* (London: Image, 1953).

Essien-Udom, E. U. *Black Nationalism* (Chicago: University of Chicago Press, 1962).

Goffman, Erving. *Stigma, Notes on the Management of Spoiled Identity* (Prentice-Hall, 1963).

Klapp, Orrin E. *Collective Search for Identity* (New York: Holt, Rinehart and Winston, 1969).

Lerner, Daniel. *Passing of Traditional Society* (New York: The Free Press, 1958).

Marcuse, Herbert. *One Dimensional Man* (Boston: Beacon Press, 1964).

May, Rollo. *Man's Search for Himself* (W. W. Norton, 1953).

Riesman, David, et al. *The Lonely Crowd* (Yale Univ. Press, 1950).

Rosenberg, Stuart E. *America Is Different: the Search for Jewish Identity* (London: T. Nelson & Sons, 1964).

Ruitenbeek, Hendrik M. *The Individual and the Crowd: a Study of Identity in America* (New American Library, 1964).

Strauss, Anselm. *Mirrors and Masks: The Search for Identity* (Free Press, 1959).

The Missing Community

Paul G. Goodman

1.

The use of history, Benjamin Nelson used to say, is to rescue from oblivion the lost causes of the past. History is especially important when those lost causes haunt us in the present as unfinished business.

I have often spoken . . . of the "missed revolutions that we have inherited." My idea is that it is not with impunity that fundamental social changes fail to take place at the appropriate time; the following generations are embarrassed and confused by their lack. This subject warrants a special study. Some revolutions fail to occur; most half-occur or are compromised, attaining some of their objectives and resulting in significant social changes, but giving up on others, resulting in ambiguous values in the social whole that would not have occurred if the change had been more thoroughgoing. For in general, a profound revolutionary program in any field projects a new workable kind of behavior, a new nature of man, a new whole society; just as the traditional society it tries to replace is a whole society that the revolutionists think is out of date. But a compromised revolution tends to disrupt the tradition without achieving a new social balance.

It is the argument of this book [*Growing Up Absurd*] that *the accumulation of the missed and compromised revolutions of modern times, with their consequent ambiguities and social imbalances, has fallen, and must fall, most heavily on the young, making it hard to grow up.*

A man who has attained maturity and independence can pick and choose among the immense modern advances and somewhat wield them as his way of life. If he has a poor society, an adult cannot be very happy, he will not have simple goals nor achieve classical products, but he can fight and work anyway. But for children and adolescents it is indispensable to have a coherent, fairly simple and viable society to grow up into; otherwise they are confused, and some are squeezed out. Tradition has been broken, yet there is no new standard to affirm. Culture becomes eclectic, sensational, or phony. (Our present culture is all three.) A successful revolution establishes a new community. A missed revolution makes irrelevant the community that persists. And a compromised revolution tends to shatter the community that was, without an adequate substitute. But...it is precisely for the young that the geographical and historical community and its patriotism are the important environment, as they draw away from their parents and until they can act on their own with fully developed powers.

In this chapter, let us collect the missed or compromised fundamental social changes that we have had occasion to mention; calling attention to what *was* achieved and what *failed* to be achieved, and the consequent confused situation which then actually confronts the youth growing up.

2.

Let us start with the physical environment.

Technocracy. In our own century, philosophers of the new technology, like Veblen, Geddes, or Fuller, succeeded in making efficiency and know-how the chief ethical values of the folk, creating a mystique of "production," and a kind of streamlined esthetics. But they did not succeed in wresting management from the businessmen and creating their own world of a neat and transparent physical plant and a practical economics of production and distribution. The actual results have been slums of works of engineering, confused and useless overproduction, gadgetry, and new tribes of middlemen, promoters, and advertisers.

Urbanism. As LeCorbusier and Gropius urged, we have increasingly the plan and style of functional architecture; biological standards of housing; scientific study of traffic and city services; some zoning; and the construction of large-scale projects. But nowhere is realized the ideal of overall community planning, the open green city, or the organic relation of work, living, and play. The actual results have been increasing commutation and traffic, segregated ghettos, a "functional" style little different from packaging, and the tendency to squeeze out some basic urban functions, such as recreation or schooling, to be squeezed out altogether.

Garden City. The opposite numbers, the Garden City planners after Ebenezer Howard, have achieved some planned communities protected by greenbelts. But they did not get their integrated towns, planned for industry, local commerce, and living. The result is that actual suburbs and garden cities are dormitories with a culture centering around small children, and absence of the wage earner; and such "plans" as the so-called shopping centers disrupts such village communities as there were. The movement to conserve the wilds cannot withstand the cars, so that all areas are invaded and regulated.

3.

Let us proceed to economic and social changes.

New Deal. The Keynesian economics of the New Deal has cushioned the business cycle and maintained nearly full employment. It has not achieved its ideal of social balance between public and private works. The result is an expanding production increasingly consisting of corporation boondoggling.

Syndicalism. Industrial workers have won their unions, obtained better wages and working conditions, and affirmed the dignity of labor. But they gave up their ideal of workers' management, technical education, and concern for the utility of their labor. The result is that a vast majority couldn't care less about what they make, and the "labor movement" is losing force.

Class Struggle. The working class has achieved a striking repeal of the iron law of wages; it has won a minimum wage and social security. But the goal of an equalitarian or freely mobile society has been given up, as has the solidarity of the underprivileged. The actual result is an increasing rigidity of statuses; some of the underprivileged tending to drop out of society altogether. On the other hand, the cultural equality that has been achieved has been the degradation of the one popular culture to the lowest common denominator.

Production for Use. This socialist goal has been missed, resulting in many of the other failures here listed.

Sociology. During the past century, the sociologists have achieved their aim of dealing with mankind in its natural groups or groups with common problems, rather than as isolated individuals or a faceless mass. Social science has replaced many prejudices and ideologies of vested interests. But on the whole, social scientists have given up their aim of fundamental social change and an open-experimental method determining its goals as it went along: the pragmatist ideal of society as a laboratory for freedom and self-correcting humanity. The actual result is an emphasis on "socializing" and "belonging," with the loss of nature, culture, group solidarity and group variety, and individual excellence.

4.

Next, political and constitutional reforms.

Democracy. The democratic revolution succeeded in extending formal self-government and opportunity to nearly everybody, regardless of birth, property, or education. But it gave up the ideal of the town meeting, with the initiative and personal involvement that alone could train people in self-government and give them practical knowledge of political issues. The actual result has been the formation of a class of politicians who govern, and who are themselves symbolic front figures.

The Republic. Correspondingly, the self-determination won by the American Revolution for the regional states, that should have made possible real political experimentation, soon gave way to a national conformity; nor has the nation as a whole conserved its resources and maintained its ideals. The result is a deadening centralism, with neither local patriotism nor national patriotism. The best people do not offer themselves for public office, and no one has the aim of serving the Republic.

Freedom of Speech. Typical is the fate of the hard-won Constitutional freedoms, such as freedom of speech. Editors and publishers have given up trying to give an effective voice to important but unpopular opinions. Anything can be printed, but the powerful interests have the big presses. Only the safe opinion is proclaimed and other opinion is swamped.

Liberalism. The liberal revolution succeeded in shaking off onerous government controls on enterprise, but it did not persist to its goal of real public wealth as the result of free enterprise and honestly informed choice on the market. The actual result is an economy dominated by monopolies, in which the earnest individual entrepreneur or inventor, who could perform a public service, is actively discouraged; and consumer demand is increasingly synthetic.

Agrarianism. Conversely, the Jeffersonian ideal of a proud and independent productive yeomanry, with natural family morals and a co-operative community spirit, did in fact energize settling the West and providing the basis for our abundance. But because it has failed to cope with technological changes and to withstand speculation, "farming as a way of life" has succumbed to cash-cropping dependent on distant markets, and is ridden with mortgages, tenancy, and hired labor. Yet it maintains a narrow rural morality and isolationist politics, is a sucker for the mass culture of Madison Avenue and Hollywood, and in the new cities (e.g., in California, where farmers have migrated) is a bulwark against genuine city culture.

Liberty. Constitutional safeguards of person were won. But despite the increasing concentration of state power and mass pressures, no effort was made to give to individuals and small groups new means easily to avail themselves of the safeguards. The result is that there is no longer the striking individuality of free men; even quiet nonconformity is hounded; and there is no asylum from coast to coast.

Fraternity. This short-lived ideal of the French Revolution, animating a whole people and uniting all classes as a community, soon gave way to a dangerous nationalism. The ideal somewhat revived as the solidarity of the working class, but this too has faded into either philanthropy or "belonging."

Brotherhood of Races. The Civil War won formal rights for Negroes, but failed to win social justice and factual democracy. The actual result has been segregation, and fear and ignorance for both whites and blacks.

Pacifism. This revolution has been entirely missed.

5.

Let us proceed to some more general moral premises of modern times.

Reformation. The Protestant Reformation won the possibility of living religiously in the world, freed individuals from the domination of the priest, and led, indirectly, to the toleration of private conscience. But it failed to withstand the secular power; it did not cultivate the meaning of vocation as a community function; and in most sects the spirit of the churches did not spring from their living congregations but was handed down as dogma and ascetic discipline. The final result has been secularism, individualism, the subordination of human beings to a rational economic system, and churches irrelevant to practical community life. Meantime, acting merely as a negative force, the jealous sectarian conscience has driven religion out of social thought.

Modern Science. The scientific revolution associated with the name of Galileo freed thinking of superstition and academic tradition and won attention to the observation of nature. But it failed to modify and extend its method to social and moral matters, and indeed science has gotten further and further from ordinary experience. With the dominance of science and applied science in our times, the result has been a specialist class of scientists and technicians, the increasing ineptitude of the average person, a disastrous dichotomy of "neutral" facts versus "arbitrary" values, and a superstition of scientism that has put people out of touch with nature, and also has aroused a growing hostility to science.

Enlightenment. The Enlightenment unseated age-old tyrannies of state and church and won a triumph of reason over authority. But its universalism failed to survive the rising nationalisms except in special sciences and learning, and its ideal of encyclopedic reason as the passionate guide to life degenerated to the nineteenth-century hope for progress through science and learning. And we now have an internationalism without brotherhood or peace, even concealing science as a strategic weapon; and a general sentiment that the rule of reason is infinitely impractical.

Honesty. The rebellion for honest speech that we associate with Ibsen, Flaubert, etc., and also with the muckrakers broke down the hypocrisy of Victorian prudishness and of exploiting pillars of society; it reopened discussion and renovated language; and it weakened official censorship. But it failed to insist on the close relation between honest speech and corresponding action. The result has been a weakening of the obligation to act according to speech, so that, ironically, the real motives of public and private behavior are more in the dark than ever.

Popular Culture. This ideal, that we may associate in literature with the name of Sam Johnson and the Fleet Street journalists, in the plastic arts with William Morris and Ruskin, freed culture from aristocratic and snobbish patrons. It made thought and design relevant to everyday manners. But it did not succeed in establishing an immediate relation between the writer or artist

145

and his audience. The result is that the popular is controlled by hucksters and promoters as though it were a saleable commodity, and our society, inundated by cultural commodities, remains uncultivated.

6.

Finally, some reforms directly connected with children and adolescents.

No Child Labor. Children have been rescued from the exploitation and training of factories and sweat shops. But, relying on the public schools and the apprentice-training in an expanding and open economy, the reformers did not develop a philosophy of capacity and vocation. Nor, since there were many small jobs, did they face the problems of a growing boy needing to earn some money. In our days, the result is that growing youths are idle and vocationally useless, and often economically desperate; and the schools, on the contrary, become apprentice-training paid for by public money.

Compulsory Education. This gave to all children a certain equality of opportunity in an open expanding industrial society. Formal elementary discipline was sufficient when the environment was educative and provided opportunities for advancement. In our circumstances, formal literacy is less relevant, and overcrowding and official interference make individual attention and real teaching impossible; so that it could be said that the schools are as stupefying as they are educative, and compulsory education is often like jail.

Sexual Revolution. This has accomplished a freeing of animal functioning in general, has pierced repression, importantly relaxed inhibition, weakened legal and social sanctions, and diminished the strict animal-training of small children. The movement has not so much failed as that it is still in process, strongly resisted by inherited prejudices, fears, and jealousies. By and large it has not won practical freedom for older children and adolescents. The actual present result is that they are trapped by inconsistent rules, suffer because of excessive stimulation and inadequate discharge, and become preoccupied with sexual thoughts as if these were the whole of life.

Permissiveness. Children have more freedom of spontaneous behavior, and their dignity and spirit are not crushed by humiliating punishments in school and in very many homes. But this permissiveness has not extended to provide also means and conditions: Young folk might be sexually free, but have no privacy; they are free to be angry, but have no asylum to escape from home, and no way to get their own money. Besides, where upbringing is permissive, it is necessary to have strong values and esteemed behavior at home and in the community, so that the child can have worth-while goals to structure his experience; and of course it is just these that are lacking. So permissiveness often leads to anxiety and weakness instead of confidence and strength.

Progressive Education. This radical proposal, aimed at solving the dilemmas of education in the modern circumstances of industrialism and democracy, was never given a chance. It succeeded in destroying the faculty psychology in the interests of educating the whole person, and in emphasizing group experience, but failed to introduce learning-by-doing with real problems. The actual result of the gains has been to weaken the academic curriculum and foster adjustment to society as it is.

7.

Let us consider the beginning, the ending, and the middle of these little paragraphs.

The headings printed in italic type are, in their summation, a kind of program of modern man. It is evident that every one of these twenty-odd positions was invented and discovered as a response to specific historical conditions. The political positions were developed to oppose the absolutism of the kings who had unified the warring feudal states; the program for children and adolescents has been a response to modern industrialism and urbanism; and so forth. But it does *not* follow, as some sociologists think, that they can therefore be superseded and forgotten as conditions change.

Consider the following of C. Wright Mills: "The ideals that we Westerners associate with the classic, liberal, bourgeois period of modern culture may well be rotted in this one historical stage of this one type of society. Such ideals as personal freedom and cultural autonomy may not be inherent, necessary features of cultural life as such." This is like saying that tragic poetry or mathematics was "rooted" in the Greek way of life and is not "inherently" human. This kind of thinking is the final result of the recent social-scientific attitude that culture is added onto a featureless animal, rather than being the invention-and-discovery of human powers. This is effectually to give up the modern enterprise altogether. But we will not give it up. New conditions will be the conditions of, now, this kind of man, stubbornly insisting on the ideals that he has learned he has in him to meet.

Yet the modern positions are not even easily consistent with one another, to form a coherent program. There have been bitter conflicts between Liberty and Equality, Science and Faith, Technology and Syndicalism, and so forth. Nevertheless, we will not give up one or the other, but will arduously try to achieve them all and *make* a coherent program. And indeed, experience has taught that the failure in one of these ideals at once entails failure in others. For instance, failure in social justice weakens political freedom and this compromises scientific and religious autonomy. "If we continue to be without a socialist movement," says Frank Marquart, "we may end up without a labor movement." The setback of progressive education makes the compulsory school system more hopeless, and this now threatens permissiveness and sexual freedom; and so forth. So we struggle to perfect all these positions, one buttressing another, if we are to fulfill our unique modern destiny.

There is no doubt, too, that in our plight new modern positions will be added to these, and these too will be compromised, aborted, their prophetic urgency bureaucratized and ironically transformed into the opposite. But there it is.

8.

If we now collect the actual, often ironical results of so much noble struggle, we get a clear *but exaggerated* picture of our American society. It has: slums of engineering — boondoggling production — chaotic congestion — tribes of middlemen — basic city functions squeezed out — garden cities for children — indifferent workmen — underprivileged on a dole — empty "belonging" without nature or culture — front politicians — no patriotism — an empty nationalism bound for a cataclysmically disastrous finish — wise opinion swamped — enterprise sabotaged by monopoly — prejudice rising — religion otiose — the popular culture debased — science specialized — science secret — the average man inept — youth idle and truant — youth sexually suffering and sexually obsessed — youth without goals — poor schools.

This picture is not unjust, but it is, again, exaggerated. For it omits, of course, all the positive factors and the ongoing success. We have a persisting grand culture. There is a steady advance of science, scholarship, and the fine arts. A steady improvement in health and medicine. An economy of abundance and, in many ways, a genuine civil peace and a stubborn affirming of democracy. And most of all there are the remarkable resilience and courage that belong to human beings. Also, the Americans, for all their folly and conformity, are often thrillingly sophisticated and impatient of hypocrisy.

Yet there is one grim actuality that even this exaggerated picture does not reveal, the creeping defeatism and surrender by default to the organized system of the state and semimonopolies. International Business Machines and organized psychologists, we have seen, effectually determine the method of school examinations and personnel selection. As landlords, Webb and Knapp and Metropolitan Life decide what our domestic habits should be; and, as "civic developers" they plan communities, even though their motive is simply a "long-term modest profit" on investment while millions are ill housed. The good of General Motors and the nation are inseparable, says Secretary Wilson — even though the cars are demonstrably ruinous for the cities, ruinous for the young, etc. Madison Avenue and Hollywood not only debauch their audiences, but they pre-empt the means of communication, so nothing else can exist. With only occasional flagrant breaches of legality, the increasingly interlocking police forces and the FBI make people cowed and speechless. That Americans can allow this kind of thing instead of demolishing it with a blow of the paw like a strong lion, is the psychology of missed revolutions.

9.

For our positive purposes . . . it is the middle parts of our paragraphs that warrant study: the failures, the fallings-short, the compromises. Imagine that these modern radical positions had been more fully achieved: we should have a society where:

A premium is placed on technical improvement and on the engineering style of functional simplicity and clarity. Where the community is planned as a whole, with an organic integration of work, living, and play. Where buildings have the variety of their real functions with the uniformity of the prevailing technology. Where a lot of money is spent on public goods. Where workers are technically educated and have a say in management. Where no one drops out of society and there is an easy mobility of classes. Where production is primarily for use. Where social groups are laboratories for solving their own problems experimentally. Where democracy begins in the town meeting, and a man seeks office only because he has a program. Where regional variety is encouraged and there is pride in the Republic. And young men are free of conscription. Where all feel themselves citizens of the universal Republic of Reason. Where it is the policy to give an adequate voice to the unusual and unpopular opinion, and to give a trial and a market to new enterprise. Where people are not afraid to make friends. Where races are factually equal. Where vocation is sought and cultivated as God-given capacity, to be conserved and embellished, and where the church is the spirit of its congregation. Where ordinary experience is habitually scientifically assayed by the average man. Where it is felt that the suggestion of reason is practical. And speech leads to the corresponding action. Where the popular culture is a daring and passionate culture. Where children can make themselves useful and earn their own money. Where their sexuality is taken for granted. Where the community carries on its important adult business and the children fall in at their own pace. And where education is concerned with fostering human powers as they develop in the growing child.

In such an utopian society, as was aimed at by modern radicals, but has not eventuated, it would be very easy to grow up. There would be plenty of objective, worth-while activities for a child to observe, fall in with, do, learn, improvise on his own. That is to say, it is not the spirit of modern times that makes our society difficult for the young; it is that that spirit has not sufficiently realized itself.

In this light, the present plight of the young is not surprising. In the rapid changes, people have not kept enough in mind that the growing young also exist and the world must fit their needs. So instead, we have the present phenomena of excessive attention to the children as such, in psychology and suburbs, and coping with "juvenile delinquency" as if it were an entity. Adults fighting for some profoundly conceived fundamental change naturally give up, exhausted, when they have achieved some gain that makes life tolerable again and seems to be the substance of their demand. But to grow up, the young need a world of finished situations and society made whole again.

10.

Indeed, the bother with the above little utopian sketch is that many adults would be restive in such a stable modern world if it were achieved. They would say: It is a fine place for growing boys. I agree with this criticism.

I think the case is as follows: Every profound new proposal, of culture or institution, invents and discovers a new property of "Human Nature." Henceforth it is going to be in *these* terms that a young fellow will grow up and find his identity and his task. So if we accumulate the revolutionary proposals of modern times, we have named the *goals of modern education.* We saw that it was the aim of Progressive Education to carry this program through.

But education is not life. The existing situation of a grown man is to confront an uninvented and undiscovered present. Unfortunately, *at* present, he must also try to perfect his unfinished past: this bad inheritance is part of the existing situation, and must be stoically worked through.

11.

Let me repeat the proposition of this chapter: *It is the missed revolution of modern times — the fallings-short and the compromises — that add up to the conditions that make it hard for the young to grow up in our society.*

The existing local community, region, and nation is the real environment of the young. Conversely, we could define community spirit and patriotism as the conviction in which it is possible to grow up. (An independent and not too defeated adult confronts a broader historical international, and cosmic scene as his environment for action.)

Modern times have been characterized by fundamental changes occurring with unusual rapidity. These have shattered tradition but often have not succeeded in creating a new whole community. We have no recourse to going back, there is nothing to go back to. If we are to have a stable and whole community in which the young can grow to manhood, we must painfully perfect the revolutionary modern tradition we have.

This stoical resolve is, paradoxically, a *conservative* proposition, aiming at stability and social balance. For often it is not a question of making innovations, but of catching up and restoring the right proportions. But no doubt, in our runaway, one-sided way of life, the proposal to conserve human resources and develop human capacities has become a radical innovation.

Right proportion cannot be restored by adding a few new teachers formally equivalent to the growth in population. Probably we need a million new minds and more put to teaching. Even Dr. Conant says that we must nearly double our present annual expenditure on education for teaching alone, not counting plant and the central schools he wants. And this does not take into account essentially new fields such as making sense of adult leisure.

It must be understood that with the increase in population and crowding, the number and variety of human services increase disproportionately, and the laissez-faire areas, both geographical and social, decrease. Therefore the *units* of human service, such as school classes or the clientele of a physician (and even political districts?), ought to be made *smaller,* to avoid the creation of masses: mass teaching, mass medicine, mass psychotherapy, mass penology, mass politics. Yet our normal schools and medical schools cannot cope with even the arithmetic increase.

Right proportion requires reversing the goal in vocational guidance, from fitting the man to the machine and chopping him down to fit, to finding the opportunity in the economy that brings out the man, and if you can't find such an opportunity, make it. This involves encouraging new small enterprises and unblocking and perhaps underwriting invention. Again, if at present production is inhuman and stupid, it is that too few minds are put to it: this can be remedied by giving the workman more voice in production and the kind of training to make that voice wise.

Probably, right proportion involves considerable decentralizing and increasing the rural-urban ratio. Certainly it involves transforming the scores of thousands of neglected small places, hopelessly dull and same, into interesting villages that someone could be proud of. A lot of the booming production has got to go into publicly useful goods, proportionate to the apparently forgotten fact that it is on public grounds, because of public investment, and the growth of population, that private wealth is produced and enjoyed. We have to learn again, what city man always used to know, that belonging to the city, to its squares, its market, its neighborhoods, and its high culture, is a public good; it is not a field for "investment to yield a long-term modest profit." A proportionate allocation of public funds, again, is not likely to devote more money to escape roads convenient for automobiles than to improving the city center. (If I may make a pleasant suggestion, we could underwrite a handsome program for serious adult leisure by a 10 percent luxury tax on new cars; it would yield over a billion.)

Since prosperity itself has made it more difficult for the underprivileged immigrant to get started, right proportion requires devoting all the more money and ingenuity to helping him find himself and get started. (In such cases, by the way, ingenuity and friendly aid are more important than money, as some of our settlement houses in New York have beautifully demonstrated.) And some way will have to be found, again, for a man to be decently poor, to work for a subsistence without necessarily choosing to involve himself in the total high-standard economy. One way of achieving this would be directly producing subsistence goods in distinction from the total economy.

In arts and letters there is a right balance between the customary social standard and creative novelty, and between popular entertainment and esthetic experience. Then, to offset Hollywood and Madison Avenue, we must have hundreds of new little theatres, little magazines, and journals of dissenting opinion with means of circulation; because it is only in such that new things can develop and begin to win their way in the world.

It is essential that our democratic legislatures and public spokesmen be balanced by more learned and honorable voices that, as in Britain, can thoughtfully broach fundamental issues of community plan, penal code, morality, cultural tone, with some certainty of reaching a public forum and some possibility of being effective. For there is no other way of getting the best to lead, to have some conviction and even passionate intensity, to save America from going to managers, developers and politicans by default.

Certainly right proportion, in a society tightly organized and conformist, requires a vast increase in the jealous safeguard of civil liberties, to put the fear of God back into local police, district attorneys, and the Federal Bureau of Investigation.

Here is a program of more than a dozen essential changes, all practicable, all difficult. A wiser and more experienced author could suggest a dozen more.

12.

Let me expand one of these: Making sense of adult leisure.

What are the present goals of the philosophers of leisure, for instance, the National Recreation Association? and now imagine those goals achieved. There would be a hundred million adults who have cultured hobbies to occupy their spare time: some expert on the flute, some with do-it-yourself kits, some good at chess and golf, some square dancing, some camping out and enjoying nature, and all playing various athletic games. Leaf through the entire catalogue of the National Recreation Association, take all the items together, apply them to one hundred million adults — and there is the picture. (This costs *at present* forty billion dollars a year, according to the guess of Robert Coughlan in *Life.*) The philosophy of leadership, correspondingly, is to get people to participate — everybody must "belong."

Now even if all these people were indeed getting deep personal satisfaction from these activities, this is a dismaying picture. It doesn't add up to anything. It isn't important. There is no ethical necessity in it, no standard. *One cannot waste a hundred million people that way.*

The error is in the NRA's basic concept of recreation. Let me quote from a recent editorial in *Recreation:* Recreation is "any activity participated in...merely for the enjoyment it affords....The rewards of recreational activities depend upon the degree to which they provide outlets for personal interests." But enjoyment is *not* a goal, it is a feeling that accompanies important ongoing activity; pleasure as Freud said, is always dependent on function.

From the present philosophy of leisure, no new culture can emerge. What is lacking is worth-while community necessity, as the serious leisure, the σχολη of the Athenians had communal necessity, whether in the theater, the games, the architecture and festivals, or even the talk.

That we find it hard to think in these terms is a profound sign of our social imbalance. Yet we do *not* need, as Dr. Douglass claimed...a new ethics, a new esthetic." For the activities of serious leisure are right there, glaring, in our communities, to avoid shame and achieve grandeur.

But the question is: If there is little interest, honor, or manliness, in the working part of our way of life, can we hope for much in the leisure part?

13.

The best exposition of what I have been trying to say in this chapter is the classic of conservative thinking, Coleridge's *On the Constitution of the Church and State.* His point in that essay is simply this: *In order to have citizens, you must first be sure that you have produced men.* There must therefore be a large part of the common wealth specifically devoted to cultivating "freedom and civilization," and especially to the education of the young growing up.

READING 9

America vs. America

James A. Michener

THE PURITAN NOOSE

Within the Christain ethic American society has always inclined toward Puritanism. Any local businessman who wanted to get ahead, any political leader who hoped for long life, has had to pay public homage to Puritan morality, and even the more liberal European Catholic Church, when implanted on our shores, found it expedient to advocate a censorship of, say films, along ridiculously pruitanical lines. I suppose that no single strand of middle-class values has been rejected more totally in recent years than this strangling rope of Puritanism which once bound us so strongly, and against which the young have rebelled with such contempt.

We have lived primarily within a Christian ethic, once largely Protestant, of late increasingly Catholic. Our father figures have been austere men like John Knox, John Calvin, Martin Luther, and Thomas Aquinas. To the perceptive young person today these moral leaders, who used to terrify me with their rectitude, seem slightly ridiculous. One evening, when I tried to introduce the matter of religious ethics to a young group, one girl said, "Please! Today the Pope is just as confused as we are."

THE THREE R'S

A cornerstone of middle-class life has been reliance upon education. Through it, immigrants were salvaged and the children of the laboring class set free. A conspicuous feature of American life has been the fact that the upper classes have done precious little in this country for the education of anyone but themselves, whereas the middle and laboring classes have striven consistently for a free, widely dispersed education. I myself, a product of that middle-class faith in education, believe it has been the principal differentiator between America and the rest of the world.

Some years ago in Hawaii a barefooted Japanese cleaning woman demonstrated the middle-class attitude toward education. She told me one day as she was sweeping my apartment that she was worried about her two sons and asked if she might talk with me. I assumed that her boys had gotten themselves mixed up with girls or had stolen a car, but her problems were rather different. "First son, senior Harvard Law School. Top ten. When he graduate he can go into big law firm New York. Or into government? Which one?" I said that since he was a Japanese boy trying to make his way in a Caucasian society it might be wise to establish himself first with his peers, then move into government. She agreed. "Second son, freshman M.I.T. Next year they starting accelerated course advanced calculus"—those were her exact words. "In regular calculus he get only only B-minus. Should he try new course?" With wages earned by sweeping apartments, she had sent her sons to two of the best universities in America, five thousand miles from Hawaii.

MAKING IT

A central belief of the middle class in which I grew up was that the son of a ditchdigger could become a college president, whereas the careless son of the top family in town could easily make mistakes from which he would not recover. These twin beliefs were not legendary; each year they were illustrated by specific lives in our community, and are still being illustrated. I have lived in a good many countries in the world, and in no other is social mobility so easily attainable, or so dominant a factor in national life. I realize that I am begging the core question of "Mobility to what?" Young people ridicule the legendary middle-class struggle to achieve upward mobility because they see that a man is often no better off "ahead" than he was when he started. For the moment I shall avoid that challenge.

COMPETENCE

At home, in school, and in church I was reared on the stern belief that in the long run competence set the limits as to what a man could become, and this was drummed into my generation wherever we turned. If you wanted to play third base in the big leagues you had to learn how to handle ground balls smashed toward the bag. If you shied away from stabbing your hand out at the speeding white bullet, you were not going to be a third baseman. You could be something else, but not that. This was true, we were taught, of all professions. If you wanted to be a lawyer, you went to law school. If you wanted to go into business, you mastered arithmetic and the art of quick decision. The penalty for sliding through life without having mastered any competence was a sentence to mediocrity.

By no means did we equate competence with formal education. Horse traders, garage mechanics, and trainmen stood high in our value judgments; and I can still remember the approval with which one of my teachers read that admirable passage from Emerson in which he described how much he admired the farm girl who knew how to subdue a fractious calf by letting the animal suck on her finger as if it were a teat. "I admire people who know how to do things," said Emerson, the high priest of middle-class values, and we shared his enthusiasm. To this day I retain a sense of awe in the presence of anyone who knows how to do something.

HIERARCHY

I have always felt that in America our middle-class values were strongly rooted in a sense of hierarchy, and the fact that we have eschewed the trappings of royalty has blinded us, I think, to the other fact that we are the most royalist of peoples. I remember when Arnold Bennett unleashed one of his periodic attacks on the British royal family to the great distress of some Englishmen who were at that moment visiting America. They were outraged that Bennett had dared to speak ill of royalty but were consoled by their New Jersey host, who explained, "Never worry about what your English fools like Arnold Bennett say of your royal family. England may go off the gold standard. She may have a Socialist government. But she will never discard or in any way abuse the royal family, because the people of Iowa would not permit it."

I find this principle of hierarchy, or class consciousness if you prefer, strongly ingrained in American life, and much of the protest of the young today has been a legitimate rejection of our country-club pretensions. On the other hand, I do feel that our responsible affection for position and order has been a strong factor in accounting for our stability.

RESPONSIBILITY

At the core of middle-class life has stood the doctrine of responsibility. Not only was a man largely responsible for himself and his family, but groups of families were responsible for their community. If I were asked to specify a major difference between life as it is actually lived in the United States and in Japan or Spain, for example, I would stress the fact that in those other countries there is no public tradition of support for art museums, hospital complexes, universities, and a multitude of other public charities, whereas this sense of responsibility has been strong in America. For tragic and historic reasons, we have not up to now been willing to allow this responsibility to operate in certain areas like race relations or the preservation of our cities, but the tradition for the exercise of such responsibility exists and is available for new creative uses. I would judge this commitment to responsibility to be a major characteristic of American middle-class life.

ACCUMULATION

No one should underestimate the powerful urge felt by the middle class toward accumulation, either of money, or property, or the sillier accouterments of success. I judge this to be one of our strongest motivating factors and one most subject to abuse. The tradition began, I suppose, on the frontier, when it was patently better to have 640 acres of cleared land than a quarter of an acre.

I spoke recently with a man who had just bought a comfortably sized insurance business, and even before he had moved into his new office he was planning for a second, a third, and a fourth office in nearby towns. He explained, "Of course I could make a comfortable living from my new office, but only for a few years. In this business you build volume or the major insurance companies take away your franchise. It's impossible to stay little. You grow big or you perish."

If our middle-class mania for accumulation is subject to abuse, it is also subject to ridicule, and many a father who has spent the years from 22 to 52 in a mad race to accumulate now finds himself powerless to answer his children who ask, "Why did you do it, Pop? What good did you get out of it? What have you to show for the rat race except two cars and three picture windows?" These are terrifying questions to throw at a man in his fifties, for they undermine his hitherto unquestioned faith in accumulating.

OPTIMISM

One of the most appealing of the middle-class virtues has been the tendency toward optimism. There has been reason for this, for in spite of wars, depressions, and other setbacks of considerable dimension, the American middle class has been living in an expanding economy, in which social justice has made conspicuous gains. The middle-class response has been a general euphoria. After all, Kaiser Wilhelm and Adolf Hitler were defeated. Communism was more or less contained, and although a stubborn Democratic party did make frequent incursions to power, the Republican party did return at comforting intervals to run things pretty much as we had grown accustomed to seeing them run. It did not seem preposterous for the middle class to cling to its optimism.

Of course, at its most blatant our optimism took the pathetic form demonstrated by George Babbit of Zenith City and was properly riduculed. One of the most disastrous cultural influences ever to hit America was Walt Disney's Mickey Mouse, that idiot optimist who each week marched forth in Technicolor against a battalion of cats, invariable humiliating them with one clever trick after another. I suppose the damage done to the American psyche by this foolish mouse will not be specified for another fifty years, but even now I place much of the blame for Vietnam on the bland attitudes sponsored by our cartoons.

When the original version of this essay was published, I received much criticism for this passage on Mickey Mouse. Some vilified me for having spoken ill of one of our nation's folk heroes. Others rebuked me for having taken seriously what was intended merely as a fairly tale, and one that they revered. And a great many asked, "You didn't mean what you said seriously, did you? Wasn't it all a put-on?" I suppose nothing proves more clearly that I did mean what I said than the seriousness of the criticism that overtook me. I do indeed believe that the narcotic nonsense of these cartoons — and similar daydreams of American life — dull our sensitiveness to real problems. Ask a thoughtful Negro of my generation how much damage was done him by the Amos 'n Andy radio series, not because that amiable program made fun of the Negro but because it deprecated him and sidetracked the rest of us for a whole generation from taking his point of view seriously. I object most strenuously to this abuse of the arts.

READING 10

The Revolt Against Democracy
Edgar Z. Friedenberg

There is a widespread conviction among dissenting youth today that they are oppressed by a fundamentally illegitimate authority.

For the younger members of a gerontocracy like ours to regard the authority of the older generation as oppressive is a rational act; that such authority should be logically regarded as oppressive is implicit in the fact that it occasions revolt. But for authority to be regarded likewise as illegitimate is something new. It makes conflict far more disruptive. It is, in fact, the characteristic that most clearly distinguishes today's intergenerational conflict from that which commonly occurs between successive generations.

Legitimacy is the chief lubricant of the social mechanism; it prevents friction by inducing collaboration among its several parts even in situations in which conflict of interest is apparent. The extreme sample is the quiet dignity with which the condemned so often cooperates with their executioners. In the ultimately terrifying situation, the victim takes what comfort he can from identifying himself as a member of the society which has officially certified him as so worthless that he must be publicly destroyed. By so doing, he is not alone in his moment of mortal terror.

In a social system that has exhausted its legitimate authority, however, executions are regarded as publicly planned assassinations that invite resistance, escalation and ultimately, role-confusion, as Danton and Robespierre discovered. Declining legitimacy leads to a rise in coercive violence, which is usually attributed to the disorderly provocation of those who have no respect for "authority" or "law and order." Analysis of the actual events more often discloses that the contrary is true: violence is launched and maintained by terrified officials who feel their authority threatened. As their legitimacy ebbs, they fall back on the resources for coercion which their official position affords, and modern technology has made these resources enormous. Whether this results in the re-establishment of legitimacy depends on whether a stable regime can be built on the wastelands of terror. In the past it has usually been possible, but it does take time — more than a generation.

Terror thus is not a very useful device for restoring the faith of the younger generation in the legitimacy of the authority of their elders. Indeed, the authorities in this country have so structured their recent confrontations with the young as to reveal their own cognizance of the illegitimacy of their authority. This is the era of *plainclothes* police cracking the skulls of students, of *undercover* narcotics agents busting students for smoking pot. A uniform is an asset to the officer of a society whose legitimacy is accepted; the uniform, as with the soldier, legitimates even lethal hostility, if there is any legitimacy left. But out of uniform the adversary is a spy, and he himself becomes the legitimate object of condemnation. The widespread use of covert surveillance and coercion in a society indicates that the forces that bind it together have become even less legitimate than those that link hostile belligerents in the traditional context of war.

Authority, however, is no less dangerous because it lacks legitimacy; rather, because of its own anxieties, it is more dangerous. The more sensitive and intelligent young people I know today consider themselves to be living in some degree the lives of outlaws. They attempt to resign themselves to the prospects of being busted for smoking pot or dropping acid, imprisoned for draft evasion either directly or under a loose charge of conspiracy, or locked away in a concentration camp if resistance to the Vietnam war or revolt in the urban slums results in the declaration of a State of National Emergency or invocation of the Internal Security Act of 1950. All these are valid fears. There *is* real danger of becoming a political prisoner in the United States today through the normal operation of due process. Our military adventures and our treatment of poor and black people are political questions, and therefore offenses related to opposition to such policies are political offenses. It is less clear that classifying marijuana as a "dangerous drug" — in the absence of substantial evidence to that effect — and making its use a felony, and its distribution under some circumstances punishable by life imprisonment, are legal definitions designed to curb political offenses. But they are, and the very fact that the political character of such laws seems paradoxical makes the political function of the pot issue worth scrutinizing.

Smoking marijuana is essentially a ritual action by which young people assert a moral position. Careful research has shown that both the dangers and joys associated with its use have been grossly exaggerated. The satisfactions it affords are derived far less from its mildly stimulating effect on the central nervous system — which may be agreeable or disagreeable, depending on the circumstances — than from the sense of affirming a particular view of the world and of one's place in it. Potblowing is ideological; examination of the ideology it expresses reveals several characteristic components. The most important of these are:

1. People who are enjoying themselves without harming others have an inalienable right to privacy.
2. A drug whose effect is to turn its users inward upon their own experience, enriching their fantasy life at the expense of their sense of the need to achieve or relate to others, is as moral as alcohol, which encourages a false gregariousness and increasingly pugnacious or competitive behavior.
3. Much of the solicitude of the older generation for the welfare of the young merely expresses a desire to dominate and control them for the sake of adult interests and the preservation of adult status and authority.

Pot is clearly less dangerous than pot-busts. It is also less dangerous to youth than the Selective Service System; parents who become hysterical and punitive about the dangers of drug abuse while being equally insistent that their sons go quietly to Vietnam when summoned are more concerned with the embarrassment of having children who are in trouble with the law than with their children's welfare. So we are back again to the issue of legitimacy, which is what the potblower's ideology basically questions. On their own terms, there can be no doubt that their position is valid: there are no demonstrable dangers to either the individual or society sufficient to justify or even explain the treatment accorded marijuana users. The effects of the drug are less obnoxious than those of alcohol; the solicitude of adults masks intense hostility and anxiety.

Institutionalized hostility toward marijuana users is intelligible, however, when the potblower's ideology is considered in relation to the class structure of American society. For that ideology expresses essentially an upper-middle to upper-class attitude toward life; indeed, for this century, it expresses one that is remarkably aristocratic. To value privacy and a rich inner life at the expense of achievement and the development of social skills in manipulating and competing with others — to value these is to reject the fundamental and official attitudes of American society, to fly in the face (and perhaps up the nose) of the school system, the Little League and the core virtues of the Land of Opportunity. The fact that marijuana is too mild a drug to do much for the fantasy-life does not affect the controversy. People get out of psychedelic drugs about what they expect and the use of marijuana has evolved in such a way that custom provides what the drug cannot — as it does for alcohol. Pot-parties have therefore become almost a photographic negative of cocktail parties: communal experiences at which the joint is passed from mouth to mouth like a peace pipe or communion cup; the scene is tranquil rather than gregarious, with no one-upping permitted; there is not even much moving around.

Pot, then, both evokes and symbolizes a whole set of attitudes and behavior that are anathema to the lower-middle classes: laziness and fantastic ease, growing with one's neighbor instead of competing with him, drifting into bed with the partner of your choice rather than conning her into it as proof of your none-too-evident manhood. Pot-busts have become primarily a form of interclass hostility, in which the working class attacks the sloth, depravity and decadence of gilded, long-haired youth.

Interclass hostility of this kind is ancient, of course. What is novel, and very dangerous, in the form of pot-bust is that the customary class roles have been fundamentally reversed. For here it is the lower of the adversary classes, which, armed with legitimacy, attacks the upper in the name of law and order. And the upper defends itself, when it does so at all, by appealing to such values as civil liberty, the right to privacy, and freedom from arbitrary search and seizure which, although recognized in general terms in the Constitution or reflected in certain court decisions, have never been accepted by the American masses which see them as essentially a form of privilege.

And so they are; and this is the heart of the conflict. For what American society most apparently lacks today is a device by which social class differences may be legitimated. This, in fact, is what our institutions have evolved, since Jackson's time, to prevent. Privilege in America is illegitimate *per se*. Or in de Tocqueville's words, written in Jackson's day:

> The Americans hold, that, in every state, the supreme power ought to emanate from the people; but when once that power is constituted, they can conceive, as it were, no limits to it, and they are ready to admit that it has the right to do whatever it pleases. They

> have not the slightest notion of peculiar privileges granted to cities, families or persons: their minds appear never to have foreseen that it might be possible not to apply the same laws to every part of the state and to all its inhabitants.

This is not quite accurate. The Bill of Rights *does* conceive of limits to the supreme power of the people, and attempts to establish them — which is why the working class so often perceives the Supreme Court as opposed to law and order. The people certainly *do* have a notion of peculiar privileges granted to cities, families or persons — it is what they are most determined to prevent. They *do* foresee that it might be possible *not* to apply the same laws to every part of the state, and to all its inhabitants — which is why they enjoy lurid fantasies of the university as a privileged sanctuary for draft-dodgers, addicts and perverts. What they *don't* grant, even as a possibility, is that such privileges, and such a sanctuary, might have social value.

And for most of them, perhaps it would not. This is not an issue that need be debated, for American society is as receptive to the claim of vested interest as it is hostile to that of privilege. There are social classes in America as elsewhere, and a society that recognizes and defers to the special interests and needs of oil-producers, speculative builders and labor unions can hardly justify rejection of the special interests of middle-class youth, which sorely needs a place to call its own. American society as a whole would surely be far better off if its most sensitive and articulate youth did not feel themselves to be outlaws. No more need be demanded on behalf of hippies or turned-on youth than is accorded Standard Oil or the friendly Chase Manhattan Bank: that their needs be recognized and reflected in the law of the land, and that they be allowed to go about their business unmolested without having to prove that what is good for them is good for the entire world.

But even this cannot be vouchsafed under our system. The answer adults give the beleaguered and fugitive young when finally forced to admit that the marijuana laws are Draconian and irrational, and the Selective Service Act capricious and inequitable, is to assert that for the sake of a stable and orderly society even unjust and unwise laws must be respected, and that procedures exist by which laws may be changed to make them wiser and more just. Unfortunately the idea that unwise and unjust laws — which reflect the hostilities and assuage the inferiority feelings and envy of the masses — can be effectively changed by due process and lawful means in a mass democracy is probably false. American law and public policy are almost always unresponsive to moral issues or minority needs, unless these find expression in terms of raw power. The fall of the Johnson administration, and subsequently of the Democratic party, under the impact of war protest may seem to belie this statement; so may the actual social progress the nation has made in the past fifty years. It is the blindness of the New Left to this record of past achievement, in fact, which most offends the surviving members of the Old Left. But neither case is a convincing indication that the American social or legal structure might be capable of a generous response to the demands of dissenting middle-class youth today. It seems very obvious that the Johnson administration would have been unaffected had the Vietnam war been prosecuted more successfully. Failure is punished by the electorate; but the war protest did not occasion the failure. Lyndon Johnson's defeat was not brought about by Benjamin Spock, Tom Hayden or Eugene McCarthy, but by the Vietnamese themselves. And they did not do it by winning their case before the bar of American public opinion or through the channels of American legal process.

The accomplishments of the Old Left are more solid, and unquestionably theirs. It is quite true that virtually all the social legislation they fought for in the thirties — against opposition fully as repressive as anything the New Left faces today — has not only been enacted but is now taken wholly for granted. What is sad, as Norman Thomas observed a few years before his death, is that nobody seems to have much pleasure out of it. But the goals of the New Left have a different political, and a different moral, significance than those of the Old; their tasks are not really comparable and they cannot really be allies.

Broadly speaking, the reforms of the thirties were economic and addressed to the improvement of social justice and the abatement of the grossest economic insecurity. What was achieved was solid, and new to a country which still provides much less in the way of social services, especially to the ill and aged, than an Englishman or Scandinavian would expect as a matter of right. In any case, the radicals of the thirties emphasized economic need and the improvement of the political power of the working class far more than civil rights, civil liberty or personal freedom. This was not because they were oblivious of these issues, but because they saw economic threat and vulnerability to poverty and economic pressure as the most serious threats to freedom. Job security and a decent wage, and essential social services, were to serve as shields against coercion by bosses and the slings and arrows of outrageous fortune. The Wagner Act and the Federal Minimum Wage Law were thought of not only as guaranteeing certain important economic and political rights, but also as part of the foundation on which human liberty would rest.

As such, they have not been particularly effective. They serve as necessary instruments of social justice in guaranteeing certain important economic rights to the organized working class, which is quite sufficient to justify them as legislation. But the working class has not proved to be devoted to liberty; it is more inclined to be devoted to George Wallace or Mayor Daley. It supports the war more zealously than the financial and industrial leadership of the country — a paradox in terms of the stereotypes of the thirties, which envisioned rough, honest, warmhearted labor as the undauntable defender of peace and international brotherhood against the rapacity of capitalist warmongers. The capitalist warmongers have proved rapacious enough. Nevertheless, I do not think the American economy as a whole is as committed to a policy of perpetual military and political malevolence as the mass of the American people; it is too easy to conceive of other and more pleasant ways of profiting by our not-altogether-free associations with our neighbors. Where generals and corporate executives support the Vietnam war out of economic and status interests, both labor leaders and the working-class people one meets from day to day actively hate the draft-dodgers, peaceniks and troublemakers who harass their country while their boy is risking his life to defend it against the savage and treacherous gook. *If he hadn't — if he had ever started to talk like those long-haired punks, they'd have had his ass themselves.* However, the various factors add, support for the war is now strongest in the working class, at least among parents; their sons, chased by the draft, may be less enthusiastic. But resistance to the war remains primarily a middle-class value.

The reforms of the Old Left have thus added to the difficulties of the New by greatly strengthening the political power of what has proved to be the most repressive segment of the population — the real control-addicts, in William Burroughs' phrase: the supporters of law and order, so long as the law does not shackle their local police or protect fresh kids and hippies. The reforms of the Old Left have created also one final problem of legitimacy that the New Left is, I think, reluctant to face. For the Old Left reforms proved ultimately popular; they benefitted the masses at the expense of the classes, which not only gave the old radicals great satisfaction, it made their programs legitimate *per se.* They were on the side of democracy and they knew it; with the final triumph of FDR they could prove it. It is true that the forces of law were often arrayed against them, sometimes with a brutality equal — discounting the greater technological efficiency of the sixties — to anything the war-resistors encounter now. But when this happened in the thirties, just as when it happened later to civil rights workers in the South, it was the law itself which had become illegitimate. This thought affords little protection to the body in confronting a group of murderous sheriff's deputies, but it does enhance the victim's self-esteem.

What seems to be the hardest today for young radicals to face, in their conviction that authority has become illegitimate, is the implication that the source of the illegitimacy is the American democratic process itself. It is one thing to assert that "the system" is corrupt, that the mass media conceal essential data and misrepresent what they do report, that political parties do not respond to the will of the electorate. It is another, and more difficult for a radical American, to grant that what is wrong with America may be characteristic of mass democracy itself.

Yet this seems to be the more valid conclusion. The mass media, for example, do not, I think, mislead people so much as they confirm them in the fantasies they wish to hold. When, as in the Chicago Convention coverage, they do not, all hell breaks loose as the public, in paroxysms of rage and self-pity, demands that its prejudices be confirmed. The public does not accept discordant interpretations of reality any more than a neurotic patient accepts an unwelcome interpretation; it was Walter Cronkite, not the public, who learned from the experience. And the American political process *does* respond to the will of the people;

it is the mass of the people that does not respond to the moral imperatives of Vietnam and the plight of the poor and the black — or, rather, it responds with greater hostility as its own destructiveness mounts.

As the twentieth century, along perhaps with everything else, approaches its conclusion, it becomes apparent that democracy and fascism are not contrasting and opposing political systems, but different stages of evolution in the responsiveness of society to the fears, envies and resentments that pervade the lives of lower status groups. Democratic political structures are devised to legitimate the demands to which these feelings naturally give rise, and to increase the political power of the masses, and hence their capacity to command a better life. But in a society as open, invidious and competitive as ours, the kinds of people who succeed are usually incapable of responding to human demands; and the political power of the masses is used merely to express the hatreds and the envy, and to destroy anything that looks like genuine human satisfaction, especially among the more vulnerable members of the higher social classes. Higher status youth — whose style of life infuriates the working class and whose status by no means compensates for their political helplessness as a disfranchised group with few established civil rights in law — have become the chief target of the working-class sense of outrage and defeat. It is difficult for white, middle-class parents to imagine — and most don't want to — the degree of harassment to which their adolescent children are subjected by hostile and vigilant school authorities, and by police who feel, and are, perfectly free to disperse groups of youngsters whose behavior is not at all threatening and who could not, if adults, be held to have given probable cause for suspicion of any offense.

Tyranny has taken many forms in history, but the graceless vulgarity and egregious, clumsy brutality of fascism are its most hideous form; and these grow best out of the democratic process itself. The masses came into the stage of history too late to be credited with having invented tyranny — even the Russians have made no such claim — but they have made something new and more terrible of it by depriving it of style.

Those who complain of the failures of democracy, are expected to provide a better political plan and, even more confidently, expected to recoil in fear or perplexity from the demand that they do so. Winston Churchill's much-quoted comment that democracy is the worst system of government in the world — except for all the others — is supposed to have settled the matter.

But, in fact, there is no reason to feel embarrassed by this demand. Our political system, like the rest of our society, has not become the way it is in response to free and conscious choice, and — unless we commit national suicide — it cannot be transformed by an act of will. It reflects, rather, the effects of years of use and abuse, insight and misunderstanding, discipline and indulgence — both often equally ill-considered — of its inherited structures. There is no question of choosing elitism or oligarchy or fascism or anything else instead of democracy. There is only the question of how our present democratic system can respond to the demands placed on it by the needs of the people whose lives it affects, including those subject to its military and economic caprice who do not live within our borders. It is not possible to change or exchange political systems at will — even revolution does nothing like this; the new one grows back, often monstrously deformed, on the roots of the old.

The comprehensive public school, in its commendable attempt to give children of all social classes some experience of one another's lives, has become an institution in which lower- and upper-class children alike find themselves held hostage — if they do not escape — to the values and behavior pattern prized by the lower-middle class and imposed by it as a universal norm of conduct and moral judgment. Release with a satisfactory credential depends on the student's good conduct, and that of his parents, in not rejecting those norms or the values of the school system itself.

The pattern of anxieties thus established in the name of socialization has done much to cement our society together — as well as to make it more rigid when facing the need to devise alternative norms. But that need is now pressing, and the society is coming apart anyway. A major force in its disruption is the irritation that the upper and lower classes feel with each other; our society is splitting right down the middle-middle. And in a society that denies the legitimacy, if not the very existence, of class interests, and whose political leaders prattle of "law and order" as a remedy for "violence in the streets" — as if they had not seen a dozen times by now that the violence in the streets is often committed by the forces of law and order — nothing realistic can be done to recognize the serious nature of the conflict between those interests, or to resolve it.

It is almost certain that any effective measures to keep the American social system from bitter dissolution must indeed transcend present structural limits and political arrangements. The crucial question is whether this is possible. The present political structure of America is precisely what is wrong, and there is no *a priori* reason to assume that it bears within itself the seeds of its own reform. But I am sure that if any radical improvement in the quality of our national life can be made — and our survival depends on this — the devices by which it can be done will seem outrageous, and will, indeed, cause widespread outrage. But as perhaps most surviving American Indians and Vietnamese might agree, there is no great risk in devising a system more outrageous than that which America already has, and has had for nearly two centuries.

READING 11

A Special Kind of Rebellion
Daniel Seligman

The phrase itself is beginning to grate, but it seems more evident every week that the "generation gap" is a rather serious matter. It would be nice to believe that it isn't — that what we are witnessing is only the latest act in history's continuous-run tragicomedy about the rebellion of restless, rootless youth against the world of its elders. A fair number of Americans are in fact clinging to some such agreeable notion about the generation gap. The notion is agreeable because it implies that this young generation too will eventually come to terms with its elders and their institutions; that the arguments now swirling around the campuses will pass; and that at some point, looking back through a nostalgic haze, we will perceive the young rebels of the 1960's as legitimate successors to the flappers of the 1920's, the campus radicals of the 1930's, and the "beats" of the 1950's, all of whom influenced our society in one way or another but were ultimately absorbed into it.

And yet it may not turn out that way at all. There are, in fact, reasons for viewing this rebellion as something special. One reason often cited is the sheer numbers of the young nowadays: if we define "the younger generation" as those eighteen through twenty-four, then 22,800,000 Americans — about one out of nine — are part of it. The number is certainly imposing; however, it should be used warily. In talking about a particular generation's influence, the critical figure is its relative, not its absolute, size. And despite the widespread belief that the U.S. is now being engulfed by an unprecedented tidal wave of youth, the parents of this young generation actually represented a bigger chunk of society when *they* were young; in 1938 one out of eight Americans were members of the younger generation.

But there is undeniably something special in the educational level of today's youth. Educated youth have to be taken seriously in any society; even when they condemn it bitterly, they are presumed to be its future leaders. Almost eight million members of the younger generation today are or have been in college (versus about two million for that 1938 group). No other society in history has ever had to deal with *mass* educated youth.

These particular masses, furthermore, are condemning society in the most sweeping and extravagant terms. Some of their views have a quite revolutionary potential, involving challenges to constituted legal authority and to democratic procedures in general. Some formulations challenge the "moral authority" of the business system. Some are more concerned with established ideas about personal conduct and with other familiar bourgeois notions about style and taste, work, and play, what's reasonable and what isn't, and what, in general, people should do with their lives. These revolutionary attitudes are not, of course, held by all or even most of the young; even on the campuses, they are held only by a minority.

The minority is fairly sizable, however, and it appears to be growing. Its members include the well-publicized activists who are — or, more precisely, play at being — "revolutionaries" in the traditional sense of the word; but they also include a much larger group that, without having done much about it, has accepted, almost casually it seems, many new-left formulations about the utter depravity of American society.

SOME VOTES FOR CHE GUEVARA

This summary of youthful attitudes is based partly on a considerable amount of on-campus reporting by contributors to this special issue of *Fortune*, who together visited about forty colleges and universities. The summary also reflects extensive plowing through recent scholarly literature on youth; the "youth sub-culture" has become a large new field of inquiry for social scientists, some of whom are solemnly rendering the rites and customs of young Americans in accents reminiscent of Ruth Benedict on the Kwakiutl Indians. In addition, *Fortune* commissioned and Daniel Yankelovich, Inc., a major attitude-research firm, executed, a depth survey of the beliefs of college-educated men and women who are eighteen through twenty-four. A detailed report on the survey follows this article; however, several of the main findings should be noted here.

The most important finding of all has to do with a sharp division on the campuses between those who are "practical-minded" and are in college because it looks like the natural route to the high-paying high-rank jobs, and those who, in effect, take good jobs and affluence for granted and are in college for a variety of less tangible reasons. This division seems to be extremely significant: students on one side of the line have attitudes about a wide range of issues that are strikingly different from those on the other side. Something like three-fifths of college students are on the "practical" side of the line. In general, their feelings about what they want from life and their beliefs about some public issues are remarkably similar to those of young men and women who have never attended college; whatever it may have done for their career prospects, higher education has certainly not revolutionized their basic values.

It is hard to find a label for the two-fifths who are in the minority, since they are defined, not by any particular beliefs or practices, but mainly by their *lack of concern* about making money. On the assumption that, as our society grows more affluent, some such unconcern will become widespread, we will refer to this minority as the "forerunner" group. Not surprisingly,the forerunners are more likely than the practical students to have privileged backgrounds. They are most likely to be majoring in the humanities. They are not only disdainful of "careerist" values, but are somewhat more likely than most students to be vague about their own career expectations; in general, however, they seem interested in finding work that is intellectually challenging and somehow relevant to their social concerns. The college environment seems to have fortified them in these attitudes. It has also led them to embrace positions that are dissident and extreme on many different public issues.

Half of the forerunners (versus only 25 percent of the practical group) said that none of the three major presidential candidates in last year's election held views close to their own. All three actually ran behind Che Guevara in a list of "personalities admired" by the forerunners.

About two-thirds of the group believe it appropriate to engage in civil disobedience to further causes they support. Almost 10 percent say they would support civil disobedience *no matter what issues were involved.* (Presumably, a good many in this group don't really mean what they say; it is hard to envision many of them supporting disobedience by, for example, the Ku Klux Klan. Still, the response suggests a strong predisposition to nihilist attitudes.)

Two-thirds of the forerunners support draft resistance — i.e., efforts to disrupt and refusal to cooperate with the Selective Service System.

Well over half, when shown a list of reasons that have been advanced to justify going to war, registered doubts about all of the following: protection of "national interests," preserving "our honor," "protecting allies," and "keeping commitments"; only 14 percent said it was clearly worth going to war to keep commitments.

About half of the group indicated that they have less faith than their parents in democratic processes.

About half believe that the U.S. is a sick society.

THE INVISIBLE DISSIDENTS

The existence of all these dissident attitudes were certainly no secret; nevertheless, those large percentages come as a surprise. Serious studies of activists have repeatedly made it clear that they are a small minority. Not one-tenth of 1 percent of American students pay dues to the largest and best-known radical organization, Students for a Democratic Society. A Harris poll taken last spring showed the activist population to be somewhat less than 2 percent of all those in college. The proportion who get involved is likely to swell rapidly in times of "confrontation," when passions are intense, then to subside. A Gallup poll taken last June showed that only 20 percent of undergraduates had ever engaged in any protest activity; many of these had presumably done so only once, and in many instances the issues were unrelated to the students' views of American society — e.g., they concerned campus regulations.

What the *Fortune*-Yankelovich survey suggests, then, is that behind the small and highly visible activist minority is a much larger and generally "invisible" minority of forerunners holding similar dissident attitudes. It is in this forerunner group, a universe of some 2,300,000, that the problem of the generation gap is centered.

To most older Americans they are a puzzling group. Viewed from a distance, or viewed for that matter by their own parents, they look very much as though they were among the most privileged members of the most affluent society in history; yet they seem to be challenging the institutions of that society — the institutions in which the democratic capitalist order is rooted.

Their attitudes are all the more puzzling in that they emerged so suddenly and unexpectedly. Though it scarcely seems credible today, our main concern about youth in the late 1950's and early 1960's was that it was passive and uninvolved: to many Americans the "silent generation" was as much a source of concern then as the activists are today. In 1962, after a few faint stirrings on the campuses, Kenneth Keniston, associate professor of psychology at the Yale Medical School, and one of the most attentive followers of student political tendencies, wrote in the *American Scholar* that those involved in the "political revival" had a quite distinctive style: "restrained, reflective, cautious, intellectual and even pedantic...One sees the restraint of these students in their picketing and petitions rather than protests and parades, in their carefully planned study-and-discussion groups, in their debates at which they give their opponents the platform..."Keniston added: "For one, I see little likelihood of American students ever playing a radical role much less a revolutionary one, in our society." The notion that students would soon be forcibly taking over university buildings, physically intimidating administrators, preventing controversial visitors from speaking on campus — and all this against a background of bullhorn-amplified new-left ranting about American imperialism — was unthinkable then.

A TURN TO POLITICS

One special reason for puzzlement about the forerunner group is that its dissidence is reflected largely in political terms. We know, mainly from Keniston's own pioneering work, that in the 1950's there were intelligent, well-educated, well-to-do college students who were profoundly alienated from traditional American values; but his work made it clear that their alienation was apolitical — one reason the 1950's *were* silent.

Recalling this group in a 1966 address to the American Psychological Association, Keniston referred to its "distrust, lack of interest in group activities, and scorn for politics and politicians..." The contrast between the alienated students who set the style for dissidence in the 1950's and the radicals who dominate the stage in the 1960's is fascinating. In the 1950's the dissidents simply ignored poverty and radical injustice in the U.S. although these were of course far more widespread than they are today. The alienated youth was — in an inescapable cliche of the late 1950's — a "rebel without a cause." His cultural heroes were apt to be "beats" like Jack Kerouac; if he was intellectually inclined, he drifted to existentialist writers like Jean-Paul Sartre, whose basic message was the meaninglessness of human existence. In the 1960's the heroes of student dissidents were almost invariably political figures, a special favorite being Che Guevara. Intellectually inclined dissidents are likely to have read, or at least attempted, Herbert Marcuse, a neo-Marxist whose basic message is the need for revolution against Western liberal political institutions. (Marcuse, professor of philosophy at the University of California at San Diego, was almost totally unknown in the U.S. two or three years ago; in the *Fortune* survey he was checked as a "personality admired by 9 percent of the forerunners, putting him just two percentage points behind Lyndon Johnson.)

Well, what happened? How did it come about that the withdrawn, alienated, apolitical dissidents of the 1950's were replaced in this decade by what might almost be called a mass movement of student radicalism? The answer appears to have several different constituents.

First, a major change in the international political environment has obviously diminished students' interest in showing their loyalty to American institutions; indeed, the notion that one might be expected to do so would now be greeted with derision by most sophisticated students. In the 1950's, even after Senator Joseph McCarthy was no longer riding high, students and professors often felt it natural to register their patriotism and to suppress ideas that might be thought helpful to international Communism. In the late 1960's patriotism seems square and old-fashioned; when the forerunner group was asked to examine a list of feelings associated with the war in Vietnam, and asked which they held themselves, 54 percent checked "disgust with our government" and only 22 percent checked "patriotism." In addition, a kind of reverse (Joe) McCarthyism now operates to suppress certain kinds of ideas that might be advanced by militant anti-Communists; for example, it is simply not respectable on some campuses to mention the idea that mass protest against the Vietnam war encourages the enemy and thereby prolongs the war.

Principally responsible for this transformation is the belief that the U.S. is no longer a society beleaguered by international Communism. Until the atmosphere changed dramatically, in the wake of the 1962 Cuban missile crisis, it seemed natural to most Americans to look at world Communism and see Hitler all over again: there were the forcible suppressions of opposition parties in Eastern Europe, in violation of wartime agreements; there was the Communist take-over of China and the threat of further takeovers in Southeast Asia, and Taiwan; there was the coup in Czechoslovakia; there was the Soviet-supported invasion of South Korea; there were three efforts to squeeze the West out of Berlin, each accompanied by a variety of ambiguous but still menacing threats; there was Castro's success in taking over and Communizing Cuba, followed by the covert Soviet efforts to introduce offensive missiles there; there was a Soviet dictator, Khrushchev, who announced that the next war would be fought on American soil, and who looked frighteningly unstable at times, as in his shoe-banging escapade at the United Nations; and there seemed for a while, to be a missile gap that might leave us at the man's mercy.

THE PRESSURE IS OFF

In the year or two following the missile crisis, the Soviet leaders generally stopped making threats and rattling rockets and the Communist monolith split in several different ways; in any case, the pressure suddenly appeared to be off. It was precisely in this period that student agitation began to assume sizable proportions — and not only in the U.S. but in other countries that had shared the feeling of beleaguerment, notably France, Italy, and Germany (including Berlin). It is noteworthy that there has been no upheaval on Israeli campuses. Israel has, by some standards, a more serious generation gap than almost any other Westernized nation: its youth can well point out, bitterly, that political power remains in the grip of elderly men who grew up in Europe decades ago, and who have consistently excluded the Sabras — the younger, native-born Israelis — from any share of that power. There is a great deal of evidence that the Sabras view the older generation as hidebound and irrelevant. There is a long tradition of dissidence among Jewish students. There is, however, no student upheaval because Israel continues to be a beleagured nation.

Three other developments also contributed to the new turn to political activism on the campus. These were the rapid swelling of the student population, the increased pervasiveness of television coverage, and the steadily increasing affluence of American students.

Something like 6,700,000 Americans are now full-time college students; the number is double that of a decade ago. Some of the growth has been absorbed by creating new universities or new campuses for existing ones. But a great deal of the growth reflects sizable increases on particular campuses. At Brandeis University in Waltham, Massachusetts, for example, the total has swelled from 1,300 to 2,800; at the Milwaukee campus of the University of Wisconsin it has gone from 5,000 to 12,000. At some point in any such growth the small proportion of students interested in political protest begins to represent a significant number — a number large enough to overcome the students' sense of isolation. With 2 percent of 2,800 students there are organizational possibilities; with 2 percent of 12,000 you can fill a fair-sized hall.

Television has also worked to dissipate any sense of isolation among radical students. Indeed, TV has made it possible to mobilize thousands of students from different campuses, in very brief periods of time. Events like the 1967 March on the Pentagon, or the converging of thousands of students on Chicago before the Democratic Convention, would scarcely have been possible if the announcements that they were scheduled, and the authorities' plans for handling them, had not been repeated endlessly on the networks' news programs.

Having money in your pocket also makes it easier to turn to political forms of protest. In, say, the early 1950's, quite a few radically inclined students could not have made it to the Pentagon or Chicago because they didn't have the money to get there. But there is a much more important point about the affluent student in an affluent society: he is quite beyond the reach of many constraints traditionally felt by those in college and still felt, apparently, by the practical-minded group in the *Fortune* survey. For someone in that group, expulsion from college, or a police record, or extensive involvement with the new left, might seem to jeopardize the career that would elevate his status in society; at the least, any of these would look like a betrayal of the family that proudly sent him off to college after years of saving and self-denial. For one of the affluent forerunners, on the other hand, any such scenario just sounds like soap opera. Whatever else may be bugging him, his own social status is high and secure. He presumes that expulsion from one college would involve no more than a transfer to another and a setback of maybe a semester. He presumes his parents will forgive anything except dropping out altogether; as long as he is working toward a degree, he can call himself a Maoist and proclaim our society rotten, but he's preserving his options and he and his parents know it.

THE TROUBLE WITH DAD

All the changes discussed thus opened up some new possibilities for students. Some differences in their own psychology may account for the manner in which these have been exploited. The alienated student of the 1950's, Keniston has shown at some length, came from a family dominated, forcefully and intrusively, by the mother. The father was perceived by the son as a cipher and often viewed with contempt. Having no role model to identify with, the son might drop out of college and, to some extent, out of society itself, i.e., join the "beats." Alternatively, he might hang on in college but succumb to overpowering feelings of pessimism, helplessness, and cynicism that plainly precluded political action. The hippies of the 1960's often have similar backgrounds. The activists have generally grown up in more healthy family situations — although there are still some serious tensions. Typically, the bond between mother and son is strong, but the mother is less domineering and the father, in his situation, plays a considerable role in shaping the son's values. Both parents are apt to be politically liberal and their children have absorbed these attitudes. However, they have also absorbed a strong sense that their fathers "compromised" their liberal beliefs in building careers.

Keniston and virtually every other student of the subject have concluded that activists tend to come from "democratic" homes in which children are encouraged to speak up. They are inclined to cherish self-expression above self-control, compassion above tough-mindedness, spontaneity and sincerity above caution and restraint. Keniston identified his young activists as "protest-prone." For them, too, there are tensions as the point of career may seem like following their parents in "hypocrisy." To reject a career outright, however, is to raise a large question: what kind of stable and meaningful adult life is available to the rejector? Many activist students relieve their tensions by deferring explicit career commitments and giving themselves wholeheartedly to the Movement. Keniston, who is politically sympathetic to the young radicals he studied, concluded that their work in the Movement was psychologically very important to them. "Just as their entry into the New Left coincided with the 'cure' of many of the anxieties, depressions, and other problems of earlier years, their continued well-being may be partly dependent upon the continuation of Movement work. Whatever their inner resources, these young men and women have many needs that may be hard to fulfill outside of their Movement."

Why are there now so many of them? Part of the answer must be, simply, that the attributes we associate with activists' families — relative affluence, "democratic" child-rearing practices, liberal political views — have become more prevalent. In addition, there is television.

IT COMPELS COMMITMENT

Television's role (noted above) in mobilizing large numbers of widely spread youths for political action is fairly clear. Its role as a molder of youths' personalities is a more confusing matter. Much of the confusion has arisen out of the extravagant assertions and peculiar vocabulary that Marshall McLuhan has brought to the subject: whether the medium is "hot" or "cool" (McLuhan says the latter), or whether one receives messages "sequentially" (from reading) or "simultaneously" (from TV), are matters whose significance many of his readers find persistently unclear. Less confusing are his assertions that television "compels commitment and participation," that it is a medium of "high involvement." Nobody really knows, despite a torrent of research papers on the subject, whether television really increases violence in our lives. But everybody knows that television *coverage* of violence has brought an entirely new dimension into news reporting: it is just about impossible for most Americans to remain calm while watching racial clashes, for example, or while watching the torments of a wounded soldier in Vietnam. Everybody also knows that television is not so effective in dealing with complex, abstract issues.

A society whose families breed more and more protest-prone youth is obviously breeding trouble for itself. If the society is simultaneously hit by new communication media that encourage "commitment" and discourage analysis of complex issues, it would appear to be in worse shape still. And if, finally, both events occur in a period of very rapid change, the problem is maximized.

To grow up in a period of rapid change is, obviously, to have a quite different sense about time — i.e., about the time it takes to get things done. This difference is a major contributor to the generation gap and a major difficulty in ordinary communication between the young and their parents. A middle-aged liberal, for example, would be unhappy over the extent of poverty in the U.S., but he would be proud about the considerable reduction of the problem in recent years. Under the widely accepted definition developed by the Social Security Administration, the number of persons living in poverty in the U.S. has been about cut in half in the past decade; the proportion has been reduced from 22 percent of the population to 11 percent. The son of the middle-aged liberal is apt to find this record unimpressive. For one thing, he views "the past decade" as a long, long time. In addition, having lived his entire life hearing about one fantastic scientific achievement after another, it is natural for him to assume that prosaic-sounding problems like those presented by poverty ought to be soluble more rapidly if anyone really wanted to solve them.

The dialogue between the generations has been additionally complicated by another consequence of rapid change. In many well-to-do families, the son does not respect his father's authority because he has no reason to view his father's experience as relevant to his own. In the world of highly specialized, endlessly organized, increasingly internationalized white-collar executives, sons are often not even clear what their fathers *do* all day, and it is usually unrealistic for them to suppose that they might sometime be doing the same thing. Thus, rapid change contributes to what might be called a **crisis** of authority for the father. The value of his — indeed, of his generation's — experience of the world just isn't what it used to be.

LIFE AFTER INDUSTRY

It seems clear that college students are more than ever beset by massive uncertainties about the direction of their lives. They are aware, moreover, that their lives will be powerfully influenced by the direction of social change itself in the decades ahead. And, it seems likely that the society they see emerging is one about which — given their psychology — they must have quite ambivalent feelings.

There are, of course, a great many visions of the future in circulation these days. Of those that are serious — that are intended as forecasts rather than parables — the vision that has almost certainly had the greatest impact on the campuses is one that describes an emerging "post-industrial society" in the U.S. The concept of some such society was first elaborated in 1962 by Daniel Bell, a former journalist (he had been a staff writer on *Fortune* for ten years), who is now professor of sociology at Columbia.

Bell believes that the post-industrial society will resemble our own in being politically democratic and in having a mixed economy. However, it will differ from our own in several critical respects, the most important of which are these: Services will replace industry as the mainstay of the economy and the major source of employment, just as industry earlier replaced agriculture. Professional and technical work will predominate in the new economy, and social status will rest mainly on intellectual achievement. Innovation will increasingly depend on comprehension of scientific theory and codification of an endlessly evolving body of theoretical knowledge; thus universities, the main repositories of codified knowledge, will gradually replace corporations as the main sources of innovation. Decision making in large organizations (including universities) will become more formalized, with the "systems" approach enlarging its jurisdiction and requiring that educated people (even those in the humanities) increase their knowledge of quantitative methods.

This vision of the future has been accepted by many social scientists. Even some who prefer a different vocabulary, or who have emphasized aspects of change that Bell minimized, are in substantial agreement about the direction of events. Zbigniew Brzezinski, a professor of political science who is also at Columbia (he returned last year from a tour of duty with the State Department's Policy Planning Council), has written of a "technetronic society" toward which we are moving. Here too we encounter the belief that the job market will be dominated by services, as cybernetic devices increasingly replace men in goods production; we also encounter the new preminence of intellectuals, the central role of universities, and the likely extension of intellectuals of scientific modes of decision making.

These prospects may look exhilarating to some but will surely alarm others. The fainthearted may note, first of all, that the future society looks like one in which no one ever really has it made. How could he in a world where status derives from intellectual attainments and where these in turn depend on comprehension of a theory that is always in flux? Furthermore, the very idea of a career — of an occupation into which one settles, more or less permanently, at some point before he is thirty — may come to seem unrealistic. The familiar presumption of steady advancement as one gains more experience will presumably look archaic in a world where the grounds of science continue to shake under one's feet.

A HARNESS FOR LIFE

The fainthearted may console themselves with the reflection that the post-industrial society will be boundlessly affluent, and that anyone who just wants to relax and enjoy it may be under no pressure to do otherwise. There will, however, be some serious problems for those with ambition. In many respects, the post-industrial society looks like a "meritocracy" — a world in which the best are routinely brought to the top, and determination of who are best is considered a major task of society. Superior students are of course used to continual testing; but many of them are also desperately tired of it. Bell believes that many have begun to resent the pressure even as undergraduates. "They know that the university is the gatekeeper to society in a completely new way," he observed recently. "They have the sense that it's terribly important to get into one of the good graduate schools — and there are still only twenty or so that really count. Formerly, though, they could see an end to the process when they left graduate school. Now they are getting the feeling that the system is putting this harness on them for life."

Brzezinski, somewhat more than Bell, has made the future society sound pressure-ridden and heartless. "The key to successful adaptation to the new conditions," he wrote in *Encounter* a year ago, "is the effective selection, distribution and utilization of social talent... Objective and systematic criteria for the selection of those with the greatest gifts will have to be developed, and the maximum opportunity for their training and advancement provided."

THE MERITOCRATIC NIGHTMARE

When Sigmund Freud became interested in dreams about seventy-five years ago, one of the first discoveries he made was the near-universality, among those who had advanced degrees, of what he called the "examination dream." In it the dreamer imagines himself to be back at the university and about to take an examination. For some reason — his own negligence, perhaps, or a misunderstanding of what the professor expected — he is hopelessly unprepared and almost certain to fail. This dream, which is still common among university graduates all over the world, is invariably marked by feelings of acute anxiety; the dreamer often wakes up in a cold sweat, and has a vast sense of relief when he realizes that he is not after all, back at the university. Freud observed that the dream occurred, typically, during the night before an event that involved some new kind of challenge — some "test" in which there was a possibility of failure and humiliation.[1] The dream is mentioned here for what it suggests about the psychic scars left by formal examinations. For those who have endured them, they remain throughout life the prototype of situations in which one is put to the test and self-doubts are confronted. A world in which test and self-doubts are confronted. A world in which testing is more or less continual is obviously not going to be comfortable for intellectuals; against a backdrop of ease, they will be competing as fiercely as businessmen ever did.

For many young graduate students there is another disquieting thought. Some of the intellectual disciplines they have worked so hard to acquire may prove irrelevant in the new society. The systems approach looks profoundly worrisome to many intellectuals, especially those in the humanities, who had cast themselves in the role of independent critics but have recently begun to sense that serious criticism is expected to involve, not insights accepted on faith, but quantitative statements backed up by, say, multivariate analysis. Writing in the fall 1968 issue of *The Public Interest,* Seymour Lipset, professor of social relations at Harvard, referred to the "heightened resentment among humanistically inclined, 'general' intellectuals toward the increased emphasis on intellectual technology and expertise. . . These trends have contributed to the rise among many intellectuals and students. . .of a backlash opposition to systematic and quantitative social science, to large-scale social research, to the very conception of the utility of efforts at value-free objective scholarship in policy-relevant fields. Many intellectuals react. . .with a populist stress on the virtues of direct action against evil institutions and practices."

Young men brought up to cherish spontaneity and "self-expression" might well react against an emerging society that looks cold, impersonal, and dominated by large science-oriented bureaucracies. The rebels of the 1960's have reacted typically, by asserting their faith in values that represent a kind of defiance: love, friendship, simplicity, and "doing your own thing" — which in practice generally means doing whatever you want to do, no matter what the rules say. There is also an extraordinary new emphasis on what used to be called "togetherness." It is reflected, for example, in the recent rise of communal settlement. Though their rules, permanence, and sleeping arrangements vary considerably, communes of anywhere from a dozen to fifty people may now be found in or near just about every major university town in the U.S. these days; there may be as many as a hundred in California alone. In their insistent concern with developing warm human relationships, many of today's young rebels afford a striking contrast to those of the 1950's. The beats emphasized their coolness, romanticized their loneliness, (e.g., in novels like Jack Kerouac's *Lonesome Traveler*), and derided togetherness.

THE POTENTIAL IS THERE

The main political expression of these new moods is of course the new left, which may be the only political movement in U.S. history to have been developed by and remained under the control of youth; in the past the young expressed themselves politically in organizations that were, in effect, auxiliaries of adult movements, e.g., Young Republicans, the Young People's Socialist League. By conventional political standards, there is not much reason to take the new left seriously. It is almost totally without central organization, and it lacks a coherent philosophy, with those who might be considered part of the movement ranging from Gene McCarthy fans to black-flag anarchists.

Yet it is by no means clear that the movement will be easy for our society to live with. Many of its members practice what has been called the "politics of conscience" — which is a politics that leaves no room for compromise; a recurrent theme in news about new-left activists is their assertion that a certain demand involves a moral issue. This often means, in practice, that the issue is regarded as not susceptible to resolution by democratic processes. Associated with the politics is an insistent questioning of the legitimacy of institutions representing authority: the universities, the selective-service system, the business world, and ultimately the government.

A few years ago, the new left might fairly have been characterized as a lunatic fringe on the campuses. It is a long way from having a majority now, but it is also a lot more than a fringe. The *Fortune* survey shows that nearly a fifth of the forerunners feel a "sense of solidarity and identification" with the new left. Adding to these a little scattered support among practical-minded students, it seems reasonable to suppose that something like 750,000 students now identify with the movement. A figure of that magnitude suggests a potential for disorder in our society that has barely been tapped.

In talking about this tremendous and extraordinary new generation, one must still use the word "potential." We are observing it now at a critical point in time. Its members are old enough to be concerned about their future, and to be pondering the career options open to them (including the option to drop out). But they are still young enough to be flexible; they have, even most of those in the new left, preserved their options. At the moment they seem quite capable of bringing the disorders that have beset the campuses into much of their parents' world — into business and government. They may end up smothering a great deal of rational discourse in the U.S. under the blanket of their own certainities. They also seem capable of working out career decisions and political attitudes that will make them the most productive generation in American history. We should begin to discern their choice in another year or two.

NOTES

1. The function of the dream, Freud believed, was to provide a kind of reassurance about the impending challenge. In effect, the dreamer is telling himself that there is no need to worry, that he had earlier faced up to and dealt successfully with the serious challenge presented by the examination. Those who flunk out of universities are said not to have the dream.

READING 12

Personal Roots: Turmoil, Success, and the End of the Line
Kenneth Keniston

Adolescence is by definition a period of physical change, and it should also be a time of intellectual and psychological change. The start of adolescence is defined by the bodily changes that move the child toward becoming a sexual adult. And if he is not too severely damaged by his childhood, the adolescent also moves toward a greater maturity of thought and personality. His thinking, formerly tied to the concrete and immediate, is freed, and he becomes capable for the first time of logical and deductive reasoning, of comparing the actual with the ideal, of relating himself to the distant past and to the present, and of understanding his place in society, in history, and in the universe. Given a relatively benign environment and the freedom necessary for adolescent development to occur, the early adolescent begins to reassess himself in relation to his own body's new potential, to his social world, and to his family, gradually moving toward greater psychological autonomy and self-direction.

But beyond these general changes, the particular form of the adolescent experience is affected by what the individual brings with him from childhood by way of special sensitivities and strengths, and by what is available for him and what happens to him in the course of his adolescence. With adolescence, the relevant environment begins to enlarge past the childhood world of family and school, eventually to include the entire social and historical world. Moreover, the relevant environment now comes to include the distant reconstructed past and the imagined future, so that the adolescent increasingly relates himself not only to his immediate world, but to his tradition and to his vision of the future.

The form and quality of the adolescent experience therefore varies enormously, even within middle-class American society. Many, and perhaps most, young men and women pass through adolescence with only minimal external turmoil, and sometimes with very little conscious internal upheaval. Others — the young radicals I interviewed, were among them — recall an adolescence that was tumultuous, complex, and full of both inner and outer tensions. As these young radicals described their childhoods, conflict and struggle were largely outside — in their families, in their communities, between their parents and friends. But as they entered adolescence, what was outside began to be experienced inside. "Conflict" now came to mean not what happened in the world, but what happend within one's self. In childhood, their sense of specialness was largely external in origin, a matter of the way they were seen by others; whereas in adolescence, they confronted the question, What does it mean to me to be special? Similarly, in childhood these young men and women lived out in a relatively unquestioning way the principles of their family; but in adolescence, some of these principles became their own and were used against the parents from whom they had learned. With adolescence, then, their narratives begin to focus more on the inner life.

TURMOIL-FILLED ADOLESCENCE

With the beginning of adolescence, a drastic reversal in behavior, accompanied by major psychological changes and conflicts, generally occurred. The preadolescent pattern of outgoing activity changed, often in a few months, to a new style of seclusiveness, a feeling of social awkwardness and moral inferiority coupled with intense intellectual concerns and, at times, with extreme religiosity. The outgoing preadolescent became, almost overnight, the shy, awkward, and tormented early adolescent.

The issues to which the turmoil of this period was consciously connected were sex, and relationships with peers. One young man described his relationships with his friends in early adolescence:

> I was fairly /pause/ removed, I'd just go home after school and read. I had a few close friends, but I was never a big social-type kid.../K.K.: In what way did you feel removed?/ Like I couldn't do it. /K.K.: Not that it was beneath you?/ No. A lot of times I'd get upset if I wasn't invited to a party or something. It really had meaning to me, but not enough to make me change. I don't know what the formula is, but I know that it hurt me because I wasn't in there pitching socially all the time. Yet it never hurt me enough to change....But then, starting in ninth, tenth, eleventh, and twelfth grades I began to change, because there was this large group of people with the same kind of values...

One young woman described similar feelings in early adolescence:

> I just hated those years...I felt very awkward. It was just awful because you were in that transitional stage, you were very nervous about your relationship with the boys, you felt very awkward and very unsure of yourself. I felt all of that....

Another young radical is now very explicit about his feelings of social inferiority with his former friends:

> I still had friends; I went out visiting. But I was conscious of the fact that I wasn't as I had been before. These parties — there was a kind of very fast-moving crowd by the end of the eighth grade. That really aggravated all of this, knowing — not so much being upset because there was a lot going on and I wasn't getting any — but that there were all these things going on, and all my former friends were involved in it, and I was outside of this thing. I didn't

know how to relate to it. I was treated by them as being outside of it, and socially I began to feel inferior. That was the most important thing.

In addition to these problems in joining the teenage culture of their peers, many connected their upset during early adolescence to their sexual feelings. One young man said:

In terms of sexual hang-ups, I think that's probably important, too. I don't know what it means, whether it's stronger in me or whether I was just more conscious of it, but without knowing the name of it, and without knowing it was a widespread thing, I was very conscious of the Oedipal thing....I remember being very conscious of it and very disturbed by it. I don't remember consciously feeling anything in the least bit of antagonism toward my father at all. But I remember having definite fantasies about going to bed with my mother, and being very disturbed about them....I would imagine that kind of thing must have been involved in my — I don't know.

Others mentioned their anxieties about masturbation, about their sexual fantasies, and about their feelings toward girls.

For some the beginning of adolescence was followed by a great intensification of largely self-generated religious feelings, often despite a relatively non-religious childhood and background.

The religious thing is very important....In eighth grade — that was the worst time. Looking back on it, from the early tenth grade on, I thought, "God, I must have been really miserable then." But the religious thing was very meaningful....[It] got much stronger. I was always interested in it, but — I don't remember if it was in eighth or ninth grade — I got very involved with [a Jewish youth group]. It was a very meaningful thing to me....I used to get this really calm, relaxed feeling after services. It reminds me of talking with my father about a year ago. He said that religious services meant nothing to him, but he liked to go because it made him feel so calm....Anyway, my parents began to worry about me....

That this religiosity was not just a reflection of his parents' values is shown by their alarm.

Another recounted an even more intense religious phase:

Well, I had gone to Sunday school an awful lot, but I never took it very seriously. Then all of a sudden, maybe in eighth grade, I started to take it seriously. It became very grasping, as if there was a force there that wanted to take control of my entire life. Because for instance, I would pray. Then I would say to myself, "You weren't properly respectful when you prayed and you have to pray again. And again, and again, and again, and again."

This went on for about two and a half years. For instance I had to carry a copy of the Bible around with me for a long time. And every evening I would pray very extensively, and also I would have to be rigid. It was all very sexual. I would have to be very rigid in bed at night and not move a muscle. . . . I think it was connected with masturbation.

The facility with which this young man now connects his religious scrupulosity to his anxieties about masturbation is typical of the psychological-mindedness of these young radicals.

Another young man spoke of his intense involvement during early adolescence with his parents' conflicts:

I guess it was when I was about thirteen. They had a big fight one night and I got very angry, I told him, "Get the hell out or I'll kill you." And he left, I'm sure for a lot of reasons. And this was one of the maybe two or three times when they considered getting a divorce. . . .

When he left, after about a month, it really became clear to me (at least it seemed to me at the time) that [the rest of the family] did nothing but sit around in the corner and cry most of the time. It must have been two or three months until. . . it sort of seemed to me that the only thing we could do was to try to work out some sort of compromise.

In recalling this event now, he is no longer sure that his father's departure and return was solely his doing; but his involvement in his family's conflict profoundly affected his adolescence.

In early adolescence, too, feelings of loneliness, solitude and isolation came markedly to the fore. Several young men and women began adolescent diaries, which they kept for many years, prefacing them with such thoughts as "Since I have no one to talk to, I will have to talk to myself." Turning toward themselves rather than toward their peers, these young radicals began a habit of self-analysis that continued in later years. Yet a journal is rarely an adequate companion, and feelings of loneliness were common:

For a long time, it seemed like, in junior high school I really felt terribly alone, I think that probably I was much stronger in the eyes of my classmates than I would have believed myself to be. What they thought didn't rate anything in my book. Deference was paid to me because it was thought that I might go further than those other kids. But I thought about the fact that I was different.

Such feelings of aloneness and difference came up again and again. The more neutral childhood sense of specialness had been transformed into something lonely and largely negative. Some felt that they were especially filled with evil thoughts, others felt unable to relate to their peers, and others even wondered about their sanity and intactness.

Without exception, then, those I interviewed told of intense inner turmoil during the early adolescent years. The conflicts they had portrayed as being largely outside them during childhood were now within them. In the internalization of what had been external, accident and happenstance also played a role: in one case, a catastrophic family illness disrupted the household for three years. Another young radical was expected to assume major responsibilities for the care of a sibling; and in still another case, a young man was intensely involved in family conflicts. But what differentiates their accounts of adolescence from those of childhood is that in childhood the *inner* experience of turmoil was not in the forefront; whereas in reviewing their adolescent years, they now begin to view outer events as the product of their inner lives, rather than vice versa.

Some of the ways in which these radicals reacted to inner and outer turmoil can be inferred from the statements already cited. One reaction was asceticism, rigorous self-discipline, and an effort to deny the flesh. Another was intense and at times scrupulous religiosity, which they often now connect to sexual anxieties. Many also reported an intense preoccupation with intellectual matters in early adolescence. One said, describing eighth grade:

> I became sort of disillusioned with most of the work I was doing . . . And I started to read. The academic work, I didn't consider it critical. I started reading a great deal and got involved in reading philosophy and psychology and literature — no political science, and no economics, nothing like that . . . . I would literally start at one end of the library and just work back and forth and read everything that there was. I didn't study any longer. I just read all day long. I'd read three or four books a day . . . . It was all sort of philosophical, and at fourteen years, I became an existentialist. That was generally what I did for the next three years.

Discussing this period in a later interview, he commented:

My mind was very sharp during that period. I was just as sharp as
a whip. I can understand what monks are now. I just seemed to
have felt that my mind was very sharp, very tight, during all of
those years, seventh, eighth, and ninth grades.

In connecting the sharpness of his mind to monasticism, he seems
to suggest that his voracious intellectuality was connected to his
ascetic denial of the flesh. Others also indicated that they now
considered their intense intellectual concerns in early adolescence
a defense against their inner turmoil.

At the same time, most of them devised stratagems for filling
their loneliness with thought. Sometimes these thoughts were
ritualistic prayers, sometimes grandiose political and
philosophical ideas, at other times, elaborate self-analyses. One
young man elaborated an extraordinary fantasy world that both
connected and complemented the troubles of his daily life:

I was very rarely that deeply involved /with my family in a day-to-
day way/. . . . Most of the other time was in fact spent trying to
build a world that was different. . . . Much of what was happening
was going on in my mind. I really created a sort of world of my
own. . . . It was an almost all-encompassing fantasy world. I
created a kingdom where things happened every day. And when
not much was happening in the real world, I would just tune in on
that. Things were happening there all the time.

Almost everything that happened in the real world was
translated into the images of that world. It was a world with a king,
with nobility, with peasants, with wars, with beautiful
women. . . . In fact, a lot of the problems that I was faced with in
daily life would be set in there. And decisions would be made. . . . In
terms of King Arthur and his Court sitting around figuring what to
do with invading Welsh. . . .

The whole kingdom was me. There were good guys and bad
guys. But I had a kind of historian's attitude toward the kingdom.
Everybody has his point to make. . . . I would have said that this
country, let's say was controlled by a very puritanical fighting
nobility, but that a middle-class revolution was going on. And it
would have presented a not inaccurate picture of actually what was
going on in my mind. I would have been conscious of that as well.

What I was trying to do was that I had become so rigid in my
family, now I was trying to break out. Other parts of my personality, more spontaneous parts, were trying to assert themselves.
This was a very tough fight. . . . It was very instrumental, but
finally it reached the point where the kingdom, that whole way of

life, had to dissolve itself because it was no longer instrumental to live experience twice or three times removed from real life. /That happened/ when my life became somewhat righer, when other people became more important.

Two or three years after this upsurge of adolescent turmoil, many of the interviewees entered into a period of rebellion against their parents, usually focused around parental "unfairness" and "injustice." The particular issues at stake in these mid-adolescent rebellions centered largely around the individual's views that his parents attempted to restrict him excessively, did not allow him sufficient freedom to be "himself," tried to control his life, tried to plan his future, and so on. Both the intensity of the rebellion and the feeling of moral outrage and betrayal that accompanied it seem unusual:

> I feel that they were really grossly unjust to me, just *really* insensitive to what kinds of social needs a child has — or that anybody has. They have the same needs, and that's why I have those needs . . . . So we used to have big fights about that.

Another interviewee rebelled at the responsibilities he was expected to take within his family:

> I reacted very violently . . . . I just got furious . . . /my parents and I/ had these tremendous shouting matches, just *pure* shouting matches, as to just where responsibility lay . . . . I was feeling very rejected and very unattended to. But my parents understood that, they knew it very well . . . .

These incidents illustrate the peculiar quality of adolescent rebellion in many of these radicals: at the very time that they rebelled, they realized that their parents "understood" and "knew" why they were rebelling. Put differently their rebellion characteristically consisted in using against their parents the parents' own principles, and inspiring *their* guilt.

One young woman, for example, described her mother's reaction after a family crisis during which her mother had neglected her:

> My mother felt very guilty for ignoring me for all that time. And she tried to make it up to me, she tried to give me presents and attention. But by that time I had learned to be independent . . . . So I didn't want her interfering with my life then. I was sixteen and I

had been independent since I was thirteen. She didn't have any place in my life any more. I resented her trying to do that again.

In all these rebellions, the issue of parental and filial principle is important. Rebellion characteristically consisted of angry outrage and betrayal upon discovering that the parents themselves did not practice the values they espoused. In particular, these adolescents felt outraged when their parents, who had consistently urged them to be independent, free-thinking, and autonomous, intervened in adolescence to attempt to control their lives.

In addition to the reasons given by these young radicals for their adolescent rebellions, there sometimes seemed to be another, less mentioned, reason. In at least a few of these families, the net weight of the family tradition seemed especially great, and mid-adolescent rebellion seems to have been unconsciously directed less at the real faults of individual parents than at a family legacy or even an honorable tradition, which the individual had to repudiate lest it overwhelm him. For example, one young radical grew up surrounded by a family and family friends whose lives were successfully and happily organized around left-wing politics. His parents' best friends were Old Leftists whose works he later read; his own best friends were their children. His family, as he judged it both then and now, had a valuable tradition of intellectual and political accomplishment. And his parents appear to have understood him and treated him well throughout his youth. It seems difficult to understand his adolescent rebellion solely in terms of the specifics to which he connects it. Perhaps equally important for him is the fact that this intensely admired family tradition seems to have been overwhelming precisely because he admired it so. It may therefore have required an unusually strong act of repudiation in order for this young man to achieve a separate individuality, a separate identity as a radical.

For a minority of those interviewed, the turmoil of early adolescence led directly to the development of psychological symptoms. Some of these symptoms, had they come to the attention of a psychiatrist at the time, would have seemed relatively ominous. They include, for example, the previously mentioned elaboration of a fantasy world more real and engrossing than the actual world, the emergence of elaborately obsessional fears of sexual intimacy, an abortive suicide gesture, and the development of a transient paranoid view of the world. Most of those interviewed, however, developed no overt symptoms, but described themselves, as often unhappy, subjectively isolated, inwardly frustrated and unfulfilled. These symptoms and feelings, and the rebellion against parents that often accompanied them, dissipated slowly as adolescence progressed.

THE RESUMPTION OF SUCCESS

Merely to discuss the turmoil, the rebellion, and, in some cases, the symptoms of early adolescence would be to overlook the continuing psychological strength shown by these young radicals. Whatever their inner turmoil, in the midst of their rebellions and despite symptoms that would have incapacitated many, these particular young men and women "functioned" extremely well. Even in early adolescence, those with the most intense conflicts often seem to have been strikingly successful despite them. And as adolescence progressed, almost all overcame their earlier feelings of seclusiveness and withdrawal; relationships with the opposite sex were established — slowly and painfully, but surely — and the preadolescent pattern of leadership of peers coupled with academic achievement was almost invariably resumed.

Looking back now on the early adolescent years, most of these I interviewed admitted the anguish, but felt that they had in some way learned or grown as a result of it. One said:

> I felt like I was carrying a considerable burden. But on the other hand, it didn't seem to me at all as much of a burden as it would seem to me now, or to an older person at the time. It seemed perfectly natural. I was old enough, I could do almost everything I wanted to. [Long pause] On the other hand, clearly that way of growing up had its disadvantages. But it had its advantages, too.

And another put it this way:

> For three years, like, maybe it did mess me up an awful lot. But it was a matter of how I dealt with it. And then I came out of it, you know, in the last years of high school and then went on to college. I had gotten a lot of experience and strength and perception from it. So I guess it all depends, I'm sure I can still be very hung up about

all that if I look back on it from one point of view. . . .But I usually
don't. I don't know why that is. I guess it's the way people are put
together.

The events of later adolescence make these retroactive judgments
of the "experience and strength and perception" that grew out of
earlier turmoil convincing. For in senior high school, and usually
continuing on into college, these young radicals describe a pattern
of outstanding success and leadership.

Most of those I interviewed tended to minimize or deprecate
their actual achievements. One young woman, for example,
initially said, "I was very much a typical college student. . . ."
But later, in answer to a more specific question, she said:

> I worked on the newspaper. I was chairman of the Social Life
> Committee, and I was on the Student Council. . . .I got mostly A's.

A similar story of academic and social accomplishment
emerged from the narrative of most of her fellow workers in
Vietnam Summer. In high school, and even in college, their major
energies were most often turned to academic success.

> In the eyes of the high-school administration, the most radical
> thing I did was that I was the one who led the move to graduate
> after three years. I went to summer school after my freshman year,
> I took six majors in my sophomore year and five and a half in my
> junior year. There were other kids who would take advanced
> courses in math, English, and science in the eighth grade, and they
> could graduate in their junior year. About five of them decided to
> do that.
>   I caught holy hell from the principal—"See what you have
> done," and all that. He thought that was really bad, because it was
> undermining the whole purpose of the honor system. The purpose
> was to get people to have more experience, more classwork and
> maturity behind them when they went to college, not to get them to
> college sooner. . . .I went off to college very, very fast, in order to
> get in and get going. I thought I was really sure about what I
> wanted to do. . . .There was huge pressure on me because my
> brother had goofed off and hadn't done well in college. . . .It might
> have been a good thing to take a year off then. [K. K.: But that
> didn't occur to you at the time.] The pressure was on. Boom boom.
> [K. K.: What pressure?] Just going to college, I don't know. To get
> away from the folks and school, and having graduated in three
> years, and all. . .

The pressure on this young man was unusually intense, but others implied a similar parental interest in their academic performance, and almost all reported little difficulty in doing outstanding work in high school and college. Their talents and academic motivations were sometimes rewarded with national scholarships and advanced admission to desired colleges.

But despite academic success, most of these young men and women became increasingly disregardful of formal academic requirements, and more and more dubious about the value of academic performance per se. One young radical said, for example:

> I went through college with a fair amount of ease. I never studied. I could always get by without studying and play around a lot. I didn't take school that seriously. I never thought that you had to study to get a lot out of it. If I had a professor who I didn't like or who I thought was a poor professor, I wouldn't study for him and I would get a C and it wouldn't bother me. But if I had a professor that I liked and thought was a good teacher, then I would work very hard for him. . . . I always felt that the people who really studied hard were kind of dull people. I would see them getting into a box of not being really creative at all. I think they'd just be studying a lot and not learning anything. . . .

Others found they learned most from what they did and read outside of class:

> In my senior year [in high school], I spent a lot of time reading bizarre things—I was just ape-shit on books. . . . I read a lot of French literature. I read St. Augustine, the Modern Library on Santayana. I wanted to drink them all in—poetry, novels, philosophy, a lot in my education that I hadn't been taught. . . .

Like this young man, most young radicals began to scorn the ease with which they could get good grades, and a number decided that classroom work was largely irrelevant to their real education. The conventional intellectual achievement that had been so highly valued by their parents gradually was disparaged; it was replaced by a determination to "learn for myself." This emerging ambivalence toward the "merely academic" is an enduring issue to these young radicals: it is related to the pervasive theme of "specialness" in their lives. For increasingly, these young radicals felt (or realized) that the conventional education that appeared to suit their classmates did not fully meet their needs.

Some of these future radicals were at this stage in their life very far from political commitment. One young man was particularly soured on political life:

> My parents had always said, "Look, man, you ought to go in the foreign service. You ought to go into politics. You ought to go into public service" This all weighed on me as a great burden. I felt, "Okay, maybe those people who have gifts do owe them to society. But how can I get involved in any kind of politics in this country? It's ugly, disreputable, No honorable man would be a politician." It may be unfair, but I just said categorically, "You'll never see me in public life."
>
> You know, it was a kind of shame. Because personalitywise, my gifts were more in that direction than they were in being introspective, or at least in being isolated. [In high school] you have two bags—the politics bag and the artsy-craftsy bag.... I thought, "Okay, my bag is going to be literature. I'm going to study literature in college, and maybe I'll write someday."

Looking around at the movements for peace and civil rights, this young man reacted negatively:

> I thought, "Oh, boy, here are all those guys with peace hangups. They feel guilty about their middle-class existences. They're just getting their hang-ups out on the black people. A bunch of liberals going out with hearts of gold and no sense." There was some element of truth in that, but I made it into a gross generality, which allowed me to dismiss all of it. At the time, though, I recognized that there was some very courageous people involved, and I respected them for doing it.

For almost all, the years of high school and college were years of growth and change. One described the impact of his years in college:

> So I went to college, and college meant I was living with people, other people my age. The atmosphere was very liberal...but for about a year, I went around being very rigid.... I didn't have very many friends other than the political ones. We formed ourselves a little clique.... We didn't involve other people in decision-making at all.
>
> But I sort of gradually changed. I made new friends in the second year. I got two new roommates that I was very close to. You know, I made a lot of close friends. That really helped me out a lot. It didn't change my basic politics, but it just helped me personally. I think that you can't have very strong political ideas or do a lot of political things without that interacting with your personality.

For others, personal growth meant establishing relationships with the opposite sex. One young radical, whose earlier adolescence had been particularly filled with anxiety over his relationships with girls, commented that later:

> The girl friends that I went out with were the major relationships that I had. I considered them all very close friends of mine, I loved them all very much. I never went out with somebody, or very rarely just for a date or two. I would get very involved, and there were lots of problems, but I really valued them as friends. They were major personal influences.

Recognizing that his sister had been exposed to many of the same influences that had inspired his own early adolescent problems about sex, he invited her to visit him and his girl friend:

> I was very happy at the fact that my girl and I at that time were getting along very well. We were sleeping together and had a wonderful equal time.... Because that was probably the first relationship that my sister saw where two people really loved each other, also the first physically close relationship that she had ever been close to.... I always really made an attempt when I was talking with my sister, a strong attempt, to give her a positive image of personal relationships. I talked with her...about sex and people being nice, and how nice it was....I talked about those kinds of things because I realized what kind of an image we had gotten from my parents.

For this young man, the struggle to attain intimate and sexual relationships with the opposite sex was particularly difficult. But others also felt that intimacy with the opposite sex had been a major factor in their growth. One, for example, discussing the disappearance of his earlier psychological problems, commented:

> I think that the reason for /their disappearance/ was my increasing capacity to love and become deeply involved in real people. Sexual expression, making love, was very important in breaking down those walls, draining the wells of suspicion and loneliness on which these problems fed.

The outward picture, then as these young men and women approached adulthood, was one of renewed success in almost every area: academic, interpersonal, organizational.

PORTENTS OF RADICALISM

Despite their outward success, these young radicals were in many ways exceptional young men and women even before they became radicals. Not only were they unusually talented and often considered leaders of their peers, but they also brought from earlier life a sense of their own ultimate differences from others, very high principles, and an unusually strong sense of independence. These qualities anticipate their later radicalism. And even before they began to think of themselves as radicals, these same qualities often brought them into conflict with their environment.

Those who came from politically active families, whether liberal or radical, sometimes began in high school to take minority stands that brought them into conflict with school authorities:

> /In senior high school/ we got involved in this newspaper. We called it *The Forest Hills Stinker*. We started distributing this in school. It was a paper where the columns debated issues. We did editorialize, but only in one sense—we always put the good position on the left and the bad position on the right. /Laughs/ But that's the only thing we did: there were no editorials in it. We thought it was a pretty good thing.
>
> Well, we got kicked out of school because we refused to stop distributing it on school grounds.... The rules were that you had to get permission, so we tried. We went as far as to knuckle under to the system and tried to get permission. But we weren't granted permission and we kept on distributing it anyway. David's mother was on the school board so he didn't get kicked out. Tommy and I both got suspended for—J don't know for how long—a week, something like that....
>
> /K.K.: What did your parents do?/ Well, there wasn't much *to* do about it. You just sat it out. They said, "This is your decision, and if you think what you're doing is right, okay." I could afford to sit it out in terms of the schoolwork.

Another tells a comparable story of preradical social action in high school:

> There were thirteen of us, thirteen seniors. We all thought we ought to do something. We wanted to leave some kind of positive legacy, aside from the broken windows. See, it was a school like a lot of other schools in Suburb Town that had an honors program. We had the best teachers and the advanced stuff and we got college credit for stuff in the ninth grade. The other kids were really getting a shitty education....

Anyway, we sat down and wrote up a list of what we thought ought to happen. A free student newspaper, student say in the curriculum. Wow, the reaction to that was amazing!....This was after the decision about the prayers and Bible reading in the schools, so one of the things we said was that they should not have benediction at convocations, assemblies, and graduations.

Then the thirteen of us—I was the chairman—and the girl who was president of the Student Council, we took these things to the principal. He acceded to some of our demands, and told us that others were out of his hands and that we had to see the Board of Education. Five of us went to see the Board. Another kid went, too, whose father was on the Board. We thought that would help. [Laughs] We were thinking of it tactically. They agreed to get rid of the convocation and benediction at graduations and assemblies. But they said that they had already invited people for the coming year, so we had to understand that Rabbi Israel and Reverend MacNamara were going to have to be there....

But then we found out the next year, and the year after...they still have it. They would tell kids anything to get them out of their office. And the student newspaper is still controlled.

...Here I should note that one consequence of early political involvement was to interest the future radical in the motivation that underlay his own political commitment.

I read Eric Hoffer's *The True Believer*, and it didn't ring true to me at all, I couldn't identify with it at all. I couldn't put a lot of the people I knew into that group either. I think I'm being honest with myself when I say that my friends seemed to have my motivations, too.

A similar interest in the sources of political action had developed in others, and the amount of thought and reading they had devoted to this subject was apparent in their conversations with me.

The independence of these young men and women showed itself in their relationships with their peers as well. One young woman, for example, discussed her experiences with cliques of girls in high school and college:

Like for instance there was a group of seven girls. And I was identified with that. And then I had one very good girl friend in it. The whole structure was very tight....But I made it a point to break out of that group and to establish relationships with other people. I don't know why. I was the only one of the group who did that....

> The same thing happened in college. I was again part of a group in college, and out of a silly little incident, which was to me a matter of major integrity, I broke away . . . . /She talks about fight between two girls./ I refused to participate in the sniping at her. . . . I defended her. And for some reason that was a major incident. . . . I felt very lonely, but it was important to me not to take part in that. I just couldn't do it. But it was, there were hard times.

Despite her loneliness and her emphasis on these being "hard times," she was a recognized student leader on her campus.

The combination of independence, political involvement, and demand for intellectual relevance that was developing in these young men and women sometimes made it hard for more conventional colleges to meet their needs, or, for that matter, to tolerate them. One young man illustrates this conflict in his account of the conservative liberal arts college he first attended:

> When I went out there for an interview, I told them I had been working with SNCC and so on, and they said, "You're just the kind of kid we're looking for." But when I got there, there were very few people like that. Just kids with names like Reichlog and Rolvag. Of course, there were thirty-five kids in the SDS chapter, but they took a lot of finding. . . .
>
> During the year, we got letters sent to us from the president of the school, saying that if we didn't like the school we shouldn't try to change it, we should leave. So eleven of us transferred. Six of the eleven had the highest point averages in the school. They were by far the best students in the school, these eleven. And a lot of faculty left too. . . .
>
> And then I knew I didn't want to stay there because when I was a freshman I got into the Hegel seminar, which was only for junior and senior philosophy majors. It was a good course. But I was the only freshman in the course: there were five juniors and five seniors and me. I got one of the two A's in the course. It was absurd, because they were all philosophy majors. I saw that if I stayed there much longer, there wasn't going to be much more stimulation that I had already found.

He eventually transferred to a college with a strong work-study program where he prospered.

Their peers and teachers recognized a "difference" about these young men and women, sometimes responding by electing or appointing them to positions of responsibility, but at other times questioning their reliability, and sometimes even pointing out to them a latent radicalism of which they themselves were not aware at the time:

> One night when I was in college, I had dinner with /a conservative professor/ and he proceeded to get quite drunk, and he said, "You know, you're a fucking traitor. You're going to be one of *those* guys. You're going to be a quisling for your own country." I was really stunned. But already, even then, there were differences developing.

What is striking in such accounts is the future radical's sense of astonishment and outrage that he should be considered unreliable or irresponsible by those whom he respected. Some of those I interviewed were considered "radicals" by those who knew them long before they had come to think of themselves as such.

One young woman, for example, had applied for an overseas job after college:

> The person who was interviewing me said, "This is a job that's open, this is what you must fit into." That bothered me; it bothered me that I had to fit into this slot. And then I went to have a psychological examination for the whole thing. He was a psychiatrist who was paid by them. And he said, "You would probably not fit very well into the structure of this world, because if you were told to do something you didn't think was the right thing to do, you wouldn't do it.... You're too independent to really work under this kind of structure...." What he was really telling me was that I'm not good at taking orders.
>
> That upset me very much, and I went directly to the dean and said what he had told me. She said, "He's probably right, you know. You wouldn't take orders and you might not be comfortable in it." At first, I was incensed, but afterwards I decided that he had probably been right.

Another of those interviewed had applied for a job with the government:

> They wouldn't let me in because they said I was "too cosmopolitan."....They were basically right; they searched it out. Well, they knew me better than I knew myself....I was trying to get in the door, or, being in the door, trying to bring new ideas into the door with me, trying to get into another room. But I wasn't able to make it. I could never get me in and all my baggage too. /K.K.: What baggage do you mean?/ Well, now I'd say that one piece of baggage that I never would have been able to get rid of is that, even when I was very young, I had seen too much poverty and exploitation to really be able to believe that the liberals were right....

In retrospect, this young man understands what his interviewers saw in him; but at the time he was hurt and puzzled.

Despite the many precursors of their later radicalism, it would be wrong to conclude that these young men and women were rebels before they became radicals. Once their early adolescent rebellions against their parents had run their course, most of them "settled down" to a period of several years of success in general conformity to the expectations of their environment. Although they sometimes found themselves in conflict with others, this conflict sprang less from generalized rebellion than from their independence of mind or from principled objection to what they saw happening around them:

> I wasn't really a rebel, I was just stubborn.... I'm not, you know, totally alienated. I didn't have a sudden break with my past. But I can see now that even in college I did have certain questions, say, about the value of exams, even about the value of honors I made in college. And I think I had always been doing that, but I never had enough reinforcement, except from some of the faculty. And this now, I think, has changed....

Yet in retrospect, the principals, college presidents, psychiatrists, government interviewers, peers, and professors who described these young men and women as somehow unreliable, as too "cosmopolitan," as troublemakers who should leave college, as "too independent," or even as future "quislings," clearly saw something that was really there. And increasingly, these young radicals-to-be became aware of it themselves. On the surface, they were successful, well-organized students, often leaders of their contemporaries. Their superficial problem was a surfeit of adult options. But subjectively, these options did not seem particularly interesting to them. Indeed, the open avenues toward adult achievement and success were, psychologically, no longer experienced as available at all. What one termed the "Establishment options" attracted them little. It was not that they disparaged technological academic, or financial success, but that they dimly felt there was something else more important. One young man, describing his thinking in college, said:

> In my confused mind at the time, I said, "I'm not going to relate to machines, I'm not going to relate to books, I'm not going to relate to money. I am going to relate to people, on a very, very personal basis of service.".... I talked around, I talked to people who I was very close to.... The decision was very indicative of the way I was going to move. It wasn't really that professionally calculated. It

was almost a process of elimination. The other things didn't matter that much.

Others, increasingly convinced that their formal education was largely irrelevant to their needs, considered dropping out of college. Some left, but others stayed.

> I wasn't sure if I wanted to stay in school or not. But I knew that there was a hell of a lot more reading I had to do in my field. And if I wasn't in some kind of institution, I probably wouldn't do it. I'd probably just get totally involved in politics. So I figured I wanted to go to school and try to combine the two.

Little by little, then, these young men and women began to experience a sense of inner frustration, discontent, and stagnation, coupled with a vague search for alternatives to the futures that lay open before them. They were, as one put it, "nearing the end of the line."

NEARING THE END OF THE LINE

It would be wrong to overdramatize the "crisis" from which each of these young men and women moved toward the New Left. Indeed, to call it a crisis at all may suggest a degree of agitation and self-consciousness that this period did not possess. What actually seems to have happened was that at some point, usually during or after the college years, these future radicals began to feel they were "wasting" their lives, and that despite outward success, they were in some sense marking time. Many had periods of dejection, discouragement, and "downness," when the world seemed flat, tasteless, and stale. Others seemed to have felt something like shame at the perceived meaninglessness of their lives. And still others came to question their basic abilities:

> /In college/ things were a little tougher. I had to face up to that, and that really shook me. I didn't know how to face failure or the threat of failure. I had never been taught about that. . . . I began to question seriously my own abilities. I began to wonder, "Well, where are you really at? Where do your abilities really lie?". . . I did a lot of soul-searching, and I said to myself, "You are really very immature. . . ."

One young man, for example, became increasingly dissatisfied with the college groups in which he was an acknowledged leader. He was troubled by the reintensification of old psychological symptoms and became progressively more involved in leadership positions in campus political organizations—an involvement that was accompanied by the diminution and eventual disappearance of his symptoms. Another, headed for the career his parents desired him to enter, began to do poorly in his required courses, and out of the ensuing crisis withdrew from college. His parents reacted strongly:

> They were furious. When I called them, it upset their intellectual values. I called them at home and said, "Look, I'm coming home." They insisted upon coming to see me, but I refused. I said, "Look, I think this is the right thing for me to do. Whatever the reason behind it we can talk about it on the phone, we can talk about it later, but you cannot come up here to see me." So they didn't. I just took a leave of absence. I was in good academic standing.... I felt very isolated and I felt very away from things that were morally—I can't even say politically—because I'm not even sure I had any politics then.

This young man's difficulty in describing the precise reasons for his crisis was typical. He can only say that he felt "very away from things that were morally—I can't even say politically..." One missing dimension in his life was moral, and its absence is somehow related to his later political involvement. But at the time, and even now, he had difficulty in pinpointing precisely *what* was wrong.

For almost all, the sense of approaching the end of the line was related to similar feelings of vaguely articulated moral irrelevance. These young men and women were not possessed of any sense of destiny. But they retained from earlier life an unusual orientation to moral principle, together with a feeling of their own difference. For them, more than for most of their contemporaries, it was not enough merely to "have principles"; it was necessary to live by their principles. The increasing sense of the inadequacy of their own lives and of the options before them was therefore related to a growing feeling that the direction in which they were moving was ethically inadequate and therefore personally irrelevant. Once again, the issue of principle—and the shame that arose from failing to follow its lead—was crucial.

Beyond these communalities, there were also great differences in the extent of the crisis that readied these young men and women to move toward the New Left. For one or two, the "crisis" was marked by an event or experience that can in retrospect symbolize the dissatisfactions of many months or years. But for most, no single episode can be found that adequately summarizes their growing sense of failure; a sense paradoxical and difficult to understand because of their continuing outward success. A few were aware that something was going wrong with their lives, and self-consciously sought alternatives. Most, however, were not aware, and only in retrospect can describe the increasing sense of emptiness and frustration. Nor did any of these young men and women actually *reach* the end of the line, in the sense, that they arrived at a point when they felt they could not go on. Rather, their growing feeling of wasting their lives was increasingly countered by a new involvement with the Movement for Social Change.

In the gradual evolution of a readiness for radicalism, then, many factors were fused with varying weights depending on the individual and his circumstances. Perhaps the continuing sense of specialness made it more psychologically possible for these young men and women to turn toward a movement that represents a special minority of young Americans separated from most of their contemporaries. Clearly, the role of principle, and specifically the shame of an unprincipled life, was important for all. But beyond these consistencies, the sense of nearing the end of the line also reflected different and sometimes opposite things for each person: a fear of becoming too like one's ineffectual father, or a guilt at not implementing the father's principles; the frustration that followed an honest attempt to "join the Establishment," or the psychological impossibility of even getting near it; the sense of the barrenness of middle-class American life as seen in his own family, or the implicit desire to extend to all Americans the warmth and excitement of his own family. What these young radicals shared was merely the growing awareness that their lives were inadequate.

ADOLESCENCE AND POLITICS

The adolescent experience of the young radicals who led Vietnam Summer is obviously exceptional from many points of view, just as these young radicals differ from those in the conventional political scene in a variety of other ways. Political action for them is not a job but a calling; they strongly resist a "professional" approach to their work; they insist on the importance of personal commitment and conviction; they come from unusual families; their psychological development differs from that of most Americans of comparable talent. Were they to be compared with equally able age-mates planning to make their careers in conventional party politics, these radicals would undoubtedly be more intense, more oriented to principle, less inclined to view their political commitment as a "career."

Any simple comparison between the precursors of politicization in these young radicals and in others is therefore bound to be fallacious. There are many paths to political action, and the path taken by these particular young radicals is unusual: it may be unique to them. But even with all of these qualifications, examination of their experience does permit the development of tentative hypotheses concerning the personal roots of radical commitment, and allows us to delineate at least *one* pathway through adolescence to political action.

Many of the events and feelings in the early adolescences of these young radicals will be well known to anyone familiar with the psychoanalytic literature on adolescence. This literature, strongly influenced by experience with upper-middle-class adolescent patients in Europe, stresses such issues as early adolescent turmoil centered around the onrush of sexuality, the development of defenses of intellectualization and asceticism as a way of warding off uncontrollable instinctual drives, and rebellion against parents as a means of breaking the bonds of childhood dependency. If such accounts are taken as descriptions of "typical" adolescence, then the adolescent experiences of these young radicals are extraordinarily true to the norm.

But as clinicians with experience on both sides of the Atlantic have observed, adolescent development among most middle-class American youths usually takes a different form. The most common adolescent pattern in America involves what Peter Blos terms "uniformism": a turning away from the family toward the peer-group culture, acceptance of its norms as infallible and regulatory, and the use of conformity to peer-group norms as a means of simultaneously regulating one's own impulses and attenuating one's family ties. Erik Erikson's account of typical

American adolescence similarly emphasizes the "ego restriction" by which many Americans effectively ward off feelings and personal relationships that might otherwise produce more turmoil and drastic changes in behavior. My experience with American college students supports these observations: most commonly, the problems of early adolescence are dealt with by submersion into the teenage culture. In many instances, involvement with the peer group helps prevent the "normal" (to the European) turmoil of early adolescence; in some cases, it may also serve to prevent a real adolescence.

Compared to their more "typical" American contemporaries, then, these young radicals seemed to have undergone an unusually "European" adolescence. At the same time, they really did *have* an adolescence, with all of the anguish and the possibilities for growth that this stage entails. I have already noted the individuality of these radicals as young adults. I have also noted that, paradoxically, those who came from what to an outside observer would appear to be the "best" families often underwent a severe struggle to emancipate themselves from these families. It may be that the very closeness, warmth, and encouragement toward independence in some of these families were what made adolescence both possible and necessary. Put differently, many of these families seem to have given their children the strength and the need to challenge, reexamine, and partially reassimilate their parents' values, and eventually to achieve an unusual degree of individuality for themselves. If we consider adolescence not merely as an awkward and painful stage to be outgrown as soon as possible, but as a phase essential to attaining the fullest possible human development, then one characteristic of these young men and women is that they were fortunate enough to possess the familial, personal, and environmental resources to allow them a full adolescence. In this regard, too, they differ from many of their contemporaries.

In discussing the evolution of political and religious ideas, some have argued that adult commitments often grow out of the resolution of "the adolescent crisis." In the turmoil and confusion of adolescence, new instinctual and intellectual forces are released that unbalance the childhood equilibrium of the personality, requiring a new resolution and synthesis that may include, for the first time, "ideological" commitments to politics, world view, and religious belief. A superficial reading of the events of these young radicals' earlier lives may suggest that such an account is applicable to them.

But closer examination of the events I have discussed indicates that their development was actually more complex. These young men and women underwent *two* crises, not one; and the characteristics of these two crises were quite different. The second occurred only after the first was adequately resolved; political commitments grew out of the second and less stormy period of personal reorganization. The first crisis was clearly the major turmoil, guilt, loneliness, anxiety, and misery of early adolescence. It is this stage that is so well described in the European psychoanalytic literature. Yet for most of these young men and women, the storms of early adolescence did *not* lead directly to political commitment, but rather to a resumption of the pre-adolescent pattern of success, to a reordering and reorganization of the personality, to an impressive, although in retrospect transient, stability, and to the development of a whole repertory of new relationships—to same-sex friends and contemporaries, and so on. This new equilibrium, in most cases, lasted several years, and only gradually outlived its usefulness.
several years, and only gradually outlived its usefulness.

Out of the preliminary equilibrium of late adolescence, then, a second crisis—what I have called the sense of "nearing the end of the line"—gradually evolved. This second crisis, which several called an "identity crisis," differed markedly from the first. It involved far less anxiety and conscious turmoil; it remains more difficult to describe and understand; and it is most easily described in philosophical, ethical, and existential terms. In this second crisis, traces of earlier problems can still be detected: problems of identification, the recurrence of psychological symptoms, irrational behavior, and neurotic anxieties are still apparent. Nevertheless, this second crisis emerges primarily from *the failure of success*. Although the equilibrium established in late adolescence was enough to satisfy the world and to open doors to many good things American society offers its more fortunate adults, there was something about the prospect before them that seemed unsatisfying to these particular young radicals. Faced with the move from late adolescence into the adult roles of the established society, they balked, became mildly depressed, and, without fully understanding at the time what they were doing, gradually became involved in the New Left. In these particular young men and women, the move toward radical politics was not a direct outgrowth of what is ordinarily considered "the adolescent crisis." They had long since resolved their first adolescent crisis in a way that almost everyone but themselves would have judged eminently successful. Commitment to the New Left developed out of a later crisis, one that occurred as entry into the Establishment became more imminent. And this second crisis seems less a part of adolescence itself than a crisis at the threshold between adolescence and conventional adulthood.

The hesitation at the door of adulthood by these young radicals can be judged in two very different ways. On the one hand, reluctance to seize the options before them can be interpreted as a reluctance to "grow up": it would probably be so judged by many Americans. And evidence could be adduced from the material I have presented to support this view: conventional adulthood might mean the loss of that sense of specialness that had been so long with these young men and women; it might mean becoming like the ineffectual side of their fathers, all of whom were in some sense involved in conventional American life. Delaying may therefore represent a childish reluctance to abandon the uncompromising adolescent insistence on purity of principle. But judged from another perspective, their hesitation may reflect strength rather than weakness. These young men and women usually had already "proved" that they could succeed in the terms that American society uses to define success. Most of them had excelled, but had gained scant satisfaction from their own excellence. So judged, their reluctance to take up the jobs, fellowships, offers, and rewards before them might indicate that they were able to demand more, not less, of themselves and of life.

But however we judge the adolescences of these young men and women, it is clear that as they approached adulthood, they were seized with a disquiet that they still find difficult to explain. Whatever its origins, this sense of having tested the psychological possibilities of one way of life and found them wanting was a prelude to their becoming radicals.

Rebellious Youth:
Causes and Cures

A section on some causes of youthful rebelliousness must begin with a few comments on causation. The first selection, by sociologist Ralph W. England, Jr., focuses on one possible cause of youthful rebelliousness: allegedly increasing hedonism. For England the idea of hedonism included the growth of a market catering to teenagers, the power of disc jockeys to influence adolescent behavior, television programing of teenage dance shows, the rise of adolescent magazines, consciousness by teenagers of being a significant population group, increased leisure, more money, and fewer responsibilities.

The second article, by sociologist Jackson Toby, supplements the first essay by centering on another possible cause of youthful rebelliousness: affluence. This term seems to have the same meaning for Toby that hedonism has for England. Toby sees affluence as a principal cause of increased youthful rebelliousness, because an abundance of materials creates additional expectations and more dissatisfaction. However, whereas England is impressionistic, Toby attempts to make causal inferences from the correlations of statistics on the availability of various kinds of material goods.

The third article, by criminologist Robert M. Carter, also focuses on the possible causal connection between affluence and rebellious youth. However, his perspective is narrower than Toby's. Carter's analysis rests on his observations of youths in the San Francisco area rather than in three countries, as Toby's does. Carter's examination of causation is impressionistic, although it may still be valid. Moreover, unlike Toby, Carter considers not only causations but ways to prevent and treat juvenile delinquency.

The fourth selection, by Edmund W. Vaz, also a criminologist, examines another possible cause of rebelliousness: peer-group pressures on youths to validate their claims to maturity. Vaz is in a better position than the other authors to make valid causal inferences because his study is narrow and more methodologically scientific than those reported in the previous essays. The stratified sampling enhances the methodological sophistication of Vaz's study. Further enhancing the scientific nature of this research is the rigorous limitation on the boundaries of the study—the precise definition of its parameters. Finally, by his study of delinquency and deviance among affluent youths, Vaz suggests that affluence is not a cause of such behavior and thus takes issue with the previous three authors.

The fifth essay, by sociologist Fred J. Shanley, illuminates the issue of causation in a much different manner. Unlike the first four articles, this one is a survey of the professional literature on this subject. Shanley's comment about single-factor and multi-factor causal model-building merits further consideration. The main problem with single-factor models is that they are simplistic. They encompass only a slice of complex reality. By contrast, the principal difficulty with multi-factor models is the establishment of a priority of causality—that is, which factors are more important and which are less so?

The sixth article, by criminologist G. Thomas Gitchoff, supplements the previous articles by devoting far more attention to prescriptions for curing—or at least mitigating—rebelliousness among youths than to possible causal factors.

The seventh essay, by psychiatrist Roy Menninger, Jr., like Gitchoff's, focuses on prescriptions rather than causes. Like Gitchoff, he favors an expansion of police social-service functions. However, Menninger also suggests that perhaps the ultimate solution to affluent delinquency is for older people to furnish youths with a significant role in society.

A Theory of Middle Class Juvenile Delinquency

Ralph W. England, Jr.

Since 1948 the number of children aged ten to seventeen coming before juvenile court authorities has more than doubled, while the number of children within these ages in the total population has increased by only 19 percent.[1] Despite the caution with which one must regard juvenile court data, police arrest statistics and the testimony of numerous persons working with youth support the Children's Bureau figures.[2] There exists non-statistical evidence that an unprecedented share of the apparent increase in delinquency is being contributed by "normal" youngsters from middle class families in communities and neighborhoods lacking previous experience with serious misbehavior among their children. Rowdiness in and out of school, abuse of driving privileges, joy-riding thefts, excessive drinking, vandalism and sexual misconduct are among the principal forms of disapproved acts seemingly becoming more frequent among teenagers from "better" backgrounds. And the problem is not merely a phenomenon of metropolitan areas: towns and smaller cities in which delinquency of any kind was nearly non-existent before the war are reporting similar difficulties.

A number of researches have shown the existence of considerable unrecorded delinquency among socially advantaged youths,[3] but few theoretical attempts have been made to explain such behavior. In an article published in 1942 Talcott Parsons touched briefly upon the existence and nature of a "youth culture."[4]

> Perhaps the best single point of reference for characterizing the yough culture lies in its contrast with the dominant pattern of the adult male role. By contrast with the emphasis on responsibility in this role, the orientation of the youth culture is more or less specifically irresponsible. One of its dominant notes is "having a

217

good time" in relation to which there is a particularly strong emphasis on social activities with the opposite sex.
. . . it is notable that the youth culture has a strong tendency to develop in directions which are either on the borderline of parental approval or beyond the pale, in such matters as sex behavior, drinking and various forms of frivolous and irresponsible behavior.
/The youth culture/ shows strong signs of being a product of tensions in the relationships of younger people and adults.

The last sentence foreshadows his later theory that in the process of acquiring a masculine role-identity middle class boys react against the feminine identification of their childhoods by engaging in "masculine protest" behavior of a rough, destructive kind. The relative inability of youths today to observe directly their fathers' occupational roles, coupled with the ubiquity of feminine roles in the home, forces an eventual rebellion not only against "feminineness" but against the "goodness" which seems to the child an integral part of femininity.[5]

A number of objections to this theory can be raised. (a) In the process of "protesting masculinity" why is the trait of adult male responsibility shunned while other presumed traits of the male (loud, aggressive, rambunctious behavior) are adopted? (b) One can imagine middle class boys who live in dormitory suburbs and large cities having some difficulty picturing their fathers' occupational roles, but this may not be true in smaller cities and in towns where the fathers' places of work are more readily accessible for visits, and where their roles are less likely to be obscured by employment in bureaucratic organizations. (c) How can the participation of girls in the youth culture be explained by Parsons' theory? (d) Are mothers' roles especially ubiquitous in communities where commuting time for the father is not so great that he cannot be with his family meaningfully except on weekends? "Catching the 7:05" each morning before the children are up and returning in the evening shortly before their bedtime is a pattern found only in our largest cities. (e) Is it to be assumed that the seeming increase in middle class delinquency since the Second World War is the result of a post-war increase in sons' difficulties in identifying with their fathers' roles, in the absence of basic post-war changes in our society's occupation structure?

The present paper begins with a backtrack on Parsons' thinking to his idea that hedonistic irresponsibility characterizes the youth culture of the United States, and a departure from this in another direction from that taken by him. The theory to be presented here is that some middle class delinquency is the result of an interaction between certain aspects of our general cultural system and an emerging teenage system, producing norms entirely functional to the latter but not to the former.

THE TEENAGE SYSTEM

The groundwork for the emergence of a teenage culture in our society was laid a century and more ago when youngsters were gradually removed from functional roles in the economy through restrictive apprenticeship codes, protective labor legislation, the compulsory education movement, and the withdrawal of children from agricultural activities attendant upon urbanization. However diverse the forces were which led to this removal from productive roles, the result was that for probably the first time a major society deactivated a large and energetic segment of its population without clearly redefining the status and function of that segment. The resulting ambiguity of status, the blurring of the lines separating childhood from youth and youth from adulthood, has been commented upon by many observers; the middle class teenager, with his typically lengthened period of ambiguous status compared with working class youngsters, is faced with contradictory expectations. He is not expected to engage in productive labor, but neither is he encouraged to loaf; he is discouraged from early marriage, but is allowed to engage in proto-courtship; he cannot vote, hold public office, or serve on a jury, but is expected to be civic-minded; he is given many privileges and a large measure of individual freedom, but without the obligatory ties to significant others which, for the adult, help keep privilege and freedom from deteriorating into license.

Bloch and Neiderhoffer[6] have recently suggested that certain attributes of adolescent life (tattooing, hazing, the adoption of nicknames, etc.) serve as latter-day rites of passage into adolescence to lessen the anxiety-producing absence of adult-sponsored rites. For several generations the teen years have been a singularly faddist time of life, and peculiarities of dress, speech, values and interests are increasingly conspicuous among this population group. It seems reasonable to presume, as have Bloch and others, that these widely-shared peculiarities are highly functional to teenagers, and are not simply youthful fancies. Some might, indeed, be the equivalent of primitive rites of passage; others might serve to maintain the new status; still others might be the ordinary *impedimenta* of a burgeoning youth cultural system.

It is the writer's contention that certain post-World War II changes—mainly in communications—have speeded the development of long-nascent tendencies arising from the ambiguous status of our teenage population. These changes have had the general, if inadvertent, effect of making teenagers newly aware of themselves as a nation-wide segment of our society by fostering communication within this population group. Probably none of these changes singly could have produced this effect, but their conjuncture following the war provided means for teenagers to enter into at least secondary contact far beyond the pre-war confines of their respective communities.

1. Perhaps basic is the exploitation of an enlarged market for teenage goods and services following our post-war rise in living standards and the consequent possession of large amounts of spending money by youngsters. An estimated nine billion dollars are spent annually by teenagers.[7] National advertising campaigns, many found only in the new teen magazines, publicize products tailored to the interests and needs of this age group: motor scooters, acne creams, portable phonographs and radios, western and rock-and-roll movies, auto accessories, hot-rod conversion kits, unusual clothing, mail-order dance lessons, etc. The wide distribution of these items is contributing to the growth of a nationally shared but age-restricted material culture.

2. Post-war changes in local radio broadcasting with increased reliance on canned material, particularly popular music, has brought into prominence the disc jockey, whose seeming chumminess with entertainers gives him some of the glamour of show business. Despite competition from television the number of operating commercial broadcasting stations increased from 890 to 3,680 between 1945 and 1958,[8] many of them being located in smaller communities throughout the country. The

number of disc jockeys has been estimated at 2,500,[9] compared
to a handful before the war, and their audiences apparently are
drawn mainly from among persons in their teens and early
twenties. The recent disturbance in Boston where a disc jockey
was accused of inciting his young followers to riot, and the
power of these men to stimulate teenage interest in charity
drives, contests and the like, are suggestive of their role in
teenage communications.

3. Similar to the above, but with the added element of visual
   impact, is TV programming of teen dance shows, from Dick
   Clark's nationally broadcast American Bandstand to the one-
   channel town's airing of the local equivalent with a lone disc
   jockey providing the recorded music. The particular image of
   teenage life thus promulgated by many of the country's 544
   operating commercial television stations (contrasted with six in
   1945[10]) probably reaches a large audience.

4. Young people's magazines have been published for many
   decades in the United States. With few exceptions, their
   common stamp was one of staid, moralistic conservatism which
   viewed adolescence as a period of preparation for an adulthood
   of similar qualities. Since 1944, however, when *Seventeen*
   began publication, a number of magazines have appeared
   whose kinship to the older *Youth's Companion* and *American
   Boy* is only faintly discernible. At least eleven of these are
   currently in the market, led by *Seventeen*, whose monthly
   circulation is slightly over one million copies. *Co-Ed, Teen,
   Cool, Hep Cats, Modern Teen, Ingenue* and *Dig* have combined
   circulations of about 1,500,000.[11] These publications are
   similar in format to movie and TV magazines read by many
   adults, but their picture stories emphasize younger personnel
   from the entertainment industry, and they contain a thin
   scattering of teenage love stories, youth "forums," puzzles and
   articles on automobiles and high school sports. In sharp
   contrast with the moralistic flavor of earlier youth magazines,
   the post-war group is distinguished by its portrayal of
   hedonistic values within an essentially amoral setting: the teen
   years are not ones of preparation for responsible adulthood, but
   of play and diversions.

5. A final influence contributing to the teenagers awareness of
   themselves as a distinct population group may be the very fact
   that the post-war years have seen public attention directed
   increasingly toward our youth because of the apparent increase

in juvenile problems. Teenagers seem very much aware that such problems exist, even if their outlines are not clear to the youngsters. [12]

Given the existence of a large population segment permeated with anxiety arising from its ill-defined status, and communicating, however imperfectly, on a national scale, one observes elements necessary for the development of something akin to a minority group psychology: a shared sense of grievance and alienation among substantial numbers of persons readily identifiable by some conspicuous trait—in this case, being in the teen years. Listing further points of similarity between minority groups and today's teenagers, one could mention *leaders and spokesmen* in the persons of disc jockeys, young entertainers and some educationists; a distinctive set of material and non-material *culture traits; sentiments of exclusiveness* toward most adults and toward "square" (*i.e.*, adult-oriented) youngsters; and *culture heroes*, selected mainly from among entertainers and athletes.

While the theory being presented here does not hinge on teenagers constituting a true minority group, it does assume that on a national scale there is evolving a complex of attitudes and values tending to control and motivate teenagers in ways consonant with the role implied by their position as a youthful group having leisure, relatively ample spending money and few responsibilities. The theme of this emerging culture seems to be one of an increasingly institutionalized but immature and irresponsible hedonism, as Parsons suggested.

It is evident that not all teenagers behave as if they were participants in such a culture. The degree to which any particular youth is controlled and motivated by the norms of the teenage system may be a function of the extent and intensity of his affiliation with youthful autonomous cliques, for these, rather than individuals, appear to be the social units of the teenage world. The relative importance of clique-membership may in turn be inversely related to a teenager's commitment to groups—usually adult-dominated—which purvey conventional normative systems, and which have the inherent disadvantage, in competing for teenagers' loyalties, of requiring accommodation to adult demands.

While strong peer-group appeal is exhibited among both working class and middle class youngsters, there may exist class differences both in the content of the youth culture shared by teenagers from the two strata, and in the duration of the culture's importance in the lives of its followers. Those teenagers currently labeled "hoods" by other youngsters are marked by levis and leather jackets, motorcycles and jalopies, frankly promiscuous girl friends, truculent, aggressive behavior in school, and a sneering avoidance of extracurricular school social activities. For these youngsters delinquent motivations may indeed stem from their experiences with snobbish discrimination within the high school social structure, as Cohen maintains.[13] But their earlier entrance into the labor market and their lower age at marriage enable them to acquire adult roles—and to become saddled with adult responsibilities—sooner than middle class teenagers. By contrast, the middle class "social crowd"—more seemly and fashionably dressed, smoother mannered, driving late-model cars, peopling the parties and proms in their communities, and indulged by their prosperous and permissive parents—constitute the spending market alluded to earlier, and may be proportionately greater participants in the teenage communications network and in that part of the teenage culture depicted in it.

DELINQUENCY AND THE TEENAGE CULTURE

An ethos of irresponsible hedonism is not in itself productive of delinquent motivations, and I am not suggesting that middle class delinquency is simply a manifestation of unchecked impulses, as the term "irresponsible hedonism" connotes. The relationship between this ethos and delinquency is more complex. If the teenager's urgent need for status affirmation is met by the teenage culture, then it becomes necessary for him to reject influences from the adult world which threaten it, and to accept only those giving it support. The threatening influences are attitudes and values running counter to short-run, irresponsible hedonism, such as hard work, thrift, study, self-denial, etc., while those supportive of it are cultural elements adaptable to it. It is the writer's contention that delinquent motivations among middle class teenagers arise from this adaptive process, in which the teenage world, peopled by immature and inexperienced persons, extracts from the adult world those values having strong hedonistic possibilities, with the result that the values of the

223

teenage culture consist mainly of distorted and caricatured fragments from the adult culture. These highly selected and altered values then serve to motivate and give direction to members of the youth world, sometimes in ways adults define as delinquent. Some examples of such value transformation will make my meaning clear.

1. Abuse of driving privileges by some teenagers is a persisting problem in most communities. Open mufflers, drag-racing, speeding, playing "chicken," or just aimlessly driving about constitute nuisances and sometimes dangers on public streets and highways. To emotionally mature adults automobiles primarily represent—and are operated as—means of transportation, but in the process of adaptation to the adolescent ethos they are redefined as playthings whose important qualities are less those pertaining to getting from place to place than to glitter, power and speed, and teenagers tend to operate them in ways appropriate to these qualities. Youth's intense interest in cars is reflected in the current number of magazines (twenty-one) devoted to the automobile. Eighteen of these were founded since 1945, and fourteen since 1950. Their reported combined monthly circulation is about 2,300,000. *Hot Rod Magazine* leads this group, with about 490,000 paid monthly circulation.[14] Some 2,000 so-called "speed shops" supplied by 100 manufacturers distribute parts and accessories for youth car enthusiasts.[15]

   A more serious problem with respect to automobiles is the increasing number of cars "borrowed" for joy rides by middle class (or at least "favored group") teenagers.[16] Larceny is customarily defined as taking another's property with intent to deprive the owner permanently of its use; joyride thievery seldom involves this criminal intention, and apprehended youngsters are quick to point out—quite accurately—that they were "merely having a little fun." (It is worth noting that cars borrowed for joy rides almost invariably embody qualities extraneous to mere transportation. Flashy convertibles are especially vulnerable.)

2. The competitive spirit, valued in our larger society as a spur to achievement, but hedged about with customary and legal restrictions, becomes productive of bitter and childish rivalries when it is applied to high school intermural contests. The youngsters, aroused by pep committees, coaches and alumni, transform competition into a hedonistic travesty: witness the

growing problem of fights, car chases and vandalism attendant on important games.

3. Whether or not we are a sex obsessed society, as European observers sometimes contend, the meaning of sex to our teenagers is confused and contradictory. On the one hand, pre-marital chastity and forbearance are upheld as prime moral values. On the other, sex is heavily exploited in most of the popular media of entertainment. The image of sex, love and romance presented by these media is one rejected by most adults whose views have been tempered by the realities of life, but the middle class youngsters of the teenage world, bemused by their burgeoning sex drives in the prolonged and presumably chaste interval between puberty and marriage, and betrayed by their inexperience, are inclined to accept this image as valid. More importantly, this image is considerably more congenial to their ethos than one conveying restraint and self-control; sex and love are redefined as ends in themselves, and have acquired sufficient preeminence in the teenage system since 1945 to motivate youngsters of twelve to begin "going steady," and of sixteen to contemplate marriage seriously.

4. Among the adult values attractive to the teenage ethos, the use of alcoholic beverages is perhaps the one most readily lending itself to distortion, for the temperate use of alcohol by adults themselves requires a degree of restraint seldom found in youngsters. Normatively, alcohol is utilized by the middle class as a social lubricant and as an adjunct to food, and strong social pressures help limit its use to those functions. By custom (as well as by law) teenagers are forbidden generally to use alcoholic beverages on their own for any purpose. But its fundamental hedonistic quality—its capacity to intoxicate—makes it so highly adaptable to the teenage ethos that when alcohol is used, this quality is emphasized, and drinking to excess becomes the norm. A further difficulty arises from the obligatory secretiveness of teenage middle class drinking: it must be done quite apart from adult eyes in automobiles, public parks, rented cottages and motels where drinking parties can easily get out of hand.

SUMMARY

Post-war changes in communications processes are heightening in-group feelings within a large population segment which, during the last one hundred years, has experienced increased status ambiguity as the productive roles of this group have diminished. The intensive preoccupation with play among today's teenagers results from the circumstance that hedonistic pursuits, evoked by the youngsters' present position in the social structure, are becoming the status-defining "function" of this emerging national interest group. In order to retain the need-satisfactions produced by this new status clarification, the group's values and norms must support its play function by constituting a hedonistic ethos, and must neutralize non-hedonistic pressures from the adult world either by denigrating them entirely or by altering them to conform with the teenage culture. Once incorporated into that culture, they become controlling and motivating forces for those teenagers sharing the system, but in directions sometimes inconsistent with adult norms.

NOTES

1. *Juvenile Court Statistics: 1956,* Children's Bureau Statistical Series, No. 47, U. S. Children's Bureau, Washington, D.C., 1958.

2. Herbert A. Bloch and Frank T. Flynn, *Delinquency: The Juvenile Offender in America Today* (New York: Random House, 1956), p. 29.

3. F. Ivan Nye, James F. Short, Jr. and Virgil J. Olson, Socioeconomic Status and Delinquent Behavior, *Amer. Jour. of Soc.,* 63: 381-89 (Jan. 1958), note 3; Frank E. Hartung, "A Critique of the Sociological Approach to Crime and Correction," *Law and Contemp. Prob.,* 23: 730-734 (Autumn, 1958), p. 730.

4. Talcott Parsons, "Age and Sex in the Social Structure of the United States," *Amer. Soc. Rev.,* 7: 604-616 (Oct., 1942).

5. Talcott, Parsons, "Certain Primary Sources and Patterns of Aggression in the Social Structure of the Western World," *Psychiatry,* 10: 167-181 (May, 1947).

6. Herbert A. Bloch and Arthur Niederhoffer, *The Gang.* (New York: Philosophical Library, 1958), Ch. 5.

7. Consumer Reports, "Teen-age Consumers," 22: 139-142 (March, 1957).

8. Statistical Abstract of the United States: 1958, U. S. Bureau of the Census, Washington, D. C., p. 519.

9. *Newsweek,* 49: 104-105 (April 1, 1957).

10. Statistical Abstract, *op. cit.,* p. 519.

11. *Consumer Magazine and Farm Publication Rates and Data for May 27, 1959,* pp. 400, 411-419, Circulation figures for *Datebook, Teens Today* and *16* are not currently listed in *Rates and Data.* A "Teensters' Union" has recently been organized by *Modern Teens* magazine, ostensibly "for the improvement of teenage society."

12. A crude measure of the increased public attention to our youth can be obtained by a count of *Readers' Guide to Periodical Literature* entries under "Youth—United States." For the respective two-year periods of May, 1945 to

April, 1947; April 1951 to March 1953; and March, 1957 to February, 1959 the number of entries was 24, 42 and 60.

13. Albert K. Cohen, *Delinquent Boys: The Culture of the Gang.* (Glencoe, Ill.: Free Press, 1955).

14. *Rates and Data, op. cit.,* pp. 65-74.

15. *Consumer Reports, op. cit.,* p. 139.

16. William A. Wattenberg and James T. Balistrieri, "Automobile Theft: A 'Favored Group' Delinquency," *Amer. Jour. of Soc.,* 57: 575-579 (May, 1952). In studying 3,900 cases of juvenile auto theft in Detroit, the authors observed that not only were the boys from somewhat better neighborhoods than other delinquents, but were well socialized in their peer-group relationships. The 'favored group' characteristic has reportedly been observed also in Britain. See T. C. N. Gibbens, "Car Thieves," *Brit. Jour. of Delinquency* (April, 1958).

Affluence and Adolescent Crime

Jackson Toby

In 1960 a United Nations Congress on "The Prevention of Crime and the Treatment of Offenders" met in London. Delegates from countries on every continent compared notes. The verdict was pessimistic: Crime rates were increasing in nearly all countries, especially among adolescents, and rich countries were having as serious problems as poor countries.[1] In 1964 another United Nations Congress met in Stockholm and came to similar conclusions about adolescent crime. Economic growth, though it raised living standards, did not seem to reduce crime rates. Some criminological experts went further: Affluence was itself a causal factor in the worsening crime problems of contemporary society.

What did these crime problems consist of? Rape? Murder? Assault? From crime reports in the daily newspapers of the large cities of the world—New York, London, Tokyo—one might think that crimes of violence were rising rapidly and constituted a major component of "the crime problem." In some places this was happening, but it was not a consistent trend. For example, in Scotland and in England and Wales, there was a steep rise in the crime rate between 1927 and 1962 (see figure 1), but in neither country were crimes against the person an important factor. In Great Britain, crimes against the person consisted of less than 5 percent of crime in general. Furthermore, crimes against the person were not increasing faster than all crimes together; in Scotland, crimes against the person rose more slowly. Criminologists who disregarded the selective horror stories of daily newspapers and looked at crime statistics coldly have observed that the crime problem revolved mainly around theft. Insofar as crimes of violence increased, they were mainly crimes like armed robbery rather than rape and murder. This thought may not console the gas station attendant shot during a holdup attempt, but it helps to explain the motivations of people who behave in ways summarized in the unrevealing category, "crime."

No. of crimes
per thousand
population

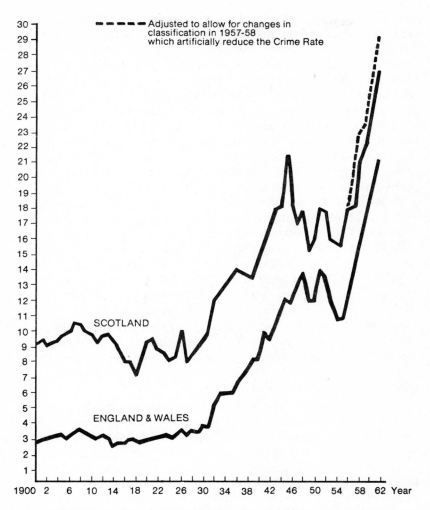

FIGURE 1 Crimes Made Known (Scotland) and Indictable
Offences Made Known (England and Wales) Related to Popula-
tion Age 8 Years and Over, 1900-1962. (Source: J. V. M.
Shields and Judith A. Duncan, *The State of Crime in Scotland*,
London: Tavistock Publications, 1964, p. 20.)

CRIME AND THE REVOLUTION OF RISING EXPECTATIONS

The preponderance of crimes against property sheds light on the tendency of crime rates to rise in the most affluent countries. People steal, not because they are starving, but because they are envious, and they are more likely to be envious of the possessions of others in countries with rising standards of living. Why should this be so? Because the rise in living standards is associated not only with an improvement of the style of life of elite groups; it is associated also with the trickling down of television sets, refrigerators, transistor radios, and automobiles to segments of the population who had not anticipated such good fortune. Industrial societies, which produce the new luxuries, distribute them more democratically than the less affluent agrarian societies did. Paradoxically though, the trend toward increasing equality in the distribution of consumer goods generates expectations of further equality. When expectations are rising faster than the standard of living, the greater availability of consumer goods makes for greater rather than less dissatisfaction. This revolution of rising expectations is both cause and effect of the soaring ownership of automobiles, television sets, and radios not just in the United States or even in Europe but in Africa, Asia, and South America (see table 1A). Traffic jams are now fully as serious in Tokyo as they have long been in New York and London; rivers of cars flow toward Tokyo every morning from as far away as Mount Fuji.[2] Suburbanization is no longer an American phenomenon; the automobile has transformed the world.

Table 1A reflects the level of affluence in selected countries — at least insofar as radios, television sets, and automobiles can be regarded as indices of affluence. Thus, table 1A shows the United States, Canada, and Sweden to be among the countries of the world rich in durable consumer goods whereas India, Nigeria, and Pakistan are among the poor countries. But for persons interested in the effect of affluence on crime, it is not only the level of affluence that is important, but the rate at which affluence is increasing. Table 1B shows that the rate at which affluence is increasing is comparatively slow for the richest countries. Thus, the rate of increase of ownership of radios in the United States and Canada is of the order of 12 percent per year. India's annual rate of

TABLE 1A. Indices of Affluence for Selected Countries, 1963

Country	Number of radios per 100 population	Rank	Number of TV's per 100 population	Rank	Number of cars per 100 population	Rank
U.S.A.	97	1	33	1	36	1
Canada	48	2	25	2	25	2
Sweden	39	3	24	3	20	5
Denmark	35	4	20	5	13	11
Belgium	33	5	12	10	11	13
Luxembourg	33	6	5	21	15	7
West Germany	31	7	15	8	13	9
Finland	31	8	10	11	7	19
France	30	9	9	12	17	6
United Kingdom	29	10	24	4	14	8
Norway	29	11	8	14	10	14
Austria	29	12	6	17	9	15
Switzerland	28	13	6	18	13	10
Iceland	28	14	(1)	(1)	12	12
Netherlands	26	15	13	9	7	18
Argentina	25	16	6	20	3	22
Chile	24	17	0.4	31	1	30
New Zealand	24	18	6	19	24	3
Israel	24	19	(1)	(1)	2	25
Panama	22	20	4	22	2	26
Australia	20	21	16	7	23	4
Japan	20	22	16	6	1	29
Venezuela	20	23	7	16	4	21
Ireland	19	24	7	15	8	16
Italy	19	25	8	13	8	11
Peru	18	26	1	26	1	31
Mexico	17	27	3	24	2	28
Jamaica	13	28	1	30	3	23
Spain	13	29	3	23	2	27
Portugal	12	30	1	27	2	24
Greece	9	31	(1)	(1)	1	32
Paraguay	9	32	(1)	(1)	0.4	36
South Africa	7	33	(1)	(1)	6	20
U.A.R.	7	34	1	29	0.3	39
Ghana	7	35	(1)		0.4	37
Brazil	6	36	2	25	0.1	40
South Korea	6	37	(2)	34	(2)	---
Turkey	5	38	(2)	35	(2)	---
Philippines	4	39	0.2	32	0.3	38
Ceylon	4	40	(1)	(1)	1	33
Iraq	2	41	0.7	22	1	34
Burma	1	42	(1)	(1)	0.1	35
India	1	43	(2)	36	0.1	42
Nigeria	1	44	(2)	33	0.1	45
Pakistan	0.5	45	(1)		0.1	41

1Statistics not available.

2Less than 0.05 per 100 population.

SOURCE: "United Nations Statistical Yearbook, 1964," New York Statistical Office of the United Nations, 1965, pp. 23-42, 391-398, 714-716.

increase of radio ownership was 36 percent in the decade 1954-64, and Nigeria's was 89 percent. True, these countries started from very low levels of ownership. Still, if we are interested in the impact of affluence on the revolution of rising expectations, the increases are dramatic. The situation with respect to automobile ownership is somewhat different. The richest countries have a comparatively slow rate of increase in automobile ownership. But it is not the poorest countries that have the fastest rate of increase but countries of the second rank: Italy, Greece, Spain. (Germany and Japan also have high rates of increase, but this can be interpreted as due to "catching up" after the Second World War.) The poorest countries have annual rates of increase only slightly higher than the richest countries, doubtless because an automobile is such a large investment in poor countries. If the increases in ownership of durable consumer goods contribute as much or more to envy as the level of ownership, this would help to explain why crime is increasing in most countries of the world.

TABLE 1B.   Changes in Affluence, 1954-64[1]

Country	Percent increase in radio ownership per 1,000 population	Percent increase in automobile ownership per 1,000 population
U.S.A.	134	125
Canada	111	147
Sweden	116	292
West Germany	127	469
Argentina	132	136
Japan	155	977
Switzerland	114	296
Italy	175	581
Spain	227	499
Greece	152	457
Philippines	388	165
Ceylon	339	53
Burma	797	184
India	362	172
Nigeria	891	176

1For Argentina, Japan, and the United States, the 10-year interval was 1953-63. For Burma and India, the 10-year interval was 1952-62.

SOURCE: Calculated from data in various volumes of "United Nations Statistical Yearbook."

Industrialization and suburbanization may be thought of in relation to the world of adults. But the revolution of rising expectations has consequences for the young too. As car registrations grow, so do the desires of adolescents to drive (as well as to own cameras, transistor radios, and new clothes). Few adolescents can get legitimate access to a car, partly because of the age of licensing drivers, partly because of the cost of vehicles. In Japan, for example, the custom is to pay workers in accordance with age as well as skill; so adolescent workers (as well as schoolboys) have almost no chance to buy a car unless they come from rich families. Relative to adults, they are impoverished despite the growing affluence of Japanese society. Interestingly enough, the crime rate in Japan has risen most rapidly for the 14 to 17 age group (see table 2), and has not increased at all for adults.[3] In 1941, the Japanese police apprehended 334,417 suspects of whom 7 percent were 14 to 17 years of age; in 1964, 726,910 suspects were apprehended of whom 19 percent were 14 to 17. Although table 2 shows the crime trend for the entire 14 to 17 age group, in 1954 the 14- and 15-year-olds and the 16- and 17-year-olds were separated in Japanese crime statistics, making it possible to study arrest data since then in greater detail.[4] For ages 20 to 24, the crime rate was 17.1 per thousand persons of those ages in 1955, and it was still 17.1 in 1964. For ages 16 to 17, the crime rate increased from 8.8 per thousand in 1955 to 14.5 per thousand in 1964. For ages 14 and 15, the increase was the greatest of all: From 5.8 thousand persons of those ages in 1955 to 14.1 in 1964.

Can the increase in the crime rate of Japanese 14- and 15-year-olds be fully explained by a desire to share in the new affluence? Probably not. There are other factors, including the decreased authority of adults over children since the defeat of the Japanese in the Second World War. A case history of a Japanese delinquent shows some of these interrelated motivations in vivid form. The following are excerpts from 3 days of conversation with a 19-year-old boy interviewed recently in a training school for delinquents near Tokyo.[5]

> Sept 15, Toshiko graduated from junior high school and entered in a vocational school to learn how to drive and repair cars. He stayed 6 months although the course was supposed to last 1 year. He said that his friends urged him to quit in order to "live an adult life." He

TABLE 2.   Increase in Juvenile Crime in Japan

| Age of suspects | Suspects apprehended by the Japanese police | | | |
| | In 1941 | | In 1946 | |
	Number	%	Number	%
Over 20	281,708	84	333,694	75
18 and 19	19,780	6	51,910	11
14-17	22,731	7	44,479	11
Under 14	10,198	3	12,401	3
Total	334,417	100	445,484	100

| Age of suspects | Suspects apprehended by the Japanese police | | | |
| | In 1951 | | In 1956 | |
	Number	%	Number	%
Over 20	452,602	73	427,192	77
18 and 19	58,030	10	48,301	9
14-17	75,626	12	52,457	9
Under 14	32,777	5	26,663	5
Total	619,035	100	554,613	100

| Age of suspects | Suspects apprehended by the Japanese police | | | |
| | In 1961 | | In 1964 | |
	Number	%	Number	%
Over 20	422,430	66	488,080	67
18 and 19	62,758	10	55,108	8
14-17	96,126	15	135,334	18
Under 14	57,572	9	48,388	7
Total	638,886	100	726,910	100

SOURCE: "Juvenile Problems in Japan," Tokyo: Central Council on Juvenile Problems, Prime Minister's Office, 1962, p. 38; "Summary of the White Paper of Crime, 1965," Tokyo: Training and Research Institute of the Ministry of Justice, March 1966, pp. 17-18.

wanted to smoke, to stay out late at night in the entertainment districts of Tokyo, to play *pachinko* [a popular Japanese slot machine game], and to wear fashionable clothing. Before he was imprisoned Toshiko wore bell-bottomed trousers and short jackets, the costume of a *chimpira* gang. He and his friends wished to feel superior to other Japanese and therefore wore what they thought to be American-style clothing. Toshiko's mother disapproved, but his father, a hard-working clerk, did not say anything. Like his friends, Toshiko wore thin underwear instead of the heavy underwear worn by the older generation. [There is very little central heating in Japan, and heavy underwear is protection against a cold, damp climate.]

After leaving the vocational school, Toshiko and his friends maintained their interest in cars. They broke into at least 11 cars over a period of several weeks, using a master key to get inside and shorting the ignition wires to start them. They picked up bread in the early morning from in front of grocery stores and ate it while driving around. When the gasoline was used up, they would abandon the cars—first taking care to remove the radios, which they sold for as much as 2,000 yen [$5.50] each.

Toshiko and his friends also broke into shops at night. They would select a little shop without a watchman. It would have to be located where a car, previously stolen for the purpose, could be parked nearby while the break-in was in progress. There were usually three to five in the group, one or two looking out for the police. They would either jimmy the door or apply a chemical paste to a window and set it aflame, enabling it to break easily and quietly.

Sometimes they picked a quarrel with a drunk, beat him up, and went through his pockets. Aside from drunks, however, they did not usually bother conventional people. More usually, they would extort money from members of rival *chimpira* groups. Toshiko would walk down the street until he saw a likely victim. Two confederates would be nearby but not visible. "Hello, fine fellow. Lend me your face." This was a challenge for the victim to go to a less busy place for a fight. Not seeing Toshiko's friends, the victim would agree; he was angry. After the fight started, the confederates would join in, using wooden bats as well as fists. Soon the victim had enough and was willing to agree to give the victors what they wanted. They preferred money. But the victim might not have any. If not, they would take his fountain pen, watch, railroad ticket, and even his clothing. If he had on expensive shoes or a new suit, they might accompany him to a pawn shop where he would exchange these things for old clothes and cash, the latter for Toshiko and his friends. (They would give a small amount to the victim, 10 percent or less.)

Since Toshiko was stealing and extorting yen with his friends, he had enough money to spend long evenings in the entertainment

districts of Tokyo. Subways and buses stopped running at mid-
night, whereas he did not usually leave his favorite bars until 2
a.m., so he was forced to pay expensive night rates to taxis in order
to get home. This dissatisfied him; he preferred to pay for beer and
whiskey or, if he was looking for cut-rate intoxication, for sleeping
pills rather than for transportation. He asked his father to buy him
a car so that he might drive himself home in the small hours of the
morning. His father was outraged. Toshiko did not work; he slept
until noon or later every day; he spent his nights in the bars of
Shibuya [an entertainment district]; and he had the effrontery to
ask his father, a poorly paid clerk, to buy him a car. [His father did
not himself have a car.] A violent argument ensued in the course of
which his father hit him; he hit his father back.

This blow must have been even more surprising to Toshiko's
father than the original request for a car. While paternal authority
is not now what it was once in Japan, it is still considerable. In
traditional homes, the wife and children do not eat with the father,
who is served literally on bended knee. That a son would dare to
argue openly with his father is a sign of the increased equality between the generations in urban Japan. That he would hit his
father, no matter what the provocation, is, to a Japanese, almost
unbelievable.

Toshiko's father ordered him out of the house. He left home and
moved in with a friend where he stayed for a week. Then he came
home and apologized. His father would not forgive him. For a few
weeks he stayed first with one *chimpira* and then with another. As
soon as he found a girl who worked in a bar as a hostess and could
help support him, he rented an apartment. [Such a girl is called
dambe in Japanese slang, meaning "one who pulls money in on a
string."] It was important to him that she not become pregnant
because she could not continue to work, so Toshiko was careful to
use contraceptives during sexual intercourse. This was not his
usual practice with casual pickups.

The significance of Toshiko is not that he is Japanese or even
that he is delinquent but that he represents one aspect of the
revolution of rising expectations: the dissatisfaction of
adolescents with their share in the new affluence. From this point
of view, Toshiko is an international phenomenon that can be
observed in Stockholm and Tel-Aviv as well as in Tokyo and
Newark. Sweden offers an unusual opportunity to observe the
effect of affluence on delinquency because circumstances that tend

to raise the delinquency rates of other countries are, for the most part, absent from the richest country in Europe. Sweden was not a belligerent during the Second World War and did not suffer the disruptive effects of bombing and population loss, as did Japan. Sweden has no ethnic minorities, except for Lapp reindeer herders in the northern section, and therefore need not be concerned about prejudice and discrimination as a cause of crime. Sweden is culturally homogeneous; except for temporary workers from Latin countries, there has been no large-scale immigration for centuries. In the United States and Great Britain, on the other hand, an appreciable part of the crime problem results from the limited economic and social opportunities of colored persons. In Israel, much crime results from "melting-pot" problems. Since immigrants from the Middle East and Africa are more difficult to educate and to train for industrial occupations than those from Europe and America, young Israeli from "Oriental" backgrounds are more likely to feel materially deprived. Statistics show that Oriental youngsters become delinquent more frequently than European youngsters.[6] The following are excerpts from an interview with a 20-year-old Yemenite prisoner in an Israeli reformatory; they illustrate one byproduct of the revolution of rising expectations in a culturally heterogeneous society:[7]

Happy's parents came to Israel in 1939 from a town in Yemen when they were young adults. Born in 1944, Happy does not seem to have many pleasant childhood memories. He mentioned two birthday parties when he was very young. I think he mentioned them to suggest how little his parents did for him as he grew older. He stopped going to synagogue at the age of 10. By the age of 15, he began smoking and gambling on the Sabbath. This was shocking behavior to his Orthodox parents, and they objected. "But I did not hear." Happy finished elementary school at 15 and went for a year to a vocational school.

When he was free, he lived in Tel-Aviv. He would wake up about 10:30 a.m. Although his mother was in the house, he would take something to eat for himself. Then he would go to a street with trees and benches where he would meet his friends. If any of the boys had money, they would go to play snooker [a form of pool] or to a day performance in the movies, taking a girl if possible. If there were unaccompanied girls near the meeting place who didn't work and had nothing to do, they might be picked up. If the boys had no money, they sat, talked, got bored, and annoyed people. If there was a plan to steal a car in the evening and break in, they talked about the job. If no job was planned, they talked about girls, about jobs they did pull or would pull.

Happy wanted to be considered *bomba* [tough] rather than *fryer* [a sucker]. A *fryer* wants to be accepted by the gang, but he never succeeds. "This kind of boy hasn't had the kind of childhood we had, and he doesn't know how to take care of himself." He is permitted to associate with the *chevra* [gang] because he gets money [presumably from his parents] for gasoline, for a party, or to pay the bill in a restaurant. A *bomba*, on the other hand, is daring and aggressive. He steals the latest model cars, and he is successful with *freyereet* [girls who are easy to seduce].

The *chevra* gambled three or four evenings a week for about 5 hours at a time, playing poker, rummy, 21, coin tossing, dice, or a game with a numbered board called "7 times 3." Happy was not usually very lucky. He lost as much as $50 in an evening. The gambling stopped by Saturday evening when the *chevra* went to the movies or to a dance club. Sometimes a boy won too much, and the others suspected him of cheating. They might beat him up and take his money.

Happy and his friends drank liquor at every opportunity, sometimes during a card game sometimes at a coffee shop, sometimes at a party. They drank Stock 84, for which they paid $1.20 to $1.40 for a half pint. When they had little money, they bought a big bottle of medicinal brandy for 70 cents

Alcohol increased the probability of fights. "When you are a little drunk, sometimes you start pushing someone around." Once Happy kicked a dog when he was "high." The lady who owned the dog shouted at him; he shouted back. The owner's husband joined the argument. Soon the *doda* [literally "aunts" in Hebrew but meaning "police"] were called. But fights occurred for other reasons. Happy recalled one time when he was playing cards out-of-doors on a Saturday afternoon A member of an extremely Orthodox sect came over to the *chevra* and told them to stop gambling on the Sabbath. In the course of the furious argument that ensued, the Orthodox man threw a nearby bicycle in the middle of the game. They stopped the game and beat him up badly. If members of the *chevra* made remarks about a girl in the movies, and her boyfriend resented them, this could start a fight. Or sometimes a member of the group took a couple of friends and *laredet alay* [literally "went down on" but meaning "beat up"] a boy who was saying insulting things about him or about the group.

On Happy's right hand is a tatoo consisting of a half moon and three stars, which [he said] means, "We are against the law." Although he made this tatoo in the reformatory, this could well have been the motto of his *chevra* in the community. Car thefts were a favorite activity. At first cars were stolen only for joy-rides. The competition consisted of stealing newer model cars and large cars. "The car is always full—as many as the car will hold." Girls were sometimes reluctant to come for fear of getting involved. Once Happy left his straw hat with a feather in a car he had tried to start unsuccessfully. The gang went back to get the hat after having stolen another car. The *doda* gave chase; but Uri, the driver, outdistanced them. After a while, they decided to use the cars they stole to help in burglaries. For example, they broke into a supermarket through airvents in the back—forcing the grill—and took cigarettes and cognac and chocolate away in the car. Then they went back to the room of one of the boys and had a party.

Once, when they passed a Willys station wagon filled with appliances, they stole them and sold them to a *client* [fence] recommended by a friend. The loot consisted of: Clothes, irons, fans, transistor radios, and electric shavers. Four boys each got $200. Happy hid his share under a tile in the courtyard of his house and continued to ask his mother for a pound or two [33 or 66 cents] for spending money. Happy spent all of his share in a month. (He kept the clothes he bought in a pal's house—so as not to arouse his mother's suspicions.) This success aroused the interest of the *chevra* in transistor radios, and they broke into appliance stores, preferably from the back but sometimes from the front when the street was clear. Sometimes they broke into two stores in a week, sometimes none at all. They also broke into dry goods stores—but this was not so profitable. From every car they stole, they took the radio. Sometimes they stripped cars without moving them.

In some ways, the crimes of Happy and his gang are not startling. They remind criminologists of the Irish, Polish, and Italian juvenile gangs in Chicago a half century ago—or of Negro gangs today in Philadelphia, New York, or Cleveland. Gangs consisting of the sons of poverty-stricken migrants to the city are commonplace. But the juvenile gangs of Sweden are less easy to understand because poverty, in the old sense of hunger, ragged clothes, and disease, does not exist in Sweden. As in many countries, there has been a housing shortage in Sweden, especially in the cities; this shortage dates from the post-war rise in the birth rate. But existing housing is modern and pleasant. Slums cannot be the breeding place of crime in Stockholm, Malmö, or Gothenburg, the three largest cities of Sweden, because there are no slums. Nevertheless, delinquency has been a troublesome problem for the Swedes. Table 3 shows the rise in adolescent offenders from 1946 to 1955. During those years, the conviction rate rose 38 percent in the age group, 15 to 17; the corresponding rise for the 18 to 20 age group was 57 percent. Note that the increase in Swedish delinquency rates, unlike the increase in

Japanese delinquency, was more pronounced among older adolescents. There may be a good explanation for this. Sweden is a radically equalitarian country, whereas Japanese tradition stresses the submission of the young to the old. Swedish youngsters, 15 to 17, are the beneficiaries of many governmental services including excellent youth clubs, and they can earn almost as much as adults if they choose to leave school and go to work. So even though they may feel deprived, they are not likely to feel as deprived as Japanese youngsters of the same age.

In spite of these favorable circumstances, Swedish adolescents commit crimes. And in addition to committing crimes, they behave in ways that are, if not illegal, disturbing to adults. For example, in the 1950's gangs of raggare [cruisers] drove around the downtown districts of the large cities in American-made cars looking for girls. At one time raggare automobiles interfered sufficiently with traffic flow in Stockholm that city officials invited leaders of the main groups, the Car Angels, the Car Comets, the Teddy Boys, and the Car Devils, to City Hall to discuss the problem. On New Year's Eve of 1957, a crowd of 3,000 persons, about two-thirds of them under 21, gathered in the center

TABLE 3. Number of Offenders Recorded in the Penal Register of Sweden per 100,000 of the Base Population, 1946-55

Year	Age of offenders and their crime rates		
	15-17 years	18-20 years	21 years and older
1946	485	473	155
1947	469	506	148
1948	482	460	128
1949	485	535	144
1950	522	569	157
1951	637	697	188
1952	651	697	204
1953	634	718	202
1954	677	708	210
1955	671	743	235

SOURCE: "Post-War Juvenile Delinquency in Sweden," Stockholm: Department of Justice and the Swedish Institute, July 1960, p. 6 (mimeographed).

of Stockholm and bombarded police with empty tin cans and other objects. They forced several cars to stop and wrenched off their doors. One car was overturned and wrecked.[8] Gate-crashing has also been a problem in Sweden, as it has in the United States.[9] As a Swedish governmental report put it, "Groups of young people force their way uninvited into a party, or break into a private house or apartment, in the absence of the owners, and proceed to break china, mutilate furniture and deface walls."[10]

That the rise in Swedish delinquency is indirectly related to Swedish prosperity is not self-evident. But there does not seem to be any major social trend—except the increase in affluence—to blame for the delinquency problem. There are also some direct connections between delinquency and affluence. In Sweden, as in the United States, auto theft is predominantly a crime of adolescents, as figure 2 shows.[11] Furthermore, while the rate of auto theft in Sweden rose from 29 per 100,000 population in 1950 to 126 per 100,000 population in 1957, the rate computed per 10,000 automobiles registered rose only from 90 per 10,000 registrations in 1950 to 116 per 10,000 registrations in 1957.[12] What does this mean? That the temptation to steal cars was proportional to the number of cars in use and the number of adolescents who felt dissatisfied with their share of them. Of course, older Swedish adolescents did not have to steal cars in order to drive them. Unlike the situation in Japan, teenage boys in Sweden who work in unskilled jobs may nevertheless earn enough to afford a secondhand car. The *raggare* gangs do not consist entirely of delinquents any more than the American hotrod clubs consist of delinquents. But some *raggare* boys and girls are not satisfied with their share in Sweden's high living standards. And they can be very delinquent indeed, as the following excerpts from an interview with a former member of the Road Devils show:[13]

> Lappen was an unwanted child.[14] He arrived just as the marriage of his parents was breaking up. Shortly after Lappen's birth, his father left his mother for another woman. Lappen's brother Bengt, 2 years older than he, was kept at home, and Lappen was temporarily sent to live with his maternal grandparents in Lapland; his mother could not take care of both children. Lappen's mother earned 600 crowns a month [about $120] in a butcher shop. By Swedish standards this was a low income, and Lappen reported that he envied the clothes and spending money of some of his friends whose family earned 1600 crowns a month [the man of the

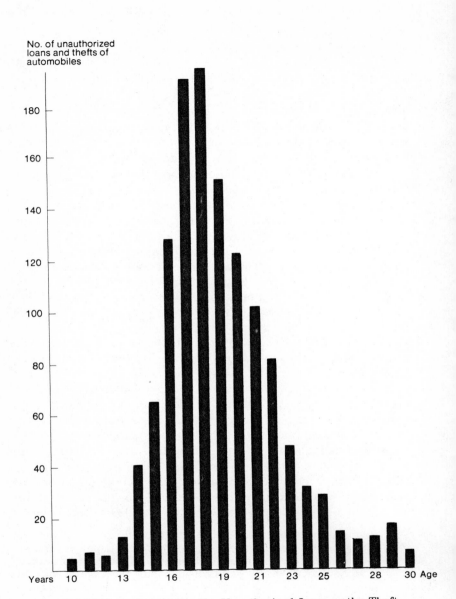

No. of unauthorized
loans and thefts of
automobiles

FIGURE 2 Arrests for the Unauthorized Loan or the Theft
of Automobiles in Fourteen Medium-Sized Swedish Cities,
1950-1956, by Age of Offender. (Source: *Post-War Juvenile
Delinquency in Sweden*, Stockholm: Department of Justice
and the Swedish Institute, July 1960, p. 16 [mimeographed].)

family earned a thousand and the woman 600*J*. When Lappen was 9
or 10 years old, he and three friends from relatively poor families
began stealing candy and fruit from local stores so that they could
have the same things as the other boys in the neighborhood. (Stig
was 1 year older than Lappen, Borje 1 year older, and Jan 1 year
younger.) The other neighborhood boys admired the courage of the
thieves. "We took greater and greater chances because we had to
show that we were just as good as those whose parents had a lot of
money." The boys who did not need to steal stole anyway out of a
sense of adventure. Lappen and his three friends became the
leaders of a gang. Lappen's gang controlled 10 or 15 square blocks.
Between the ages of 10 and 15, Lappen participated in many fights.
As many as 200 boys were involved in some of the biggest fights.
The fights were with gangs from outside the neighborhood and
were usually over "honor and girls, if I may say so." Lappen differentiated between two types of boys from outside the neighborhood: Boys who came from essentially the same class and boys
who were *sossar* [important]. Fights with boys from the same social
level were relatively friendly. "We only fought to show who was
best. After the fight, we were all friends." In addition to fighting,
Lappen and his friends increased the scope of their stealing activities. They "borrowed" rowboats and bicycles. They also
"borrowed" automobiles for joyrides.

When Lappen attended school he played hookey at least 1 day
a week. He said it was because he "had it so easy. The next day I
came back and knew what they had talked about." The teachers did
not find out about his truancy because he would write notes to
them and forge his mother's signature. His mother urged him to go
to school. However, she didn't tell the teacher he played hookey
when she had an interview with the teacher because " . . .she wanted
it to be good for me in school. Mother wanted me to be something,
to go to the university, but I wouldn't. My interest was motors. I
wouldn't sit on a book" Lappen's relationship with his mother has
never been **very good**. "She lives her life and I live mine. I like her
but I do not love her."

At the age of 15, just about the time he quit school, Lappen
had his first sex experience. His gang [the South End Club] had
obtained a meeting room in a local youth club. Lappen had
carefully observed the caretaker's keys, and he had made a
duplicate from memory. Consequently, he, Stig, and Borje had a
key to the meeting room. One evening he took a girl friend into the
room and locked the door. Stig and Borje were outside to see that
members of the youth club did not try to come in. Other members
of the gang were in the game rooms of the club to keep the
caretaker busy enough so that he would not disturb Lappen. Since
there was no bed or sofa in the room, his first experience with
knulla [intercourse] occurred on a table. Subsequently, he engaged
in *knulla* frequently, usually in the home of girls whose parents

243

were working. Although he and his friends were *raggarbrud* *[promiscuous]*, they resented it when girls were unfaithful. He told me of one member of the gang who was in love with a girl. When he discovered that he had been sharing her with numerous others, he was enraged. He told his friends. On some pretext the jealous lover and seven of his friends, including Lappen, rowed to a deserted island near Stockholm with the girl. They confronted her with her infidelity and, as punishment, forced her to remove her clothes, and then all except the injured boy friend had sexual relations with her in turn. They rowed back to the mainland leaving her to swim back as best she could.

When he left school, Lappen got a job as a car mechanic. On and off for the next 3 or 4 years, he worked in this occupation, earning 200-250 crowns a week *[$40-$50]*. Like many other Swedish boys of similar social background, he is fascinated by cars, especially big American cars. He eventually became a member of one of the four most important *raggare* clubs of Stockholm, the Road Devils. Lappen and his friends drank heavily, drove recklessly, and cruised around the city of Stockholm picking up girls who were "looking for a good time." They held noisy parties and dances. Some members stole accessories for their cars. Those who did not own a car "borrowed" cars for joyrides. Lappen was probably more delinquent than most of the *raggare*. He rolled homosexuals and drunks. He burglarized stores with one or two confederates—usually using *schmacha* *[the smash and grab technique]*. His last *schmacha* was a jewelry store window. He got enough jewelry and watches to sell to a fence for 2,000 crowns. With this money he bought his own car and gave up stealing.

As Lappen described his life as a *raggare* boy, it was a life of fun, of laughs. "I lived an expensive life and I done exactly what I want. If I wanted to go to Copenhagen, I gotta go to Copenhagen. When we would drive to a little town, the girls knew we came from Stockholm and looked up to us." There was dancing and singing in the streets. "When I want to dance, I dance." Every weekend there would be parties in the homes of various girls or boys that he knew. He would start out on a Saturday evening at one party and would move on to others as the inclination moved him. He would usually bring vodka or Scotch or Spanish brandy as his contribution to the merriment. Ten to twenty young people would be present at a given party at one time, but there would be constant comings and goings. For example, Lappen would usually get to three or four parties by Sunday morning. "If I didn't have fun, I'd get home by 3 or 4 a.m. If I had fun, I'd get home by 6 or 7." Sometimes, however, the parties lasted all through Sunday.

In 1957 Lappen was convicted for breaking and entering and sent to Fagared, a youth prison near Gothenburg. When he was released, he did not return to Stockholm. Instead he took a room in Gothenburg and got a job as an auto mechanic. Somehow, while he was in the institution, he had fallen in love with a local girl. He distinguished his love for this 17-year-old girl from the many intimate relationships that he has had with girls in his neighborhood and in the *raggare*. (Girls are also members of the *raggare* clubs, but they rarely own cars.) "That year 1958 I shall never forget. It was the happiest year of my life. For the first time, I had a family. I played cards with her father and listened to the radio." The girl's father, an office worker, took a liking to Lappen. He discovered that the boy was living in a lonely furnished room and offered to rent a room to him in their house. Lappen eagerly accepted. During the period when he lived in his girl friend's house, he was, according to his account, a model young man. He didn't drink; he went to bed early; he worked steadily; and he spent his spare time with his girl friend. Unfortunately, she became pregnant. When they told her parents, he at first thought that they would allow him to marry her, which is what both of them wanted. But a few days later the father told him that he "was no longer welcome in the house." Without further discussion, Lappen left. The girl, being only 17, could not marry without her parent's consent. They insisted that she go to a hospital and have an abortion. Lappen returned to Stockholm. His letters to her were returned unopened. Soon he went back to his old life with the *raggare*. Twice he and another Road Devil broke into safes although Lappen was very nervous, and he let his partner handle the explosives.

"The boys in this place are like gamblers. If we win, we get money. If we lose, we are locked up. Because we are good losers, we can smile." He recognized that, when he got out of prison, he faced a choice between two very different ways of life. "I know that the right kind of life is to work and have a family, something to hope at. Maybe I had it too easy the last year now and it is difficult to get back to normal life. On the one side, I found a lot of fun and on the other side, the right side, there was only a hard life." I asked Lappen what the chances were of his not getting into trouble any more. "If I learn to trust people, I won't have any more trouble." I think what he meant was that he would not commit further crimes if he developed another relationship like the one he had with the girl from Gothenburg and her family.

Case studies like those of Lappen, Happy, and Toshiko illustrate the mechanism whereby affluence leads to crime: through arousing feelings of material deprivation that cannot be satisfied legitimately. It is unlikely that adolescents from such different cultures would react to affluence so similarly unless there were a common causal process at work. Bear in mind though that the Lappens, Happys, and Toshikos are in the minority in their countries. Feelings of deprivation do not inevitably lead to crime. On the contrary, they are rarely acted upon. Under what conditions does the impulse to steal lead to theft? If affluence not only arouses predatory motives but gives the potential predator some prospect for "getting away with it," it greatly increases the probability that the motives will find expression in action. As the next section of this report will show, urban industrial societies do precisely that for adolescents: They loosen social controls and thus provide the opportunity for delinquency.

AFFLUENCE AND PARENTAL CONTROL
OVER CHILDREN

One of the effects of affluence is to increase the life expectancy of everybody in the society, including, of course, parents. This means that a child in a rich industrial society has a far better chance of having both his parents alive and well during his adolescence. Another effect of affluence is to increase the divorce and separation rate. Why? Because industrialization enables women to support themselves—and their children, if need be.[15] Hence marital unhappiness is more likely to result in divorce or separation in rich industrial societies than in poor underdeveloped societies. But the most important effect of affluence on the family is to strip it down to jet-age size (mother, father, and their dependent children) and to isolate it physically and emotionally from other relatives. This is not true of all families even in the United States. And some industrial societies—Japan is a good example—have gone less far in deemphasizing generational ties than has Sweden, Israel, and the United States. Still, families in industrial societies are characteristically small; they move from community to community as employment opportunities arise; they lack the bulwark of kinship and communal support that poorer societies had.

These effects of affluence on the family help to explain why delinquents come from broken or inadequate families in industrial societies. Broken and inadequate families cause delinquency in rich societies because these societies assign major responsibility to parents for the control of their children. In poorer rural societies, where in addition to their biological parents, neighbors, grandparents, uncles, aunts, and other assorted relatives supervise children, the death or divorce of parents does not lead to juvenile delinquency. In short, a truism of criminologists, that delinquents come from less stable families than nondelinquents, is a truism only for affluent industrial societies. And even for us it is not clear *why* it is true. Two quite different mechanisms have been suggested by experts to explain this relationship between parental inadequacy and juvenile delinquency:

Mechanism 1. Parental rejection and neglect damage the personality of the developing child. Lack of impulse control results from pathological socialization. The psychopathic or neurotic boy reacts with violence to trivial provocations, sets fires, and steals purposelessly.

Mechanism 2. Parental inadequacy and neglect, by reducing family control, thereby orient the boy toward his agemates in the neighborhood. The family and the peer group are in a sense competing for the allegiance of boys in high-delinquency neighborhoods. If the peer group is delinquent, a boy's desire for acceptance by his peers tempts him to participate in delinquent activities.

Some evidence supports both mechanisms; research is needed to distinguish the more important one. Such clarification would be useful because if mechanism 1 predominates, juvenile delinquency will probably continue to rise in all urban industrial countries. It is unlikely that most family catastrophes can be prevented. Assuming that the emotional scars resulting from death, divorce, or the mental illness of a parent cause delinquency, then delinquency may be part of the price of living in a rich society. On the other hand, if mechanism 2 predominates, more effective programs of delinquency control can be designed than are available at present. Assuming that the main problem is a breakdown of family control over the child, thereby exposing him to the corrupting influences of the street corner gang, then supportive institutions can be developed to backstop parents. [16]

Supportive institutions may be needed anyway. After all, although "problem" families have less effective control over adolescents than "normal" families in affluent societies, under contemporary conditions all families have weak control over adolescents, especially over boys. This weakness of adult control is most obvious under pathological circumstances such as slum neighborhoods or broken homes. Its ultimate source, however, is not pathology but the increasing social fluidity resulting from the allocation of education, recreation, work, and family life to separate institutional contexts. These changes in social organization affect everyone in contemporary societies, but their impact is especially great on adolescents because adolescence is a period of transition. Youngsters must disengage themselves from the family into which they were born and raised and establish themselves in a new family unit. They must eventually withdraw from the system of formal education and assume an occupational role. While preparing to make these transitions and learning preparatory skills, many adolescents are socially adrift—except for such solidarities as they form with youngsters in the same situation as they. This is one reason for the development of "teenage culture." It is not the whole explanation. The affluence of industrial societies creates the material basis for an adolescent market. That is to say, adults in the United States, Sweden, Great Britain, the Soviet Union, Israel, and other industrial societies give adolescents substantial discretionary purchasing power, which enables adolescents to demand (and obtain) distinctive clothing, motion pictures, phonograph records, recreational facilities, and eating and drinking places.[17]

Teenage culture helps to ease the transition between the family into which the child was born and the family the young adult will create by marriage. Peers give the adolescent an emotional anchorage, but they constitute an unpredictable influence. Unless adolescents are organized under adult sponsorship, as boy's clubs, Scouts, and church youth groups are, they may mutually encourage one another to engage in a wide variety of unconventional or rebellious behavior. Delinquent gangs represent an antisocial development of adolescent autonomy; they are of course less pleasing to adults than scouting or 4-H clubs. Gang formation is possible in contemporary societies because the institutional structure, in adjusting to the requirements of urban industrial life, has (unintentionally) undermined effective adult supervision of adolescents. Of course, some families maintain better control over adolescents than others; and adolescent girls are generally better supervised than adolescent boys. The very technology of industrial societies emphasizes the independence of the adolescent from parental observation. In the age of the automobile, an adolescent's home may be the place where he sleeps and little else. The car is not the only means of avoiding adult surveillance, but the car symbolizes the looseness of the ties between adults and adolescents because it is such an effective instrument for escaping the eyes of adults.

The increased freedom of adolescents from adult control cannot be revoked. Not only technology but ideology is on the side of youthful independence. Contemporary societies are organized with the unit of participation the individual rather than the family. The child is not a representative of his family in the classroom or in the play setup; as an adult he will participate in the economic and political systems as an individual also. This principle of individualism, implicitly embodied in social organization, is explicitly defined (outside of Iron Curtain countries) in the concept of "freedom." Adolescents are jealous of this prerogative. The freedom offered to adolescents is not always used wisely; the freedom to choose is the freedom to make mistakes. Delinquency is one mistake. On the other hand, many adolescents use their period of unsupervised freedom creatively: to establish commitments to educational and occupational goals, to learn how to relate to the opposite sex and, ultimately, to marry and have children. It would be throwing out the baby with the bath water to attempt to establish preindustrial control over adolescents to prevent some of them from using their freedom destructively.

AFFLUENCE AND EDUCATION: COUNTERVAILING FORCES ON DELINQUENCY

The new affluence has an important impact on the material aspirations of young people: on the desire for cars, transistor radios, cameras, and clothes. But affluence has also an impact on education. As table 4 shows, substantial proportions of adolescents in industrial countries now remain in school instead of going to work, which was the usual pattern up to a generation ago. Even for secondary education, the change is recent, as table 5 shows.

TABLE 4. School Attendance in Contemporary Nations in Various Recent Years

Country	Base year	Percent of age group enrolled in school			
		5-14 years	15-19 years	20-24 years	5-24 years
United States	1958	89.9	66.2	12.0	69.9
Iceland	1957	73.2	57.9	6.8	56.7
Societ Union	1958	71.5	44.6	8.2	49.1
Canada	1958	87.3	45.9	9.3	63.0
Norway	1957	77.3	35.7	9.5	55.2
Netherlands	1958	85.5	32.8	4.7	57.4
Sweden	1960	82.6	32.3	11.0	54.0
Belgium	1957	95.4	31.5	5.5	60.2
France	1958	90.1	30.8	3.8	58.6
Luxembourg	1957	76.3	25.2	5.4	44.0
Switzerland	1956	78.6	22.9	3.4	44.7
Ireland	1957	92.6	19.6	4.2	55.3
Denmark	1957	76.4	18.5	5.6	48.9
Germany. F.R.	1958	80.2	17.6	4.6	42.3
United Kingdom	1957	98.8	17.6	3.9	59.6
Yugoslavia	1956	66.3	16.9	4.1	37.8
Greece	1956-57	74.5	16.9	3.3	40.8
Italy	1957	78.8	15.7	3.9	42.5
Spain	1958-59	74.9	13.3	3.3	39.6
Austria	1957	84.8	13.1	3.7	46.5
Portugal	1957-58	56.2	8.8	3.1	32.6
Turkey	1959-60	44.7	3.3	1.1	25.1

After Ingvar Svennilson (in association with Friedrich Edding and Lional Elvin), "Targets for education in Europe in 1970," Paris: Organization for Economic Cooperation end Development, January 1962, pp. 107-108.

TABLE 5. The Increasing Number of High School Graduates in the United States, 1870-1956

School year ending	High school graduates	
	Number	Percent of population 17 years old
1870	16,000	2.0
1880	23,634	2.5
1890	43,731	3.5
1900	94,883	6.4
1910	156,429	8.8
1920	311,266	16.8
1930	666,904	29.0
1940	1,221,475	50.8
1950	1,199,700	59.0
1956	1,414,800	62.3

SOURCE: U.S. Bureau of the Census, "Historical Statistics of the United States, Colonial Times to 1957," Washington: Government Printing Office, 1960, p. 207.

Why does affluence have this effect on educational aspirations? One reason is the increased public support of education made possible by large national incomes. Another is the greater resources of individual families, making it possible for them to forego the financial contributions of working adolescents. Both of these factors make for an increased supply of educational opportunities. Education is a substantial investment, both for society and for the individual family; rich countries can make this investment more easily. The demand for education—as opposed to the supply—depends on the motivation of young people themselves. This has been negatively demonstrated in recent crash programs in slum schools (e.g., the Higher Horizon program in New York) where substantial new resources did not make dramatic improvements in student accomplishments. Research is needed to clarify the conditions under which students are motivated to seek as much education as they can master. It is known that parental encouragement is important. And what if parents are not encouraging? Can teachers and other school personnel make up for this deficit? To some as yet unknown extent, they can.

The potentialities of fostering educational aspirations can perhaps be gauged by an unplanned experiment in the consequences of high aspirations. American children of Japanese, Chinese, and Jewish backgrounds do extraordinarily well in school and go to colleges and universities in disproportionate numbers. They also have extremely low delinquency rates. [18] What is the connection? These same ethnic groups are often considered drivingly ambitious. Do not their educational aspirations reflect this ambition? Japanese, Chinese, and Jewish parents want to insure their children a share in business and professional occupations; education is the means to this end. Being members of minority groups, they are perhaps more keenly aware of the necessity of education for socioeconomic success, but they are motivated in esentially the same way as white Anglo-Saxon Protestants. The connection between higher education and high-income employment is well understood and provides a principal motivation for college attendance. [19]

What about Negroes? Unlike the Japanese, Chinese, and Jews, American Negroes show massive educational disadvantage. But recent studies prove that Negro educational retardation does

251

not reflect lack of interest in education. Negro school children, even though they may be performing poorly in the classroom, are as likely as white children to say that they want to go to college. [20] They are less likely to perceive education as feasible for them; hence they are less likely to plan on going and to put in the consistent studying that can make college attendance a reality. In the light of their underutilization of the educational escalator, it is no coincidence that Negro adolescents have a high delinquency rate. Whereas education is a legitimate opportunity for Japanese adolescents, delinquency constitutes for Negro adolescents a tempting alternative to poverty—what one sociologist has called an "illegitimate opportunity."[21] It would be oversimplifying to maintain (1) that all delinquents are envious and (2) that they would not be delinquent had they realized that education could get them a high standard of living. Some delinquents are not envious. Some envious adolescents are not delinquent. Some adolescents are not willing or able to wait for the economic payoff of education; they share the sentiments of a famous economist who said, "In the long run we are all dead."

Nevertheless, there is fragmentary but consistent evidence from various industrialized countries that the longer a youngster stays in school the smaller are the chances that he will commit crimes. For example, table 6 presents some Swedish data showing that the criminal conviction rate for boys born in Stockholm in 1940 was 10 times as great if they completed primary school than if they completed *gymnasium*. The data in table 6 are unusually clean cut; few countries have as good criminal records as Sweden where it was possible to trace 94 percent of the cohort of Stockholm boys from birth until the age of 21.

Table 6 shows clearly that educational accomplishment prevents criminality, but it does not tell why. Therefore it does not immediately suggest policy recommendations. Would raising the age for compulsory school attendance reduce adolescent delinquency? Not unless mere custody of children in school is the reason for the correlation between educational attainment and nondelinquency. This is rather unlikely to be the case. The correlation almost certainly reflects the motivations of young people themselves. That is to say, the significance of graduation from *gymnasium* is that graduation from *gymnasium* fulfills the aspirations of Swedish young people. Most of them were in-

TABLE 6.   Boys Born in Stockholm in 1940 Who, by the Age of 21,
Acquired a Record in the Criminal Register, by Educational Attainment

Highest educational attainment	Boys with criminal records		All boys
	Number	Percent	
Gymnasium	10	2.0	488
Realskola	34	9.9	445
Primary School	185	20.2	918
Unknown	7	14.3	49
Total	236	12.4	1900

SOURCE: Unpublished study of comparative adolescent delinquency being conducted by Jackson Toby, Carl-Gunnar Janson, and Shuichi Miyake.

terested in obtaining business and professional occupations. Some may have been interested in education for its own sake. But committing crimes would be incompatible with the fulfillment of either of these goals. Arrests label a boy to himself as well as to his classmates and teachers as belonging to a different world, a world the values of which are opposed to those of the school and incompatible with it.

Table 7 is a refinement of the data of table 6 taking into account the fact that the 1900 boys came from different socioeconomic circumstances. It is known that boys from working class families are less likely to seek higher education than boys from business, professional, and white-collar families. It is also known that boys from working class families are more likely to be arrested for delinquent behavior than boys from more elite occupational backgrounds. Table 7 examines the joint effect of socioeconomic background and educational attainment on criminality, thus providing an answer to the question: Which takes precedence? The answer is fairly clear. Those Stockholm boys who graduated from gymnasium had a low offense rate, and it did not make much difference whether their fathers were high status or low status. Three of the 71 working class boys who completed gymnasium had a criminal record as compared with 2 of the 235 boys from upper class families. At the minimal education level, on the other hand, parental status had an appreciable effect on criminality. Whereas 21 percent of the 618

TABLE 7. The Crime Rates of Boys Born in Stockholm in 1940, by Educational Attainment and the Socioeconomic Status of Their Families

| Highest educational attainment | Boys with criminal records | | | | | |
| | In the upper class | | In the middle class | | In the working class | |
	Number	Percent	Number	Percent	Number	Percent
Gymnasium	4	1.7	3	1.6	3	4.2
Realskola	4	5.3	15	8.6	15	8.0
Primary School	0	---	57	20.0	128	20.7
Unknown (49 cases)	---	---	---	---	---	---
Total	8	2.4	75	11.8	146	16.6

SOURCE: Unpublished study of comparative adolescent delinquency being conducted by Jackson Toby, Carl-Gunnar Janson, and Shuichi Miyake.

working class boys with minimal education had a criminal record, none of the 25 upper class boys with minimal education had one. What are the implications of this finding? That a youngster who commits himself to education is unlikely to become delinquent regardless of his family background.

But why does educational commitment have this effect? Criminologists do not know for sure. One likely possibility is that youngsters who pursue successful careers at school are consciously doing so in order to enjoy the "good life" as adults. They desire to share in the material rewards of an affluent society, just as delinquents do, but they utilize a legitimate path to socioeconomic advancement. This is probably not the whole explanation. Whatever the initial motivation for desiring success at school—to please concerned parents, to obtain a well-paying job as an adult, to learn—involvement in the school program has consequences for the student's conception of the world. A relatively uneducated delinquent does not know as much about the pleasures an affluent society can offer as a university student. The university student may obtain pleasure out of reading a book, attending a concert or ballet, visiting a museum, appreciating natural beauty, fighting for social justice—as well as out of driving a powerful car, getting "high," and wearing fashionable clothes. Delinquents in affluent societies characteristically desire material pleasures intensely—so much so that they are willing to risk freedom for them—but they are aware only of a small part of the opportunities for gratification that their societies offer. Furthermore, opportunities they are unaware of are those that are awakened or cultivated by the educational system. These considerations suggest that another reason that education prevents crime is that education broadens the range of desires of young people and stimulates some desires that bear little relation to money income. This is, of course, speculation. Research is needed to establish the precise mechanism whereby educational achievement prevents crime.

CONCLUSION

Poverty is nothing new. It is affluence that is new. But the relationship between subjective dissatisfaction and objective deprivation is more complicated than was at first thought. Poverty cannot cause crime but resentment of poverty can, and, curiously enough, resentment of poverty is more likely to develop among the relatively deprived of a rich society than among the objectively deprived in a poor society. This is partly because affluent industrial societies are also secular societies; the distribution of goods and services here and now is a more important preoccupation than concern with eternal salvation. It is also because the mass media—to which television has been a recent but important addition—stimulate the desire for a luxurious style of life among all segments of the population. These considerations explain why the sting of socioeconomic deprivation can be greater for the poor in rich societies than for the poor in poor societies. They also throw light on the high crime rates of affluent societies and on the increase of adolescent delinquency rates with the increase in general prosperity. Relative to adults, adolescents feel like a poverty striken and powerless minority, and how they feel has consequences for how they behave.

The fact that adolescents mostly go to school and adults mostly go to work helps to explain the phenomenon of "teenage culture." It is not the whole explanation. The affluence of industrial societies creates the material basis for cultural differentiation. That is to say, industrial societies allocate to adolescents substantial discretionary purchasing power, and this enables adolescents to demand (and obtain) distinctive clothing, motion pictures, phonograph records, recreational facilities, and eating and drinking establishments. From the viewpoint of understanding delinquency, however, the extension of formal education is probably more important than the development of the adolescent market. The reason for this is that mass formal education has created serious problems of life goals for adolescents with educational disabilities. For academically successful adolescents, school is a bridge between the world of childhood and the world of adulthood. For children unwilling or unable to learn, school is a place where the battle against society is likely to begin.

Orientation to consumption seems to be an increasing characteristic of industrial societies. It permeates most strata, not merely adolescents, and it contributes to other phenomena besides delinquency, e.g., ostentatious expenditures for food, clothing, travel, housing. However, the impact of commercialism is greatest on working class adolescents because the impact on them of the educational system is less positive than for middle class youth. If they leave school as soon as they legally may, they have less opportunity to experience art, literature, serious music, science, religion, and meaningful work, than they have of being attracted to the gadgets and entertainments available in the marketplace. This isolation of school-leaving youths from what are generally conceded to be the accomplishments of industrial civilization may partially account for violent crimes. As Nelson Algren put it in his paraphrase of a literary idea of Richard Wright, " . . . When a crime is committed by a man who has been excluded from civilization, civilization is an accomplice of crime." [22] Selective exposure to industrial society is not merely an internal problem. Anthropologists have called attention to the selective "diffusion" of culture traits to underdeveloped societies. Trinkets, tools, hard liquor, and Coca Cola are easier to export than arts and sciences or even religion.

H. G. Wells once remarked. "Human history becomes more and more a race between education and catastrophe." Is delinquency a catastrophe? Some might argue that delinquency is a small price to pay for life in a rich society where most people, including adolescents, have the freedom to choose the direction of their destiny. It is true that delinquency is rare in subsistence economies (where there is less to envy) and in totalitarian states (where social controls coerce would-be rebels). On the other hand, crime does cost a society something, not only the losses to victims but also the wasted years of delinquent youths. Most ex-delinquents regard the years spent in raising hell on the streets as well as those in prison as irretrievable mistakes. Mass education can prevent some of this waste. The appeal of education, like adolescent delinquency itself, is stimulated by affluence. But affluence needs reinforcement if youngsters from homes where parents do not value education are to believe that education is for them too. The primary benefit of education is of course intrinsic: the greater realization of the potentialities of young people. But a secondary consequence is to deflect adolescents from the destructive possibilities open to them in a free society. If the experience of American society with its Japanese, Chinese, and Jewish minorities is any precedent, the indirect consequence of educational upgrading will be the reduction of adolescent delinquency. True, these ethnic groups possessed special cultural values favorable to education, which were transmitted to children without planning. However, it seems likely that planned programs of educational upgrading, adequately financed and enthusiastically publicized, could duplicate the Japanese, Chinese and Jewish unintended experiments in delinquency prevention. Is it worth a try?

NOTES

1. Second United Nations Congress on the Prevention of Crime and the Treatment of Offenders, "Report Prepared by the Secretariat," New York: Department of Economic and Social Affairs, 1260, pp. 8-18.

2. In 1964, the number of registered automobiles in Japan was 6,775,971, about 47 times as many as were registered in 1945. The number of traffic deaths in Tokyo was 1,050, about 9.8 per 100,000 population and about 9.9 per 10,000 registered automobiles. The latter rate is much higher than for large cities in the United States. "Summary of the White Paper on Crime, 1965," Tokyo: Training and Research Institute, Ministry of Justice, March 1966, p. 6.

3. "Crime rate" refers to the number of persons investigated by the Japanese police for a penal code violation per thousand persons of the base population.

4. "Summary of the White Paper on Crime, 1965," p. 18, op. cit. n. 2.

5. The interviews were conducted in Japanese with the help of a skilled interpreter, Masahiko Kikuchi, during March and April of 1964. The opportunity to visit the training school and interview inmates was graciously provided by the Correction Bureau of the Ministry of Justice and in particular by Director Osawa. Mr. Kakuichiro Ogino, and Mr. Akira Tanigawa.

6. Children born in Israel had a delinquency rate in 1960 of 5.6 per thousand of juvenile court age. Children born in Europe or America had exactly the same rate. But children born in Asia had a delinquency rate of 11.4 per thousand in the base population, and children born in Africa a rate of 17.6 per thousand. "Statistical Abstract of Israel, 1963," Jerusalem: Central Bureau of Statistics, 1963, p. 688.

7. The interview was conducted in Hebrew with the help of an Israeli colleague, Aryeh Leissner. The opportunity to visit a reformatory and interview prisoners was graciously provided by Dr. Zvi Hermon, Scientific Director, Prison Service of Israel.

8. "Post-War Juvenile Delinquency in Sweden," Stockholm: Department of Justice and the Swedish Institute, July 1969, p. 19 (mimeographed).

9. Robert Wallace, "Where's the Party—Let's Crash It!" "Life, vol. 55 (July 5, 1963), pp. 62-67.

10. "Post-War Juvenile Delinquency in Sweden," op. cit., p. 20.

11. In 1965 there were 486,600 auto thefts reported in the United States, 51 percent more than in 1960 and more than double the percentage increase in automobile registrations. Sixty-two percent of the persons arrested for auto theft were under 18; 83 percent of the persons arrested for auto theft were under 25.

Federal Bureau of Investigation, "Uniform Crime Reports of the United States, 1965." Washington: Government Printing Office, 1966, pp. 17-18.

12. "Post-War Juvenile Delinquency in Sweden," op. cit. n. 8. p. 14.

13. This interview was conducted in English in a reception center for young offenders near Uppsala, Sweden, in 1960. In addition to studying English in school, as all Swedes do, the prisoner had been a merchant seaman and had visited English-speaking countries. The opportunity to visit a reception center and interview inmates was graciously provided by Torsten Eriksson, Director-General , Swedish National Prisons Board.

14. "Lappen" is a nickname meaning Laplander. At the age of 6, he spent 6 months in Lapland with his maternal grandparents when his mother was too sick to take care of him. When he returned to Stockholm, his friends noticed traces of a Lapland accent and dubbed him "Lappen." "I liked that name because not everyone knew my real name. If someone told it to the police, they might not catch me."

15. In 1890, women constituted 15.8 percent of the white civilian labor force; in 1957, they constituted 34.1 percent. In 1890, divorced, separated and widowed women constituted 28.6 percent of working women; in 1957, these categories constituted 40.4 percent of working women. U.S. Bureau of the Census, "Historical Statistics of the United States, Colonial Times to 1957." Washington: Government Printing Office, 1960, p. 72.

16. In Sweden, unmarried mothers not only receive allowances for their children. They are visited regularly by social workers who attempt to give some of the guidance that a husband-father might provide. Nevertheless, children from broken families have a higher delinquency rate than children from intact families. The supportive institution is not fully successful.

17. Mark Abrams, "The Teenage Consumer," London: London Press Exchange, 1960.

18. Jackson Toby, "Educational Maladjustment as a Predisposing Factor in Criminal Careers: A Comparative Study of Ethnic Groups," Ph.D. Dissertation, Department of Social Relations, Harvard University, 1950.

19. Jackson Toby. "The American College Student: A Candidate for Socialization." "American Association of University Professors Bulletin," vol. 43 (June 1957), pp. 319-322.

20. U.S. Office of Education, "Equality of Educational Opportunity," Washington: Government Printing Office, 1966.

21. Richard A. Cloward, "Illegitimate Means, Anomie and Deviant Behavior." "American Sociological Review," vol. 24 (April 1959), pp. 164-176.

22. Nelson Algren, "Remembering Richard Wright," "The Nation," vol. 192 (Jan. 28, 1961), p. 85.

Delinquency in the Upper and Middle Classes
Robert M. Carter

In any attempt to determine the nature, distribution and extent of delinquency among upper and middle class youth, attention must be directed to the newly emerging suburban communities of our country. These suburban communities house our middle and upper class populations.

One of the important changes in America today is the rapid urbanization of our society and the creation of enormous population centers that surround and engulf our major cities. While we readily note statistical changes in our population, we fail to recognize that the society of the megalopolis is something more than new numbers and a new distribution of the population.

This urbanization pattern is partially characterized by the entrance of minority groups (predominantly Spanish-American and Negro) into the metropolitan areas and by the migration of whites from the central core cities to the suburbs. While vast areas of our central cities are being transformed into racial slums, the upwardly mobile, affluent white population flees to suburbia in the hope of escaping the pressures and problems of urban life: high taxes, traffic congestion and transit difficulties, smog and air pollution, garbage disposal and probably of greater significance, the "changing neighborhood patterns"—a euphemism for the spread of minority groups in the central city.

SUBURBIA AND SUBURBAN MAN

Suburbia has become the acquired, if not the natural, environment of the middle and upper classes. Although the suburbanite may have escaped the known problems and pressures of the urban community, he has encountered new difficulties—unforseen, as yet unresolved and, in many ways, more complex than those from which he fled.

Suburbia is many things. In general, it is a series of unincorporated (or recently incorporated) affluent communities housing a young, primarily all-white, middle and upper class population. Suburbia has excellent schools, shopping centers, well-organized activities for children, barbecue pits, community and private swimming pools, golf courses and two-car families. In the words of the chambers of commerce, the suburbanite finds "gracious modern living at its best . . . the unexcelled combination of outdoor living in close proximity to highly developed shopping and employment areas with homes situated in the midst of tree-covered hills and valleys" or "nesting along tree-lined streets and lanes."

Those who have examined suburban man as carefully as an anthropologist studies primitive man find that many traditional images of national life have disappeared in suburbia. What has emerged is a man without direction or ambition except for a desire to obtain material security, a man so conscious of his fellows that he has no convictions of his own. Lacking the stern code of conduct of the 19th century "inner-directed man," separated from the Protestant ethic that maintained individuality 50 years ago, the suburbanite seeks direction from a passing parade of experts who dictate the design of his house, the education of his children, the choice of his friends and the use of his income. He willingly turns the direction of community affairs over to others and passively observes the national issues of the day. In the suburbs, individuality, privacy and pride of craftsmanship have been exchanged for group cooperation and something obscurely defined as the "social ethic."

Each characteristic and institution of suburban life testifies that the "lonely crowd" is everywhere. The suburbanite does not live in a house that expresses his individuality or blends landscape and architecture. Instead, he either builds a house that expresses the values of the real estate experts or settles in a large housing development of quarter-acre parcels. His house, as much like his neighbor's as possible, is crammed with mechanical conveniences that reflect a preoccupation with consumption. Arranged for

261

entertainment, these houses are built to encourage family and neighborhood sociability. They are erected as symbols of material well-being and "togetherness," the new social ethic in practice.

The use of time in the suburbs is important. Most observers find an array of schedules that reveal the suburbanite's inability to live as an individual. The commuter schedule for the husband, the nursery and social schedule for the wife and the school schedule for the growing child govern suburban life. Time spent going to and from work, time spent hauling children, time spent in class; the weekday for work, the weekend for "career maneuvering" or improving social status; time is the master of suburbia. Forever active, constantly harassed, the suburbanite hurries everywhere, caught up in a series of events never of his own making but from which he cannot readily withdraw. He is plunged into participation in an endless circle of meetings, appointments, arrivals and departures.

The school emerges as the all-important focus of existence and from the school, to parents and children alike, comes the constant message of "adjustment." Teachers stress cooperation and togetherness. Competition and individuality are subdued; the cry is for a common outlook.

Although family life is "important," and love and constant association are expected, the means for holding the family together are obscure. The commuter father is no longer a figure of authority. Rearing the child and running the suburb are left to the mother and the schools and the experts on whom both rely. The desires and demands of children—their play space, their training, their future careers, their happiness—become the predominant forces in suburbia.

ALIENATION AND CRIME

A social commentary of our times would be dominated by terms that describe a growing distance between men and their former objects of affection. Alienation, estrangement, disaffection, anomie, withdrawal, disengagement, separation, noninvolvement, apathy, indifference and neutrality—all are terms that point to a sense of loss and a widening gap between men and their social world. Ours is an age not of synthesis but of analysis; not of constructive hopes but of destructive potentials; not of commitment but of alienation. American alienation takes the form of a rebellion without a cause. It affects not only those at the lowest level but those at the top. It is not only imposed on men by their society; it is increasingly chosen by them as a response to society. The rejected have no reason to embrace their society, for it offers them little. To almost any American Negro or any unemployed worker whose job has been lost through automation, alienation makes good sense and needs no complex explanation. But we also have alienation of the average, adjusted, affluent American and estrangement of the fortunate, the talented and the privileged. Part, but not all, of the problem may be a result of our technologic society, in which computers, soft landings on the moon and the Pill lead its members to wonder about their appropriate place.

If our general observations on suburbia and the increase in alienation are correct, one of the manifestations would be a noticeable rise in deviance, delinquency and crime in the new suburban communities. The overall pattern reported by the Federal Bureau of Investigation is relevant. In 1964, the FBI noted that suburban crime had increased 17 percent over 1963 and, furthermore, that persons under the age of 18 accounted for over one-half of the total number of arrests for serious crimes in suburban communities. In 1965, the FBI reported that suburban crime had increased an additional 8 percent, with youthful offenders again representing a majority of those arrested. While complete data for 1966 are not yet available, the FBI tentatively reports still another increase, of 13 percent, in suburban crime.

Crime and delinquency in suburban communities are increasing at an alarming rate. Part of the increase is due to those qualities of American life and suburban culture described previously. In addition, if we look at law enforcement in these suburban communities, we find that the laws are enforced by a 19th century anomaly, the county sheriff, and a lilliputian police department. Despite good intentions, these agencies are in the main unable to cope with the crime problem confronting them. They provide an example of the lag in the administration of justice behind the facts of community life. The problems of crime and delinquency cannot be met by law enforcement agencies operating within traditional political boundaries. As yet, governments and civic machinery have not been developed which can cope with and serve the new suburban communities, not only in the areas of crime and its correction but in most other areas, such as education and transportation. Obviously, some changes in our conventional notions of government are essential, including the development of models and systems that are coexistent with the new metropolitan communities.

A SEPARATE ADOLESCENT WORLD

The problems of adolescents in America in the late 1960's are not entirely different from those of other age groups. However, the young do occupy a peculiar status in our social structure. Our teenagers are suspended between childhood and adulthood. The prolongation of adolescence in our industrial, technologic society exempts the adolescent from the world of work and propels him into the world of school, play, leisure or deviance. In a very real sense, our young people are cut off from the larger society in which they will someday play a part.

The process by which this has come about has not been particularly swift or dramatic. At one time, our youth were an integral part of the labor force but the development of protective labor legislation and compulsory education removed them from functionally useful roles and left them without an adequate definition of their new status. For perhaps the first time, a large and energetic segment of our society was deactivated without a redefinition of its status and function.

This extension of adolescence and prevention from entrance into useful economic relationships has generated a distinct adolescent social world. When a society does not make adequate preparation, formal or otherwise, for the induction of youth into adult status, corresponding forms of behavior appear. This improvisation is typically described as the "teen culture" or subculture.

There are delinquency-generating features in this newly emerged subculture. Thus American society, which once contained only "adults" or "children" has produced a third category—the adolescent. A system of shared understandings, peculiar to adolescents, has evolved and this system further isolates our youth from the context of the larger society. If the teenager's urgent need for status affirmation is met by the teenage culture, then it becomes necessary for him to reject the influences of the adult world that threaten it and to accept only those that support it. These highly selected and altered values serve to motivate and give direction to members of the adolescent world, sometimes in ways adults define as delinquent.

PATTERNS OF DELINQUENCY

But what is the nature and extent of delinquency in our upper and middle class communities? What methods may be implemented to bring about prevention, treatment and control? There is, of course, a vast void in our knowledge about such delinquency. However, we may turn to a study currently under way at the University of California for some partial answers. This study, conducted by the School of Criminology at the university and supported by the President's Committee on Juvenile Delinquency and Youth Development, is examining deviance and delinquency in two San Francisco Bay Area communities. These communities and their patterns of usual deviance reflect the situation in most American middle and upper class suburban communities.

Two patterns are of particular significance. The first is that the amount of *official* delinquency given in various administrative reports grossly understates the amount of *actual* delinquency and deviance. Preliminary findings indicate that suburban communities have significant amounts of "unofficial" delinquency. Unofficial delinquency consists of those acts which come to the attention of official community agencies (e.g., law enforcement, schools) but which are handled without processing through the normal judicial channels. They are disposed of in some other fashion by a very powerful, but not clearly defined, informal social system.

A separate category of unofficial delinquency includes acts which are *not* reported to official agencies but are known only to the residents of the community and are handled in a nonjudicial manner. Normally the "solution" is reached by the families of the victim and the offender. An example of this group is a case of neighborhood vandalism in which the offender's family makes restitution to the victim without referring the matter to an official agency.

Unofficial delinquency illustrates a phenomenon we have called "absorption"—the attempts of parents, schools, neighborhoods and communities to handle the problem of deviant and delinquent youth without referral to the official agencies. If there has been such a referral, the community attempts to remove the offender from the official process by offering a solution, a technique or a method of dealing with the youth outside the normal judicial channels. In a sense, absorption refers to the "tolerance level" of the community. It appears from our data that *the process of absorption is the major approach to delinquency in affluent communities.* In our cohort studies, we have found that some 70 percent of the youngsters who come into official contact with law enforcement agencies are dealt with informally, such as by reprimand, with or without the parents present. Of the youngsters processed beyond the law enforcement level to a probation agency, another 70 percent are removed from official channels as "solutions" to their deviant or delinquent behavior are offered. And of those who proceed beyond the probation department to the juvenile court, a similar percentage are disposed of informally (without a *formal* judgment of delinquency). In short, only a small percentage of delinquent acts in affluent suburban communities are officially judged delinquent; this is a product of the informal processes of absorption.

The second major pattern which appears in our study of middle and upper class delinquency is the power of the social systems of youth. Much of adolescent behavior, both deviant and nondeviant, is influenced, if not controlled, by peers. Our data indicate that of the official cases of suburban delinquency, about 75 percent of the acts were committed by two or more youths. If we add to this those delinquent acts which were committed primarily for a peer group audience, the figure rises to nearly 90 percent. We have observed clear patterns of residential clustering of young delinquents. This, in turn, leads to educational clustering of the delinquents since the school population is usually based on home address. We suspect that a "tradition" of delinquency exists in some parts of the communities and, through a well-established feeder system into the schools, the tradition may well evolve in certain schools.

The specific patterns of delinquency are interesting and provocative. For example, we have found that the majority of delinquent acts are against property—such as theft, burglary and larceny. What can account for attacks on property by well-groomed, well-dressed youths with money in their pockets, who more often than not drive to the scene of their delinquency in the family car? We have observed time-sequence patterns of delinquency, which may be a reflection of suburban life. In general delinquency is at a low during the school day, when the school provides a form of baby-sitting for adolescents. Delinquency increases substantially after classes and remains high until dinnertime. It disappears almost completely as the father returns home and is joined by his children for the dinner ritual. Delinquency rises again after dinner and remains high until late in the evening when, by mutual agreement of youth and adults, it is time to return home to ensure a good night's sleep for tomorrow's identical pattern.

The picture of suburbia which has emerged thus far is perhaps not as attractive as that described by land developers. The nature and dimensions of suburban life, coupled with the growing feeling of anomie among all segments of our population, may well explain many of the increasing patterns of delinquency in suburbia. (And we must remember that the official data on delinquency are gross underestimates of actual delinquency.)

Preliminary findings from the upper and middle class delinquency study in the San Francisco Bay Area include the following points, most of which have been discussed previously:

1. The official indices of delinquency and deviance far understate the nature and extent of the actual situation.
2. Delinquency is primarily a group phenomenon.
3. The capacity of communities to absorb delinquency by informal techniques—without referral to, or processing through, official agencies—is diminishing. Since this informal handling seemingly produces a low rate of recidivism and avoids the problems of officially labeling youngsters as "delinquent," this reduced capacity of absorption may have disastrous consequences for the youth.
4. Adults have little understanding of the social systems of youth. Nor do they understand the strong influence of these social systems on the activities, attitudes and conduct of youth. In a sense, two separate worlds exist—that of the adult, and that of the adolescent.

TREATMENT AND CONTROL

We believe community absorption of deviance is a worthwhile target. Absorption, of course, does not just happen; a favorable environment must be created. Such an environment includes several key elements. First, there must be a redefinition of deviance, that is, an increase in tolerance on the part of the community, its individual members and its agencies and organizations. A second essential component is to make explicit the alternatives to traditional strategies for dealing with deviance, alternatives which focus on the community's absorption of delinquency. The third factor is the need to develop community awareness of the problems of youth and ways to cope with these problems.

How may these principles be specifically applied? Since the social systems of youth guide their behavior and misbehavior to a large extent, it is essential to engage such social systems in programs aimed at controlling and preventing delinquency. Furthermore, since the capacity of a community to absorb misbehavior is, in part, a product of a dialogue and understanding between the adult and youthful social systems, it is essential to bring these two social systems together and utilize the strength of each. Young people must be involved with adults in decision-making activities. In short, they should have a significant voice in planning activities which involve them. Finally, those strategies that contain delinquency within the community (normally the individual solutions of desperate parents) should be given a collective force and character.

STEPS IN MANAGEMENT

Let us examine briefly the application of these general themes and principles to two communities currently under study. Both communities have established a youth commission or council which contains an almost equal number of adults and youth. These organizations serve as basic policy-making and operating bodies. Each has a full-time university staff member as its director, two part-time field-work assistants and a large number of youth "consultants" from all parts of the adolescent community. The youth council acts for the community and emphasis is placed on the fact that a community effort is required. The adult and youthful representatives of these councils are persons who represent both formal and informal organizations within the community. In these councils, adults and young people formulate plans and policies on an equal footing. Communication and dialogue between the adult and youthful worlds are facilitated and increased. The councils have developed programs which relate to the previously outlined themes.

The programs are especially notable in that they not only incorporate specific activities that were previously absent but also reflect the participation of youth in the decision-making process. Four of these programs will be reviewed here.

Auto Center. The planning and creation of an auto center has involved young people since its inception. They helped select a location and participated in such activities as the installation of electricity and plumbing, under supervision of city inspectors. The program permits a youth to use one of the stalls in the auto center for 25 cents an hour. For this fee, he can use a complete set of automotive tools and receive expert help in body work or mechanical problems from "youth consultants"—usually local junior college students with an aptitude in these areas. Each stall is sponsored by a service club, thus ensuring continued interest by formal groups within the community.

Teen Center. The creation of the teen center was directed by council members and youth from the community, whose participation ranged from overall planning to painting and renovating of the center building. The center is under the direction of a committee of 25 teenagers who plan social activities and formulate teen center policy. They make their own rules for conduct, work schedules, clean-up and policing for social functions.

Employment. The employment program includes a cooperative effort with the Department of Employment. Representatives from that agency appear at the youth council office daily to provide employment counseling.

A course in baby-sitting, with training by the Red Cross, is another component of the youth employment program. Persons needing qualified baby-sitters can obtain names by calling the youth council. The course has been well publicized and has been enthusiastically received by adults in the community. Many have become aware of the overall programs of the council through this service.

Still another component is the development of "youth business," through a house-to-house canvass of 7,000 homes. Jobs in child care and garden work (for example) have been created in this way. While registration of jobs and referral of applicants are made through the Department of Employment, canvassing is done by the youths.

Motorcycle Club. One of the important youthful subcultures centers around motorcycles. It was found that young motorcycle riders, frequently identified by adults as deviant, would welcome a motorcycle club. Consequently, several teenagers on the council and in the community joined to create a formal organization. They sought and obtained sponsorship from the local Junior Chamber of Commerce, drew up a set of bylaws for their organization, established rules for conduct and behavior and opened a bank account. Both adults and teenagers have spent thousands of hours on motorcycle activities and we suspect that there has been a redefinition of the motorcycle rider, formerly called "deviant."

Many other similar programs could be enumerated but the programs themselves are not as important as what they signify. In our research and demonstration project, we set out to bring the adult and youthful worlds closer together and to have youth participate in decision-making activities. We wanted to create an environment in which modification and redefinition of deviance could occur. In addition, we wanted an environment in which a community could increase its capacity to absorb its deviance by developing a latent sense or feeling of community. Success or failure cannot, of course, be equated with numbers or types of programs except as they relate to these goals.

READING 16

Delinquency and the Youth Culture:
Upper- and Middle-Class Boys

Edmund W. Vaz

Juvenile delinquency among upper-class boys remains shrouded in mystery. So scanty is our knowledge of this group that a public image of the upper-class adolescent is non-existent, and not the barest trace nor suspicion is available of him as delinquent. Although the hard knot of delinquency (behavior that is apt to try any public tolerance) is located in the bottom levels of the working class, limited studies (using self-reported techniques) have revealed delinquency throughout the class structure.[1] But nothing is known about the delinquency of boys who attend expensive private schools. Knowledge of the informal handling and special treatment by officials of upper-class boys, the inaccessibility of upper-class institutions, and the absence of a socially recognized image of the upper-class youth as delinquent has, perhaps, discouraged systematic theory and research. But if knowledge is to accumulate in this area, sociological research must pinpoint these boys for study. Both their legitimate and illegitimate conduct must be uncovered and made known, the frequency of their acts, the style that it takes and the conditions under which it occurs. Are there subcultural dimensions to upper-class delinquency? To what extent are these boys peer oriented? Is their delinquency related to the system of roles and expectations among these boys and to the social status of schools (both public and private) which they attend? Are the socially approved interests and activities of these boys the source of their delinquencies? To what degree are certain kinds of delinquency institutionalized among these youths? Answers to these kinds of questions (and these are only a few) are needed if we are to understand and explain the behavior of these boys.

The major focus of this paper is on the attitudes, delinquent acts, and selected aspects of the youth culture of upper-class boys attending private and public schools. But there is considerable overlap in the attitudes and behavior of upper- and middle-class boys, and a comparative analysis of this material is presented. Little is known about the legal and illegal behavior of these boys which is good reason for cautious speculation. Our discussion takes us beyond the data offered here; however, an effort is made to bring together and expand some of the ideas discussed in previous work. [2]

As part of a larger study an anonymous questionnaire was used to gather data from boys (aged 13 to over 19) in five public schools and one upper-class boys' private school located in five Canadian communities. This group consists of all boys in the secondary grades at the time of our visits. However, this paper reports on boys aged 15-19 years only. The communities vary in size from an industrial city of over 100,000 population to residential suburbs and townships. The public schools are situated in typically middle-class areas, the private school in an upper middle-class residential area. Questionnaires were administered under similar conditions in all schools. Multiple methods were used to guarantee anonymity of respondents and necessary precautions were taken to insure honesty and reliability of responses.

Most boys who attend private schools come from the upper end of the social and economic spectrum. [3] Today this includes boys from upper and upper-middle socioeconomic strata. Few middle-class families can afford to send their children to expensive private schools. [4] In our analysis three criteria were used for the socioeconomic classification of subjects: father's occupation, father's level of education and the size of organization in which father works. Three socioeconomic categories were established from the Blishen Occupational Scale. [5] Using father's occupation, subjects were initially classified into one of three categories according to the Blishen Scale. Cases that were unclassifiable (where father's occupation was omitted or reported ambiguously) were reviewed and classified according to father's education level. Respondents whose father had undertaken postgraduate university training were classified into category 2; those who had completed university (e.g., B.A., B.Sc., etc.) without postgraduate work were grouped into category 3. No difficulty was encountered in the classification of respondents into category

1. All category 1 respondents correspond precisely with the occupations listed in the corresponding category on the Blishen
Scale. In this paper categories 1 and 2 are grouped and termed
"upper class"; category 3 subjects are hereafter referred to as
"middle class." The private school studied in this project does not
likely recruit students from the highest reaches of the upper
socioeconomic strata. Very likely our private and public school
"upper class" subjects come from mainly lower upper and upwardly mobile, upper middle-class socioeconomic levels.

A youth culture is not endemic to a society, but is apt to
develop under special conditions. Institutional change in the
social and economic spheres of Canada and the United States has
made possible the emergence of a relatively prestigious youth
culture. Cityward migration from rural areas and the decreasing
size of families have characterized both countries.[6] The growth of
unionization, which helps protect the semi-skilled and skilled from
competition   from   new   recruits,   and   the   growth   of
professionalization which makes entry into these occupations
dependent upon "educational qualifications" have helped foster
the almost universal consensus that children should remain in
school and be kept out of the labor market.[7] Thus, more children
have remained in school for longer periods of time which has
helped generate a youth culture.

Change has occurred also in family size, role structure,[8] and
in the redistribution of power in the family. This has given greater
individuality and freedom to family members and fostered th
proliferation of peer-group contacts among young people. Furthermore, there has occurred an increasing "democratization" of
family life in rural, but predominantly in urban areas with the
resultant erosion of roles governing parent-child relationships in
particular,[9] and adult-child contacts in general. Parents now
experience considerable anxiety and uncertainty in the raising of
children.[10] They turn to contemporaries for advice, to the mass
media, to "experts," and ultimately, in desperation, to the
children themselves.[11] Schools have grown increasingly "permissive" (reflecting change in educational "philosophies") and
lack traditional authority. Baltzell writes, "The changes at the
/private/ school since the war have been far-reaching and
progressive. A less puritanical and more permissive atmosphere
has been consciously created in order to set a more democratic,

tolerant, and possibly other-directed tone to school life."[12] In some instances power seems to have been transferred from teachers to pupils.[13] The vacillation in attitude and policy of teachers and high schools towards students, the continual revision of curricula and standards, and the seemingly indiscriminate experimentation with teaching "techniques" mirror the vast social change. However, it also suggests, perhaps, not so much a commitment to "progressive" education and "scientific findings" as is often alleged, but a desperate search for purpose and stability in education.

A latent function of structural change in society has been the emergent prominence of the adolescent. As a target of exploitation adolescents have been cajoled, flattered, idealized, and have quickly become victim to the glamorizing significance of active participation in the teenage culture.[14] Of course this has greatly influenced the production requirements of big business. But the adaptability of corporate industry through publicity and the mass media has promoted the "needs" of adolescents, and reflects the strategic significance of sustaining the youth culture for the general economy.

Given a prominence perhaps hitherto unknown among young people, the public image of the adolescent has become his own role model. The undue attention and publicity given the fads and collective displays of teenagers and young people, besides their vociferous commentary on the "social ills" of society, serve to alert them to their own conduct and pronouncements as a growing source of power and recognition. Highly sensitive to adolescent affairs, almost any event or opportunity which conceivably might increase their publicity or improve their collective self-image seems to be legitimate prey for the teenage challenge. This has spawned a variety of groups among young people, many of which are perhaps irresponsible, often delinquent. Because standards and norms are in rapid flux, final judgment of these youths and their actions is often postponed. To be a teenager today is to be supremely valuable, and adolescents know this. The status, rights and obligations of the adolescent have become legitimized, morally valid.

The notion of a mass youth culture suggests that it cuts across social class lines and that the majority of young people are unable to escape its dominant themes, interests and values. The "world" of upper-class boys is no longer all of a single weave. For an ever increasing number of adolescents the contemporary high school has become the great leveling ground where differences become largely neutralized, students homogenized. [15] Aloofness is the shortest path to social pariahdom among teenagers. Once a boy enters high school he becomes quickly absorbed with the interests and attitudes of peers and teachers from all social strata, and peers expect enthusiastic participation in their activities.

Not even the private school can escape the mainstream of the teenage culture. Although these institutions often emphasize training in leadership and "character formation" their purpose is subverted by the prevailing youth culture. Today there is often close coordination between private and public schools in education associations, outside programs and intellectual contests. Also the private school population is becoming increasingly diverse, and upper-class "courting mores" have changed, no longer is "steady dating" considered "middle class." [16] However, all this does not deny the importance of social class for understanding adolescent behavior. [17] But class variations in teenage conduct are apt to be more a matter of emphasis than of kind, [18] and in part mirror their respective adult class cultures. Typically this will be seen in the styles of teenage behavior from different classes. Nor does this preclude the emergence of adolescent subcultures, cultural pockets of values, interests and norms sufficiently distinct to set them off from their parent class culture. Although little Canadian data are available, some of these subcultures may be of a delinquent nature.

Previous studies have shown clearly that middle-class boys are often peer oriented, and that they are interested primarily in non-intellectual socially-oriented activities. [19] Although our information is limited to three items it gives us a brief glimpse of these dimensions of upper-class adolescent life and allows us to compare upper and middle-class youths. The first item was used to establish the degree to which these lads were oriented to peers and parents. We asked: "Let us say that you had always wanted to belong to a special club in high school and then finally you were asked to join. But you discovered that your parents did not approve of the club. And since your best friend was not asked to join you would have to break up with your best friend. Which of these things would be hardest for you to take?" [20]

Table 1 makes clear that all three groups (especially private and public school upper-class boys) appear more oriented toward peers than parents. This seems to be a common characteristic among contemporary youth.[21]

The next item enquired into the dating habits of these boys. Each adolescent was asked the following question: "On the average how often do you take a girl out during the week?"

These data indicate that upper-class boys (private and public school both) more often date girls than do middle-class boys.[22] Eighty-five percent of private school upper-class boys date at least once a week; less than 53 percent of the other groups do so. The largest percentage of each group dates once a week; proportionately about twice as many private as public school boys date this often.

The following item provides some indication of the general interests and youth culture orientation of these teenagers. Each boy was asked to check those items which applied "to most of the boys here at school." Table 3 presents the selected items in rank order of response frequency.

Table 3 suggests five major points: (a) each group of boys is strongly oriented to girls, sports, cars, and "fun and kicks," (b) proportionately more private than public school boys are interested in "fun and kicks," (c) cars are considerably more important to public than private school boys, (d) proportionately more private than public school youths report that boys study hard in school, and (e) correlatively, public school lads are less concerned with academic matters than are private school boys.

The responses of these boys suggest a commonality of interest among them all. The evidence that considerably more private school boys report that boys "study hard" mirrors the enforced emphasis on academic matters in private school. However, this does not preclude these boys from being influenced by the youth culture. In contrast, the public high school is often the focus of youth culture events, but typically lacks a strong scholastic orientation.

DELINQUENCY AMONG PRIVATE AND PUBLIC SCHOOL UPPER- AND MIDDLE-CLASS BOYS

In this paper the delinquent acts of boys are self-reported and are taken from an anonymous checklist of behavior items included in

TABLE 1. Peer Orientation of Private and Public School Upper- and Middle-Class Boys

Response Category	Percentages for Boys Aged 15-19		
	Upper Class		Middle Class
	Private	Public	Public
Breaking with your best friend	69.0	60.8	54.9
Parents disapproval	31.0	38.5	43.5
Non-responses	0.0	0.7	1.6
Total	100.0	100.0	100.0
N =	58	288	428

TABLE 2. Time Spent Dating Among Private and Public School Upper- and Middle-Class Boys

Response Category	Percentages for Boys Aged 15-19		
	Upper Class		Middle Class
	Private	Public	Public
Twice or more times a week	25.4	20.1	19.2
About once a week	59.3	31.9	27.3
Hardly ever or never	15.3	47.7	53.5
Non-responses	0.0	0.3	0.0
Total	100.0	100.0	100.0
N =	59	287	428

TABLE 3. Orientation of Private and Public School Upper- and Middle-Class Boys

Response Category	Percentages for Boys Aged 15-19		
	Upper Class		Middle Class
	Private	Public	Public
Interested in girls	77.9	74.3	77.6
Sports-minded	74.5	65.6	70.3
Out for "fun and kicks"	57.6	49.3	50.9
Crazy about cars	52.5	59.0	65.0
Studies hard	49.1	23.3	30.2
Snobs	28.8	13.5	18.5
Not much interested in school	25.4	37.1	33.1
Non-responses	0.0	0.0	4.0
N =	59	288	428
		$P =$ .905	

a larger questionnaire. Each item is a violation of the law or an offense which could result in official action being taken.

Table 4 indicates that of the 17 delinquency items, 14 are reported by proportionately more upper-class private school boys, two items (car theft and driving a car without a license) by upper-class public school boys, and one item (drunkenness) by middle-class boys. Two items, "serious" theft and "remained out all night without parents' permission," are disproportionately reported by upper-class private school boys. The responses of public school groups (upper and middle class) are very similar on almost each item. A few further points are noteworthy. Petty theft is reported by over 70 percent and 64 percent of upper- and middle-class boys respectively. We suspect that this type of theft is practiced by all boys, at one time or another, irrespective of social class. Stealing for "fun" is not restricted to lower-class boys. It is more than this. The values of adventure, courage and masculinity are integral components of the male role. Notwithstanding differential class emphasis, they are taught early by all parents, and are something a youngster ought not to overlook to be accepted as a boy. Among boys courage is often an important indicator of masculinity, and petty theft and varying kinds of vandalism usually validate a youth's claim to "manliness." In a private school where girls are absent the pressures to demonstrate one's masculinity are perhaps at a premium, and situations multiply where these kinds of behavior are encouraged, which helps explain why private school boys are more "delinquent" on most items. The data reveal that petty theft, "serious" theft, fist-fighting, and stealing money are considerably more prevalent among these boys. In the public schools the daily presence of girls very likely serves as social controls, not because girls are especially moral, but because youngsters will neither know (since theirs is a predominantly boy's "world") nor believe that girls steal, and will look upon them as virtuous. Girls define stealing as wrong, and although young boys may ridicule the femininity of girls they will likely respect their virtue and curtail their behavior accordingly.

Our data on petty theft are likely a reflection (in part) of the earlier years of these boys, but as they assume more sophisticated roles, petty theft, vandalism, fist-fighting, and stealing money decrease markedly. We note that gambling, taking a drink, driving beyond the speed limit, and driving without a license, assume

TABLE 4. Self-Reported Delinquent Behavior of Private and Public School Upper- and Middle-Class Boys

Type of Offense	Percent Admitting Offense (15-19 years)			Percent Admitting Offense More than Once or Twice		
	Upper Class		Middle Class	Upper Class		Middle Class
	Private	Public	Public	Public	Private	Public
Taken little things of value (between 12 and !50) which did not belong to you	37.9	15.5	15.2	8.6	4.8	2.3
Remained out all night without parents' permission	42.4	27.3	25.9	11.9	11.1	8.4
Gambled for money at cards, dice, or some other game	69.5	68.8	65.4	30.5	35.8	38.8
Taken a car without owner's knowledge	10.0	13.9	11.3	1.6	3.1	3.0
Destroyed or damaged public or private property of any kind	67.8	52.3	52.3	23.8	14.6	14.7
Taken a glass of beer, wine, or liquor at a party or elsewhere with your friends	72.9	65.0	66.4	44.1	34.6	36.2
Tried to be intimate with a member of the opposite sex	49.2	39.2	38.3	15.3	18.4	17.3
Driven a car without a driver's license	59.4	63.2	61.5	30.6	28.9	22.8
Taken little things that did not belong to you	74.5	71.5	64.7	27.1	19.8	15.4
Skipped school without a legitimate excuse	57.7	41.0	41.6	17.0	12.2	14.5
Driven beyond the speed limit	69.4	57.1	48.8	59.3	42.1	38.6
Engaged in a fist fight with another boy	63.8	53.0	58.2	13.8	8.0	9.6
Been feeling "high" from drinking beer, wine, or liquor	37.2	38.9	40.4	22.0	17.8	29.4
Broken into or tried to break and enter a building with the intention of stealing	16.8	9.0	7.7	3.3	.07	1.1
Bought or tried to buy beer, wine or liquor from a store or adult	33.9	27.1	24.5	17.0	11.4	12.6
Taken money of any amount from someone or place which did not belong to you	45.8	36.8	29.2	11.9	10.4	4.7
Placed on school probation or expelled from school	13.6	7.3	4.7	3.5	1.0	1.1
N =	59	288	428 P = .956			

279

more importance for older boys. This might be termed "sociable delinquency" since it tends to emerge from predominantly "social" events. Finally, the data suggest that breaking and entering, being placed on school probation, automobile theft, and purchasing liquor, are relatively unpopular delinquencies among upper- and middle-class boys.

ATTITUDES OF PRIVATE AND PUBLIC SCHOOL UPPER AND MIDDLE-CLASS BOYS TOWARD SELECTED YOUTH CULTURE ACTIVITIES

To speak of a youth culture is to refer to a relatively coherent, integrated system of attitudes, norms and values that relates to a distinguishable body of interaction. Our material has suggested that upper- and middle-class boys both are peer oriented and concerned mainly with non-academic, fun-laden interests, and that their self-reported delinquencies are often "social" in quality.[23]

The roles that individuals occupy lead them to classify objects, persons and activities in appropriate ways. Customarily the individual defines and evaluates everything in his environment in terms of the significance which it has for him and what he proposes to do with it. When attitudes are integrated about some general class of behavior or social "objects" and include an affective conception of the desirable properties of the behavior or "objects" we may legitimately refer to values.[24] If we think of values falling along a continuum, at one end we might have those values that are "true matters of conscience," at the other, values that deal with norms of expedience and technical efficiency.[25] Not all values and rules that circumscribe adolescent behavior are of the former kind, nor does their violation evoke feelings of guilt. But certain kinds of conduct traditionally defined immoral such as drinking, gambling, physical intimacy and sexual intercourse remain relatively serious matters in the eyes of the community although it seems increasingly unable to control them.

We believe that during an earlier period these kinds of behavior very likely generated feelings of guilt, and provoked considerable anxiety among young people—more so than today.[26] Both the attitudes and behavior of young people have very likely undergone considerable change in these matters. We suggest that never before have these kinds of deviance been practiced on such a wide scale among middle- and upper-class youths. And there is little reason to suspect that adolescents of a previous period were more adept at concealing their delinquencies. Firm family controls and the social organization of their everyday lives likely diverted these young people from extensive peer-group relationships and activities which, in turn, precluded them from engaging in widespread deviance of this nature. Discussing young people of the past the Lynds write, "*[I]n* 1890 a 'well-brought up' boy and girl were commonly forbidden to sit together in the dark. . . . Buggy-riding in 1890 allowed only a narrow range of mobility; three to eight were generally accepted hours for riding, and being out after eight-thirty without a chaperon was largely forbidden."[27] As for sex, Frederick Allen writes, "boys and girls knew they were expected to behave with perfect propriety towards one another and only rarely did they fail to do so"; indeed, boys followed a code under whose terms "a kiss was virtually tantamount to a proposal of marriage."[28] How odd these remarks seem when compared with accounts of the behavior and attitudes of contemporary adolescents. Indeed, the absence of anything resembling a youth culture in the past prevented adolescents from successfully claiming legitimacy for many of the behavior patterns accepted (albeit, sometimes reluctantly) by contemporary parents. Today, activities such as drinking, physical intimacy and other forms of heterosexual conduct are less often true "matters of conscience," and although adolescents are not "morally freewheeling" their attitudes towards these types of conduct point to the emergence of a morality over which they have greater control.

As the youth culture develops and acquires greater importance in the lives of adolescents, particular kinds of conduct— some delinquent—become increasingly institutionalized. The large number of boys who do not disapprove of certain types of delinquency suggests an increase in the institutionalization of this activity, although this is perhaps not yet widespread. This is not to suggest the structural collapse in our system of morals. Nor is the gradual change in morality an adventitious dimension of the youth culture, limited to a segment of especially delinquent boys. Expectedly, the attitudes and values of the youth culture tend towards greater inclusiveness. There appears a configuration of relatively consistent attitudes and sentiments towards delinquent types of situation which reflect what is proper and improper, virtuous and wicked, ugly and beautiful among these youths. This is both cause and consequence of the larger structural change taking place—an emerging general system of rules and values congruent with the increasingly permissive forms of adolescent conduct. Thus its principal function is its practicality.

The following data, gathered from a set of five items, are hardly definitive, but suggest a direction for future research. Each item is designed as a "life-situation" geared to the level of everyday reality of adolescents and assumed to be typical of the youth culture. The closer one approaches the level of interpersonal relations, the press of circumstances and the fear of consequences become more immediate conditions of conduct. Perhaps these conditions are likely to be more meaningful to the teenager and thereby elicit attitudes correspondingly valid.

Table 5 indicates that approximately 75 percent of all groups approve of this behavior. As many as 93 percent of the private school upper-class boys find this acceptable. "Having a couple of beers" appears so widely acceptable one suspects that it is a normative pattern among these boys.

A second item focused on "social" drinking in the company of girls. It is customary, especially among the middle classes, that masculine kinds of conduct (e.g., drinking liquor) will be restricted in the presence of women. Responses to the following item point in this direction.

In this instance it is clear that the major difference in responses is attributable to private school boys who dispropor-tionately favor "spending an evening like this." Yet approval is not limited to this group; over 53 percent of all boys (upper and middle class) approve of this activity.

Among middle- and upper-class families (especially in large urban areas) light drinking in the home among older adolescents is often permitted, seldom condemned, although drunkenness is strongly disapproved. Since a relatively large percentage of boys approve of drinking we should not expect to find drunkenness among peers tabooed altogether.

If private school upper-class boys strongly approve of boys drinking in the company of girls, proportionately few (27 percent) condemn boys who get drunk occasionally. Although there is

TABLE 5. Attitudes of Private and Public School Upper- and Middle-Class Boys Toward "Social" Drinking

Ralph and a couple of his 12th grade classmates have nothing to do Friday evening. They decide to go for a drive together. There isn't much doing in town, so they return to Ralph's house for a couple of beers, and shoot the breeze together. Later the boys go straight home to bed. How do you feel about this? (Check one.)

	Upper Class		Middle Class
	Private	Public	Public
I do not approve that they spend an evening this way.	6.8	26.7	24.1
It is alright, I guess, to spend an evening this way.	30.5	30.6	33.9
It is OK to spend an evening this way.	62.7	42.4	41.1
Non-responses	0.0	0.3	0.9
Total	100.0	100.0	100.0
N =	59	288	428

TABLE 6. Attitudes of Private and Public School Upper- and Middle-Class Boys Toward "Social" Drinking With Girls

John, Jean, Frank, and Mary are grade 12 high school students. Saturday evening they go out driving together. Everyone is friendly, laughing and joking. Later the boys and girls begin necking in the car. Finally they all decide to return to John's house for a couple of beers and to listen to records. How do you feel about spending an evening like this? (Check one.)

	Upper Class		Middle Class
	Private	Public	Public
I do not approve that they should spend an evening this way.	23.7	42.0	43.0
It is alright, I guess, to spend an evening this way.	40.7	35.4	32.7
It is OK to spend an evening this way.	35.6	22.6	24.$
Non-responses	0.0	0.0	0.2
Total	100.0	100.0	100.0
N =	59	288	428

TABLE 7.   Attitudes of Private and Public School Upper- and Middle-Class Boys Toward Drunkenness

You are attending a party at your friend's house Saturday night. His parents are away and he is having some of the boys and girls over. Everyone is enjoying himself. There are records and dancing. Cokes and beer are available and there is food to eat. Later in the evening one of the boys appears to be feeling "high" from drinking too much beer. He is *not* behaving rudely except that he is feeling "high." How do you feel about this boy feeling "high?" (Check one.)

	Upper Class		Middle Class
	Private	Public	Public
I do not approve of his actions.	27.1	46.6	47.4
It is alright, I guess, since he is at a party.	33.9	19.4	22.9
It is OK. It happens to a lot of fellows.	39.0	34.0	29.2
Non-responses	0.0	0.0	0.5
Total	100.0	100.0	100.0
N =	59	288	428

greater similarity in the responses of the public school groups, over 50 percent of all groups approve of this behavior. It is very likely that parties are "special" events among all adolescents during which new attitudes and sentiments are expected and special sets of rules are operative. Under these circumstances drinking and "feeling high" may fall easily within the range of acceptable behavior. At the same time events such as parties and dances are integral to the youth culture and, as the data have shown, there is continuity (with other events) in the attitudes of these boys.

Today heterosexual relationships and dating among young people are considered "healthy" activities, and are strongly encouraged (even during preteen years) by adults. Certain kinds of intimacy such as kissing and "necking" ("once it doesn't go too far") are permitted. Certainly among the upper and middle socioeconomic strata events such as parties, dances and "socials" are organized for early teenage participation. Given these conditions it would be surprising to find many boys (irrespective of social class) who disapprove of some kind of intimacy on a first date. Since boys are very likely to successfully challenge the rules of behavior, advanced kinds of intimacy (as suggested in the item) are apt to be acceptable among all groups. Table 8 shows that differences among groups are small, and that over 63 percent of all groups approve, at least conditionally, that to "neck and pet" on a first date is acceptable.

We have suggested that a change in morality is emerging among these boys and much of our data points this way. But to talk of a developing youth culture and a change in morality is to imply a course of social change, a period of transition during which relatively stable values, attitudes and norms of an earlier era are being recast. It does not imply that all segments of the culture structure change at an equal rate, nor that the values, attitudes and sentiments of young people have been transformed overnight. Given our Puritan heritage some especially "sensitive" areas, such as sexual conduct (rooted in deeply felt values), are perhaps more resistant to change. But as young people gain greater license from formal adult control, and assume the management of their own affairs, they shoulder greater responsibility for their sexual conduct. In the process their sentiments and attitudes are reshaped; regulatory codes evolve, which in turn influence the conduct of sexual matters.

The data reveal that a considerable percentage of these boys approve of relatively advanced stages of physical intimacy. This is

TABLE 8.   Attitudes of Private and Public School Upper- and Middle-Class Boys Toward Sexual Intimacy on First Date

Janet and Bob are in grade 12 in high school. They know each other because they are in the smae biology class. But Saturday night will be their *first* date together. After the dance, on the way home, Bob stops the car and kisses Janet. Soon he kisses her again and they begin to neck and pet. How do you feel about this? (Check one.)

	Upper Class		Middle Class
	Private	Public	Public
I do not approve of their actions.	37.3	35.4	31.8
It is alright, I guess, how they wish to act.	40.7	40.3	46.0
It is OK.	22.0	23.6	21.5
Non-responses	0.0	0.7	0.7
Total	100.0	100.0	100.0
N =	59	288	428

not to say that they advocate sexual promiscuity. Sexual congress remains a delicate issue for these boys even with girls of "bad reputation." Table 9 shows that the majority of upper-class boys and 48 percent of middle-class boys disapprove of the described behavior, and that only about 10-12 percent approve outright. Yet 34 percent of the private school boys, and as many as 42 percent of middle-class boys, agree that sexual intercourse is more or less acceptable.

For centuries in Western society sexual intercourse has been associated with affection.[29] Emergent rules governing sexual patterns among young people are influenced by both previously established and contemporary adult values and conduct. Among boys coitus continues to be associated largely with affectionate involvement. In high school, girls of "easy virtue" are apt to serve as relatively acceptable means of sexual release for a small segment of "outsiders," atypical older adolescents. Perhaps these girls have always served this service. But among adolescents generally sexual intercourse is likely associated with romantic love, and under special conditions is normatively tolerated. "Going steady" certainly legitimates sexual experimentation among teenagers. Perhaps sexual intercourse with love brings little discredit. Unlike the past when girls could "fall from virtue" today they are more apt to slip into womanhood—with confidence.

TABLE 9.   Attitudes of Private and Public School Upper- and Middle-Class Boys Toward Sexual Intercourse

Carol is a good-looking, grade 12 student. But she has a bad reputation throughout the school. She is known to be pretty free and easy. Her classmate Robert takes her out on a date Saturday night. Before returning home Robert tries to get intimate (go the limit) with her, and *she* does *not* object. How do you feel about Robert's actions? (Check one.)

	Upper Class		Middle Class
	Private	Public	Public
I do not approve of Robert's actions.	55.9	50.3	48.1
Robert's actions are alright, I guess, since Carol did not object.	33.9	38.2	42.1
Robert's actions are OK.	10.2	11.5	9.8
Total	100.0	100.0	100.0
N =	59	288	428

DISCUSSION [30]

In the past the restricted home life of upper-class children precluded the proliferation of peer-group relationships, and a youth culture as we know it did not exist. The rights and obligations of young people were confined to relatively specific age-sex roles, and the unequivocality of parental roles was well established. Having few outside contacts and associations the child was family-reared (often by a governess who over-emphasized patriarchal and class values),[31] and later in the less secular private schools which served principally to ascribe status and socialize their youthful populations. At this time sex was a matter largely hidden from children and physical intimacy among young people was tantamount to sin. Adult dictates for adolescent conduct were entrenched in Anglo-Saxon Protestant morality—a system of rules and values especially functional for a relatively stable class structure where legitimate authority resided in adult positions in the home, school and church. Goals for adolescents were relatively clear-cut and parents believed in the ideals which were taught their children and knew what direction behavior should take. Under these circumstances children were apt to be reared according to widely institutionalized rules, and parental dictates were likely meaningful to existing conditions of adolescent life.

In a fast changing technological world the upper classes have become increasingly "democratized" and heterogeneous. Today adolescent life is much less divorced from extra-class contacts, and ambiguity is evident in parent-child relationships. The "increased concern of parents with *understanding* their children" very likely reflects a desperate bid by parents to do *something*[32] in the face of their moral ambiguity and the paucity of clear-cut rules for governing their offspring. In many cases schools and other organized clubs have taken over parental duties usually to the satisfaction of parents. In private schools regimentation is enforced by sets of rules for parents to follow with their teenage children. Furthermore, adult groups tend to support the values and sentiments that circumscribe "progressive" socially-oriented education and often endorse the institutionalized practices (dances, parties, dating, "socials," etc.) allegedly conducive to the development of "social competence" and adjustment of the child. In turn this helps sustain the adolescent culture.

The problem of rules is an important feature that helps explain delinquency among middle- and upper-class children. Rules refer to classes of events, and as such are difficult to apply to specific situations. They can never be "legislated" (even within the family) to cover each act of the child for every occasion. Nor do we deny the need for discretion. Where uniformity characterizes adolescent roles, and where teenage activities are comparatively limited, widespread institutionalized rules may be more suitable guides for behavior. Such is not the case today. Often parental rules for contemporary adolescents seem especially inappropriate to the kinds and diversity of youth culture activities. For parents to encourage, and thereby legitimate in the child's eyes, active youth culture participation with only a blurred blueprint for behavior, is to leave uncharted a vast range of events for the child. Moreover it is risky to rely on discretion when rules are vague. Under such conditions motives become the sole criteria for establishing deviance. But motives are not always meaningful to others. Within the same social class failure to appreciate another's motives reflects a difference in socio-cultural "worlds." When a teenager explains his wrongdoing by reporting, "We were just havin' fun," adults often consider this meaningless or trivial. But fun can be serious business. What is trivial to the adult is often of consequence to the adolescent. Of course motives are often suspect as when a high school student insists on wearing his hair long for "matters of principle."

When parents rely largely on the discretion of their children there is the presumption that it will not be used towards "bad" ends. But goals often emerge from ongoing situations. Social behavior is a progression of interrelated acts which rotate about the completion of goals. But usually goals are unclear, and in social interaction goals and means are oftentimes fused; what was momentarily a goal the next moment becomes the means towards new goals. Coitus among teenagers is apt to emerge from a relatively prolonged, emotionally packed process under specific conditions. At no point need either partner orient his (or her) actions initially to that end. Oftentimes the final state of affairs is a "shock" to both partners. In such a case motives are not directed towards "bad" ends. When the teenager explains, "I don't know how it happened" he is telling the only truth he knows, that is, sexual intercourse was not his original intention. Where intermediate goals and means are fused in process they are not easily distinguished nor readily recalled. It seems that rules must set limits to discretion. Where rules are unclear, and parents are ambiguous about their roles, yet report (as one father stated) that, "We trust our daughter,"[33] this probably reflects more hope than confidence that "nothing will happen."

But unlike most children in the past, adolescents are no longer subject only to adult rules. Once a youth engages in the teenage culture he becomes partly subject to its norms. In contrast to parental rules peer-group norms have their origin in the shared mundane experiences of teenagers, and refer to relatively specific situations. Although the youth culture is especially susceptible to fads and fashions it would be wrong to characterize it only in these terms. The normative system not only influences its content, it implies and imposes limits on what is considered proper and improper, moral and immoral, and helps regulate what form social relationships will take. It is commonplace that youths look to peers in matters of fashion, but they are also peer-oriented in academic output, sexual matters, dating and drinking patterns and other delinquent activities. These differentially institutionalized norms reflect a newly emerging morality among adolescents besides implying role expectations of those who claim "membership" in the youth culture.

A rule that is useful and appropriate at one time and for one purpose may well become useless and inappropriate at another time for the same purpose. For example, the broad prescription, "Be a good boy at the party," is apt to be much less meaningful today when applied to typical adolescent experiences. Yet these are precisely the kinds of gross indicators used by parents to guide their children. Does it mean that a boy ought not to hold hands with his girl friend, dance close, kiss good-night, practice different types of kissing and physical intimacy? Perhaps at this juncture peer-group norms become functional for youths, since they relate more precisely to their everyday "needs" and experiences, and also help relieve some of the anxiety of social interaction. Each of the above steps possesses its own shared understandings, and is important in the dating game, but parents are apt to overlook the normative significance of these "details"; rules are either nonexistent or go unspoken because parents are ambiguous about their validity.

To suggest that the freedom of today's adolescents is a result of their manifest maturity and evident sense of responsibility is false. We hold varying expectations about the ability of young people to police their own behavior and exert self-control. Responsibility and self-control are socially defined expectations and obligations of the roles that we occupy and they vary accordingly. But where uncertainty characterizes role expectations, and where the general norms governing adult-child relationships are under strain, this precludes agreed-upon criteria for evaluation. Adamant approval or disapproval of typical teenage conduct is apt to be an isolated posture among middle- and upper-class parents since it mirrors role confidence and moral certainty. Parents will approve of the value of dating yet be of two minds regarding "heavy necking"; they will tolerate light beer drinking in the home yet be uncertain whether they are "doing the right thing"; they will endorse social events among young people, but reluctantly tolerate "close" dancing. At the same time no parent wishes upon his child the role of social pariah. Terms are cultural inventions and change over time. Self-control and responsibility are terms no longer easily defined. The adolescent who refuses to participate in typical teenage events because he defines them "irresponsible" is apt to be considered a case for the psychiatrist, not a model of "responsible" conduct. Since our conception of an individual's responsibility for his behavior often corresponds to his self-conception, we might wonder at the standards according to which the contemporary teenager forms his self-image. The ambiguous responses of parents are hardly conducive to the growth of the adolescent self-conception in such terms. Among young people operating criteria for self-evaluation are likely peer-centered.

The conviction in one's own sense of responsibility, "moral fibre" and self-discipline is handmaiden also to the kind of socialization that one experiences. When children are reared according to firm moral principles that highlight "character strength" and "moral fibre," as young men and women they will be expected to demonstrate self-control. Moreover, the social structure will tend to facilitate role conformity. Social distance in relationships may be highly valued, peer-group relationships will be minimal, the variety of adolescent roles restricted, and expectations will tend to overlap. Heterosexual contacts will be discouraged and physical intimacy strongly condemned. Dating in the popular sense is comparatively unknown. And behavior is likely defined in categorical terms; children will be either good or bad.

Today children are seldom reared according to clearly defined moral tenets, and the value of industry, moral integrity and "character strength" are often taught in a whisper.[34] If educational practices, rooted in fingertip awareness of moral considerations have grown wobbly, social cues have gained significantly in the socialization of children.[35] So alien have these values become that they carry an odd ring when discussing adolescent behavior. Since they are not crucial criteria for peer evaluation, the contemporary adolescent seldom defines himself in these terms.

This does not imply that children are reared in a moral vacuum. Remnants of the Puritan ethic still comprise the hazy moral milieu of most middle- and upper-class families. But in the midst of rapid social change moral principles are difficult to teach convincingly. Given the danger of being thought radical in matters of propriety, comportment, and affairs political, it is perhaps equally ill-advised to risk being different in morals. With this kind of training one's "moral fibre" becomes flexible, easily adjustable to emerging peer-group requirements. During this period of transition, when values and attitudes are still unclear in society, the majority of youths do not yet experience coitus nor do white-collar boys often engage in victimizing delinquency. We suggest that adolescents seldom undergo traumatic experiences in moral matters; stages of physical intimacy are learned through role occupancy and are usually taken comfortably in stride according to normative expectations. Moral flexibility allows for easy adaptation to normative teenage activities and relationships, and conformity helps fortify operating norms.

None of this denies the considerable compliance of upper-class adolescents with parental demands. Indeed teenage obedience remains necessary and helps the teenager adapt to the youth culture. Recurrent compliance with parental wishes helps convince parents of the responsibility, maturity and self-control of their children.[36] The comparative absence of assaultive delinquency among middle- and upper-class children or the fact that adolescents often stabilize their physical intimacy at a point prior to coitus does not, however, necessarily reflect special self-control. But generally parents are unable to explain behavior in other terms. Reluctant to admit loss of control over their children, and the felt moral confusion of their own roles, they often cling to the time-worn concepts of "character strength," "moral fibre," and self-control. More likely, however, teenage conduct reflects conformity to operating peer-group norms which cover a wide variety of situations, relationships and stages of relationship. Intense participation in peer-group events increases sensitivity to cues, behavior subtleties, and norms of action. Coitus between adolescents is neither "accident" nor loss of self-control, but behavior which falls within a range of relatively permissible acts. If coitus is not proscribed among peers, "going steady" serves to cushion condemnation should it become public knowledge—and teenagers know this. This suggests a further elasticity in the rules governing the conditions under which sexual intercourse between adolescents is partially tolerated.

What happens is that the upper-class gets the delinquency that it "deserves." The cardinal values and interests of adolescents contain the seeds of delinquency. It seems to be the case for many boys that attending dances *means* late hours, dating *means* varying degrees of physical intimacy, possession of an autombile *means* speeding, "dragging" and "parking," and "hanging" with the boys *means* rough-housing and special kinds of vandalism. Conformity and deviance among these boys very likely reflect the same set of values, interests and attitudes. What tips the scales in favor of drinking, drunkenness, sexual intercourse or "raising hell" is not likely a difference in values. A boy's commitment to *respectable* adolescent activities is especially important since it includes his self-involvement and his continuing effort to support status-role claims. Equally important, it engages the adolescent in a daily round of teenage events (opportunities for status gain) in which particular kinds of delinquency are potentially possible. We have in mind events such as parties, dating, dances, "socials," sports events, motoring along the highway, "hanging" about the drive-in—almost any teenage occasion where boys and girls participate jointly. At no time are these situations likely defined delinquent nor are their consequences perceived potentially delinquent. The boys' motives are seldom predatory; the interaction is neither shocking (and thereby not inhibiting to others) nor especially serious, but un- folds as a progression of increasingly self-involving and therefore self-maintaining steps. The adolescent is seldom faced with the choice between delinquent and non-delinquent behavior and therefore seldom initiates delinquent acts to help "solve his problem." There is no "problem."[37] The bulk of delinquency among these youths is an emergent property arising from daily youth culture activities. The effort to maintain one's status serves to support the activity and increase joint participation and behavioral innovation. The perceived risk of delinquency is minimal since the joint activity is seldom begun nor continued for ulterior motives.[38] The prevailing teenage vocabulary helps structure perception under these everyday circumstances.

Active participation in the youth culture helps teenagers achieve status and increases opportunities for further social participation. It also supports parental expectations that their children be "popular," and becomes a major source of motivation for future peer-group activity. The socially active youth who is caught in this normative web of events is pressured to conform or opt out. This choice is not as easy as it may seem, especially where adolescent attitudes tend to reinforce operating behavior. Reversal of behavior at this stage is both difficult and costly for the adolescent. It means the loss of social standing among peers (and is perhaps equally painful to parents), it means the loss of cherished opportunities for desired events, it means the loss of close friends and increased difficulty in dating. It means, no less, a change in "worlds" for the adolescent, and ultimately leads to a transformation in self-conception.

The choice of behavior is not willy-nilly among these boys. The conduct of youths is often their attempt to meet peer-group standards. But it is more than this. There is more than a single role available to boys in the youth culture, and much of their behavior can be seen as an effort to claim particular kinds of roles, at the same time presenting carefully selected selves, or groping behaviorally for a self, for evaluation. The "swinger," the boy with a "style," the "terrific personality," the "grind," the "sports star," and the boys with a "smooth line"—these are social roles seemingly endemic to the youth culture. To be a successful claimant to a particular role means to act in prescribed ways, to hold the correct attitudes, to display the appropriate sentiments, and to avoid the wrong moves. One cannot possess a "smooth line" without accepting the opportunities to practice one's expertise; the role of "sports star" includes both athletic participation, social activities and heterosexual relationships. The "great guy" will be expected to "go along with the boys," "skip school," and engage in a "drag." It will be difficult to be a "swinger" and not "take a drink," or perhaps smoke "pot," while the boy who has a "style" is apt to be preoccupied with the opposite sex. [39] Since peers occupy so much of a teenager's time and comprise a major source of his rewards they gradually become the lens through which he defines his self. What he is and who he is, that is, how successful he is in achieving his self-claims, depend on those sources of rewards, counsel and motivation, *i.e.*, those intimate relationships that help sustain the vital elements in his self-conception. Since the teenager wishes to be seen in as good a light as possible he will not want to jeopardize the allegiance nor provoke the antagonism of peers and thereby "risk losing himself in a total way."

We do not deny the importance of the family in the socialization of these youths, but we have recognized the obscurity of parental roles and rules, and we have seen that many middle- and upper-class parents look to other institutions to "complete" the task. Parents are often defined "square" in teenage matters which means simply that their rules and counsel do not "fit" the reality of the adolescent "world." Today adults can seldom agree on what is deviant among many kinds of typical adolescent conduct in the middle and upper classes. Certain activities have become so widespread that society can do little to restrict such conduct. To increase the surveillance of teenagers or severely restrict their freedom is impossible. Given the strategic significance of the youth culture for society both men and boys would suffer. It would handcuff adolescent participation in the youth culture and dangerously jeopardize the economic and social success of newly emerged occupations and institutions. To impose a stricter moral code on youth (if this were possible) would be to undermine seriously cherished values and beliefs concerning the education and socialization of children. The alternative seems to be to adapt to these conditions. The seriously considered proposal to lower the drinking age is one sign of this adjustment. The teaching of sex in schools is another example of society's adaptation to a situation it cannot otherwise control. The ultimate consequence of this instruction is caught neatly in the motto, "If you can't be good, be careful."[40] Use of the category "joy-riding" as a less serious offense in handling juvenile cases in court is also to the point.

Finally, some writers have noted the sophistication of adolescents who acknowledge their own behavior as a "stage" in "growing up."[41] Yet the particular role of adolescent is not apt to be a tongue-in-cheek affair for the growing boy. Strong identification occurs in recurrent interaction with close friends, and disapproval, ridicule or loss of status carries more injury among peers than among others. There is too much at stake for the teenager to "work" his peers.[42] More likely is he to "work" one parent against the other to secure his own ends. The ambiguity of parental rules and their considerable ignorance of the adolescent "world" make this especially convenient.

NOTES

*Appreciation is expressed to Central Michigan University for a small grant covering computer services.

1. Nye, Short, Jr. & Olson, *Socioeconomic Status and Delinquent Behavior,* 63 Am. J. Soc. 381 (1950); Vaz, *Self-Reported Juvenile Delinquency and Socio-economic Status,* 8 Can. J. Corr. 20 (1966).

2. See Scott & Vaz, *A Perspective of Middle-Class Delinquency,* 29 Can. J. Eco. & Pol. Sci. (1963); Vaz, *Middle-Class Adolescents: Self-Reported Delinquency and Youth Culture Activities,* 2 Can. Rev. Soc. & Anthro. 52-70 (1965).

3. Porter, *The Vertical Mosaic* 285 (1965).

4. The private school discussed here is not to be confused with "Preparatory" or "Tutorial" private schools. Although it is not the most expensive of its kind in Canada its tuition fees run over $1,000 per year. The "highest standards" of propriety, personal appearance and "character formation" are stressed, and scholarship is strongly fostered. Discipline in school is regimented through a system of upper-grade prefects. Also a set of regulations for students is distributed to parents who are expected to adhere to its directions. Out-of-town students often live with "masters" which serves as a further control. Modelled after the British "public" school there is a quiet homogeneity about the private institution which is patently absent from the larger, heterogeneous public high school.

5. Blishen, Jones, Naegele & Porter, Canadian Society: Sociological Perspectives 477-85 (1961). Based on the Blishen scale, category 1 ranges from judges (90.0) to architects (73.0) and includes also occupations reported as "president of a company," category 2 ranges from statisticians (72.9) to transportation managers (60.1), and category 3 extends from dispatchers, train (58.5) to personnel service officer (50.5).

6. Mills, *White Collar* 3-35 (1956); *see also* Elkin, *The Family in Canada* 15-30 (1964).

7. *See* Cohen, *Foreward* to Musgrove, *Youth and the Social Order* at xiv (1964).

8. For factors contributing to change in the family *see* Ogburn, *Why the Family is Changing*, in Ross, *Perspectives on the Social Order* (1963); Elkin, *op. cit. supra* note 6, at 95-112.

9. For a review of work done in Canada involving parent-child relationships *see id.* at 105-06; Reisman, Glazer & Denney, *The Lonely Crowd* (1955).

10. Heise, New Horizons for Canada's Children (1961); Reuter, *The sociology of Adolescence*, 43 Am. J. Soc. (1937).

11. Coleman, *The Adolescent Society* 291 (1961).

12. Baltzell, *An American Business Aristocracy* 459 (1962). Although Baltzell writes of a very high level group, the private schools he discusses are of the kind studied in this project.

13. See the paper by Cohen, *Teachers vs Students: Changing Power Relations in the Secondary Schools*, a public lecture given at the University of California, Berkeley, August 22, 1961.

14. For an excellent review of the teenage culture *see* Bernard, *Teen-Age Culture: An overview*, 338 *Annals* (1961).

15. It is true that under such circumstances marginal differentiation likely takes on special significance.

16. Baltzell, *op. cit. supra* note 12, at 459-62; *see also* Mays, *The Young Pretenders* 35-36 (1965), concerning youth in England.

17. *See* Hollingshead, *Elmtown's Youth* (1961).

18. Bernard, *supra* note 14, at 5.

19. Coleman, *op. cit. supra* note 11. For Canadian data *see* Vaz, *supra* note 2.

20. Some of the items used in this project were taken from Coleman, *op. cit. supra* note 11. We are much indebted to this study.

21. *Ibid.* For data on younger children in England read Musgrove, *op. cit. supra* note 7, at 92-105. A preliminary analysis of data gathered among Swiss boys by the writer reveals that they are strongly parent oriented.

22. Perhaps dating takes on greater significance among boys in a private school where girls are a rarity and students spend longer hours in school.

23. Recent research reveals that both boys and girls of the middle class commit similar kinds of delinquency. See Barton, Disregarded Delinquency: A Study of Self-Reported Middle-Class Female Delinquency in a Suburb (Unpublished Ph.D. Dissertation, Indiana University, 1965).

24. Katz & Stotland, *A Preliminary Statement to a Theory of Attitude Structure and Change,* in Koch, *Psychology: A Study of a science* 432 (1959).

25. Williams, *American Society* 402 (1960).

26. Admittedly this is a hypothesis that is difficult to substantiate.

27. Lynd & Lynd, *Middletown* 137 (1956).

28. Allen, *The Big Change* 11 (1952). In discussing sexual patterns before marriage among adults Goode writes, "Cautiously stated, it seems likely that a considerable increase has occurred in the toleration of certain kinds of sexual or premarital behavior, such as petting or even sexual intercourse, before and after marriage with someone other than the marital partner." However, it is uncertain whether any change has taken place regarding sexual relations with the future spouse alone; *see* Goode, *World Revolution and Family Patterns* 37 (1963); *see*

also Kinsey, Pomeroy, Martin & Gebhard, *Sexual Behavior in the Human Female* 422-24 (1953).

29. Reiss, *Sexual Codes in Teen-Age Culture*, 333 *Annals* 53 (1961).

30. For the ideas in this discussion I am indebted to Albert K. Cohen, his writings and lectures. Of course he is not responsible for their present formulation. *See also* Cohen, *Deviance and Control* (1966).

31. Baltzell, *op. cit. supra* note 12, at 546.

32. Naegele, *Children in Canada—Past and Present*, in Heise, *op. cit. supra* note 10, at 18-29.

33. Conversation with a middle-class parent.

34. We recognize that changes in "moral fibre" and "character strength" may be especially difficult to measure.

35. The increased significance of "social" factors in the formal and informal socialization of children is seen in Reisman, Glazer & Denney, *op. cit. supra* note 9, and in Seeley, Sim & Looseley, *Crestwood Heights* (1956).

36. Since many of the "means" and "social objects" crucial for participation in the adolescent culture are either partly or completely controlled by parents, *e.g.*, the family car, a boy's clothes, pocket money, and his time, compliance with parental demands becomes necessary. Relatively recurrent obedience to parental expectations leads to predictable accessibility to such "objects" which allows adolescents to plan ahead for future social engagements. Yet it is precisely such obedience to parental wishes that often confounds middle- and upper-class parents when they learn of their sons' delinquencies.

37. By this we mean that among middle- and upper-class boys generally delinquency is not a "solution" to any particular common "problem" among them.

38. The importance of risk-taking in deviant behavior is discussed in Lemert, *Social Structure, Social Control, and Deviation*, in Clinard, *Anomie and Deviant Behavior* (1964).

39. Interestingly, however often a middle- or upper-class boy "drags," truants from school or is "expert" with girls in one or another sexual activity, and irrespective of his court appearances for this kind of conduct, he is not likely to acquire the role of "delinquent." The process and functions of acquiring the role of "delinquent" among these boys is in need of research.

40. Dr. G. F. Millar, chairman of the provincial subcommittee with the sex education program for the province of Saskatchewan, was asked why the new course (in sex education) is being attempted in an already overcrowded school program. He replied: "I readily agree that sex education is the proper function of the home. However, for various reasons, many young people are not receiving sex education from their parents. The result of this ignorance and inadequate standard among young people is frightening. Look, for example at the statistics for illegitimate births among teenage girls; they have gone up about 50 percent in the last 10 years. Then there's the increased incidence of venereal disease." Reported in *The Globe and Mail*, Toronto, Jan. 21, 1967.

41. Westley & Elkin, *The Protective Environment and Adolescent Socialization*, 35 *Social Forces* 243 (1957).

42. Berger, *Invitation to Sociology* 122-50 (1963).

Middle-Class Delinquency as a Social Problem

Fred J. Shanley

INTRODUCTION

An examination of the existing body of juvenile delinquency literature suggests the social scientists' relative disinterest in the problem of middle-class delinquency. For some scientists, this lack of interest stems from their judgment regarding the limited significance of middle-class delinquency[1] as a social problem. For example, Ohlin says

> "It seems quite probable that the apparent official tendency to take more seriously the delinquencies of lower-class youth involves, in part, at least an implicit recognition of the greater, potential, long-run social costs which flow from participation in delinquent subcultural activities. . . . The delinquent patterns of behavior of the lower-class child are likely to be more deeply ingrained, more integrated, more fully rationalized, and more stable because he incorporates a culturally defined and socially supported role."

Ohlin goes on to point out that the delinquent behavior of middle-class youth often seems to be "petty in comparison and lacking possibilities for the development of criminal careers" because the delinquent behavior does not represent "a reflection of socially expected forms of role behavior among members of a delinquent subculture."[2]

Nevertheless, the findings of a few recently completed research projects suggest that the delinquency records of certain *subgroups* of the middle-class delinquent population are serious enough to represent a social problem of significance, and that such behavior warrants additional study.

Empey and Erickson,[3] for example, identified a group of middle-status adolescents whose delinquent behavior is both serious and repetitious. In their report, they compare the delinquents' official and unofficial law violation patterns, sub-classified by number of official and unofficial offenses committed and also by social status. The findings indicate that it was middle-status boys, as contrasted with lower- and upper-status boys, who committed the most serious offenses, including forgery, breaking and entering, destroying property, and arson. Furthermore, not only did the middle-status boys report two-thirds of the serious violations but the persistent offenders of that group were disproportionately high on the majority of all offenses.

The writer, in a study of suburban secondary-school students, identified a subgroup of *aggressive*[4] middle- and upper-class delinquents whose patterns of police contact[5] were generally comparable to those of delinquents in lower-class neighborhoods. For example, 77 percent of this suburban delinquent group had two or more police contacts, 43 percent had four or more, and 16 percent had seven or more contacts. Related percentages of police contacts[6] for a sample of Negro delinquents in the Los Angeles Metropolitan Area were 72 percent, 41 percent and 22 percent.

To provide a second measure of the seriousness of the offenses of this suburban delinquent group, their record of juvenile court petitions was compared with the record of the above mentioned Negro delinquent group. Fifty-six percent of the middle-class group had one or more petitions filed, 27 percent had two or more, and 9 percent had four or more petitions filed. Related percentages for the Negro delinquent group were 60 percent, 38 percent, and 10 percent. The similarity of the distributions for the two groups provides striking evidence of the seriousness of the police record of this particular group of middle-class adolescents.[7]

Herskovitz, et al.,[8] studied the law violation patterns of institutionalized middle- and upper-class delinquents. The most frequently committed offenses for the group were auto theft, other theft, vandalism, sexual offenses, breaking and entering, and physical assault. In considering the character of these offenses, the author's comment "Dealing first with the issue of socioeconomic level, we note there were comparatively few differences in the nature of the offenses committed. . . . With two exceptions, burglary and auto theft, delinquency seems to be delinquency, irrespective of slums or suburbs, material advantages or underprivilege, gangs or no."[9]

The three studies referred to above indicate that the law violation patterns of these particular samples of middle-class delinquents are serious enough to represent a social problem of importance in their own communities. The findings also suggest the need for further research designed (a) to document in a more comprehensive fashion the degree of significance of middle-class delinquency as a social problem, (b) and to investigate more systematically the etiology of that phenomenon.

Within the context of this general position, then, the balance of this article is devoted, first, to a summary of literature regarding the etiology of middle-class delinquency and, second, to the identification of research questions that are judged to be important for future study.

SURVEY OF DELINQUENCY LITERATURE

1. Theoretical Formulations[10]

With regard to middle-class delinquency causation, Cohen speculated that sweeping changes in the labor market and in educational objectives and practices in America have resulted in a value orientation shift for certain middle-class youth toward "irresponsible, hedonistically oriented behavior involving the courting of danger, liquor, sex, cars, etc."[11] Cohen also points out that "many families which are middle-class in economic terms ...may be decidedly working-class in terms of the experiences they provide their children"[12] and thus do not properly prepare them to compete in the general society. He also discusses a theoretical position suggested by Parsons' writings,[13] one which postulates that adolescent sex-role anxiety leads to antisocial behavior as a demonstration of masculinity. In a similar vein, Wilensky and Lebeaux[14] account for middle-class delinquency in terms of adolescent sex-role anxiety associated with the father's failure to play a strong masculine familial role and the mother's dominance as a disseminator of values.

Kvaraceus and Miller[15] speculate that middle-class delinquency can be accounted for in terms of recent cultural changes that have weakened the "deferred gratification" tradition. These changes include the increased emphasis upon installment buying and a related "have it now" philosophy, compulsory school attendance which holds students in school regardless of academic achievement, the upward diffusion of lower-class standards, and the discrepancy which middle-class youth feel between achievement expectations and ability to achieve.

England[16] points to the development of a hedonistic youth culture since World War II, emerging as a reaction to the adolescent's ambiguous status and role in our society and also as a result of the influence of fundamental changes in communication and merchandising methods. Bohlke[17] identifies "stratification inconsistency" as an important determinant of delinquent behavior. He speculates that some delinquents come from "nouveau bourgeoisie" families that are middle-class in income but lower-class in background, and that others come from middle-class families that are mobile downward. Gold[18] theorizes that a boy of any social class will be inclined to delinquent behavior if he is not attracted to norm supporting individuals and organizations such as the school and family, and if he has experienced personal failure in school and anticipates occupational failure as an adult. Cohen and Short[19] speculate that the democratization of family relations, the independence of family members from each other and the popularity of a "minimize psychic pain" childrearing philosophy have weakened the deferred gratification pattern of socialization, retarded the internalization of authority, reduced the child's ability to tolerate frustration and thus contributed to an increase of delinquency among middle-class children.

Bloch and Niederhoffer[20] theorize that deviant adolescent behavior arises when societies impede the progress of youth toward desired social maturity. When blocked from achievement of adult status, adolescents develop deviant behavior patterns which represent psychological satisfying substitutes for adult status, e.g., the gang. In contrast, Matza and Sykes[21] theorize that some forms of juvenile delinquency in our culture have a "common sociological base regardless of the class level at which they appear," because the delinquents' values clearly relate to the values of a leisure class and to "subterranean values" of the more general society. The delinquents endorse these values and express them in a more seriously deviant form when faced with intense frustration in their adolescent experience. Shulman[22] sees middle-class delinquent behavior as a reflection of spontaneous outbursts of children against parental controls, or as an end-product of the social disorganization of some American families in which marital friction or relaxed and inadequate controls result in severe emotional disturbance among children.

Shoham and Hovav[23] speculate that the middle-class adolescents' internalization of social norms is negatively affected by conflict situations encountered in the home (marital discord, parent-child norm conflict, deviant parental modeling behavior) and in the society (conflicting cultural norms). One method of conflict resolution involves the acceptance of the more consistent and easily understood norms of the delinquent gang. Goldsmith and Berman[24] theorize that, because of endocrinal changes at puberty, some adolescents find their instinctual drives in such conflict with their ego strength and with their families' normative requirements that they face a crisis of control and emotional expression. These adolescents handle the crisis by establishing a "home base" among peers and by adopting a value system which constitutes a repudiation of family values and which is often delinquent in form. Ferdinand,[25] in developing a social class typology of delinquency, theorizes that the "upper-upper" class adolescent cultivates a manner that is distinctive, personalistic, and indulgent. This behavior pattern encourages delinquent activities involving stylistic misappropriation and destruction of property, sexual delinquencies and illegal use of alcohol. The "lower-upper" and "upper-middle" class adolescents play a central role in the *adolescent* subculture, and their delinquencies reflect deviant expression of adolescent subculture values, including sex experience deviance, aggressive use of the automobile, property destruction, etc.

2. Research Studies

With reference to research studies (as opposed to theoretical speculations not directly supported by data) Herskovitz, et al.,[26] reported that the delinquent behavior of a "higher socioeconomic" sample of institutionalized delinquents was correlated with psychological conflict, developed as a reaction to negative intra-family experience, e.g., exposure to an inconsistent, indulgent, over-protective mother and a distant, hostile, aggressive father with perfectionist expectations for the child. Bandura and Walters[27] studied middle- and upper-class boys with a history of "aggressive destructive" behavior and associated that behavior with dependency frustration in the home. Jaffe[28] tested a hypothesis regarding the relationship between delinquency proneness and "value conflict" among family members, children's feelings of powerlessness and difficulties in parent identification. He found that the hypothesized relationship held for both "upper-middle income" families and "low income" families. Reiss[29] identified a "relatively weak ego" delinquent, characterized as anxious, insecure, isolated from parents and peers, and highly aggressive and destructive. This type of youth lives in a conventional neighborhood in an unbroken home that is disturbed by extremes of parental conflict and hostility. Carek, Hendrickson and Holmes,[30] in a psychiatric investigation of family life correlates of delinquent behavior, report that (a) the parents derived vicarious gratification from their children's delinquencies, (b) the parents lacked emotional convictions that the delinquent behavior was wrong, and (c) a complex interpersonal relationship existed in which there was an unconscious mutual manipulation between parent and child, with both parties keeping alive the relationship which was supportive of deviancy.

Myerhoff and Myerhoff[31] indicated that the law violations of groups of deviant middle-class suburban youth were more often capricious and manipulative than violent and that their actions appeared to represent an endorsement of the "subterranean values" of the society. Karacki and Toby[32] described a gang of fighting delinquents that did not come from economically deprived homes. Their delinquent behavior was related to an endorsement of "youth culture" values which included: (a) assertion of masculinity through physical aggression, (b) loyalty to deviant peers, and (c) a desire for immediate gratification.

Liu and Fahey[33] compared the self concept, occupational aspirations and feelings of anomie of 50 "serious delinquents" and 50 "nondelinquents." The authors speculated that the more negative aspirations and self concepts of the delinquents (irrespective of social class) reflected a conviction that there is little one can do once the marks of serious delinquency status has been imprinted. Similarly, in a study of secondary school students, Elliott[34] reported that, at every social class level, a higher proportion of delinquents than nondelinquents perceived lower opportunity for achieving adult goals. In both studies, the authors comment that the youths' perception of limited opportunity might be the effect of their affiliation with a delinquent subculture rather than a cause leading to such affiliation.

Wattenberg and Balistrieri[35] reported that the family relationships of a group of male car thieves from "favored neighborhoods" were characterized by weak affectional ties between parent and child and the exercise of limited parental supervision. Schepses[36] identified a group of training school boys from middle-class homes who committed only car thefts, usually stole the car to have a good time, but did not come from a home characterized by any single pattern of parent-child relationship. Greeley and Casey[37] found the members of an upper-middle-class gang to be academic failures and disciplinary problems in school and to come from "father-absent" families, that were upwardly mobile in a "socially disorganized" new suburb. Coleman[38] pointed out that, if youth can't achieve status in the adolescent social system by membership in the "leading crowd" or by being "popular," one method of resolving this problem is to seek status in deviant subgroups. In a study of secondary school adjustment, Shanley[39] identified a group of middle-class, aggressive students who expressed great dissatisfaction with their school experience and who had extensive delinquent records.

After investigating the ecological correlates of delinquency in an urban community, Lane[40] suggested the need for "new" lines of investigation of middle-class delinquent behavior, including studies of: (a) the relation between religious affiliation and delinquency, (b) the specific cultural determinants of "alienation" for middle-class youth, (c) upward, rapidly mobile families and delinquency, (d) the utility of the concept "contraculture" as opposed to "subculture" to describe the peer culture of middle-class delinquents. In an urban New England community, Pine[41] found that "unrecorded" delinquent behavior was associated with degree of social mobility (students whose families were mobile downward were more often delinquent) and with educational and occupational aspirations (students with low aspirations, whatever their social class, were more likely to be delinquent).

Because of the range and complexity of subject matter of the above described studies, their specific content has been reviewed and summarized in terms of eight etiological dimensions. The subject matter focus of each dimension will be briefly treated below and then related to possible research objectives in the last section of the paper.

Dimension 1—Anxiety Regarding Sex Role Identification.

The antisocial behavior of the middle-class male is seen as representing a "masculine protest" against the dominance of the mother who is "the principal examplar of morality, source of discipline and object of identification"[42] in the middle-class home. (Cohen) (Parsons) (Wilensky and Lebeaux).

Dimension 2—Delay in Achievement of Adult Status.

Delinquent behavior has been described as one response to the ambiguity of the adolescent's role in our society, his long period of dependence on parents and the related blocking of the adolescent from an early and desired assumption of his adult work and marriage roles. (Block and Niederhoffer) (England) (Cohen).

Dimension 3—Feelings of Status Deprivation.

The relationship between delinquency and status deprivation has reference here to the adolescent's recognition of his incapacity to achieve status due to lack of skill or stigmatization, e.g., recognition of the status-depriving consequences of school failure or of delinquency, or of inadequate home training. (Bohlke) (Elliott) (Greeley) (Gold) (Lane) (Liu and Fahey) (Pine).

Dimension 4—The Weakening of the Deferred Gratification Principle and the Related Emphasis Upon a Hedonistic Philosophy.

This fundamental shift in value orientation has been explained in terms of changes in labor market requirements for youth, related changes in educational objectives, upward diffusion of lower-class values, merchandising and communication media stimulae, and child rearing practices emphasizing the protection of children from frustration. Having rejected status achievement in terms of the deferred gratification principle, the adolescent seeks status among his peers with forms of hedonistic display that sometimes are expressed in delinquent form. (Cohen) (Cohen and Short) (England) (Karacki and Toby) (Kvaraceus and Miller) (Schepses).

Dimension 5—Inadequate Parent-Child Relationships.

The linkage between parent-child relationships and delinquent behavior has been described in terms of three related influences: (a) ineffective early childhood training resulting in the child's inability to control anti-social impulses, (b) added negative influence of inadequate parent-child relationships during adolescence, (c) with both these influences linked to the disturbing impact of physiological changes during adolescence. (Bandura and Walters) (Carek) (Cohen and Short) (Goldsmith and Berman) (Greeley) (Henderson and Holmes) (Herskovitz) (Jaffe) (Shoham and Hovav) (Shulman) (Wattenberg and Balistrieri).

Dimension 6—Ineffective Performance in School.

Delinquent behavior may also reflect the ineffective student's feelings of frustration associated with compulsory school attendance and his daily exposure to the "punishing" consequences of deviant academic and social school performance. (Gold) (Greeley) (Shanley).

Dimension 7—The Influence of Deviant Peer Groups.

Middle-class delinquency literature does not emphasize this causal factor. However, deviant cliques and friendship groups, formed to resolve problems of peer acceptance and peer status, would be likely to embrace values and behavioral norms that could be expressed in delinquent behavioral form. (Block and Niederhoffer) (Karacki and Toby) (Greeley and Casey) (Coleman).

Dimension 8—Capricious Experimentation with Deviant Behavior Practices.

Here, delinquent behavior is not seen as a seeking-after-status or an expression of frustration, but rather as a type of irresponsible, temporary experimentation with deviant behavior which will terminate without serious consequence upon entry into adult status. (Matza and Sykes) (Myerhoff and Myerhoff).

FUTURE RESEARCH OBJECTIVES

The results of the literature survey have suggested a number of general research objectives which the writer believes should be pursued if the phenomenon of middle-class delinquency is to be better understood.

1. Before considering the utility of the above mentioned dimensions as a stimulus for the identification of desired research objectives, attention should be given to an important investigative need of this field—that is, for research studies designed to provide basic descriptive data regarding middle-class delinquency. At present, very little data exists which are descriptive of the incidence of delinquent behavior among middle-class adolescents, the types of offenses committed, and the kinds of social settings in which these offenses occur. Regarding the matter, Cohen says, "We need to know more about the frequency, about the 'spirit', the 'quality', the 'emotional tone' of the delinquent action; about the circumstances, events, and activities which provide the context preceding, accompanying and following the delinquent act and above all, we need to know more about the collective or individual nature of the delinquent act and how delinquency varies in individual and group situations."[43] Though Cohen was referring to the field of delinquency, undifferentiated by social class, when he made these comments, the current literature review indicates that his remarks have definite relevance for the field of middle-class delinquency at this time.

2. As an extension of this general idea, the findings of studies reviewed above suggest the utility of projects designed to study subclasses of the middle-class delinquent population. For example, the research of Bandura and Walters[44] (identifying an "aggressive destructive" middle-class adolescent) and Wattenberg and Balestrieri[45] (identifying an "adaptive socialized" delinquent) suggest the utility of an "aggressive" vs. "passive" subclassification of that delinquent population. The results of the author's own study of middle-class "aggressive" delinquents also support this objective.[46]

   Empey's and Erickson's [47] work suggests another potentially significant basis for subclassification of the middle-class delinquent population, that is, into "persistent offender" vs. "single offender" groups. It is possible that a more intensive study of the types of delinquent subgroups mentioned above (and others) will reveal that the sociogenic and psychogenic correlates of their delinquent behavior are substantially different.

3. As a third research objective, there is an obvious need for the

systematic replication of the "more significant" research studies and for the testing of the major existing theoretical formulations described above. The previously mentioned etiological dimensions provide one organizing principle in terms of which a review of research alternatives could be conducted. It would appear that any one of the identified dimensions could properly be the focus of a series of specific research investigations.

For example, theoretical writings have pointed to the relationship between the weakening of the deferred gratification principle, the increased involvement of adolescents with hedonistic values, and delinquent behavior. Yet there is relatively little research data to document the extent of this value shift. Consequently, studies should be conducted to investigate the extent to which middle-class delinquents and nondelinquents differentially endorse pleasure-seeking values as well as to identify the social determinants of such a value shift.

There is also a need to study the effect of modern communication and merchandising methods upon the adolescents' value system in order to determine the extent to which American youth are influenced by such media to interpret adolescence as a period of play and diversion, rather than as a period of preparation for adulthood.

With regard to the parent-child relationship area, there is a clear need for further study of the relationship between varying patterns of childrearing practice and delinquent (nondelinquent) behavior. In this regard, the writings of Bandura and Walters,[48] Herskovitz, et al.,[49] Sears, et al.,[50] and Miller and Swanson [51] should provide a suggestive speculative base for further study.

Dimension seven interprets middle-class delinquency as a capricious, mischievous type of experimentation with antisocial acts that does not reflect "habitually deviant" attitudes or behaviors.[52] The explanation stands in sharp contrast to other theoretical explanations and suggests the utility of studies to determine the extent to which middle-class delinquents actually view their deviant acts in this fashion, and also are able to terminate such behavior in adulthood without negative effect on reputation or personal adjustment.

Finally, there is a need for investigations of the association between negative school experience and middle-class delinquency. Gold[53] and Shanley, et al.,[54] have reported such a relationship. Gold postulates that the adolescent (of whatever social class) perceives the status deprivation consequences of persistent school failure and becomes more likely to be "provoked" to delinquent behavior as a consequence. Though a number of studies have been conducted in this general area, nearly all of them have been concerned with the disadvantaged lower-class student.

4. A fourth research objective represents a logical extension of the recommendations already made and involves the linking of the separate etiological dimensions in a more comprehensive theoretical formulation. In this endeavor, one would attempt to account for deviant adolescent behavior in terms of the joint effect of major etiological forces, such as the family and the peer culture, whose influences have tended to be separately dealt with in existing theoretical work. (See Moles, Lippitt and Withey,[55] Cohen,[56] and more recently Stanfield[57] for recommendations of a similar nature.)

The complexity of such a task is clearly recognized. In fact, this type of effort may be premature until additional empirical studies have been completed which focus on more limited aspects of the adolescent's social experience and which provide a reliable body of descriptive data in these related areas. However, it is also apparent that the diverse and complex set of socializing forces represented by the family, the peer culture, the school, etc., all contribute substantially to the patterns of deviant or conforming behavior of the middle-class adolescent. If social scientists are to more effectively account for this behavior, then they must at some point begin to assess the interactive influence of such socializing forces upon that behavior.

Sherif and Sherif comment regarding this point, "The deeds and misdeeds of youth cannot be predicted solely on the basis of class membership, nor solely on the basis of family relations, nor through any theory advocating a single sovereign cause. . . . The etiology of behavior, whether acceptable or not, must include the context of membership in natural groups, in whose formation and functioning many influences participate."[58]

As an extension of this point, if one re-examines the content of the etiological dimensions previously described in this paper, one can discern a general relatedness of content that would allow the subsuming of most of the dimensions under three more general headings—those having reference to the family, the peer culture, and the school.

From such a broad base, one could attempt the development of more comprehensive theory (in testable form) descriptive of the interactive influence of these three powerful socializing agents upon adolescent behavior in the middle-class setting. The serious difficulties associated with such a theoretical undertaking are obvious, but the utilities to be derived from the end product of that undertaking (if achieved even in part) are equally obvious and attractive.

CONCLUSION

In summary, this article has reviewed the existing literature regarding middle-class delinquency, has argued for the expansion of research activity in this subject matter area and has suggested a number of investigative foci which might profitably be studied in the future. Consideration of the content of these research questions is suggestive of the complexity of the social phenomenon under study and may also provide the most persuasive argument for the general position of this paper, that is, the need for an expansion of research regarding middle-class delinquent behavior.

FOOTNOTES

1. The term "middle-class delinquency" is defined in a variety of ways by scientists whose articles are referred to in this article. However, the term "middle-class" most frequently has reference to a socioeconomic status classification determined by father's occupation or by a combination of father's occupation and education. The occupational classification will usually include sales, clerical, and skilled categories, as well as small-enterprise entrepreneurs or managers. The term "delinquent" will have reference to a number of classifications, including (a) self-reported offenders, (b) police booked offenders, (c) court petition offenders and (d) incarcerated offenders.

2. Lloyd W. Ohlin, *The Development of Opportunities for Youth* (Syracuse: Youth Development Center., 1960), 8-9.

3. LaMar T. Empey, and Maynard L. Erickson, *Hidden Delinquency: Evidence on Old Issues* (Provo Experiment, Brigham Young University, 1965).

4. The aggressive classification of the delinquent group was based upon a set of school behavior characteristics i.e., behaviors that were chronically disruptive and challenging of the school's regulatory system and of authority figures in that setting.

5. A "police contact," as defined in this paper, involves a police arrest of an individual for an offense and preparation of a written record of the arrest by the police.

6. The Central Juvenile Index of Los Angeles County Sheriff's Department was used to develop police contact statistics for this group and for the aggressive middle-class delinquent group.

7. The distributions of police contacts and juvenile court petitions for the two delinquent groups were tested for significance of difference, utilizing chi-square and were found not to be significantly different from each other.

8. Herbert H. Herskovitz, Murray Levene, George Spivak, "Anti-Social Behavior of Adolescents from Higher Socio-Economic Groups," *Journal of Nervous and Mental Diseases,* 125 (November, 1959), 1-9.

9. Ibid., 7.

10. In this section, publications will be reviewed that are more or less formally "theoretical" and that are not directly supported by research data in the publication in which the theoretical formulation is presented.

11. Albert K. Cohen, "Middle-Class Delinquency and the Social Structure," paper delivered at the American Sociological Association Meeting, August, 1957.

12. Albert K. Cohen, *Delinquent Boys* (New York: The Free Press, a Division of the Macmillan Co., 1955), 159.

13. Talcott Parsons, "Certain Primary Sources and Patterns of Aggression in the Social Structure of the Western World," *Psychiatry,* 10 (May, 1947), 167-81.

14. H. L. Wilensky and C. H. Lebeaux, *Industrial Society and Social Welfare* (New York: Russell Sage Foundation, 1958).

15. William Kvaraceus and Walter B. Miller, *Delinquent Behavior: Culture and the Individual,* Vol. 1 (Washington, D.C.: National Education Association, 1959).

16. Ralph W. England, "A Theory of Middle-Class Juvenile Delinquency," *The Journal of Criminal Law, Criminology, and Police Science,* 50 (March-April 1960), 535-40.

17. Robert H. Bohlke, "Social Mobility, Stratification Inconsistency and Middle-Class Delinquency," *Social Problems,* 8 (Spring 1961), 351-63.

18. Martin Gold, *Status Forces in Delinquent Boys* (Ann Arbor: Institute for Social Research, University of Michigan, 1963).

19. Albert K. Cohen and James F. Short, "Research in Delinquent Subcultures, *Journal of Social Issues,* 14 (No. 3, 1958), 20-37.

20. Herbert A. Bloch and Arthur Niederhoffer, *The Gang: A Study in Adolescent Behavior* (New York: Philosophical Library, 1958).

21. David Matza and Gresham M. Sykes, "Juvenile Delinquency and Subterranean Values," *American Sociological Review,* 26 (October 1961), 712-19.

22. Harry Manuel Shulman, *Juvenile Delinquency in American Society* (New York: Harper and Brother, 1961).

23. Shlomo Shoham and Meir Hovav, "B'Nei-Tovim—Middle and Upper Class Delinquency in Israel, *Sociology and Social Research,* 48 (July, 1964).

24. Jerome M. Goldsmith, and Irwin R. Berman, "Middle-Class Jewish Delinquency," *Journal of Jewish Communal Services,* 39 (Winter, 1962), 192-96.

25. Theodore N. Ferdinand, *Typologies of Delinquency* (New York: Random Hous, 1966), 96-113.

26. Herskovitz, et al., op. cit.

27. Albert Bandura and Richard H. Walters, *Adolescent Aggression* (New York: The Ronald Press, 1959).

28. Lester D. Jaffe, "Delinquency Proneness and Family Anomie," *The Journal of Criminal Law, Criminology, and Police Science*, 34 (June, 1963).

29. Albert J. Reiss, "Social Correlates of Psychological Types of Delinquency," *American Sociological Review*, 47 (December, 1952) 710-18.

30. Donald J. Carek, Willard J. Hendrickson, and Donald J. Holmes, "Delinquency Addiction in Parents," *Archives of General Psychiatry*, 4 (April, 1961) 357-62.

31. Howard L. Myerhoff and Barbara G. Myerhoff, "Field Observations of Middle-Class 'Groups'," *Social Forces*, 42 (March, 1964), 328-36.

32. Larry Karacki and Jackson Toby, "The Uncommitted Adolescent: Candidate for Gang Socialization," *Sociological Inquiry*, 32 (Spring, 1962), 203-15.

33. William T. Liu and Frank Fahey, "Delinquency, Self Esteem, and Social Control: A Retroductive Analysis," *American Catholic Sociological Review*, 24 (Spring, 1963), 3-12.

34. Delbert S. Elliott, "Delinquency and Perceived Opportunity," *Sociological Inquiry*, 32 (Spring, 1962), 216-27.

35. William Wattenberg and James Balistrieri, "Automobile Theft: A Favored Group Delinquency," *American Journal of Sociology*, 57 (May 1952), 575-79.

36. Erwin Schepses, "Boys Who Steal Cars," *Federal Probation*, 25 (March, 1961), 55-62.

37. Andrew Greeley and James Casey, "An Upper Middle-Class Deviant Gang," *The American Catholic Sociological Review*, 24 (Spring, 1963), 33-41.

38. James S. Coleman, *The Adolescent Society*, (New York: The Free Press, a Division of the Macmillan Co., 1962).

39. Fred J. Shanley, Jalil Alzobaie, and D. Welty Lefever, *Comparative Analysis of School Record Data for Aggressive, Well-Adjusted and Under-Achieving Students* (Los Angeles: Youth Studies Center, University of Southern California, 1964).

40. Ralph Lane, Jr., "Delinquency Generative Milieux: A Theoretical Problem," *American Catholic Sociological Review*, 24 (Spring, 1963), 42-53.

41. Gerald J. Pine, "Social Class, Social Mobility and Delinquent Behavior," *The Personnel and Guidance Journal*, 43 (April, 1965), 770-74.

42. Cohen, op. cit., 162.

43. Cohen, op. cit., 173.

44. Bandura and Walters, op. cit.

45. Wattenberg and Balistrieri, op. cit.

46. Fred J. Shanley, et al., op. cit.

47. Empey and Erickson, op. cit.

48. Bandura and Walters, op. cit.

49. Herskovitz, et al., op. cit.

50. Robert R. Sears, et al., *Patterns of Child Rearing* (Evanston: Row Peterson and Co., 1957).

51. Daniel R. Miller and Guy E. Swanson, *The Changing American Parent* (New York: John Wiley and Sons, 1958).

52. Meyerhoff and Myerhoff, op. cit.

53. Gold, op. cit.

54. Shanley, et al., op. cit.

55. Oliver Moles, Ronald Lippitt, and Stephen Withey, *A Selective Review of Research and Theory on Delinquency* (Ann Arbor: Institute for Social Research, 1959), 125-76.

56. Albert K. Cohen, "The Sociology of the Deviant Act," *American Sociological Review*, 30 (February, 1965), 5-14.

57. Robert Everett Stanfield, "The Interaction of Family Variables and Many Variables in the Aetiology of Delinquency," *Social Problems*, 13 (Spring, 1966), 411-17.

58. Muzafer Sherif and Carolyn W. Sherif, "The Adolescent in his Group in its Setting," Chapter 12, in Muzafer Sherif and Carolyn W. Sherif, editors, *Problems of Youth* (Chicago: Aldine Publishing Co., 1965), 290.

READING 18

Kids vs. Cops: Delinquency Prevention and the Police Function

G. Thomas Gitchoff

The problem of delinquency prevention is probably one of the most controversial among students and scholars alike. The area of delinquency prevention undoubtedly represents the greatest number of self-made experts and theoreticians expounding, creating and innovating in a hopeless vacuum.

In a period when society is undergoing rapid changes, experiencing greater technological advances and striving to understand the complexities of slum and suburban existence, the reality of any problem requires thoughtful analysis and study in order to understand its component parts. Before delinquency prevention programs are designed and implemented, there must be devised an orderly and systematic frame of reference. There should be an analysis of past work and literature, comprehensive enough to possibly suggest the proper methodology to be used and/or any alternatives. Additionally, there should be an integrated and cooperative effort and understanding on the part of concerned social institutions, agencies and communities.

It is unfortunate that many preventive efforts are, in fact, control programs. They are by their very nature instituted after delinquency rates have reached all time highs. Preventive programs in terms of meeting social, psychological or educational needs, before the fact (delinquency) are a rarity.

Generally, it might be said, the public is loath to involve itself in social issues which might require sacrifice and the expenditure of community energy and finances. Programs can only be effective if and when the public and police decide to actively involve themselves and not merely offer token gestures.

Police participation in juvenile delinquency prevention is of recent origin. Primarily due to the complex and rapidly changing social systems, the police function is becoming more involved in social service duties, heretofore neglected or not considered within their domain. The past decade has witnessed many changes and improvements in police functions and social responsibilities.

> Now police must understand and be concerned with racial prejudice, minority conflict, labor strife, juvenile gangs, addiction, and a host of their communal problems that, far more challenging mere ordinace and statutes, threaten the very foundation of a democratic society. Policemen, now more than ever, must be social practitioners, students of social and psychological phenomena, if they are to fulfill their responsibility to promote the common good of our communities and nation. A knowledge of law and arrest procedures is no longer sufficient for even the lowest police rookie.

The social aspects of police service can be expanded most directly through delinquency prevention work. This must be developed and enlarged through imaginative and creative programs. The growth of the police function is necessary in a pluralistic, mobile society. To be static, to be isolated, to blindly pursue traditional practices is to ignore the social responsibility of police service and can only result in tragedy and wasted human resources.[1]

The importance of expanding the police function toward protective and greater understanding of neglected or delinquent youth is, *ipso facto*, an area of considerable concern in need of uniform development.

The police must expand their ability to meet the challenges of modern society by favorably enhancing their own image through increased learning and the development of their capacities. This, of course, is not a one-way process. The public must also accept the responsibility of change and produce an active and cooperative citizenry within the community. People who are "police problems" are also problems for the entire community—for families, schools, welfare agencies, correction agencies, hospitals and youth shelters.[2]

The police represent the first social agency through which many juvenile offenders are brought into contact with both the official and judicial agencies. It is usually during this confrontation between the police officer and the youth that the "greatest amount of curbstone justice is dispensed." As a result of this appropriate use of police discretionary power, most first offenders never reappear on police records. As Swanson has stated:

> When an officer knows something about the reasons for different types of behavior and something about the reaction of people under such circumstances, he can carry out his responsibility without causing an increase in the individual's problem of living in a satisfactory manner. It is particularly true that a police officer's way of handling the situation may make a great difference. What a police officer does or fails to do may have a lasting effect not only upon the future plans for the child but upon his attitude toward treatment personnel and respect toward authority.[3]

Police throughout the country who are concerned about youth can do much in the area of delinquency prevention and control. The police function does not pose a threat to other youth-serving agencies. Police prevention work does not resort to "mollycoddling," and police power is never surrendered. Instead, it is reinforced with other approaches and techniques of great importance in deterring youth from a collision course with crime.

Police have much to learn to do their jobs well. Police can measure up to societal needs. They need opportunity and encouragement to grow professionally, and together with other social agencies, they must seek to prevent criminality at its roots.

The concept of "nipping crime in the bud" or early prevention before the late cure has been espoused for many years. Unfortunately, it will probably be many more years before adequate early prevention programs are developed that are uniformly effective.

In an effort to design an effective police-youth relations program aimed at reaching pre-delinquent and adjudged delinquent youth, a unique program was initiated by the Youth Commission in 1967. Based upon a mutual understanding and reeducation between authority figures (police and probation officers) and youth, the purpose was to achieve a meaningful dialogue and rapport by engaging the informal social system of hostile youth.

This required the establishing of certain principles as guide lines:

1. Determination by youth that such a program was needed.
2. Offering a program attractive and interesting to youth by having them assist in the development and implementation of such programs.
3. Engaging the local police agency.
4. Engaging the probation agency, schools, recreation, etc.
5. A realization that a police-youth discussion group did not represent a panacea, but could be effectively utilized to establish mutual understanding between youth and police, needed to convey the principles of law, order, and justice throughout the community.
6. Establishing ground rules which encouraged informal hostile discussion and guaranteed certain immunity to the participants.

It should be emphasized that the program was aimed at only that minority of hardened and alienated youths requiring special attention. Youths who would normally be attracted to the great variety of boys' clubs, recreation, YMCA, Boy Scouts, and other structured activities were not included.

As regards the usual structured activities for youths, Smith says, ". . . they are concerned with youths in the mass and not with youthful offenders as such. It is with that special problem-oriented segment of the youth population that police should be concerned rather than with the generality of young persons, the majority of whom are members of a law-abiding society."[4]

Although no empirical study has been conducted to determine the long range effectiveness of such a police-youth program, the observations and comments by all parties concerned have been highly favorable, especially from those two parties that have traditionally been diametrically opposed—youth and police!

THE POLICE-YOUTH DISCUSSION GROUP PROGRAM

The development of the police-youth discussion group originally grew out of the need "to do something" to placate riotous youth in Richmond, California, in 1965.[5] The police and the Human Relations Commission decided to meet and talk with hostile Negro youths who had been on the rampage for several nights. Through police indigenous aides, several of the youths were contacted and invited to air their grievances to the police at a roundtable discussion. The first session was conducted in a fashion not uncommon between two warring factions. Shouting, cussing, insults, derogatory epithets and general chaos seemed to be the rule rather than the exception. This highly emotional, insulting session produced one very effective result: apparently both police and youth experienced a release of pent-up hostilities that were heretofore exploding on the streets in the form of violent action.

The Richmond Police Department, hoping that some good might come from these "highly irregular" sessions, continued to conduct these meetings for several months. During this time, the group of youths participating grew from several at the beginning to thirty-five at the end of six months. The discussion group had expanded to such a large number that the police decided they had served their purpose and arranged to transfer the group to the County's Juvenile Probation Department.

During the six-month period under police guidance, there was a noticeable reduction of difficulties in handling these youths on the streets. Previous to these sessions, the majority of the youths confronted by a police officer on the street would antagonize or resist him. Subsequently, these same youths who were once so hostile and rebellious toward authority of any kind or color, could now better understand the function of law enforcement. They no longer insulted the officer when stopped for questioning or asked to "break it up" or "move on." The officers, in turn, had learned to understand these youths, and from them, how to handle situations

317

in a non-threatening manner that did not challenge their self-respect or dignity.

As a result of these successful police-youth discussion groups, the Richmond Police Department established a Human Relations Officer, whose function was to continue organizing these groups throughout the city. The continued popularity and success of this program made it necessary to expand the Human Relations Officer's duties so that currently it is now a unit composed of three full-time officers. The Richmond program is currently being viewed as a model of police-youth relations work by other departments throughout the State.

From a criminological point of view, the Richmond example dealt only with lower-class Negro youth. In an effort to apply the same principle to an all-white middle-class group of youngsters, the police-youth discussion group was transplanted in Pleasant Hill.

The implementation of the police-youth discussion group (hereafter referred to as discussion group) in a middle-class community was obviously an easier task to accomplish when compared to the lower-class group of riotous youth in Richmond.

In the case of Pleasant Hill, the youthful members of the first discussion group were obtained through the local county probation officer servicing both high schools within the city limits. Youths on probation for more serious offenses, e.g., narcotics, car theft, aggravated assault, grand larceny, were of major concern; however, some lesser offenders were also included. Additionally, the schools were encouraged to refer "troublesome" pre-delinquents to the discussion group.

For the first discussion group, a deputy sheriff, one of eleven contracted by the city to provide police protection, was chosen to meet with the youths. He was chosen especially for his youthful appearance and his ability to express himself and relate well with the younger generation. He was also the arresting officer of many of the youths in attendance. Additionally, the probation officer in charge of all the youths present was also in attendance.

What might have appeared to be a prearranged structured session weighted in favor of the authority figures was, in reality, a highly vocal gripe-session with very little restraint on anyone's part. The youths were just as vicious in their vocal attacks on their own probation officer as they were with the police officer.

Challenges and counter-challenges, vulgarity, and insults permeated the recreation room where the discussion group met. Rapid-fire questions by youths accusing the police officer of brutality, unjust arrests, and illegal search and seizure procedures were answered by pinpointing the exact circumstances of the case being discussed. The officer then gave "his side" of the story and added some of the major points omitted by the youth. The officer knowledgeably explained the reasons for his actions and readily pointed out that he too was human and subject to make an occasional error in judgment. This statement, alone, had the effect of gaining the youths' support and to realize the officer was in fact something more than a badge, gun, and club wrapped neatly in a uniform; he was a personable human being.

During the several month period, the discussion group was growing in popularity and rapidly increasing in membership. Originally begun with a hard-core of eleven youths, the group soon reached an unwieldy membership of thirty-five, requiring a limit to be set until future arrangements could be made to accommodate all those wanting to attend. The ideal number was considered to be fifteen to twenty with meetings set at two per month, lasting two to three hours per session.

It should be stressed that the greatest importance was placed on attempting to develop a meaningful dialogue and mutual understanding between the juveniles and the authority figures. No stone was left unturned to attain this goal. After the initial hostile sessions, the youths began to view the officers as friends and were soon on a first name basis. What previously had been the "cop" or "fuzz," unanimously hated, was now considered a personable friend, "doin' a job I wouldn't want," as one youth put it.

Realizing the favorable results obtained, it was decided to bring in other officers assigned to the Pleasant Hill area who had frequent contact with these youths. Admittedly, the other police officers were somewhat skeptical of another "do-gooder" program until they themselves became deeply involved. Those who previously had doubts were subsequently "sold" on the discussion group. The reeducation and favorable modification of attitudes of both the police and the youths were considered a phenomenal breakthrough in the communications gap between these two traditional enemies.

From the outset, the discussion group concerned itself only with those youths who were the most despicable and recognized by the community as being incorrigible. This notion was based upon the fact that the great majority of young people are law-abiding, complete school, and find employment. The small number of delinquents, drop-outs and unemployable youths are, more often than not, caught up in a pattern that finds them shifting from one detention facility to another.

It was with this concept in mind that the discussion group had to serve the "unreachable" youth. Furthermore, it was felt that some type of program was needed to bring together the accused and the accuser in an attempt to develop a modicum of understanding and communication which would result in controlling the present situation and preventing future occurrences. O. W. Wilson has stated:

> Today's children will be tomorrow's citizens whose feelings will then determine the public attitude toward the police. Future police service, therefore, will be facilitated when the police establish favorable relations with the children of the community, *particularly with those who appear to be more likely to become delinquent than others.* (Emphasis mine.) When the police fail to establish this relationship or are prevented from doing so, not only will their future task be made more difficult, but, in addition, a greater proportion of the juvenile population will be launched on criminal careers in consequence of unwholesome attitudes toward the police. On the other hand, when the police deal directly with problem children and in the course of their treatment win their friendship and respect, the likelihood of the child becoming an adult offender will be materially reduced.[6]

One unique feature of the discussion group is that in our highly mobile, impersonalized and heterogeneous society, the concept of the traditional personable "cop on the beat" approach is effectively modernized. Where in past decades the local officer walked his beat and knew everyone personally, both law-abiding and law-breaker, the present discussion group approach concerns itself only with the law-breakers. Few officers today walk a beat, but instead patrol a large area in squad cars. By meeting regularly with youthful offenders, establishing rapport and a personable friendship, to the extent that everyone is on a first name basis, the "cop on the beat" approach becomes a more specialized process involving only those who most need to be involved.

The discussion group sessions are held in an informal, unstructured atmosphere, leaving the direction of the meeting to whatever subject or case the youths wish to discuss. The only rules are: (1) Whatever transpires within that session stays there and all persons in attendance are forewarned that the officer is duty bound to enforce the law if anyone admits to a crime currently under investigation, and (2) That anything may be said and any language used, but no one is allowed to touch anyone else in anger.

Patience and flexibility are the two most important traits that the officer should possess. These same traits should also be transmitted to the youths in order to dispel any thoughst they may have of expecting immediate tangible results. It has been observed that favorable results in terms of communication, understanding and rapport take place within a three- to six-month period, with meetings held twice per month.

In similar police-youth relation programs in other parts of the state, the first sessions ended in a heated debate and failure because both parties expected too much too fast. It is therefore necessary to stress the importance of being patient and not to expect a mutually shared antagonism of many years to be corrected in a matter of a few hours.

Although the discussion group is primarily based on the use of modified group therapy techniques, it is more accurately described as a "question-answer" type group session. This is due to the active role of the police officer in answering all questions as might be found in seminars. Each session begins in a highly hostile atmosphere, but settles into a fair level of debate within a short period of time. The vocabulary is kept at a level of understanding for youths and all are encouraged to interrupt the speaker any time for clarification of a point or word.

Another technique utilized to stimulate discussion and encourage understanding and communications is the psychodramatic session or role-reversal. This is done by allowing a youngster to tell his subjective side of the story. When completed, roles are immediately reversed and the youngster assumes the role of the officer and vice-versa. After both sides are heard, challenges are made to both participants and from this evolves some semblance of truth and objectivity. The psychodrama technique is not forced on the youths, but is left to them to be used at their own discretion. It should also be noted that during any of the techniques used, everyone sits in a circle including the officer. This dispels the notion that the authority figure is "talking down" to his audience, and also removes the classroom-like environment, for which these youths have a great distaste.

Ideally, the officer involved in the discussion group should be a patrolman who comes into frequent contact with the offending youth on the street. It is felt that he knows the problem areas, hangouts, etc., and is most often first on the scene. Police officers generally involved in administrative tasks and of higher rank are not felt to be effective in dealing with the hard-core youth in these types of sessions. They are usually too far removed from understanding hostile youth and have become established in their roles as administrators and therefore would find such a session extremely threatening to their security.

From a police point of view, it is the "cop on the beat" that must effectively deal with the juvenile delinquent. As Wilson stated: "Prosecution does not serve the best interests of either the offender or society. Harsh action may, in fact, create an unwholesome attitude that may arouse dormant criminality. The police should direct their efforts at keeping people out of jails and prisons, so long as this may be done without jeopardy to the public peace and security."[7]

The officer interested in becoming involved in a discussion group must possess a social awareness and a willingness to help develop favorable relations between youth and the police. The current decline of respect for law and order among young people makes it mandatory that these types of programs be implemented on a full scale. The unfavorable police image will continue to be a problem in future generations unless something is done now to remedy the situation. The social serving aspect of police prevention work with delinquent youth must be given top priority for the sake of future generations.

> Sound police philosophy is a positive one of aid and assistance to all, not a negative one of prohibition and punishment. The social welfare character of police service is not a new concept, and many police tasks have social rather than specifically criminal significance. The principles underlying the prevention of criminality are not contrary to modern police philosophy, nor are delinquency-prevention activities inconsistent with other police duties.[8]

It is hoped that, through a greater awareness by police of the problems of delinquent youth, greater stress will be placed in the near future on meeting this challenge with enthusiastic vigor.

The discussion group is considered to be a highly successful program because it has been and is continuing to be an effective vehicle for establishing favorable relations between youth and police agencies. The fact that this program has been accepted and supported by both the youth and police adds great weight to its value and effectiveness.

It is also encouraging to note that the discussion group has been utilized in both lower and middle socio-economic communities and has received support and endorsement from both areas.

As aforementioned, the discussion group is designed to elicit intensive reactions and hostilities from both youth and police, in the hopes that grievances will be aired and a mutual understanding of each other's functions and attitudes will result. This concept is especially valuable when applied to the low-minority group areas. It is here where the President's Commission on Law Enforcement and the Administration of Justice recommends greater efforts to communicate and establish meaningful dialogues. It is here, too, that the greatest need is to develop and/or expand police-community relations to reduce racial hostilities through understanding. Big city police departments can effectively implement discussion groups at district or precinct levels designed to service only the hard-core delinquents in that particular area. The program, if implemented correctly, will sustain itself on its own merits.

Examples of token efforts to appease racial minorities during the "hot times" are numerous, but generally counterfeit. This is especially true of the southern states, where racism permeates every level of officialdom. Token gestures in police-community relations only perpetuates the hypocrisy of a racist society.

The onus for any type of prevention program rests with the citizenry. Unless and until they assume an active interest and concern, the complacent community and its apathetic citizens will get their just (or unjust) rewards. It has been this way since America's founding and will continue to be so, short of a major miracle.

Effective police-youth programs are not made by top level police administrators, albeit their approval is a necessary requirement. The main effort derives from the beat officer who confronts and is confronted by the citizenry, friendly or hostile, youth or adult. It is the beat officer who must have a penchant for improving police-youth relations, if he is to successfully create meaningful communication and understanding between these traditionally opposed factions.

The area of police-youth relations is replete with myths, misconceptions, injustices, racism, and hypocrisies. To offer a remedy to this dilemma, society, its institutions, and all of its policemen would have to undergo a major socio-educational revamping concerning the true meaning and application of *justice* and *equality* for all citizens; young and old; black and white; rich and poor; strong and weak. To do this overnight or in a century may be impossible, but attempts must be made now.

Criteria for success, although not empirically tested, can be readily observed through the activity and support of the parties concerned, namely, police and youth. Both parties believe something beneficial is occurring and continue urging its existence and expansion to new groups of youth in other areas of the community. Cooperation, respect, and meaningful dialogues were once foreign to these two groups. Through the police-youth discussion group, they are now a pleasurable reality.

As a matter of evaluation based upon observation and speculation, it can fairly be stated, that when two emotional and diametrically opposed forces mutually agree that beneficial communication and understanding has been developed; then it should be logically concluded that such a program as the police-youth discussion group is indeed successful and effective. For in the final analysis, it may well be that what we sow, we too shall reap. As Geis has stated:

> We have (juvenile delinquency) not because we do not know how to prevent (it), but because we do not have enough interest or energy to do the things we already know will bring an end to delinquency. We do not lack the knowledge. We lack the will.[9]

The onus is not only on society in general, but specifically on the official agencies who must search for new alternatives to maintain their invulnerability and avoid offending the public they serve.

NOTES

1. William E. Amos and Charles F. Wellford, *Delinquency Prevention: Theory and Practice* (New Jersey: Prentice-Hall, 1967), pp. 189-190.

2. O. W. Wilson (ed.), *Parker on Police* (Springfield: Charles C. Thomas, 1957), pp. 11-17.

3. Lynn D. Swanson, "Police and Children," *The Police Chief*, International Association of Chiefs of Police, June, 1958, pp. 18-26.

4. Bruce Smith, *Police Systems in the United States*, (New York: Harper & Row, 1960), pp.234-235.

5. For detailed historical description and subsequent development and expansion of the police-youth discussion groups, see G. Thomas Gitchoff, "Community Response to Racial Tension: An Exploratory Study of the Street-gang Problem in Richmond (California)," Unpublished Master's Thesis, University of California, School of Criminology, Berkeley, September, 1966.

6. O. W. Wilson, *Police Administration* (New York: McGraw-Hill, 1963), p. 328.

7. *Ibid.*, pp. 328-329.

8. *Ibid.*, p. 329.

9. Gilbert Geis, *Juvenile Gangs*, President's Committee on Juvenile Delinquency and Youth Crime (Washington, D. C., Government Printing Office, June, 1965), p. 60.

READING 19

The Dilemma of the Generations

Roy W. Menninger, Jr.

There is nothing new in the observation that youth and age gaze at each other across a gap of suspicion, doubt, and hostility. Five centuries before Christ, Socrates bitterly attacked youth's "bad manner, contempt for authority, and disrespect for their elders," and declared that "children nowadays are tyrants." As one recent essayist put it, "all through history, denouncing the young has been a tonic for tired blood, and more important, defying elders is hygienic for the young." Perhaps because the memory of the post-war "apathetic generation" of youth is still quite vivid for most of us, the present strife between generations is all the more dramatic and dismaying.

One way to characterize the gap that separates those under thirty from those over thirty is to describe it as a conflict of values. The young, convinced that the value systems of their elders are at least misguided and at worst frankly deceitful, hypocritical, and dishonest, have shifted toward values which lead to immediate gratification. Perhaps because of the appalling unpredictability of the future in this fantastically rapidly changing world, the young have little reverence for an irrelevant past and little hope in an uncertain future. They are trying to live in the present. They have become the "now" generation. For most of us, a belief in the future is the cornerstone of our existence—we plan for it, work toward it, look forward to it, and expect a payoff in it. Acquisition of wealth and material goods makes sense to us elders because we expect the future to enable us to enjoy it. Our youth, responding to their perception of an uncertain future, prefer to focus instead on the intrinsic worth of human relationships. There is an emphasis on *being* rather than *doing*. They are preoccupied with becoming "beautiful"—capable of warm and open relationships with others. In their view, rigid external authority (which we older representatives of the system are perceived as establishing and maintaining) is destructive of the ethics and relationships they seek to create. Pressing for a measure of counterbalancing power, struggling to define and then defend their integrity, they rise to confound and attack the beliefs and the structures of their elders.

This may well describe the nature of the intergenerational strife that dismays us, but to a less objective eye our youth seem irrationally angry, inexplicably aggressive, unpardonably brash, and appallingly intolerant of everyone but themselves. In short, to our eyes they look both troubled and troubling. We are troubled by their appearance, by their ready resort to drugs, by an ease and freedom with sexuality we never knew, by their attacks on adult hypocrisies, and by their strident rejection of values we cherish. We have seen their aggressive demands humble the administration of more than one college and university, and felt a revulsion and anger curiously mixed with fascination for the flower children.

Confrontation with a few additional statistics leaves us little doubt that they are troubled people. One out of every six teenage girls becomes pregnant out of wedlock, and one-third of all teenage marriages are prefaced by illegitimate pregnancy. The number of unwed mothers under eighteen has doubled since 1940.

One teenage marriage in every two ends in divorce within five years. Three youngsters in every hundred between ten and seventeen will be adjudged delinquent this year. There are nearly half a million children hauled into juvenile court every year. The tremendous increase in the use of drugs is, of course, well known to us all. More than one-half the major crimes committed in this country involve an adolescent.

To these dismaying signs of trouble, we react. So much evidence of disrupted living evokes apprehension within most of us. What does it all mean? Will any of these things happen to my children? Do they feel so troubled, too? If they do, am I, the parent, to blame? Confronted by these chilling statistics and our incomprehension of the behaviors so many adolescents show, we understandably develop a sense of apprehension about adolescence in general. "Clearly," we think, "they are unpredictable, stormy, and potentially violent people, and the less we have to do with them, the better.

Not all of us are so consciously aware of this apprehension, but it is there, with its workings evident in our reactions of contempt, disdain, disgust, or distaste that so many express in the wake of some teenage act. This reaction of rejection is born perhaps of some awareness that adolescents are volatile combinations of sex and aggression barely under control. For most of us, it is a short and easy step to a reaction of indignant anger. Made anxious by the visible struggles of our teenagers, with their impulses of sex and aggression, and upset by their challenging, provocative behavior, we are quick to defend ourselves with counterattacks on their moral character, buttressed by righteous proclamations which emphasize our adult wisdom and our greater experience. "They are irresponsible," we say, "they have been spoiled by a generation of overpermissive Spockian parents and reared in affluence and indulgence."

Out of these anxious and angry feelings of ours come unreasonable constraints on our adolescents, vitriolic attacks on their behavior, or ready capitulation to their demands. Perhaps too commonly, we then turn our backs on them, their concerns, and their needs, and ignore them completely. In short, our first reaction—sometimes our *only* reaction—is not one of understanding their conflicts and struggles, of empathy for their anguish and perplexity, of tolerance for their false starts and

327

immature self-control, but a reaction of fearful, angry rejection and withdrawal. These fearful, angry reactions lead us to miss the whole point of much of this behavior which troubles us. And the point is this—their troubled behavior is a *symptom*, not the problem. It is an indicator of trouble, and only secondarily a cause of it.

By encouraging us to focus on the dramatically flagrant symptomatic behavior of today's adolescent, our reactions of anger and fear blind us to a clear view of a serious underlying problem—the failure of our adult society to provide the adolescent with a genuine, honest-to-goodness part in the real life action of living. In a hundred ways, today's adolescents are telling us in words, pictures, and actions that they have been left out and by-passed, denied a place in a world they already feel a vital part of, and ignored by people who are important to them. Surely it is correct to say that our adolescents' provocative behavior expresses their confusion and perplexity, but I suspect it is also their way of saying to us, "I object." They are telling us how they feel at our systematically segregating them from adult society. They are trying to make us understand how grave is our failure to perceive their legitimate needs for recognition, for involvement with adults, and for participation and genuine engagement in the real tasks of living. Unfortunately, I think we adults have failed our youth by failing to listen—or having listened, failing to hear.

It is not easy to set aside our strong, emotional reactions and reflect thoughtfully on the problem I have defined—it is far simpler to reject the views of our youth altogether, call for simple repressive measures which deal with the symptom, and ignore the problem—but let us try. It would appear that we regard the growing adolescent in a slightly schizophrenic perspective. We consider him generally immature and unready for major responsibility, clearly prone to all kinds of potentially dangerous impulsive actions. At the worst, we view adolescence as an unfortunate inconvenience, a sort of bad moment we hope will pass as quickly as possible, with the expectation that the passage of time will somehow transmute the cute little baby of yesterday into the adult of tomorrow. Most of us feel rather put upon by the very existence of the adolescent, annoyed with his presence, his unpredictability, his demands, his rapid alternation of languid parasitism with righteous independence. At times we feel the victim, even as he declares us to be the victimizer. Yet for all our conviction that the adolescent is little more than an overgrown child, we are annoyed and resentful—and even surprised—when he acts that way.

We think we understand that adolescence is a period of testing, searching, defining; we watch the adolescent examine new ideas and new philosophies, often ones we disagree with, especially as he turns to his peers and away from his parents. We understand this as a transition from childhood to adulthood, from the family into society. We *know* he needs a broad scope, a broad field, and lots of new opportunities if he is to traverse this rocky ground successfully. Yet the biggest challenge we seem able to offer is the possibility of making Honor Pep in the twelfth grade, or being elected class secretary in a meaningless popularity contest. And even these empty, honorific jobs, devoid of any challenge for growth, are available to a tiny minority of youth.

We expect that progress through the adolescent years will lead to a readiness for adult responsibilities, failing to appreciate that much of what constitutes contemporary secondary education actually gives our youths very little opportunity to participate, and hence to learn how to become responsible and effective citizens in the community. How can it? Even if educators wished to do so, their efforts are handicapped by the overriding negative, hands-off attitude which prevails among most adults. What we ask of students is not participation and thoughtful contributions, but quiet, non-trouble-making conformity—a modern-day version of the Victorian aphorism: children should be seen and not heard.

Whether we regard them as too immature, or a drug on the labor market, or unable to "understand" this adult world of ours, or better left to the exclusive task of attending school, the fact is that we preclude our youth from participation in programs which involve them where *we* are, or with activities we will eventually want them to respect and become a part of. They are cut off from any part of the world we expect them eventually to enter.

Nowhere is the starkness and meagerness of this social isolation more apparent than in the lot of the fifteen year old. Except for going to school, virtually nothing that he can do is legal. He can't quit school, he can't work, he can't drink, he can't smoke, he can't drive except to and from school, he can't marry, he can't vote, he can't enlist, he can't gamble, he can't run for office. He cannot, in fact, participate in *any* of the adult virtues, vices, activities, or responsibilities.

By what magic, then, do we expect our growing adolescents, denied opportunities for the participation that teaches, suddenly to emerge on the stage of adulthood, full-fledged, capable, mature, and responsible? Small wonder that so few are ready for these responsibilities when the time comes, when their predominant experience has been the frustration of waiting, *im*patiently, expected to forego, to postpone, to stand apart from the society which flows all around them.

How does this come to be?

One factor is the dramatic change in the economic status of the adolescent. The affluence of our society means, in effect, that the adolescent does not have to work, because the money he might earn is no longer as necessary for support of the family as it once was. Affluence provides him with the means for fantastic self-indulgence. It is estimated that last year the total of allowances and money earned by adolescents came to the staggering sum of 17 billion dollars. This amount of money, plus a large amount of leisure time, plus a lack of significant involvement in the social fabric, in the absence of the disciplining effects of work, inevitably makes for a pattern of living with the character of endless play.

A second factor is the upward extension of schooling itself. Compulsory public education for all, initially limited to the elementary grades, gradually extended to secondary school education, with the expansion of knowledge that needed to be mastered and an increasing need for more and better training of people. But out of this virtue of compulsory public education came a few unexpected disadvantages. Among other things, it has meant an extended period in which our growing adolescents are dependent upon and controlled by adults, promoting many of the undesirable effects of dependency. Moreover, this delayed entry into the adult world of work confines them involuntarily to a system of schooling which is genuinely educative for too few, and for too many is felt to be less and less helpful for future life, more and more artificial with its prison-like demands and constraints, and simply not where the action is.

Not only is adolescence extended longer and longer, but it is beginning earlier as well. With better nutrition, the age of puberty has dropped, nearly two full years, and the mass media—

especially television—has markedly accelerated the psychological maturation of the young child, exposing him to ideas and images that many of us had not heard nor seen before our late teens or twenties. In effect, our adolescents may now stay children for more than a decade after reaching biological maturity. Contrast that to the Middle Ages, or even one hundred years ago, when young adolescents were commonly in the army and often head of the household.

What are the consequences of affluence and enforced dependency? Perhaps the most serious effect is the extent to which the adolescent is infantilized—"Childized," as some have called it. He becomes more childish because we give him room, the permission, the means, and our encouragement to stay that way. This state is a deterrant to healthy growth; it provokes and sustains our perception of him as immature, and gives rise to an impressive self-fulfilling prophecy. We deny him some of the responsibilities of progressive maturity, and when he responds with childish behavior, we say, "See, I told you all along you weren't ready." As we react by giving him still less responsibility and penning him up more, *he* reacts with still greater evidence of the immaturity that justifies yet another round of adult control and demand for conformity.

I think this infantilizing of the adolescent does something more. I suspect it provokes adventure-seeking, challenging, and serious risk-taking behavior, such as taking drugs, provoking riots, playing chicken on the highway, speeding at ninety miles an hour through the city, and so forth. I would suggest that this behavior not only expresses the sense of helplesness and frustration the adolescent feels at being so irrelevant to the adult society all around him, but quite effectively conveys his anger and his resentment for being so disregarded and shoved aside by adults.

Enforced schooling combined with enforced infantilization, cemented by a systematic exclusion from work experience and participation in social process, yields an unfortunate fruit. In spite of twelve years of education, the average high school graduate emerges from his educational cocoon with no place to go and nothing to be. He has no occupational identity, no skills worth selling, no systematic practice in the arts of living in a complex society, and not much of a clue about where to go to find what he does not yet have. The exceptions, of course, are the college-bound youths, though they, by that very token, are not average. Even here, though they may continue their schooling through various kinds of higher education, these older adolescents continue to feel isolated from society and are, in fact, excluded from much significant participation in social processes, even in the school that educates them. Without voice or responsibility for the society that they are physically a part of, continuing to be aware of a pervasive sense of irrelevance to the larger adult community, and treated as unwanted children, they give vent to their distress and their resentment through overt external action—through acts of social protest, or student sit-ins, or vociferous support of un-popular causes, or through internal retreat with LSD or by becoming hippies.

These differences between the college adolescent and his drifting buddy who barely made it through high school are more apparent than real. Each in his own way is struggling to come to terms with the failure of society to prepare him better for the adult life it now expects him to lead. This is a message we cannot afford to miss; this is not simply a school problem; this is not a problem to be solved by a retreat to a simple-minded hard line stance of repression and control, with a brave call for more law and order. It is a problem for which *all* adults are responsible. It is a problem of our having failed to provide the growing adolescent—from the years of puberty onward—with the several vital ingredients he needs if he is to establish the solid identity of independent adulthood that we so anxiously and insistently demand. These ingredients are (1) a warm and extended experience with adults who are admirable, firm, loving, and involved—so that he might have the *model* for future behavior that he needs; and (2) plenty of opportunity to test and develop and prove his competence in work and service.

It is not enough to give him a generous allowance, a few rules irregularly enforced, an occasional pat on the head and a signature on the semester report cards, and assume that some combination of the demands of school and the support of his friends will do the trick. It is not enough to reserve our investment of concern with his welfare for those moments of eleventh-hour crisis when we suddenly wonder what happened and where we failed and what should we do now. It is not enough to respond to his evidence of perplexity and rejection of what we value with moralistic sermons and angry demands for conformity.

Instead, we must recognize the need for better models of responsible adult behavior for him to copy, made available to him early in his adolescence; we must recognize that he needs to be given a more substantial voice and sense of participation in the world he is a part of. We need to see more clearly where we have denied the adolescent the room he needs to experiment, to participate, to engage, and to involve himself in the fabric of living, and to *earn* his place in adult society. We need to consider how *we* can enable our youth to participate legitimately in work and in the social issues of our time, to struggle with the problems of racial prejudice, social and economic deprivation, self-government, and the development of a conception of service to others.

The adolescent is task-oriented, he is eager, he has enormous energy and a willingness to invest himself in useful and meaningful activities—but only if he has the opportunity to do so. If we fail to supply tasks which are adequate to absorb these energies, tasks that are relevant to the psychosocial task of finding himself, he will do the only thing he can—seek his own outlets, and adults be damned. This need not happen, for there are things we can do and opportunities we can provide that will give youth a better chance to be part of the action, and a bigger boost toward maturity.

The first and most important move to be made is *to get involved* with our adolescents, to listen to them, talk to them, reason with them, and even to argue with them. It is not just the hippies who have opted out and turned away; as far as our adolescent youth are concerned, it is persons like you and me who have pulled back and copped out. Whether we justify our withdrawal from them as our way of "helping" them be independent, or simply feel we do not understand them and cannot deal with them, or are acting out of fear and disgust, the result is the same. We have abdicated from a vital responsibility, and thereby robbed them of one part of the elemental mix they need—engagement with people who care, and after whom they can model themselves. What most adolescents want, and certainly what most adolescents need almost more than anything else, is a sense that adults take them seriously.

Second, we ought to introduce a more sophisticated version of the old "work-study" program which is common in many schools for a handful of students unable to make the academic grade, and not interested or not qualified for vocational technical school training. Typically, a work-study program has been viewed as compromise, an effort to keep marginal kids in school, if only part time, and blessed with low status and no prestige. The idea needs overhauling, for it contains the nucleus of some vital possibilities. Perhaps it should be that *every* student in high school might spend a part of each day, part of each week, or part of each month either working at a paying job, or serving as a volunteer in a service-to-others capacity. The paying jobs should include opportunities to work with business men, with doctors as medical aides or nurse aides, with lawyers, with architects, with policemen riding on patrol—functioning in an apprentice role. The trades should similarly participate. This would include our youth in the business and professional community where they would be working with men whose skill, wisdom, and proficiency make them good teachers of what they are doing, and excellent models of how effective and mature adults actually behave.

Such a scheme would tap the vast reservoir of teaching talent which resides in the multitude of functioning and effective adults in the community—people with whom students normally have little contact, and neither know about nor understand. This interdigitation of our youth and our working adult population would change the bad image of adolescents by giving adults an exposure to young people under circumstances quite different from the usual unhappy glimpses of noisy, irresponsible adolescents chasing each other in cars, or raising the devil in the corner pizza parlor. Our stringent work laws now keep many young people from the opportunity of earning their *own* money, depriving them of the satisfaction that this independence and self-reliance brings.

Insisting that each student participate in such a program would remove the stigma of "work" as something fit only for those who cannot study. Inclusion of volunteer service as an equivalent experience would introduce in a more systematic way the idea that there is a need for and benefit from activities which serve others rather than one's self. Normally undertaken only by the conscientious and concerned, a broad program of service would help to introduce a general expectation that all people should learn to serve others, and that society has a right to expect this from its members.

Such a scheme, introduced early into the educational pattern of the adolescent, would convey a sense of participation he now lacks and—in combination with the growing sense of responsibility that such a program could engender—would lead to a markedly enhanced concept of who he is and what he can do, based on tested experience and proven competence.

The development of social competence and more solid personal identities at earlier ages would enable us to make a third and vital move: to lower the voting age to seventeen. We speak of "appreciating" what our youth are doing in Vietnam, but is it not the ultimate in contempt for them that we ask them to face the mortal dangers there, and yet so casually dismiss their demand for a political voice here as being "immature"? We would hardly dismiss such seventeen-year-old adults as Joan of Arc or Surveyor George Washington as "immature teenagers." In an earlier time, adults were more ready to follow John Locke's advice: "The sooner you treat him as a man, the sooner he will be one."

Fourth, youth should be a part of government at *all* levels. At the very least, the sham of "student government" in countless high schools and colleges should be discarded in favor of a representational system which gives the students (and the faculty, for that matter) a genuine voice in the conduct of their own education. But beyond this, we ought to revise radically our present pattern of excluding young people as representatives of youth in our councils of government. At the national level, and in those cities and counties with representative government as well, youth should be present. Not only can they profit from the participation as a means of learning, but they can also contribute a perspective, a vigor, an idealism, which are all too often lacking. They should serve as members of both local and national citizen advisory commissions, particularly on the committees and groups grappling with problems which affect the young persons in our society—recreation, delinquency, education, and so forth. Far too frequently committees pondering the needs of our youth include only people over thirty; again, a tacit message of contempt for the contribution which participating youths could make.

It is vital, of course, that any groups thus created be real ones meeting real needs and struggling with real problems. The proposals must be genuinely accepted, studied, and acted upon, or else the move will be seen as only another example of adult hypocrisy which our youth now reproach us for.

Fifth, special youth task forces could be created to handle specific problems—to work with volunteer agencies or city departments in cleaning up ghetto areas, to develop programs in delinquency control, or to exploit the lessons learned from the success of the youths in white hats who were involved in helping control the riots of Tampa and Newark some years ago. There should be extensive student tutorial programs, which would draw upon the older and more skillful students to teach the younger and less well-prepared children.

That there is a "generation gap" there can be no doubt. Nor is there much doubt that the stresses of transition from childhood to adulthood will always produce degrees of conflict with those younger than the adolescent, and more pointedly, those older as well. This should not, however, be such cause for alarm and dismay, for it is this sort of conflict which serves to dramatize the hypocrisies and defects of our imperfect society, and helps to mobilize the energies of youth (and those who are older, too) toward some righting of these wrongs. What must be emphasized, and what I have tried to underscore here, is the extent to which our passive indifference to the *legitimate* needs of struggling adolescents has made matters materially more difficult for them, and in turn for us.

There is room for hope and optimism, if we will only recognize how much we can promote a general improvement by getting involved with our adolescents, enabling them to be involved with us and the society we are all a part of. This *shift* in our attitude and behavior will generate inumerable opportunities for their participation in the solution of the social problems which confront us, giving them the laboratory of learning they need, the share of the action they want, and the engagement with significant adults which they must have if they are to mature. This shift will insure that the inevitable intergenerational conflicts will be truly constructive of a better society.

Name Index

337

Subject Index